THE KOVELS' COLLECTOR'S GUIDE TO LIMITED EDITIONS

by Ralph M. and Terry H. Kovel

Crown Publishers, Inc.　New York

Books by Ralph M. and Terry H. Kovel

The Kovels' Collector's Guide to Limited Editions

The Complete Antiques Price List

Know Your Antiques

American Country Furniture 1780-1875

Dictionary of Marks—Pottery and Porcelain

The Official Bottle Price List

How to Use This Book

We have tried to use as few symbols as possible, but when a price list is written sometimes abbreviations are needed to conserve space.

Items are grouped by manufacturer. When the information was available we have included a very short paragraph that will furnish you with the location and years of production of the firm. Many of the limited editions are sold by one company and manufactured by another. This type of information has been kept a "trade secret" and consequently was not always available to us. The first column of each listing gives the name of the item, and the name of the artist where it is important; the second column gives the year or years of manufacture. Column 3 is the number of items in that particular edition. If the edition is limited to the number of orders before a special date we use the word "year." In many cases the exact number of the edition is released later. The next column tells the price at the time of issue. Please remember that the issue prices do not reflect the devaluation of the dollar or the changes in the price of gold or silver. They are the actual prices at the time the pieces were first offered for sale. The last column gives a current range of prices for the piece. These prices were taken from advertisements, auctions, sales, and shops from March 1973 to March 1974. These prices do reflect the devaluation of the dollar and all foreign currency prices have been converted into the dollar value as of March 1974. A single asterisk following an entry refers to a black-and-white illustration; two asterisks refer to a color illustration.

This book is divided into five chapters: Chapter 1, Figurines; Chapter 2, Paperweights; Chapter 3, Plates, Plaques, and Miscellaneous. Chapter 3 also includes Christmas ornaments and spoons. Chapter 4, Medals; Chapter 5, Bars and Ingots. This book does not contain listings for any type of prints or paper limited editions. Bottles were not included because the full listing for such limited edition bottles as Beam, Wheaton Commemoratives, Lionstone, Ezra Brooks, etc., are to be found in The Official Bottle Price List by Ralph and Terry Kovel. Some other limited edition items such as coronation or souvenir items may be missing. We have tried to include items that are most likely to be found in the United States. Limited editions made in other countries that have little interest to the American collector were not included. The limited editions included in this book date back to 1895 when the first Christmas plate was made. It was virtually impossible to find out about all limited editions since that date. We have concentrated on items during the past five years and, where it was possible, we traced back to the earlier editions made by these same companies. Information about original issue price and edition number has often been missing for some of the early editions and for future books we would certainly welcome any added information from readers.

Inquiries should be addressed to Crown Publishers, Inc.,
419 Park Avenue South, New York, N.Y. 10016.
Library of Congress Catalog Card Number: 74-84027
Printed in the United States of America
Published simultaneously in Canada by General Publishing Company Limited

INTRODUCTION

Someone once said that a limited edition is "an instant antique." The humor of that remark would be lost by the serious investor who thinks of limited editions only in terms of profit and loss. The collector who has been buying Christmas plates for years can understand exactly how the limited editions and the antique are related.

This book makes no attempt to guide you in purchasing limited editions for pleasure or profit. It is a report of the market as it appears in the United States. Our research has taken us to Denmark, England, New York, Connecticut, California, and many other parts of the United States. Some of the information that we wanted could not even be found in the manufacturers' offices because no records were kept regarding the original issue prices. Several companies have gone out of business and many of the names that we traced turned out to be mail-order advertisement addresses and nothing more. Most of the companies were cooperative in every way and offered us pictures and information. There were a few companies that absolutely refused to tell us anything about the number made in some of their limited editions or of their marketing methods. No doubt, a few companies have been missed entirely because, although we tried, it is impossible to be perfect the first time. A very small number of companies proved impossible to locate.

We have read dozens of articles about the investment possibilities of limited editions. A careful look at the issue and current prices in this book will help you to make your own determination. Not all of the claims are true, but many of the limited editions have become more valuable. Some limited editions are just too recent to have appreciated in value. It must be understood that if you are investing, you usually buy at retail, which are the prices listed in our book. When you sell, it is usually at a wholesale price which is less than the retail by at least 40 percent. You might sell at auction, but even that requires a 20 percent or higher commission. It is true that in these days of inflated money any work of art or antique keeps pace with the changes. The experts guess that there are more than a half-million people interested in limited editions. Some of these collectors will make money on the limited editions, but most collectors are interested in limited editions for aesthetic reasons, and if a profit is eventually realized, it is a bonus.

Here are a few suggestions for those who are interested in limited editions. Most of them are made and sold by reputable companies. Price and product are exactly as advertised. These are the limited editions you should buy. Be careful of the edition that has no announced limits. Be careful about any company that offers guaranteed profit. Watch out for forgeries which will certainly appear when values rise. There are already known copies of Danish Christmas plates, but fortunately these are very few. Try to restrict your collecting to items made by reputable companies. If you believe that an unknown plate or figurine has beauty, don't hesitate to buy it for your own pleasure and satisfaction. And be very careful in buying silver items with the idea that the rise in silver will give you a profit. The cost of the silver alone is much less than you paid for the original piece.

ACKNOWLEDGMENTS

The following companies and collectors helped us with material and pictures.
Thanks to

Vi and Si Altman
Clarence, New York

John E. McNichols
American Commemorative Council

Bill Veroxie
American Historical Plates

Anheuser-Busch

E. A. Babka
Antique Trader Weekly

Ivan Glickman
Arista Imports

J. R. Pitts
Aynsley China

Mrs. Chantal Simoni
Baccarat, Inc.

M. K. Sigurdsson
The Bengough Collection of
    Canadiana

Aaron Ritz
Jorgen Sannung
Bing & Grøndahl Porcelain Company

Henry Blummer
Blue Delft Co.

Mrs. Dorothy Kay
Edward Marshall Boehm, Inc.

Dr. Irving Burgues
Burgues Porcelains

Svend A. Knudsen
Bygdo Keramik

Carl's House of Silver
Englewood, N. J.

Leon A. Micheline
Carson City Mint

Donald M. Claus
Chateau, Inc.

Churchill Mint Ltd.
Sheffield, England

Arthur Goldenberg
Coin & Currency Institute

Frank B. Knight
Collector's Weekly

Steve Lynd
Columbus Mint

Dave Quammen
Commemorative Imports

S. Geary
Continental Mint

Bill Curry
Bill Curry Productions

Frank W. Reddan
Cybis

Frank Zimmerman
Danbury Mint

A. Alexander Fanelli
Dartmouth College

Daniel N. Storr
Denbyware, Ltd.

Ola & H. C. Torbøl
Desiree Porcelain Factory

George W. Ebeling
Ebeling & Reuss

Mary W. Rosenberg
Ellis Barker Silver Co.

Donald and Joan Ewing
Ewings

Frank M. Fenton
Helen Warner
Fenton Art Glass Company

Richard D. McNeill
Fisher, Bruce & Company

Harry J. Forman
Philadelphia, Pennsylvania

Fostoria Glass Company
David B. Dalzell, Sr.

David R. Brown
Peter H. Jungkunst
Josephine Seladoro
Franklin Mint

Mr. John Frank
Frankoma Pottery Company

John R. Gentile
Gentile Glass Company

Steffen Andersen
Georg Jensen Silversmiths
Denmark

Jay Bruni
George Washington Mint

W. Dan Lemeshka
Gorham Company

Theresa & Arthur Greenblatt
Amherst, New Hampshire

Judy Sutcliffe
Joan Liffring Zug
Greentree Pottery

Arthur Hald
Karin Olsson
AB Gustavsbergs Fabriker

Gary Schmidt
Harmer-Rooke

Frederick Haviland
Haviland & Company

W. D. Card
Historic Plate Company

Lucille J. Kennedy
Imperial Glass Corporation

R. San Roman
Intercontinental Fine Arts, Ltd.

Cindy Haskins
International Silver Company

Lloyd J. Glasgow
Jacques Jugeat, Inc.

Robert Weber
Judaic Heritage Society

Lars Peitersen
Kastrup Og Holmegaard Glasvaeker

Kay Mallek
Tucson, Arizona

Patricia C. Lollot
Ralph Destino
Kenton Wholesale, Inc.

Harold F. Flynn
The Kirk Collection

M. Blair
Koscherak Brothers, Inc.

L. A. Stanley
Lawrann's

William E. Weydemeyer, Jr.
Lenox

Helmut H. Lihs
Lihs-Lindner

Pat Dunlap
Faye Chu
The Lincoln Mint

Linda Kerr
Lombardo Mint

Mr. Jean-Paul Loup
River Forest, Illinois

E. Fuur
Meka A/S

Povl Nissen
A. Michelsen

Bette Benedict
Mort Barish Associates

Kathy Serratore
Mount Everest Mint

Deloris Williams
Moussalli, Ltd.

Aleta Ambrose
Noritake Company, Inc.

Stuart Drysdale
Perthshire Paperweights, Ltd.

Henry A. Pickard
Pickard, Inc.

Colin Day
Poole Pottery Limited

Hans Christian Kontni
Porsgrund Porcelain Company

R. James Harper
Presidential Art Medals, Inc.

Anthony H. Clipper
Puiforcat U.S.A., Ltd.

Robert D. Rieman
RAM China Plate Co.

Dorothy George
Reco International Corp.

Reed & Barton Corporation
Taunton, Massachusetts

Gus Preston
Remington

Klaus Peter Lohaus
Kaaren Kovvalski
Rosenthal U.S.A., Ltd.

Steen Vedel
Bredo L. Grandjean
Erik Skaarup
J. Fog-Petersen
Royal Copenhagen Porcelain
Company

Miss E. Gore
Royal Crown Derby

Mr. David Allen
Nancy E. O. Clarke
Royal Doulton, Ltd.

Barbara Krempel
San Francisco Private Mint

Matthew F. Schmid
Schmid Brothers, Inc.

Seven Seas Traders, Inc.
Addison, Illinois

Gerald H. Lowenstein
Silver Coalition, Ltd.

Hugh and Carolyn Smith
Millville, New Jersey

H. J. Oppermann
L. E. Smith Glass Co.

Mary Louise Cram
Society of Medalists

Eleanor Midlik
Spode, Inc.

Charles C. Steiff, II
Steiff Company

George Willis
Stone Mountain Memorial Assoc.

Robert P. Cook
Paul A. Straub & Co.

A/B Strombergshyttan
Sweden

Patricia J. Andeweg
Systems International, Inc.

Arthur L. Roy
Towle Manufacturing Co.

Sharon H. Casale
U. S. Bicentennial Company

United States Mint
Department of the Treasury

United States Silver Corporation
Van Nuys, California

Lynn Krynski
Valley Forge Mint

Virgil Vance
Van Brook of Lexington

Lee Benson
Veneto Flair

Douglas Bothwell
Vernonware Division
Metlox Potteries

Pat Owens
Viking Import House, Inc.

Marcia P. Lloyd
Vincent Lippe Corporation

Jan Pearce
Walter Fleisher Company

Luella Powell
Wara Intercontinental

Bill Richardson
Washington Mint

Claudia Coleman
Wedgwood

Charles H. Morgan
Weil Ceramics & Glass, Inc.

Robert E. August
Wendell August Forge

Robert R. Rupp
Westmoreland Glass Company

John F. Henier
Wheaton Industries

Williams Adams, Inc.
New York, New York

Daniel M. Price
H. Wittur & Co.

W. E. Williamson
WNW Mint Industries

SPECIAL THANKS

Our very special thanks go to the following people who
helped us beyond what would normally be expected:

Hy Brown
Painesville, Ohio

Leon Lindheim,
Author of **Coin-Wise**

Neil Cooper
International Numismatic Agency

Clifford Mishler
Editor, **Coin Prices**

Caroline Delfino
Royal Worcester Porcelain Co.

Mr. Reese Palley
Atlantic City, N.J.

Ispanky Studios and Kruckmeyer and
Cohn Jewelers for furnishing the
Spring Bouquet photograph

Mr. Frank W. Reddan
Cybis

D. Wayne Johnson
Medallic Art Company

Mr. Paul Sadows
C. B. Charles Galleries

Mr. Paul Jokelson
Scarsdale, New York

L. H. Selman
San Francisco, California

Thanks too to the staff who helped us put it all together, especially Terry Siko
who did much of the special researching and compiling.

BIBLIOGRAPHY

Altman, Seymour and Violet. *The Book of Buffalo Pottery*. New York: Crown Publishers, Inc., 1969.

Cosentino, Frank J. *Edward Marshall Boehm, 1913–1969*. Trenton, New Jersey: Edward
Marshall Boehm, Inc., 1970.

Cybis Factory Publication. *Cybis*. Trenton, New Jersey, 1973.

Dusterberg, Richard B. *The Official Inaugural Medals*. Medallion Press. Cincinnati,
1971.

Eyles, Desmond. *Royal Doulton, 1815–1965*. London, England: Hutchinson & Co.
Publishers Ltd., 1965.

International Plate Collectors Club Bulletins, Long Beach, California

New Jersey State Museum. *Cybis in Retrospect*. Trenton, New Jersey: New Jersey State
Museum, 1970.

Owen, Pat. *The Story of Bing & Grøndahl Christmas Plates*. Dayton, Ohio: Viking Import House, 1962.

———. *The Story of Royal Copenhagen Christmas Plates*. Dayton, Ohio: Viking Import House, Inc., 1961.

Royal Copenhagen Porcelain Manufactory, The. *Plates from The Royal Copenhagen
Porcelain Manufactory*. Copenhagen, Denmark: Gyldendalske Boghandel Nordisk
AS, 1970.

Royal Worcester Factory Publication. *The Collectors' Handbook of Royal Worcester
Models*. England: The Royal Worcester Factory, 1969.

Steinke, Violette. *Original Royal Delft Christmas Plates*. Publisher unknown, 1972.

Witt, Louise Schaub. *Wonderful World of Plates, Annual, Christmas and Commemorative with Collector's Price Guide*. North Kansas City, Missouri: Trojan Press, Inc.,
1970.

1

Figurines

Title	Date of Issue	Issue Limi- tation	Issue Price	Current Price
Anichini Porcelains				
Saw-Whet Owl		480	600.00	600.00
Western Meadowlark		400		475.00

Baccarat limited editions are made in France by La Compagnie des Cristalleries de Baccarat, located near Paris. The factory was started in 1765. The firm went bankrupt and started operating again about 1822. Famous cane and millefiori paperweights were made there during the 1860-1880 period. In 1953, after a lapse of 80 years, sulfide paperweights were again introduced. A series of limited edition paperweights has been made each year since 1953.

See listing for Baccarat in Paperweight section

Title	Date of Issue	Issue Limi- tation	Issue Price	Current Price
Baccarat Crystal Sculptures				
Cat, Signed Robert Rigot		500	330.00	330.00
Egyptian Falcon, 6 3/4 X 5 1/4 In.*		100	400.00	400.00
Owl, Signed Robert Rigot*		500	450.00	450.00
Penguin, Signed Robert Rigot*		500	500.00	500.00
Winged Bull, 5 1/4 X 1 3/8 In.*		250	400.00	400.00

Baccarat, Egyptian Falcon

Baccarat, Owl

Kramlik limited edition porcelain paintings are made in New Jersey, by Balint Kramlik. Kramlik, a native of Herend, Hungary, worked with Edward Marshall Boehm before producing his own limited edition porcelain paintings. Each painting is 9 x 12 inches unframed.

Title	Date of Issue	Issue Limi- tation	Issue Price	Current Price
Balint Kramlik Porcelain Paintings				
Bald Eagle		200	400.00	400.00
Black-Capped Chickadee On Cherry Blossom		100	400.00	400.00
Blue Jay, Female		200	400.00	400.00
Blue Jay, Male		200	400.00	400.00
Blue-Winged Warbler On Mountain Bay Rose		100	400.00	400.00
Brown Thrasher		200		300.00
Brown Thrasher On Carolina Rose		100	400.00	400.00
Cardinal		200		300.00
Cuckoo		200		350.00
Flemish Floral		200		400.00
Flower Market With Mockingbird		200		50.00
Green Woodpecker		200		350.00
Marguerite, French Daisy		200	400.00	400.00
Marguerite, French Daisy, Blue		200	400.00	400.00
Marguerite, Yellow Flowers		200	400.00	400.00

Baccarat, Penguin

Baccarat, Winged Bull

Boehm, Barn Owl

Boehm, Black Grouse

Medicinal Herb, Digitalis Purpurea	1973	50	150.00	150.00
Medicinal Herb, Gentiana Asclepiadea	1973	50	150.00	150.00
Medicinal Herb, Papaver Somniforum	1973	50	150.00	150.00
Medicinal Herb, Passiflora Exoniensis	1973	50	150.00	150.00
Spotted-Breasted Oriole On Clematis		100	400.00	400.00
Summer Flowers With Bluebird		200		500.00

Boehm porcelains were first made by Edward Marshall Boehm in Trenton, New Jersey, in 1950. The Malvern Boehm Studio of London was established after Mr. Boehm's death in 1969. Bone china Boehm figurines are made at the English factory. Hard paste porcelains are still made in New Jersey. Lenox China has also issued a limited edition plate series featuring Boehm birds.

See listing for Boehm in Plate section

Boehm Porcelains

Adios	1969	150	1500.00	1500.00
American Cocker, Decorated	1972		7.50	375.00 to 550.00
American Cocker, White	1950		7.50	550.00 to 600.00
American Redstarts	1958	500	300.00	2200.00 to 2750.00
Arabian Stallions	1955	130	110.00	3000.00 to 3400.00
Barn Owl*	1972	350	3600.00	3600.00 to 5000.00
Basset Hound	1957	310	27.50	1300.00 to 1500.00
Beagle	1952	400	12.50	500.00 to 600.00
Black Angus Bull	1950	250	20.00	900.00 to 1100.00
Blackbirds	1973	250	5400.00	5400.00
Black Grouse**	1972	350	2800.00	2800.00 to 3100.00
Black-Headed Grosbeak*	1969	750	900.00	1200.00 to 1450.00
Black-Tailed Bantams	1956	51	350.00	4500.00 to 6000.00
Black-Throated Blue Warbler	1958	500	400.00	2200.00 to 2850.00
Blue Grosbeak And Oak Leaves	1967	750	500.00	1200.00 to 1800.00
Blue Jays	1962	250	2000.00	10750.00 to 12500.00
Blue Tits	1973	400	2200.00	2200.00
Bobcats	1971	200	1600.00	1600.00 to 1700.00
Bobolink	1964	500	450.00	1200.00 to 2600.00
Bobwhite Quail	1953	750	200.00	2000.00 to 3400.00
Boxer, Large	1952	600	6.00	475.00 to 600.00
Boxer, Small	1952	400	6.00	400.00 to 500.00
Brown Pelican**	1972	100	9500.00	9500.00 to 10500.00
Brown Thrasher	1973	500	1700.00	1700.00
Bunny, Female	1961	532	3.00	275.00 to 325.00
Bunny Box With Carrot	1955	63	8.00	700.00 to 800.00
Bunny Milk Mug	1955	93	5.00	600.00 to 700.00
Cachette, French	1954	1766	12.50	450.00 to 550.00
Cactus Wren	1972	400	2400.00	2600.00 to 2800.00
California Quail	1957	500	300.00	2100.00 to 2600.00
Canadian Warbler, Fledgling**	1967	750	450.00	1300.00 to 1700.00
Cardinals, Decorated	1955	500	450.00	3200.00 to 3800.00
Carolina Wrens	1957	100	650.00	4000.00 to 5000.00
Cat With Kittens	1961		25.00	475.00 to 575.00
Catbird*	1965	500	900.00	1800.00 to 2500.00
Cerulean Warbler	1957	100	750.00	4600.00 to 5300.00
Chick, White	1953	321	6.00	350.00 to 400.00
Chrysanthemum & Butterfly	1972	350	950.00	1200.00 to 1400.00
Cockatoo And Flowers	1971	50	4200.00	4200.00
Collie	1954		28.00	500.00 to 725.00
Common Tern	1968	500	1400.00	4750.00 to 6000.00
Cottontail Bunny		25	5.00	850.00 to 950.00
Crested Flycatcher*	1961	500	1650.00	2300.00 to 2500.00
Cupid With Horn	1956	230	12.50	325.00 to 375.00
Dachshund	1953	235	12.50	600.00 to 700.00
Diana With Fawn	1953	42	35.00	550.00 to 650.00
Dogwood	1973	500	575.00	575.00
Downy Woodpecker	1957	500	400.00	1900.00 to 2300.00
Dutch Boy & Girl			12.00	1500.00 to 1700.00
E.M.Boehm Orchid Centerpiece**	1970	300	6200.00	8200.00 to 8500.00
Eagle, Large	1957	31		7900.00 to 8500.00
Eagle, Small	1957	76		Unknown
Eastern Bluebirds	1959	100	1800.00	6900.00 to 7200.00
English Bulldog	1959	46	25.00	1700.00 to 1900.00

Boehm, Black-Headed Grosbeak

Boehm, Green Jays

Boehm, Everglades Kite

Boehm, Foxes

Boehm, Goldcrest

Boehm, Catbird

Boehm, Fondo Marino

Boehm, E.M.Boehm Orchid Centerpiece

Boehm, Crested Flycatcher

Boehm, Brown Pelican

Boehm, Orchard Oriole

Boehm, Hunter

Boehm, Junco

Boehm, Kestrels

Name	Year	Edition	Issue Price	Current Value
Etrafon Head	1962	5000	5.00	125.00 to 150.00
Everglades Kite*	1973	300	5800.00	5800.00
Fawn	1953	54	10.00	750.00 to 850.00
Field Mouse With Vetch	1960	479	25.00	325.00 to 375.00
Flicker	1971	400	2200.00	2800.00 to 3000.00
Fluted Urn	1957	537	8.00	200.00 to 250.00
Fondo Marino*	1970	50	28500.00	8500.00 to 33000.00
Foxes*	1971	200	1800.00	1800.00
Foxhound Reclining	1950	25	22.50	600.00 to 1250.00
French Poodle	1953	154	40.00	800.00 to 850.00
German Shepherd	1959		25.00	1500.00 to 1800.00
Goldcrest*	1973	500	650.00	650.00 to 900.00
Goldencrown Kinglets	1956	500	375.00	2400.00 to 2800.00
Golden Pheasant, Decorated	1954	7		Unknown
Golden Pheasant, White	1954	7		Unknown
Goldfinches With Scottish Thistle	1961	500	400.00	2300.00 to 2600.00
Great Dane, Reclining, Fawn	1956	10	20.00	550.00 to 600.00
Great Horned Owl, Fledgling	1965	750	350.00	1400.00 to 1500.00
Green Jays With Persimmons*	1966	400	1850.00	3300.00 to 3900.00
Hereford Bull	1950	152	30.00	2500.00 to 2800.00
Hooded Mergansers**	1968	500	1600.00	2200.00 to 2450.00
Horned Larks With Wild Grapes	1973	400	3800.00	3800.00
Hunter, Bay*	1953	250	125.00	1200.00 to 1400.00
Hunter, Dapple Gray	1952			3750.00 to 4500.00
Hunter, White	1953	250		1200.00 to 1750.00
Junco*	1970	750	1100.00	1300.00 to 1500.00
Kestrels*	1968	500	1800.00	2600.00 to 2800.00
Kildeer	1964	300	1750.00	5000.00 to 5600.00
Lazuli Buntings	1973	500	1800.00	1800.00
Lesser Prairie Chickens, Decorated*	1972	300	1200.00	1650.00 to 1800.00
Lion Cub	1956	125	15.00	650.00 to 1300.00
Long-Tail Tit	1973	400	2600.00	2600.00
Madonna With Child		120	35.00	700.00 to 1100.00
Mallards	1950	500	180.00	1100.00 to 1850.00
Meadowlark	1957	750	225.00	3200.00 to 3500.00
Mearns Quail	1963	350	950.00	2800.00 to 3200.00
Mercury	1953	100	28.00	550.00 to 600.00
Mockingbirds	1961	500	650.00	2500.00 to 4500.00
Mountain Bluebirds	1963	300	1900.00	4750.00 to 5900.00
Mourning Doves	1958	500	250.00	1000.00 to 1400.00
Mute Swan**	1971	400	3400.00	7000.00 to 8000.00
Neptune With Seahorse	1953	65	35.00	650.00 to 1200.00
Nonpareil Buntings	1958	750	250.00	1050.00 to 1700.00
Northern Water Thrush	1967	500	800.00	1200.00 to 1500.00
Nuthatch With Mushroom	1971	350	650.00	650.00 to 1000.00
Orchard Oriole*	1970	750	1200.00	1500.00 to 1750.00
Ovenbird	1970	750	1050.00	1400.00 to 1600.00
Palomino Colt	1980	100	10.00	1750.00 to 2250.00
Parula Warblers	1965	400	1500.00	2100.00 to 2500.00
Percheron Mare, Decorated	1950		25.00	2700.00 to 3000.00
Percheron Mare, White	1950		25.00	1300.00 to 1500.00
Percheron Stallion, Decorated	1952		30.00	2500.00 to 2700.00
Percheron Stallion, White	1952		30.00	3900.00 to 4000.00
Peregrine Falcon*	1973	400	3400.00	3400.00
Pointer, Liver & White	1950	275	35.00	1700.00 to 1900.00
Polo Player	1957	100	850.00	4200.00 to 5000.00
Poodle, Reclining				195.00
Pope Pius XII Bust	1958	50	400.00	800.00 to 1000.00
Ptarmigans	1962	350	800.00	3000.00 to 4500.00
Pug Dog	1959	48	20.00	850.00 to 950.00
Raccoons	1971	350	1600.00	1500.00 to 1800.00
Red-Breasted Grosbeak	1950	361	10.00	1000.00 to 1800.00
Red Squirrels	1954	94	4.00	Unknown
Red Squirrels, Malvern	1972	350	2600.00	2600.00
Red-Winged Blackbirds	1957	100	700.00	5000.00 to 6500.00
Ring-Necked Pheasants	1953	500	425.00	1100.00 to 1500.00
Roadrunner	1968	500	1700.00	2500.00 to 3700.00
Robin	1964	500	600.00	4500.00 to 4800.00
Ruby-Crowned Kinglets	1957	300	150.00	1300.00 to 1500.00
Ruffed Grouse	1960	250	950.00	4800.00 to 5900.00

Boehm, Peregrine Falcon

Boehm,
Verdins With Stewart Crucifixion-Thorn

Boehm,
Mute Swans (Bird Of Peace)

Boehm, Lesser Prairie Chickens

Boehm, Western Bluebirds

Borsato, Morsels Of Wisdom

Boehm, Swan Centerpiece

Boehm, Sugarbirds

Boehm, Yellowhammer On Hawthorn

Burgues, American Goldfinches
With Morning Glories

Burgues, Baltimore Oriole

Burgues, Belted Kingfisher, Fledgling

Burgues, Bighorn Sheep

Rufous Hummingbirds**	1966	500	850.00	2000.00 to 2350.00
Saint Francis Of Assisi	1958	264	75.00	1200.00 to 2000.00
Saint Maria Goretti	1950	233	10.00	500.00 to 900.00
Scottish Terrier	1954	250	6.00	2750.00 to 3000.00
Screech Owl	1973	500	850.00	850.00
Snow Bunting	1971	400	1600.00	2000.00 to 2300.00
Song Sparrows	1956	50	2000.00	8800.00 to 9700.00
Streptocalyx Peoppigii	1973	200	3400.00	3400.00
Sugarbirds*	1961	100	2500.00	8000.00 to 10500.00
Swan Centerpiece, White		250	1900.00	1900.00
Towhee	1963	500	350.00	1750.00 to 2000.00
Tree Creepers	1972	350	3200.00	3200.00 to 3700.00
Tufted Titmice	1965	500	500.00	1500.00 to 1900.00
Varied Buntings	1965	300	2200.00	3500.00 to 4000.00
Venus	1953	96	28.00	600.00 to 700.00
Verdins With Stewart Crucifix-Thorn*	1969	750	800.00	1200.00 to 1300.00
Water Thrush				1025.00
Western Bluebirds*	1969	400	4500.00	5750.00 to 6000.00
Whippets	1954	248	50.00	3000.00 to 3400.00
White Mouse Preening	1959	469	15.00	250.00 to 300.00
Winter Robin	1971	350	1150.00	1150.00 to 1500.00
Wire-Haired Fox Terrier	1954	150	12.50	400.00 to 500.00
Wood Ducks	1951	201	15.00	1200.00 to 1400.00
Wood Thrushes	1966	400	3500.00	8000.00 to 10000.00
Woodcock	1954	500	25.00	1750.00 to 2400.00
Yellow-Bellied Sapsucker	1972	400	2700.00	2700.00 to 3100.00
Yellowhammer On Hawthorn*	1973	400	2800.00	2800.00
Young American Eagle	1969	850	700.00	1300.00 to 1500.00

Borsato Porcelains have been made by Antonio Borsato of Milan, Italy, since 1937. Limited editions were first made in 1973.

See listing for Borsato in Plate section

Borsato Porcelains

Morsels Of Wisdom**	1974	100	2600.00	2600.00

Dr. Irving Burgues, Austrian-born artist, is the designer of Burgues porcelains. His studio is located in Ocean County, New Jersey. Burgues porcelains are in the collections of many museums.

Burgues Porcelains

American Goldfinches With Morning Glories*		150	1250.00	1250.00
Anemone*		350	550.00	550.00
Baltimore Oriole, Juvenile*	1973	200	750.00	750.00
Belted Kingfisher Fledgling*		750	350.00	350.00
Bighorn Sheep**		250	2750.00	2750.00
Burro, Young		300	1250.00	1250.00
Canon Wren	1973	250	850.00	850.00
Carolina Wren With White Dogwood		350	750.00	750.00
Cassin's Kingbird		350	750.00	750.00
Cave Swallows, Male And Female		500	750.00	750.00
Chanticleer		100	1300.00	1300.00
Chickadee On Dogwood		75	950.00	950.00
Chipmunk With Acorn		750	150.00	150.00
Chipmunk With Fly Amanita**		450	400.00	400.00 to 600.00
Crab-Eater Seals		200	1250.00	1250.00
Daffodil Manco**		250	450.00	450.00
Golden-Crowned Kinglet		450	500.00	500.00
Golden-Winged Warbler In Nest		100	1100.00	1100.00
Junco On Snow		250	600.00	600.00
King Penguins**		350	850.00	850.00
Lady's Slipper Orchid, Pink*		350	800.00	800.00 to 1000.00
Lilac Charm Rose*	1973	75	700.00	700.00
Madonna		30	125.00	125.00
Magnolia, Oriental Strain*	1973	150	1600.00	1600.00
Prickly Pear Cactus*		250	900.00	900.00
Red-Breasted Nuthatch*		950	225.00	225.00
Redheaded Woodpecker*		350	1100.00	1100.00
Robin, Juvenile**		950	150.00	150.00
Robin With Marsh Marigolds**		500	550.00	550.00
Ruby-Throated Hummingbird**		300	600.00	600.00

Burgues, King Penguins

Burgues, Red-Breasted Nuthatch

Burgues, Snow Bunting, Juvenile

Burgues, Magnolia

Burgues, Lilac Charm Rose

Burgues, Pink Lady Slipper Orchid

Burgues, Robin, Juvenile

Burgues, White-Throated Sparrow

Burgues, Robin With Marsh Marigolds

Burgues, Red-Headed Woodpecker

Burgues, Snowy Owl

Burgues,
Snow Bunting With Trumpet Honeysuckle

Burgues, Water Lily

Burgues, Prickly Pear Cactus

Snow Bunting, Juvenile*		950	165.00	165.00
Snow Bunting With Trumpet Honeysuckle*		500	350.00	350.00
Snowy Owl*		500	450.00	450.00
Veiltail Goldfish, Colored**		150	875.00	875.00 to 975.00
Veiltail Goldfish, Glazed		150	875.00	875.00
Water Lily*		200	175.00	175.00
White-Breasted Nuthatches**		75	3500.00	3500.00
White-Throated Sparrow*	1973	250	800.00	800.00 to 1000.00
Wild Rose		150	2500.00	2500.00
Yellow-Billed Cuckoo		500	400.00	400.00
Yellow-Billed Cuckoo, Juvenile		950	175.00	175.00
Yellow Warbler		75	700.00	700.00

The Cybis Porcelain firm of Trenton, New Jersey, was founded in 1942 by Boleslaw Cybis, an internationally known painter and sculptor. The studio has continued production since Mr. Cybis's death in 1957. Cybis porcelains are in the collections of many museums.

Cybis Limnettes

Autumn	1973	500	125.00	125.00
Country Fair	1973	500	125.00	125.00
Easter Egg Hunt	1973	500	125.00	125.00
Independence Celebrations	1973	500	125.00	125.00
Merry Christmas	1973	500	125.00	125.00
Sabbath Morning	1973	500	125.00	125.00
Spring	1973	500	125.00	125.00
The Pond	1973	500	125.00	125.00
The Seashore	1973	500	125.00	125.00
Windy Day	1973	500	125.00	125.00
Winter	1973	500	125.00	125.00

Cybis Porcelains

American Crested Iris With Bobwhite Chick*	500	975.00	975.00
Autumn Dogwood With Chickadees**	500	1100.00	1100.00
Baby Bust	239	375.00	400.00 to 450.00
Beatrice	700	225.00	800.00 to 1400.00
Blackfeet, Beaverhead, Medicine Man**	500	2000.00	2000.00
Blue-Gray Gnatcatchers, Pair	200	400.00	1700.00 to 1950.00
Blue-Headed Vireo With Lilac, Pair	500	1200.00	1800.00 to 2100.00
Bull	100	200.00	4000.00 to 4500.00
Calla Lily*	500	700.00	800.00 to 1500.00
Carousel Goat*	500	875.00	875.00
Carousel Horse**	500	925.00	925.00
Christmas Rose	500	250.00	600.00 to 775.00
Clematis With House Wren**	500	1300.00	1300.00 to 1900.00
Columbia, 1776 Through 1976	200	1000.00	2000.00 to 2900.00
Conductors' Hands	250	250.00	475.00 to 575.00
Cree Indian, Magic Boy	100	2500.00	2500.00
Cybele	500	675.00	675.00
Dahlia	350	450.00	1100.00 to 1800.00
Dakota, Laughing Water, Minnehaha	500	1500.00	1500.00
Dutch Crocus*	700	550.00	550.00
Eleanor Of Aquitaine	750	875.00	875.00 to 1600.00
Elephant	100	600.00	3900.00 to 6000.00
Enchanted Prince, Florimund*	500	975.00	975.00
Enchanted Princess, Aurora*	500	1125.00	1125.00
Eskimo Mother*	350	1875.00	1875.00
Exodus	50	350.00	1500.00 to 3000.00
Flight Into Egypt	50	175.00	2750.00 to 3000.00
Folk Singer	283	300.00	750.00 to 1000.00
Golden Clarion Lily	100	250.00	4000.00 to 4200.00
Great White Heron	350	850.00	1600.00 to 2750.00
Guinevere	800	250.00	850.00 to 1200.00
Hamlet	500	350.00	900.00 to 1750.00
Holy Child Of Prague	10	1500.00	5000.00
Horse	100	150.00	1600.00 to 1800.00
Iroquois, At The Council Fire*	350	4250.00	4250.00
Iris	250	500.00	3000.00 to 3200.00
Juliet	800	175.00	1750.00 to 2600.00
Kwan Yin*	750	1250.00	1250.00 to 1750.00
Little Blue Heron	500	425.00	1200.00 to 2000.00

Cybis, Calla Lily

Cybis, Blackfeet, Beaverhead, Medicine Man

Cybis, Pegasus

Cybis, Dutch Crocus

Cybis, Eskimo Mother

Cybis, Shoshone, Sacajawea

Cybis, Kwan Yin

Cybis, Iroquois, At The Council Fire

Cybis, Enchanted Prince Florimund
Cybis, Enchanted Princess Aurora

Cybis, Onondaga, Hiawatha

Cybis, Turtle Doves

Moses, The Great Lawgiver	750	250.00	2000.00 to 2500.00
Narcissus	500	350.00	350.00 to 450.00
Nashua	500	2000.00	2000.00
Onondaga, Hiawatha*	500	1500.00	1500.00
Ophelia	800	650.00	750.00 to 1250.00
Pansies With Butterfly	1000	275.00	275.00 to 285.00
Pegasus	500	1450.00	1450.00 to 1600.00
Portia	750	825.00	825.00
Prophet	50	250.00	1000.00 to 2000.00
Rapunzel	1000	375.00	375.00
Ring-Necked Pheasant	150	750.00	1200.00 to 2500.00
Scarlett	500	450.00	825.00 to 1550.00
Shoshone, Sacagawea**	500	2250.00	2250.00
Skylarks, Pair	350	300.00	1000.00 to 1800.00
Solitary Sandpipers	400	500.00	1250.00 to 2000.00
Stallion	500	475.00	550.00 to 700.00
Thoroughbred	350	425.00	1000.00 to 1650.00
Tranquility Base, Apollo 11 Moon Mission	111	1500.00	1600.00 to 1800.00
Turtledoves**	500	350.00	4500.00 to 5000.00
Unicorn**	500	1250.00	1250.00
Wood Duck	500	325.00	375.00 to 500.00

Doris Lindner, see Royal Worcester

Edward J. Rohn porcelains, see Rohn

Frederick Gertner, see Royal Worcester

F.W. Goebel factory was founded in 1871 by Franz and William Goebel. In 1934, under the tradename of Hummelwerk, the German factory, in collaboration with Berta Hummel, produced the first Hummel figurines. Limited edition plates were introduced in 1971. A series of limited edition figurines commemorating the American Bicentennial was issued in 1974.

See listing for Hummel Goebel in Plate section

Goebel Figurines

Attacked By A Grizzly	1974	400	600.00	600.00
Forging Westward	1974	400	600.00	600.00
George Washington	1974	400	600.00	600.00
Paul Revere's Midnight Ride	1974	400	600.00	600.00
Signing The Declaration Of Independence	1974	400	600.00	600.00
Westward Bound	1974	400	600.00	600.00

Gorham, Rockwell, Four Seasons, Set Of 4

Gorham Silver Co., of Providence, Rhode Island, was founded in 1831. Crystal and China were added in 1970. The first limited edition item, a silver Christmas ornament, was introduced in 1970. Limited edition porcelain plates were issued in 1971. Ingots and medals were first made by the Gorham Mint division in 1973.

See listing for Gorham in Plate, Bar & Ingot, and Medal sections

Gorham Floral Arrangements

Fleurs Des Siecles, Fontainebleau		500	600.00	600.00
Fleurs Des Siecles, Versailles		500	1000.00	1000.00

Gorham Figurines

Rockwell, Four Seasons, Set Of 4	1972	5000	200.00	175.00 to 200.00
Rockwell, Four Seasons, Set Of 4*	1973	5000	280.00	225.00 to 300.00

See listing for Granget in Plate section

Granget Crystal Sculptures

Long-Eared Owl, Asio Otus*	1973	350	2250.00	2250.00

Granget Porcelains

Blue Titmouse, Lively Fellow	1974	750	1295.00	1295.00
Bobwhite Quail, Off Season				2700.00 to 3300.00
Canadian Geese, Heading South				3750.00 to 4650.00
Chaffinch, Spring Melody	1974	750	1675.00	1675.00
Dolphin Group				7500.0 to 19000.00
Golden-Crested Wrens, Tiny Acrobats	1974	700	2060.00	2060.00
Goldfinch, Morning Hour	1974	750	1250.00	1250.00
Great Blue Herons, The Challenge		200		7400.00 to 9000.00
Great Titmouse Adults, Busy Activity	1974	750	2175.00	2175.00
Great Titmouse Babies, Fledged At Last	1974	650	2395.00	2395.00

Gorham, Rockwell, Four Seasons, Set Of 4

Hairy Woodpecker With Nuthatches				2500.00 to 3000.00
Halla				1300.00 to 1400.00
Kingfisher, Detected Prey	1974	600	1975.00	1975.00
Mallard Family, First Lesson				2350.00 to 2800.00
Mourning Doves, Engaged				1400.00 to 1750.00
Pintail Ducks, Safe At Home		350		2800.00 to 3400.00
Ring-Necked Pheasants, Take Cover				5250.00 to 6350.00
Robin, A Day Begins	1974	750	1795.00	1795.00
Screech Owl With Chick, Disdain				2600.00 to 2850.00
Stag				4000.00 to 4850.00
Woodcocks, A Family Affair				1100.00 to 1500.00

Granget Woodcarvings

Eagle, Large*	1973	250	2000.00	2000.00
Eagle, Small	1973	1000	550.00	550.00
Fox, Large*	1973	200	2800.00	2800.00
Fox, Small	1973	1000	650.00	650.00
Grouse, Large*	1973	200	2800.00	2800.00
Grouse, Small	1973	1000	700.00	700.00
Lynx, Large*	1973	250	1600.00	1600.00
Lynx, Small	1973	1000	400.00	400.00
Mallard, Large*	1973	250	2000.00	2000.00
Mallard, Small	1973	1000	500.00	500.00
Partridge, Large*	1973	200	2400.00	2400.00
Partridge, Small	1973	1000	550.00	550.00
Rooster, Large	1973	250	2400.00	2400.00
Rooster, Small	1973	1000	600.00	600.00
Wild Boar, Large*	1973	200	2400.00	2400.00
Wild Boar, Small	1973	1000	275.00	275.00

Gregory Higgins' sculptures are of manganese bronze, silver, and vermeil on a mineral rock base. Each piece is signed and numbered by the artist.

Gregory Higgins Sculptures

Angelfish On Cut Jade, Sterling	750	165.00	180.00
Aquarium With Sterling Fish	500	285.00	310.00
Avocet On Natural Jade	350	570.00	700.00
Butterfly Fish On Coral, Sterling*	500	550.00	550.00
Cypress With Sterling Birds*	500	240.00	310.00
Deer*	500	240.00	260.00
Egret On Natural Jade*	500	285.00	310.00
Hummingbird With Fuchsia*	500	285.00	310.00
Hummingbirds With Fuchsias	500	670.00	680.00
Landlocked Salmon With Rapids Of Jade	500	450.00	470.00
Marsh Wrens With Nest, Bronze	500	600.00	600.00
Marsh Wrens With Nest, Sterling	500	700.00	700.00
Owl	500	240.00	270.00
Pelican With Sterling Fish On Jade*	500	285.00	310.00
Peregrine Falcon & Sterling Jesses On Jade*	500	1200.00	1200.00
Raccoon*	500	240.00	260.00
Sea Bass With Vermeil Fish, Sterling*	500	500.00	500.00
Sea Otter With Sterling Abalone*	500	230.00	260.00
Stilt With Cattails On Cut Jade*	750	175.00	180.00
Swan	500	230.00	260.00
Trout With Sterling Hook On Cut Jade, Bronze*	500	400.00	450.00
Trout With Vermeil Hook And Fly, Sterling	500	450.00	470.00
Walrus On Cut Jade*	500	240.00	290.00
Warbler On Cut Jade, Bronze	750	175.00	200.00
Warbler On Cut Jade, Sterling	750	260.00	260.00
Warbler With Sterling Eggs, Bronze	500	600.00	600.00
Warbler With Vermeil Eggs, Sterling	500	700.00	700.00
Wren On Cut Jade, Bronze	750	165.00	180.00
Wren On Cut Jade, Sterling	750	220.00	220.00

Ispanky porcelains are designed by Lazlo Ispanky at his studios in Pennington, New Jersey. Mr. Ispanky was born in Budapest in 1919, and moved to the U. S. in 1956. He works in wood, stone, and metal, as well as porcelain. The first limited edition pieces were The Hunt, Pioneer Scout, and Pack Horse. They were issued in 1966. Of the 500 Rosh Hashana pieces made, 498 have white beards and only 2 have a gray beard. The Spring Bouquet porcelain is made of 937 separate parts, 113 casted and 824 hand made.

Gorham, Rockwell, Four Seasons, Set Of 4

Gorham, Rockwell, Four Seasons, Set Of 4

Granget, Woodcarving, Lynx

Granget, Woodcarving, Fox

Granget, Woodcarving, Grouse

Granget, Woodcarving, Wild Boar

Granget, Woodcarving, Mallard

Granget, Crystal Sculpture,
Long-Eared Owl

Granget, Woodcarving, Partridge

Gregory Higgins, Deer

Gregory Higgins, Cypress With Sterling Birds

Gregory Higgins, Butterfly Fish On Coral, Sterling

Gregory Higgins,
Hummingbird With Fuchsia

Gregory Higgins,
Peregrine Falcon & Sterling Jesses On Jade

Gregory Higgins, Egret On Natural Jade

Gregory Higgins,
Sea Otter With
Sterling Abalone

Gregory Higgins,
Walrus On Cut Jade

Ispanky, Annabel Lee

Ispanky, Aaron

Ispanky, Abraham

Gregory Higgins,
Sea Bass With Vermeil Fish, Sterling

Gregory Higgins, Raccoon

Gregory Higgins,
Trout With Sterling Hook On Cut Jade, Bronze

Gregory Higgins,
Pelican With Sterling Fish On Jade

Gregory Higgins,
Stilt With Cattails On Cut Jade

Ispanky, Beauty And The Beast

Ispanky, Dawn

Ispanky, Debutante

Ispanky,
Eternal Love

See listing for Ispanky in Plate section

Ispanky Porcelains

Aaron**		350	1200.00	1200.00
Abraham**		500	600.00	600.00 to 700.00
Annabel Lee**		500	750.00	750.00 to 900.00
Artist Girl		500	200.00	700.00 to 800.00
Autumn Wind		500	300.00	500.00 to 680.00
Ballerina		500	350.00	350.00 to 400.00
Ballet Dancers		500	350.00	350.00
Beauty And The Beast*		75	4500.00	4500.00
Betsy Ross		350	750.00	800.00 to 975.00
Bird Of Paradise		250	1500.00	1500.00 to 2200.00
Cavalry Scout, Decorated		200	1000.00	1000.00 to 1100.00
Cavalry Scout, White		150	675.00	675.00
Celeste		200	275.00	350.00 to 500.00
Christine		300	350.00	660.00 to 800.00
Cinderella		400	375.00	375.00 to 450.00
Daffodils		250	950.00	950.00
Dawn*		300	500.00	500.00 to 600.00
David		400	450.00	450.00
Debutante*		500	350.00	350.00 to 450.00
Dianne	1974	500	500.00	500.00
Dragon, Emerald**		100	2500.00	2500.00
Dragon, Turquoise		100	2500.00	2500.00
Drummer Boy, Decorated		200	250.00	250.00 to 350.00
Drummer Boy, White		600	150.00	150.00 to 175.00
Dutch Iris		250	1400.00	1400.00 to 1500.00
Eternal Love*		300	400.00	425.00 to 450.00
Evening		300	375.00	500.00 to 600.00
Excalibur		100	3500.00	3500.00
Felicia*		100	2500.00	2500.00
Forty-Niner, Decorated		200	450.00	450.00
Forty-Niner, White		350	250.00	250.00 to 275.00
Freedom		250	300.00	Unknown
Great Spirit, Decorated		200	1500.00	1500.00
Great Spirit, White*		150	750.00	750.00 to 800.00
Hawaiian Beauty		150	1500.00	Unknown
Horse		300	300.00	450.00 to 500.00
Horsepower		100	1650.00	1650.00
Hunt, Decorated		200	2000.00	2000.00 to 2200.00
Hunt, White		150	120.00	1200.00 to 1400.00
Icarus*		350	350.00	350.00 to 400.00
Isaiah		300	475.00	500.00 to 750.00
Jessamy		400	450.00	450.00 to 500.00
King & Queen, Pair		250	750.00	800.00 to 850.00
King Arthur*		500	300.00	300.00
Lorelei*		500	550.00	550.00 to 600.00
Love*		300	375.00	375.00
Love Letters**		450	750.00	750.00
Madame Butterfly*		300	1500.00	1500.00
Maid Of The Mist*		350	450.00	Unknown
Maria		350	750.00	950.00 to 1250.00
Meditation*		300	350.00	400.00 to 650.00
Mermaid Group		200	950.00	1000.00 to 1150.00
Messiah		750	450.00	450.00
Morning		500	300.00	500.00 to 695.00
Moses		400	400.00	600.00 to 800.00
Mr. And Mrs. Otter		500	250.00	250.00
On The Trail, Decorated		200	1700.00	1700.00 to 1900.00
On The Trail, White		150	750.00	750.00
Orchids		250	1000.00	1000.00
Owl		300	750.00	750.00
Pack Horse, Decorated		200	700.00	1000.00 to 1200.00
Pack Horse, White		150	500.00	500.00 to 600.00
Peace, Decorated		100	375.00	500.00 to 650.00
Peace, White		100	300.00	400.00 to 500.00
Peace Riders		10	35000.00	35000.00
Pegasus, Decorated		300	375.00	500.00 to 600.00
Pegasus, White		300	300.00	400.00 to 500.00
Pilgrim Family, Decorated		200	500.00	500.00

Ispanky, Felicia

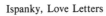
Ispanky, Love Letters

Ispanky, Great Spirit

Ispanky, Maid Of The Mist

Ispanky, King Arthur

Ispanky, Lorelei

Ispanky, Love

Ispanky, Meditation

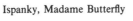
Ispanky, Madame Butterfly

Ispanky, Icarus

Ispanky, Rebekah

Ispanky,
Romeo And Juliet

Ispanky,
Spirit Of The Sea

Ispanky, Spring Ballet

Pilgrim Family, White	350	350.00	350.00
Pioneer Scout, Decorated	200	1000.00	1000.00 to 1200.00
Pioneer Scout, White	150	675.00	675.00 to 750.00
Pioneer Woman, Decorated	200	350.00	350.00 to 450.00
Pioneer Woman, White	150	225.00	225.00 to 275.00
Princess And The Frog	500	675.00	675.00 to 750.00
Promises	100	225.00	2000.00 to 2500.00
Queen Of Spring	200	850.00	1100.00 to 1300.00
Quest	50	1500.00	1500.00 to 1750.00
Rebekah*	300	400.00	400.00
Reverie	200	200.00	Unknown
Romeo & Juliet*	500	375.00	375.00
Rosh Hashana, Gray Beard**	2	275.00	Unknown
Rosh Hashana, White Beard	498	275.00	575.00 to 700.00
Spirit Of The Sea*	450	500.00	500.00
Spring Ballet*	400	450.00	450.00 to 500.00
Spring Bouquet**	50	3000.00	3250.00 to 3750.00
Storm	500	400.00	400.00 to 450.00
Swan Lake	300	750.00	750.00
Tekiah*	200	1800.00	1800.00
Texas Rangers	600	1650.00	1650.00 to 1800.00
Thrasher	300	1000.00	1000.00 to 1200.00
Tulips, Red	250	1800.00	1800.00
Tulips, Yellow	250	1800.00	1800.00

Jean-Paul Loup, the editor of Art of Chicago, joined the Betournes Studio of Limoges, France, to issue their first limited edition plates in 1971. The plates and porcelain paintings are hand-applied enamel on copper. Each plate is signed by both Michel Betourne and Jean-Paul Loup.

See listing for Jean-Paul Loup in Plate section

Jean-Paul Loup/Betournes Enamel on Copper Paintings

Bonaparte*	8	795.00	825.00 to 850.00
Boys Eating Melons And Grapes*	8	950.00	950.00 to 1000.00
Card Players*	8	375.00	375.00 to 425.00
Coronation Of Napoleon*	8	1250.00	1250.00 to 1350.00
Don Manuel*	8	500.00	500.00 to 550.00
Effects Of Insobriety*	8	950.00	950.00 to 1000.00
Four Seasons, Autumn**	200	250.00	250.00 to 300.00
Four Seasons, Spring**	200	250.00	250.00 to 300.00
Four Seasons, Summer**	200	250.00	250.00 to 300.00
Four Seasons, Winter**	200	250.00	250.00 to 300.00
Good Monk*	8	650.00	650.00 to 700.00
Holy Family*	8	950.00	950.00 to 1000.00
Late Care*	8	650.00	650.00 to 700.00
Madonna Della*	8	795.00	795.00 to 850.00
Napoleon And The Austrian Emperor*	8	500.00	500.00 to 550.00
Napoleon, Charles*	8	450.00	450.00 to 500.00
Nest*	8	650.00	650.00 to 700.00
Portrait Of Anna Codde*	8	650.00	650.00 to 700.00
Six Crafts, The Butcher**	150	200.00	200.00
Six Crafts, The Mower**	150	200.00	200.00
Six Crafts, The Plowman**	150	200.00	200.00
Six Crafts, The Reaper**	150	200.00	200.00
Six Crafts, The Sower**	150	200.00	200.00
Six Crafts, The Vinedresser**	150	200.00	200.00
Spirit Of 76*	8	795.00	795.00 to 850.00
Traveler's Halt*	8	650.00	650.00 to 700.00

Kaiser Porcelain Manufactory was founded in 1872 by August Alboth in Colburg, Germany. The plant was moved to Steffelstein, Bavaria, in 1953. Their first limited edition plate was made in 1970. That year, the company's mark was changed from AK and a crown to 'Kaiser Porcelain.'

See listing for Kaiser in Plate section

Kaiser Porcelains

American Eagle, Color	1970	400	500.00	500.00 to 600.00
American Eagle, White*	1970	1200	250.00	300.00 to 350.00
Arabian Stallion, Color**	1972	600	250.00	300.00 to 350.00
Baby Titmice, Color	1974	800	400.00	400.00

Jean-Paul Loup, Bonaparte

Jean-Paul Loup,
Boys Eating Melons And Grapes

Ispanky, Tekieh

Jean-Paul Loup, Effects Of Insobriety

Jean-Paul Loup, Card Players

Jean-Paul Loup,
Four Seasons, Spring

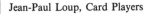

Jean-Paul Loup,
Four Seasons, Autumn

Jean-Paul Loup, Coronation Of Napoleon

Jean-Paul Loup,
Four Seasons, Winter

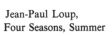

Jean-Paul Loup,
Four Seasons, Summer

Jean-Paul Loup, Don Manuel

Jean-Paul Loup, Napoleon, Charles

Jean-Paul Loup, Madonna Della

Jean-Paul Loup,
Napoleon And The Austrian Emperor

Jean-Paul Loup, Good Monk

Jean-Paul Loup, Late Care

Jean-Paul Loup, Traveler's Halt

Jean-Paul Loup, Spirit Of '76

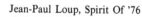

Jean-Paul Loup, Nest

Jean-Paul Loup, Holy Family

Jean-Paul Loup, Six Crafts,
The Vinedresser

Jean-Paul Loup, Six Crafts,
The Butcher

Jean-Paul Loup, Six Crafts,
The Sower

Jean-Paul Loup, Six Crafts,
The Mower

Jean-Paul Loup, Six Crafts,
The Plowman

Jean-Paul Loup, Six Crafts,
The Reaper

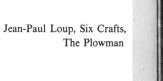

Kaiser, Arabian Stallion

Kaiser, Flushed, Color

Kaiser, American Eagle, White

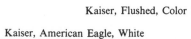

Kaiser, Encroachment, Color

Kaiser, Bluebird

Kaiser, Goshawk, Color

Kaiser, Goshawk, White

Kaiser, Triple Porpoise Group, White

Kaiser, Waiting For Mother, Color

Baby Titmice, White	1974	1200	200.00	200.00
Baltimore Oriole, Color	1970	2000	60.00	80.00 to 100.00
Bluebird, Color*	1973	2500	120.00	120.00 to 130.00
Blue Jay, Color**	1970	2000	60.00	85.00 to 100.00
Blue Jay With Wood Base	1974	1500	475.00	475.00
Cardinal, Color**	1970	2000	60.00	80.00 to 100.00
Cardinal With Wood Base, Color	1971	1500	225.00	225.00
Encroachment, Color*	1973	950	900.00	900.00
Flushed, Color*	1973	950	1000.00	900.00 to 1000.00
Goshawk, Color*	1973	800	1200.00	1100.00 to 1200.00
Goshawk, White*	1973	700	550.00	500.00 to 550.00
Hummingbirds With Wood Base	1974	1500	450.00	450.00
Kingfisher, Color**	1972	1500	140.00	175.00 to 200.00
Kingfisher, White	1971	2000	45.00	55.00 to 60.00
Owl, Color**	1970	1500	150.00	200.00 to 225.00
Owl, White	1972	2000	70.00	80.00 to 90.00
Pigeon Group, Color	1970	1500	150.00	200.00 to 225.00
Pigeon Group, White	1972	2000	60.00	75.00 to 85.00
Pony Group, Color**	1972	1000	150.00	200.00 to 225.00
Pony Group, White	1972	5000	50.00	60.00 to 70.00
Roadrunner, Color	1973	1000	350.00	300.00 to 350.00
Robin & Worm, Color	1970	2000	60.00	80.00 to 90.00
Robin With Wood Base	1974	1500	260.00	260.00
Scarlet Tanager, Color	1970	2000	60.00	80.00 to 90.00
Seagull, Color	1973	800	850.00	850.00
Seagull, White	1973	700	550.00	500.00 to 550.00
Tay-Kaiser Eagle, Color	1973	800	1300.00	1300.00
Triple Porpoise Group, White**	1971	5000	85.00	100.00 to 130.00
Waiting For Mother, Color*	1973	950	550.00	500.00 to 550.00
Wild Ducks, Color**	1970	1500	150.00	200.00 to 250.00

King's Porcelain Factory is located in Italy. Their limited edition plates, introduced in 1973, are high bas relief and hand-painted. Limited edition figurines were first made in 1974.

See listing for King's Porcelain in Plate section

King's Porcelain Figurines

Blue Jay	1974	200	900.00	900.00
European Roller	1974	350	500.00	500.00
Hummingbird	1974	300	700.00	700.00
Robins	1974	300	650.00	650.00
Titmouse	1974	250	700.00	700.00
Woodcock	1974	150	1800.00	1800.00

Kirk limited editions are made by Samuel Kirk and Sons, Inc. The firm was started in Baltimore, Maryland, in 1815. The company is well known for both antique and modern silver wares. Limited edition plates and spoons were first made in 1972.

See listing for Kirk in Plate section

Kirk Silver Figurines

Foxhounds	500	150.00	150.00
Mare And Foal	250	200.00	200.00
Pony And Girl	250	150.00	150.00

Kramlik, see Balint Kramlik

Lichtenstein Sculptures

Airmail Plane, Chrome Plated	50	300.00	350.00 to 400.00
Airmail Plane, Polished Bronze	50	275.00	325.00 to 375.00
Airmail Plane, Silver*	50	375.00	500.00 to 525.00

Lindner, Doris, see Royal Worcester

Lladro Porcelain factory of Tabernes Blanques, Spain, produced its first limited edition plate in 1971. Lladro also produces a large line of limited and nonlimited porcelains.

See listing for Lladro in Plate section

Lladro Porcelains

Allegory For Peace	150	550.00	550.00
Antique Automobile*	750	1100.00	1100.00

Eagles		750	900.00	900.00
Eve At The Tree		600	450.00	450.00
Girl With Guitar		600	650.00	650.00
Hamlet		750	350.00	350.00
Hansom Carriage		750	1250.00	1250.00
Lyric Muse		400	750.00	750.00
Madonna With Child		300	450.00	450.00
Madonna With Child, Seated		300	400.00	400.00
Oriental Horse		350	1100.00	1100.00
Othello & Desdemona*		750	350.00	350.00
Seabirds With Nest		500	600.00	600.00
Three Graces		500	950.00	950.00
Turkey Group		350	650.00	650.00
Young Oriental Man		500	500.00	500.00

Moussalli Porcelains

American Redstart With Cherries*		500	60.00	150.00
American Redstart With Flowers*	1972	500	600.00	600.00
Anna's Hummingbird			250.00	125.00 to 250.00
Baltimore Oriole		300	650.00	1250.00
Bay-Breasted Warbler*	1974	300	325.00	325.00
Black-Capped Chickadee**	1969	250	550.00	350.00
Canadian Warbler*		500	180.00	200.00 to 250.00
Cardinal		300	600.00	700.00 to 800.00
Eastern Bluebird On Rock			250.00	125.00 to 250.00
Flycatcher	1974	300	360.00	360.00
Golden-Crowned Kinglet*	1974	400	225.00	225.00
Golden Finch*		150	550.00	650.00 to 700.00
House Wren*	1972	500	250.00	275.00 to 325.00
Hummingbird In Forsythia*		500	250.00	150.00 to 325.00
Hummingbird And Honeysuckle*		500	250.00	275.00 to 325.00
Indigo Bunting**	1972	150	650.00	750.00 to 800.00
Olive Warbler*		500	200.00	225.00 to 250.00
Redbreasted Grosbeak**	1971	300	435.00	435.00
Red-Faced Warbler*	1974	300	435.00	435.00
Redheaded Woodpecker*		200	450.00	525.00 to 575.00
Red-Winged Blackbird		300	700.00	1000.00 to 1250.00
Say's Phoebe**	1974	300	360.00	360.00
Scarlet Tanager*		300	360.00	360.00
Slate-Colored Junco*		500	180.00	200.00 to 250.00
Snow Bunting**	1974	200	830.00	830.00
Tufted Titmouse**	1972	150	650.00	750.00 to 800.00
Wheatear*		300	350.00	400.00 to 450.00
Wren On Magnolia Branch*		300	600.00	725.00 to 775.00
Wren On A Rock*		500	170.00	225.00 to 275.00
Yellow-Throated Warbler		500	120.00	150.00 to 200.00

Nikerk Silver Figurines

Christmas Tree, Silver	1971	200	100.00	115.00 to 150.00
Christmas, Boy Hanging Ornament, Silver	1972	200	85.00	95.00 to 110.00

The Poole Pottery of Poole, Dorset, England, has produced pottery since 1873. Limited edition plates, which were first made in 1972, are handmade to resemble stained glass windows. A limited edition porcelain line featuring game birds was introduced in 1973.

See listing for Poole in Plate section

Poole Porcelains

Canada Goose*	1973	500	350.00	350.00

Rohn porcelain sculptures are made by American artist Edward J. Rohn of Elmhurst, Illinois.

Rohn Porcelains

American G.I.		100	600.00	600.00
Apache*		200	900.00	900.00
Coolie		100	700.00	700.00
Crow Indian		100	800.00	800.00
Gypsy		150	1450.00	1450.00
Jeanine		400	475.00	475.00
Matador*		150	2400.00	2400.00
Riverboat Captain		100	1000.00	1000.00

Lichtenstein, Airmail Plane

Lladro, Antique Automobile

Moussalli, American Redstart With Cherries

Lladro, Othello & Desdemona

Moussalli,
American Redstart With Flowers

Moussalli,
Hummingbird And Honeysuckle

Moussalli, Olive Warbler

Moussalli, Indigo Bunting

Moussalli, Golden-Crowned Kinglet

Moussalli, Bay-Breasted Warbler

Moussalli, Canadian Warbler

Moussalli, Hummingbird In Forsythia

Moussalli, House Wren

Moussalli, Golden Finch

Moussalli, Wren On A Rock

Moussalli, Scarlet Tanager

Royal Crown Derby, Welsh Dragon

Moussalli, Red-Faced Warbler

Moussalli, Redheaded Woodpecker

Moussalli, Slate-Colored Junco

Moussalli, Tufted Titmouse

Poole, Canada Goose

Moussalli, Wheatear

Moussalli, Wren On Magnolia Branch

Rohn, Apache

Rohn, Matador

Rohn, The Sherif

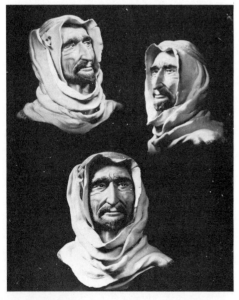

The Sherif*		150	1500.00	1500.00
Trailhand		100	1200.00	1200.00

Ronald Van Ruyckevelt, see Royal Worcester

Royal Crown Derby of England was established as the Derby factory in 1750. The name Royal Crown Derby was used after 1890. Current limited editons were introduced in 1969.

See listing for Royal Crown Derby in Plate section

Royal Crown Derby Porcelains

Welsh Dragon, Investiture Of Prince Of Wales*	1969	250	125.00	125.00

The Doulton Porcelain factory was founded in 1815. Royal Doulton is the name used on pottery made after 1902. A series of limited edition commemorative and special wares was made during the 1930s. Modern limited edition Christmas plates and mugs were first made in 1971. Royal Doulton also makes a line of limited edition porcelains.

See listing for Royal Doulton in Plate section

Royal Doulton Porcelains

Indian Brave*	1967	500	2500.00	2500.00 to 3000.00
Lady Musicians, Cello**	1971	750	250.00	250.00
Lady Musicians, Flute*	1973	750	250.00	250.00
Lady Musicians, Harp*	1973	750	275.00	275.00
Lady Musicians, Lute*	1972	750	250.00	250.00
Lady Musicians, Violin*	1972	750	250.00	250.00
Lady Musicians, Virginals**	1971	750	250.00	250.00
Prince Charles Bust**	1969	150	400.00	400.00
Queen Elizabeth & Duke Of Edinburgh Busts*	1972	1000	1000.00	1000.00
The Palio*	1971	500	2500.00	2500.00

The Royal Worcester Porcelain Factory, of Worcester, England, was founded under the name of Worcester in 1751. The name was changed to Royal Worcester in 1862. Limited edition plates, in both pewter and porcelain, were first introduced in 1972. Limited edition porcelains have been made since the 1930s.

See listing for Royal Worcester in Plate section

Royal Worcester Pewter Figurines

Colonial Craftsmen, Blacksmith	1973	2500	225.00	225.00
Colonial Craftsmen, Cabinetmaker	1973	2500	225.00	225.00
Colonial Craftsmen, Potter	1973	2500	195.00	195.00

Dorothy Doughty, English artist, was born in San Remo, Italy, in 1892. She began modelling porcelain birds for Royal Worcester in the 1930s. The first model in the American bird series was issued in 1935. The British series was begun in 1964.

Royal Worcester, Dorothy Doughty Porcelains

Apple Blossoms	1941	250	400.00	3250.00 to 3750.00
Audubon Warblers	1963	500	1350.00	4000.00 to 4200.00
Baltimore Orioles*	1938	250	350.00	5500.00 to 5800.00
Bewick's Wrens & Yellow Jasmine	1956	500	600.00	3200.00 to 3800.00
Bluebirds	1936	350	500.00	8500.00 to 9000.00
Blue Tits & Pussy Willow	1965	500	1250.00	2000.00 to 2500.00
Bobwhite Quail*	1940	22	275.00	36000.00
Cactus Wrens*	1959	500	1250.00	3500.00 to 4500.00
Canyon Wrens	1960	500	750.00	3500.00 to 4000.00
Cardinals	1937	500	500.00	8750.00 to 9250.00
Carolina Paroquet, Color	1968	250	1200.00	1900.00 to 2200.00
Carolina Paroquet, White	1968	75	600.00	900.00 to 1100.00
Cerulean Warblers & Red Maple	1965	500	1350.00	2500.00 to 3000.00
Chickadees & Larch	1938	300	350.00	8500.00 to 8900.00
Chiffchaff	1965	500	1500.00	1800.00 to 2900.00
Crabapples	1940	250	400.00	3750.00 to 4250.00
Downy Woodpecker & Pecan, Color	1967	500	1500.00	2100.00 to 2400.00
Downy Woodpecker & Pecan, White	1967	75	1000.00	1450.00 to 1600.00
Elf Owl*	1959	500	875.00	2250.00 to 2300.00
Gnatcatchers*	1955	500	600.00	4500.00 to 4900.00
Goldfinches & Thistle	1936	250	350.00	6500.00 to 7000.00
Gray Wagtail**	1968	500	600.00	1000.00 to 1250.00

Royal Doulton, Indian Brave

Royal Doulton,
Queen Elizabeth & Duke Of Edinburgh Busts

Royal Doulton, The Palio

Royal Doulton,
Lady Musicians, Harp   Royal Doulton,
Lady Musicians, Flute

Royal Doulton,
Lady Musicians, Violin   Royal Doulton,
Lady Musicians, Lute

Royal Worcester, Dorothy Doughty, Cactus Wrens

Royal Doulton, Prince Charles Bust

Royal Worcester, Dorothy Doughty, Bobwhite Quail

Royal Worcester, Dorothy Doughty,
Baltimore Orioles

Royal Worcester, Dorothy Doughty,
Gnatcatchers

Royal Worcester, Dorothy Doughty,
Elf Owl

Royal Worcester, Dorothy Doughty,
Nightingale And Honeysuckle

Royal Worcester, Dorothy Doughty,
Hooded Warblers

Royal Worcester,
Dorothy Doughty, Scarlet Tanagers

Hooded Warblers*	1961	500	950.00	4700.00 to 4900.00
Indigo Buntings	1942	500	375.00	2750.00 to 3000.00
Kingfisher Cock & Autumn Beech	1965	500	1250.00	1900.00 to 2300.00
Kinglets & Noble Pine	1952	500	450.00	4000.00 to 4200.00
Lark Sparrow	1966	500	750.00	1100.00 to 1400.00
Lazuli Buntings & Chokecherries, Color	1962	500	1350.00	3000.00 to 4500.00
Lazuli Buntings & Chokecherries, White	1962	100	1350.00	2600.00 to 3000.00
Lesser Whitethroats	1965	500	1350.00	Unknown
Magnolia Warbler	1950	150	1100.00	12800.00
Mexican Feijoa	1950	250	600.00	2800.00 to 4000.00
Mockingbirds	1940	500	450.00	7250.00 to 7750.00
Moorhen Chick	1970	500	1000.00	1250.00
Mountain Bluebirds	1964	500	950.00	1750.00 to 2300.00
Myrtle Warblers	1955	500	550.00	2500.00 to 4000.00
Nightingale & Honeysuckle**	1972	500	2500.00	2500.00 to 2750.00
Orange Blossoms & Butterfly	1947	250	500.00	4250.00 to 4500.00
Ovenbirds	1957	250	650.00	4500.00 to 4700.00
Parula Warblers	1957	500	600.00	3400.00 to 3600.00
Phoebes On Flame Vine	1958	500	750.00	4700.00 to 5000.00
Red-Eyed Vireos	1952	500	450.00	3750.00 to 4000.00
Redstarts & Gorse**	1968	500	1900.00	2450.00 to 2750.00
Scarlet Tanagers*	1956	500	675.00	3800.00 to 4200.00
Scissor-Tailed Flycatcher, Color	1962	250	950.00	Unknown
Scissor-Tailed Flycatcher, White	1962	75	950.00	1300.00 to 1600.00
Vermillion Flycatchers*	1963	500	1250.00	2400.00 to 2600.00
Wrens & Burnet Rose**	1965	500	650.00	2000.00 to 2100.00
Yellow-Headed Blackbirds	1952	350	650.00	2800.00 to 3800.00
Yellowthroats On Water Hyacinth	1958	350	750.00	4300.00 to 4500.00

Royal Worcester, Frederick Gertner and Neal French Porcelains

Colonel Of The Noble Guard	1963	150	600.00	1200.00 to 1300.00
Officer Of The Palatine Guard	1965	150	500.00	1050.00 to 1100.00
Papal Gendarme	1967	150	450.00	1000.00 to 1100.00
Privy Chamberlain Of The Sword & Cape	1959	150	500.00	1100.00 to 1250.00
Trooper Of The Papal Swiss Guard	1956	150	500.00	1100.00 to 1250.00

Doris Lindner began designing porcelain animal sculptures for Royal Worcester in 1931. Her limited edition Equestrian series was started in 1959.

Royal Worcester, Doris Lindner Porcelains

American Saddle Horse**	1973	750	1450.00	1450.00
Angus Bull	1961	500	350.00	Unknown
Appaloosa*	1969	750	550.00	950.00 to 1350.00
Arab Stallion*	1963	500	450.00	Unknown
Arkle	1967	500	525.00	Unknown
Brahman Bull	1968	500	400.00	800.00 to 8750.00
British Friesian Bull	1964	500	400.00	800.00 to 900.00
Bulldog	1968	500		800.00 to 850.00
Charolais Bull**	1968	500	400.00	800.00 to 875.00
Dairy Shorthorn Bull	1966	500	475.00	875.00 to 900.00
Duke Of Edinburgh*	1968	750	1000.00	2100.00 to 2400.00
Fox Hunter	1960	500	500.00	900.00 to 1100.00
Hereford Bull*	1959	1000	350.00	650.00 to 775.00
Hyperion	1965	500	525.00	Unknown
Jersey Bull	1964	500	400.00	900.00 to 975.00
Jersey Cow	1961	500	300.00	550.00 to 600.00
Marion Coakes-Mould*	1970	750	750.00	1125.00 to 1500.00
Merano	1963	500	500.00	1150.00 to 1250.00
Nijinsky*	1972	500	2000.00	2000.00
Officer Of Royal Horse Guards	1961	150	500.00	1300.00 to 1450.00
Officer Of The Life Guards	1961	150	500.00	Unknown
Palomino**	1971	750	975.00	975.00 to 1100.00
Percheron Stallion*	1966	500	725.00	1250.00 to 1400.00
Prince's Grace & Foal, White	1971	250	1400.00	1400.00 to 1600.00
Prince's Grace & Foal, Color**	1971	750	1500.00	1500.00 to 1700.00
Princess Anne On Doublet**	1973	750	4250.00	4250.00
Quarter Horse	1962	500	400.00	700.00 to 775.00
Queen Elizabeth	1947	100	275.00	Unknown
Royal Canadian Mounty	1966	500	875.00	1450.00 to 1600.00
Santa Gertrudis Bull*	1961	500	350.00	675.00 to 700.00

Royal Worcester, Dorothy Doughty,
Vermillion Flycatchers

Royal Worcester, Doris Lindner,
Marion Coakes-Mould

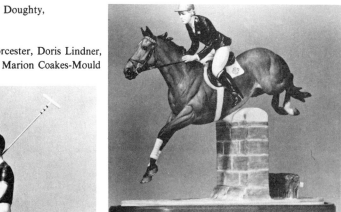

Royal Worcester, Doris Lindner,
Duke Of Edinburgh

Royal Worcester, Doris Lindner,
Nijinsky

Royal Worcester, Doris Lindner,
American Saddle Horse

Royal Worcester, Doris Lindner,
Appaloosa

Royal Worcester, Doris Lindner,
Palomino

Royal Worcester, Doris Lindner,
Percheron Stallion

Royal Worcester, Doris Lindner,
Hereford Bull

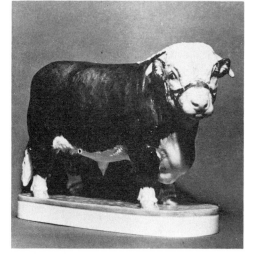

Royal Worcester, Doris Lindner,
Princess Anne On Doublet

Royal Worcester, Doris Lindner,
Prince's Grace & Foal

Royal Worcester, Doris Lindner,
Arab Stallion

Royal Worcester, Ronald Van Ruyckevelt,
Passionflower

Royal Worcester, Doris Lindner,
Santa Gertrudis Bull

Royal Worcester, Doris Lindner,
Welsh Mountain Pony

Royal Worcester,
Ronald Van Ruyckevelt, Bluefin Tuna

Royal Worcester,
Ronald Van Ruyckevelt, Dolphin

Royal Worcester,
Ronald Van Ruyckevelt, Rock Beauty

Royal Worcester,
Ronald Van Ruyckevelt, Languedoc

Royal Worcester, Ronald Van Ruyckevelt, Green-Winged Teal

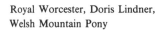

Shire Stallion	1964	500	700.00	1300.00 to 1400.00
Suffolk Punch**	1969	500	650.00	1175.00 to 1250.00
Welsh Mountain Pony*	1966	500	450.00	800.00 to 925.00

Royal Worcester,
Ronald Van Ruyckevelt,
Madelaine

Ronald Van Ruyckevelt became a designer at the Royal Worcester Porcelain Company in 1953. His first limited edition porcelain was made in 1956.

Royal Worcester, Ronald Van Ruyckevelt Porcelains

American Pintail, Pair	1970	500		3000.00 to 3200.00
Argenteuil A-108	1969	338		925.00 to 1000.00
Beatrice	1960	500	125.00	Unknown
Blue Angel Fish	1958	500	375.00	675.00 to 725.00
Bluefin Tuna*	1967	500	500.00	950.00 to 1050.00
Blue Marlin	1965	500	500.00	900.00 to 1000.00
Bobwhite Quail, Pair	1969	500		2000.00 to 2100.00
Bridget	1969	500	300.00	600.00 to 675.00
Butterfly Fish	1957	500	375.00	675.00 to 725.00
Caroline	1960	500	125.00	Unknown
Castelneau Pink	1969	429		825.00 to 875.00
Castelneau Yellow	1969	163		825.00 to 875.00
Charlotte & Jane**	1968	500	1000.00	1500.00 to 1650.00
Dolphin**	1968	500	500.00	750.00 to 900.00
Elaine**	1971	750	600.00	600.00 to 650.00
Elizabeth*	1967	500	300.00	750.00 to 800.00
Emily	1969	500	300.00	600.00 to 650.00
Felicity**	1971	750	600.00	600.00 to 650.00
Flying Fish	1962	300	400.00	500.00 to 575.00
Green-Winged Teal**	1971	500	1450.00	1450.00
Hibiscus	1962	500	300.00	1050.00 to 1100.00
Hogfish & Sergeant Major	1956	500	375.00	Unknown
Honfleur A-105	1968	290		550.00 to 600.00
Honfleur A-106	1968	290		550.00 to 600.00
Languedoc**	1971	216		1150.00
Lisette	1959	500	100.00	Unknown
Louisa	1962	500	400.00	900.00 to 975.00
Madelaine*	1968	500	300.00	750.00 to 800.00
Mallards	1968	500		3000.00 to 3200.00
Marion	1968	500	275.00	575.00 to 625.00
Melanie	1964	500	150.00	Unknown
Mennecy A-101	1968	338		675.00 to 725.00
Mennecy A-102	1968	334		675.00 to 725.00
Passionflower*	1961	500	300.00	1050.00 to 1100.00
Penelope	1959	500	100.00	Unknown
Rainbow Parrot Fish**	1968	500	1500.00	1500.00
Red Hind	1958	500	375.00	775.00 to 800.00
Ring-Necked Pheasants	1968	500		3200.00 to 3400.00
Rock Beauty*	1964	500	425.00	850.00 to 900.00
Rosalind	1964	500	150.00	Unknown
Sailfish	1962	500	400.00	850.00 to 900.00
Saint Denis A-109	1969	500		925.00 to 950.00
Sister Of London Hospital	1963	500		475.00 to 500.00
Sister Of St. Thomas' Hospital	1963	500		475.00 to 500.00
Sister Of The Red Cross	1970	750		525.00 to 550.00
Sister Of University College Hospital	1966	500		475.00 to 500.00
Squirrelfish	1961	500	400.00	825.00 to 875.00
Swordfish	1966	500	575.00	1050.00 to 1100.00
Tarpon	1964	500	500.00	900.00 to 975.00
Tea Party	1964	250	1000.00	2250.00 to 2400.00
White Doves	1972	25	3600.00	27850.00

Royal Worcester,
Ronald Van Ruyckevelt,
Elizabeth

Royal Worcester,
Ronald Van Ruyckevelt,
Rainbow Parrot Fish

Bernard Winskill, English sculptor, designed his first limited edition porcelain for Royal Worcester in 1969.

Royal Worcester, Bernard Winskill Porcelains

Duke Of Wellington**	1970	750	4500.00	4500.00
Napoleon Bonaparte**	1969	750	3500.00	3500.00

Saari Metal Sculptures

Nixon, Stainless Steel	1972	5000	25.00	25.00 to 30.00

See listing for Silver Creations in Plate and Bar & Ingot sections

Towle,
Mother & Child

Tay, Eagle

Vasari, Christ

Vasari, The Cossack

Vasari, Three Kings

Silver Creations Ships

America, Silver				700.00 to 1200.00
Cutty Sark, Silver				700.00 to 1200.00
Ferret, Silver				700.00 to 1200.00
Intrepid, Silver				700.00 to 1200.00

Sovereign Metalcasters Sculptures

President Kennedy, Sterling*	1973	Year	150.00	150.00

Tay Porcelains are designed and modeled by Giuseppi Tagliariol in Monza, Italy.

Tay Porcelains

American Woodcock**	1974	500	625.00	625.00
Blue Jay	1970	500	375.00	375.00 to 475.00
Boreal Chickadee	1974	1000	275.00	275.00
Eagle**	1970	500	1000.00	1250.00 to 1300.00
Falcon	1971	500	500.00	600.00 to 675.00
Gray Partridge	1972	500	800.00	1000.00 to 1100.00
Gyrfalcon	1974	300	1250.00	1250.00
Limpkin**	1970	500	600.00	700.00 to 775.00
Mallard Duck	1974	500	900.00	900.00
Mallard Duck, Flying	1974	500	550.00	550.00
Owl	1974	500	350.00	350.00
Pheasant**	1971	500	1500.00	2000.00
Roadrunner**	1971	500	800.00	950.00 to 1000.00
Turtledoves	1974	500	425.00	425.00
Woodcock**	1970	500	325.00	350.00 to 500.00

Towle Silversmiths of Newburyport, Massachusetts, was established by William Moulton in 1664. Towle limited editon ornaments were first issued in 1971. Plates followed in 1972.

See listing for Towle in Plate section

Towle Silver Figurines

Goal Line Stand	650	500.00	500.00
Mother & Child, Silver*		500.00	500.00

Trova Sculptures

Manscape, Gold Plated Bronze	75	295.00	350.00 to 400.00
Manscape, Silver	50	395.00	800.00

Van Ruyckevelt, see Royal Worcester

Vasari Figurines

Cellini	200	400.00	400.00
Christ*	200	250.00	250.00
Creche*	200	500.00	500.00
D'Artagnan	250	250.00	250.00
English Crusader	250	250.00	250.00
French Crusader	250	250.00	250.00
German Hussar	250	250.00	250.00
Italian Crusader	250	250.00	250.00
Leonardo Da Vinci	200	250.00	250.00
Michelangelo	200	250.00	250.00
Ming Warrior	250	200.00	200.00
Pirate	250	200.00	200.00
Roman Centurion	250	200.00	200.00
Spanish Grandee	250	200.00	200.00
Swiss Warrior	250	250.00	250.00
The Cossack*	250	250.00	250.00
Three Kings, Set Of 3*	200	750.00	750.00
Three Musketeers, Set Of 3*	200	750.00	750.00
Venetian Nobleman	250	200.00	200.00
Viking	250	200.00	200.00

Wallace Crystal Sculptures

Afternoon Of A Fawn	30	550.00	550.00
Don Quixote	30	625.00	625.00
Firebird	30	625.00	625.00
Giselle	30	700.00	700.00
Les Sylphides	30	750.00	750.00
Romeo & Juliet	30	700.00	700.00

Royal Worcester,
Ronald Van Ruyckevelt,
Elaine

Royal Worcester,
Ronald Van Ruyckevelt,
Felicity

Royal Worcester, Bernard Winskill,
Duke Of Wellington

Vasari, Creche

Vasari, Three Musketeers

Royal Worcester, Bernard Winskill,
Napoleon Bonaparte

Sleeping Beauty	30	700.00	700.00
Swan Lake	30	625.00	625.00

Wallace Silversmiths Pewter Figurines

Jones, John Paul	1000	350.00	350.00
Pitcher, Molly	1000	400.00	400.00
Valley Forge	1000	350.00	350.00
Washington Crossing The Delaware	1000	400.00	400.00

Wedgwood was established in Etruria, England, by Josiah Wedgwood in 1759. The factory was moved to Barlaston in 1940. Wedgwood is famous for its Jasperware, Basalt, and Queensware, all produced in the eighteenth century. These wares are still used by Wedgwood for its limited editions, introduced in 1969.

See listing for Wedgwood in Plate section

Wedgwood Busts

Eisenhower, Large, Black Basalt	521	200.00	200.00
Eisenhower, Small, Black Basalt	5000	75.00	75.00
Kennedy, Small, Black Basalt	2000	75.00	75.00
Lincoln, Large, Black Basalt	351	200.00	200.00
Lincoln, Small, Black Basalt	2000	75.00	75.00
Washington, Small, Black Basalt	2000	75.00	75.00

Winskill, see Royal Worcester

2

Paperweights

Title	Date of Issue	Issue Limi- tation	Issue Price	Current Price

Baccarat limited editions are made in France by La Compagnie des Cristalleries de Baccarat, located near Paris. The factory was started in 1765. The firm went bankrupt and started operating again about 1822. Famous cane and millefiori paperweights were made there during the 1860-1880 period. In 1953, after a lapse of 80 years, sulfide paperweights were again introduced. A series of limited edition paperweights has been made each year since 1953.

See listing for Baccarat in Figurine section

Baccarat Paperweights

Title	Date of Issue	Issue Limitation	Issue Price	Current Price
Apples And Pears, Combined Edition	1973	200	250.00	250.00
Carpet Ground With Zodiac Signs**	1973	150	170.00	170.00
Churchill, Winston, Overlay	1954	81	75.00	1500.00 to 2000.00
Churchill, Winston, Regular	1954	558	25.00	750.00 to 1000.00
Complex Flower**	1973	200	160.00	180.00 to 200.00
Coronation, Overlay	1953	195	75.00	550.00 to 650.00
Coronation, Regular	1954	1492	20.00	300.00 to 350.00
Dahlia	1973	200	200.00	200.00
Eisenhower, Dwight D., Overlay	1953	178	75.00	600.00 to 700.00
Eisenhower, Dwight D., Regular	1953	1389	25.00	375.00 to 425.00
Filigree, Regular, Combined Edition W/special*	1973	300	85.00	85.00
Filigree, Special, Combined Edition W/regular*	1973	300	90.00	90.00
Franklin, Benjamin, Overlay	1955	180	75.00	650.00 to 750.00
Franklin, Benjamin, Regular	1955	414	25.00	400.00 to 500.00
Gridel Elephant*	1973	250	150.00	150.00 to 165.00
Gridel Horse**	1973	250	150.00	150.00 to 165.00
Gridel Rooster*	1972	1200	150.00	150.00 to 165.00
Gridel Squirrel**	1972	1200	150.00	150.00 to 165.00
Hoover, Herbert, Overlay, Pale Blue	1971	300	155.00	175.00 to 225.00
Hoover, Herbert, Regular, Cobalt Blue	1971	2500	47.50	65.00 to 75.00
Jackson, Andrew, Overlay, Green	1972	400	155.00	175.00 to 225.00
Jackson, Andrew, Regular, Green	1972	2400	47.50	47.50 to 65.00
Jefferson, Thomas, Overlay	1954	156	75.00	550.00 to 650.00
Jefferson, Thomas, Regular	1954	594	25.00	325.00 to 375.00
Kennedy, John F. Memorial		314	65.00	450.00 to 550.00
Kennedy, John F., Overlay	1964	308	135.00	375.00 to 425.00
Kennedy, John F., Regular	1964	3572	35.00	225.00 to 275.00
Lafayette, Overlay	1955	227	75.00	525.00 to 575.00
Lafayette, Regular	1955	744	25.00	300.00 to 325.00
Lee, Robert E., Overlay	1954	137	75.00	550.00 to 650.00

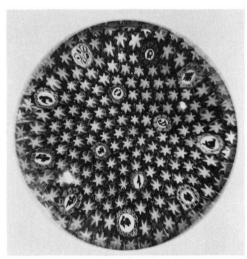

Baccarat, Carpet Ground With Zodiac Signs

Baccarat, Filigree, Regular

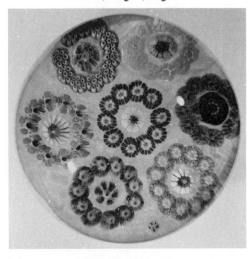

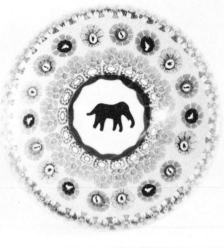

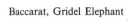

Baccarat, Gridel Elephant

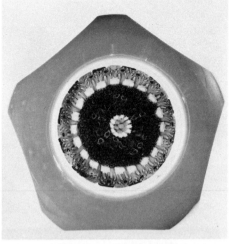

Baccarat, Mushroom Overlay

Baccarat, Filigree, Special

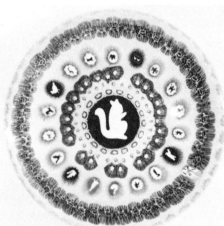

Baccarat, Pansy

Baccarat, Gridel Squirrel

Baccarat, Gridel Rooster

Baccarat, Woodrow Wilson, Regular

Cristal d'Albret,
Christopher Columbus, Overlay

Cristal d'Albret,
John James Audubon, Overlay

Baccarat, Millefiori, Concentric

Lee, Robert E., Regular	1954	913	25.00	300.00 to 350.00
Lincoln, Abraham, Overlay	1954	197	75.00	500.00 to 600.00
Lincoln, Abraham, Regular	1954	1291	25.00	300.00 to 350.00
Luther, Martin, Overlay	1956	86	75.00	500.00 to 600.00
Luther, Martin, Regular	1956	607	25.00	275.00 to 325.00
Millefiori, Concentric**	1973	150	140.00	140.00 to 170.00
Millefiori, Regular**	1973	400	150.00	150.00
Monroe, James, Overlay, Green Flash	1970	400	155.00	175.00 to 225.00
Monroe, James, Regular, Orange	1970	2500	47.50	65.00 to 75.00
Mushroom Overlay*	1973	200	180.00	200.00 to 225.00
Pansy*	1973	200	250.00	250.00
Pope John XXIII, Overlay	1966	300	145.00	325.00 to 375.00
Pope John XXIII, Regular	1966	2000	37.50	125.00 to 175.00
Pope Pius XII, Overlay	1960	284	100.00	325.00 to 375.00
Pope Pius XII, Regular	1960	2157	30.00	125.00 to 175.00
Queen Elizabeth, Overlay	1954	200	75.00	450.00 to 550.00
Rayburn, Sam, Overlay	1961	93	100.00	450.00 to 550.00
Rayburn, Sam, Regular	1961	512	30.00	275.00 to 325.00
Rogers, Will, Overlay, Green Swirl	1968	300	150.00	325.00 to 375.00
Rogers, Will, Regular, Yellow	1968	2000	45.00	100.00 to 125.00
Roosevelt, Eleanor, Overlay, Amethyst	1971	400	155.00	200.00 to 250.00
Roosevelt, Eleanor, Regular, Amethyst	1971	2500	47.50	47.50 to 65.00
Roosevelt, Theodore, Overlay, Green	1967	300	150.00	275.00 to 325.00
Roosevelt, Theodore, Regular, Amethyst	1967	2000	42.50	85.00 to 125.00
Salamander**	1973	200	350.00	350.00
Snake**	1973	100	300.00	300.00
Stevenson, Adlai, Overlay, Amethyst Flash	1969	300	150.00	225.00 to 275.00
Stevenson, Adlai, Regular, Garnet Red	1969	2250	45.00	62.50 to 75.00
Truman, Harry S., Overlay**	1973	400	175.00	175.00
Truman, Harry S., Regular	1973	2400	55.00	55.00
Washington, George, Overlay	1954	200	75.00	450.00 to 550.00
Washington, George, Regular	1954	1182	25.00	250.00 to 300.00
Wilson, Woodrow, Overlay, Yellow	1973	400	160.00	160.00
Wilson, Woodrow, Regular, Turquoise*	1973	2400	50.00	50.00

Cristal d'Albret, Ernest Hemingway, Overlay

Cristal d'Albret, Paul Revere, Overlay

Cristal d'Albret plates and paperweights are made at the glassworks of Vianne, France. Limited edition sulfide paperweights were first made in 1966. Limited edition glass plates were introduced in 1972.

See listing for Cristal d'Albret in Plate section

Cristal d'Albret Paperweights

Astronaut		1000	85.00	85.00 to 90.00
Audubon, John James, Overlay*		250	170.00	170.00
Audubon, John James, Regular		1000	68.00	68.00 to 84.00
Columbus, Christopher, Overlay*		200	150.00	225.00 to 275.00
Columbus, Christopher, Regular		1000	55.00	85.00 to 95.00
Da Vinci, Leonardo, Overlay**		200	160.00	160.00 to 180.00
Da Vinci, Leonardo, Regular		1000	62.00	65.00 to 85.00
Gustaf, King Of Sweden, Regular		1000	55.00	55.00 to 65.00
Hemingway, Ernest, Overlay*		225	160.00	160.00 to 180.00
Hemingway, Ernest, Regular		1000	62.00	62.00 to 70.00
Kennedy, John & Jackie, Overlay**		300	150.00	150.00 to 200.00
Kennedy, John & Jackie, Regular		2000	55.00	55.00 to 75.00
MacArthur, Douglas, Overlay		300	150.00	150.00 to 170.00
MacArthur, Douglas, Regular		1500	55.00	55.00 to 65.00
Prince Charles, Overlay			150.00	150.00 to 170.00
Prince Charles, Regular			55.00	55.00 to 65.00
Revere, Paul, Overlay**		200	160.00	160.00 to 180.00
Revere, Paul, Regular		800	62.00	65.00 to 75.00
Roosevelt, Franklin D., Overlay		300	150.00	150.00 to 175.00
Roosevelt, Franklin D., Regular		2000	55.00	55.00 to 65.00
Schweitzer, Albert, Overlay		200	160.00	160.00
Schweitzer, Albert, Regular		1000	55.00	55.00 to 62.00
Twain, Mark, Overlay		225	150.00	150.00 to 170.00
Twain, Mark, Regular		1000	55.00	55.00 to 65.00

Pairpoint, Amethyst Snake Pedestal, 1972

Erlacher Paperweights

Ballerina	1974	50	300.00	300.00
Butterfly	1973	50	200.00	200.00
Cardinal	1974	50	250.00	250.00
Hummingbirds	1973	50	300.00	300.00

Kosta, Annual Paperweight, 1973

Pairpoint, Faceted Red Rose

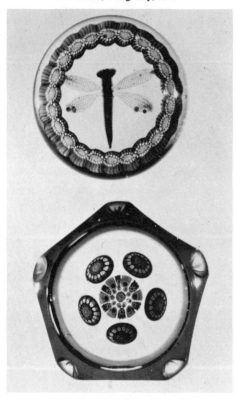

Perthshire, Dragonfly, 1970

Perthshire, Translucent Overlay,
Various Colors, 1970

Pairpoint, Red Pedestal Rose, 1972

Puss 'n Boots	1973	50	250.00	250.00
Rainbow Trouts	1974	50	250.00	250.00
Swan	1973	50	200.00	200.00
Thoroughbred	1974	50	300.00	300.00
Gentile Glass Paperweights				
Apollo XI, Moon Landing And Astronaut, Set		1800	25.00	25.00
Apollo XV		1000	15.00	15.00
Apollo XVII		1000	15.00	15.00
Beetle Family		50	250.00	250.00
Caterpillar On Ground		50	185.00	185.00
Caterpillar On 3 Leaves		50	250.00	250.00
Center Beetle		50	125.00	125.00
Devil's Fire		1800	28.00	28.00
God Bless America, Peace	1973	1800	7.50	7.50
Grape Crystal Faceted, Star Bottom		200	250.00	250.00
Grape With Leaf, Plain		200	200.00	200.00
Green Lizard With Beetle		50	225.00	225.00
Green Lizard, Plain		50	200.00	200.00
Kennedy, John F., Faceted		900	25.00	25.00
Kennedy, John F., Plain		3600	15.00	15.00
Millefiore, Broken Heart, Faceted		100	50.00	50.00
Millefiore, Broken Heart, Plain		500	35.00	35.00
Millefiore Heart, Faceted		100	50.00	50.00
Millefiore Heart, Plain		500	35.00	35.00
Old Glory, Faceted		1000	75.00	75.00
Old Glory, Plain		1000	50.00	50.00
Pearl Harbor		1000	12.00	12.00
Salamander, Circled		200	130.00	130.00
Salamander, Circled With Baby In Shell		100	250.00	250.00
Salamander, Circled With Beetle		200	135.00	135.00
Salamander, Circled With Worm		50	135.00	135.00
Salamander, Crawling		200	125.00	125.00
Salamander, On Two Leaves Attacking Beetles		50	225.00	225.00
Snake, Crawling		200	75.00	75.00
Snake, Cross-Over		100	85.00	85.00
Snake Family		50	185.00	185.00
Snake, Figure 8		200	85.00	85.00
Snake, Figure 8 With Beetle		200	100.00	100.00
Spiral Wig Stand		500	30.00	30.00
Three Cherry Crystal Faceted, Star Bottom		100	250.00	250.00
Three Cherry With Leaf, Plain		200	200.00	200.00
Washington, George, Faceted		500	25.00	25.00
Washington, George, Plain		1000	15.00	15.00
Washington, Martha, Faceted		500	25.00	25.00
Washington, Martha, Plain		1000	15.00	15.00

Kosta Glassworks of Sweden was founded in 1742 by King Charles II. The limited edition line, introduced in 1970, includes paperweights, plates, and mugs.

See listing for Kosta in Plate section

Kosta Paperweights

Annual, Mom	1970	Year	24.50	17.50 to 22.50
Annual, Dad	1971	Year	26.50	20.00 to 26.50
Annual, Twins, Pair	1972	Year	30.00	21.50 to 30.00
Annual, Miss Kosta*	1973	Year	30.00	30.00

Max Erlacher, see Erlacher

Pairpoint limited editions are made by the Pairpoint Glass Company of Sagamore, Massachusetts. Artisans in Glass, Inc., of New York is the distributor of Pairpoint limited editions.

See listing for Pairpoint in Plate section

Pairpoint Paperweights

Amethyst Snake Pedestal*	1972	50	125.00	125.00
Faceted Red Rose**		300	200.00	200.00
Opal Snake Pedestal	1973	200	80.00	80.00
Red Pedestal Rose*	1972	300	200.00	250.00 to 335.00
Red, White, And Blue Crown**		500	80.00	80.00
Yellow Rose Of Texas**	1973	500	225.00	250.00 to 275.00

The Perthshire Company, founded in 1968, is located in Crieff,
Scotland. Limited edition paperweights were first made in 1969.

Perthshire Paperweights

Christmas, Holly And Berries*	1971	250	100.00	125.00 to 200.00
Christmas, Mistletoe	1972	300	100.00	125.00 to 145.00
Close Millefiori	1973	400	140.00	140.00
Cushion Weight	1971	250	80.00	95.00 to 120.00
Dahlia*	1972	200	250.00	250.00 to 275.00
Dragonfly*	1970	250	75.00	175.00 to 225.00
End Of Day	1972	350	40.00	45.00 to 65.00
End Of Day	1973	350	40.00	40.00 to 65.00
Faceted Cushion Ground*	1972	300	130.00	130.00 to 150.00
Faceted Millefiori	1973	250	52.50	52.50
Flower In Basket	1972	1000	75.00	90.00 to 100.00
Flower On Latticinio	1973	300	135.00	135.00
Millefiori On Lace, Amethyst Base	1973	300	55.00	55.00
Millefiori On Lace, Blue Base	1973	300	55.00	55.00
Millefiori On Lace, Clear Base	1973	300	50.00	50.00
Overlay Bottle*	1971	300	200.00	225.00 to 300.00
Pansy	1971	350	125.00	150.00 to 175.00
Patterned Millefiori On Cobalt Ground	1972	300	55.00	55.00 to 70.00
Patterned Millefiori On Maroon Ground	1972	300	55.00	55.00 to 70.00
Red, White, And Blue Crown	1969	350	125.00	Unknown
Ribbon, Small Rose Florette*	1971	150	80.00	100.00 to 125.00
Small Pink Flower*	1972	1000	75.00	90.00 to 100.00
Swan In A Pond	1973	250	185.00	185.00
Translucent Overlay, Various Colors*	1970	150	300.00	300.00 to 350.00

Pairpoint, Red, White, And Blue Crown

See listing for Royale Germania Crystal in Plate section

Royale Germania Crystal Paperweights

Annual, Capitol, Blue	1970	350	180.00	300.00 to 350.00
Annual, Independence Hall, Red	1971	350	200.00	225.00 to 300.00
Annual, Washington's Inauguration, Green	1972	350	270.00	200.00 to 290.00
Annual, Constitution, Lilac*	1973	300	270.00	270.00

Perthshire,
Dahlia, 1972

Perthshire, Faceted
Cushion Ground,
1972

Smith paperweights are made by Hugh and Carolyn Smith of Milleville,
New Jersey.

Smith Paperweights

Cattail*		200	125.00	125.00
Double White Clematis*		200	125.00	125.00
Double Yellow Clematis*		200	125.00	125.00
Double Red Pointed Petal Clematis*		200	125.00	125.00
Five-Petal Blue Mountain Flower*		200	125.00	125.00
Ground Pink		150	170.00	170.00
Red Desert Flower*		200	125.00	125.00
Red Poinsettia		150	170.00	170.00
Six-Petal Purple Flower*		200	125.00	125.00
White Trillium*		200	125.00	125.00

Perthshire,
Small Pink Flower,
1972

St. Clair Paperweights

McGovern	1972	2000	25.00	25.00
Nixon	1972	2000	25.00	25.00

Perthshire, Christmas, 1971

The original St. Louis glasshouse was established in 1767 at
St. Louis, France. The name became Compagnie des Cristalleries de
St. Louis in 1829. The first paperweights were made during the 1840s.
Modern paperweights were started again in 1952.

St. Louis Paperweights

Carpet Ground, June	1972	250	180.00	170.00 to 190.00
Corrugated White Canes, White Carpet Ground	1973	250	180.00	130.00 to 180.00
Dahlia On Latticinio	1973	250	140.00	140.00 to 170.00
Dahlia, White	1974	250	190.00	190.00
Flat Bouquet On Opaque White Ground**	1972	250	150.00	150.00 to 160.00
Flower On Opaque Orange Underlay*	1973	250	190.00	190.00
Honeycomb, Red	1974	250	230.00	230.00
King Of France Commemorative	1967	2000	210.00	225.00 to 240.00
Lafayette Sulfide	1967	500	200.00	300.00 to 350.00
Marbrie, Blue Yellow & White**	1971	250	210.00	200.00 to 225.00
Marbrie Magnum				200.00 to 220.00

Perthshire, Ribbon,
Small Rose Florette, 1971

Royale Germania,
Annual Paperweight, 1973

Smith, Double Yellow Clematis

Smith,
Double Red Pointed Petal Clematis

Perthshire, Overlay Bottle, 1971

Smith, Double White Clematis

Smith, Red Desert Flower

Smith, Six-Petal Purple Flower

Smith, Cattail

Smith, White Trillium

Smith,
Five-Petal Blue Mountain Flower

St. Louis, Flower
On Opaque Orange Ground,
1973

St. Louis, Millefiore Garland, 1973

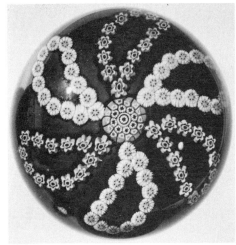

St. Louis, Three-Color Crown, 1974

St. Louis,
Stylized Flower
On Opaque Absinthe Ground,
1974

St. Louis, Piedouche

Van Son, Commemorative Paperweight

St. Louis, Penholder, 1973

Millefiori Cluster	1972	250	140.00	160.00 to 180.00
Millefiori Garland*	1973	250	210.00	210.00
Millefiori, Latticinio Ribbon		250	160.00	170.00 to 200.00
Mushroom, White Overlay		250	220.00	210.00 to 220.00
Patterned Millefiori	1972	250	120.00	150.00 to 170.00
Penholder*	1973	125	325.00	325.00
Piedouche*		250	250.00	300.00 to 325.00
Pinwheel, Blue & White Swirl**	1971	250	140.00	140.00
Pinwheel, 5-Color Swirl		250	160.00	140.00 to 170.00
Red Flower Faceted**		250	140.00	140.00
Red Honeycomb	1974		250.00	230.00
Scattered Canes And Lace Tubes	1972	250	160.00	170.00 to 200.00
Schumann, Robert, Commemorative	1969	1000	225.00	300.00 to 350.00
Star-Shape Millefiore		250	140.00	120.00 to 150.00
Stylized Flower On Opaque Absinthe Ground*	1974		190.00	190.00
Three-Color Crown Weight*	1974		180.00	180.00
Turquoise Ground	1972	250	180.00	180.00 to 200.00
Yellow Flower, Faceted		250	140.00	140.00

St. Louis Seals

Blue	1974	1000	50.00	50.00
Red	1974	1000	50.00	50.00

Van Son Paperweights

Commemorative, Black & Yellow**	1972	1500	25.00	20.00 to 30.00

Whitefriars paperweights are made by Whitefriars Glass Ltd. of Wealdstone, Middlesex, England. The original Whitefriars glasshouse was established in 1680. Paperweights were first made in 1848. They were discontinued for many years until modern paperweights were again made in the 1960s. Until recently the company was known as James Powell & Sons (Whitefriars, Ltd.).

Whitefriars Paperweights

Olympics	1972	500	65.00 to 75.00
Queen's Anniversary	1972	500	65.00 to 75.00

Whittemore paperweights are made by Francis Dyer Whittemore, Jr. of Landsdale, Pennsylvania. His first paperweights were made in 1964. Each weight is marked with a 'w' within a cane.

Whittemore Paperweights

Christmas, Candles & Holly	1971	100		325.00 to 375.00
Christmas, Stocking & Candy Canes	1972	100		325.00 to 375.00
Iowa State Flower, Iowa Rose		100		325.00 to 375.00
Minnesota State Flower, Lady Slipper		100		325.00 to 375.00
Monument Valley, Marigold Carnival	1972	Year	20.00	15.00 to 20.00

3

Plates, Plaques, and Miscellaneous

Title	Date of Issue	Issue Limi- tation	Issue Price	Current Price
A. Michelsen, see Michelsen				
A. Y. Jackson, see Wellings Mint				
Addams Family Plates				
Christmas, Christmas Dinner	1972		10.00	8.00 to 10.00
Mother's Day, On The Tracks	1972		10.00	8.00 to 10.00
Agazzi, see Count Agazzi				
Air Force plate, see Quality Systems				
Alice in Wonderland plate, see Collector Creations				

The Amen 'Festival of Lights' plate was commissioned by Carl's House of Silver of Englewood, New Jersey. The plate was designed by Irving Amen and manufactured by Reed & Barton Silversmiths.

Title	Date of Issue	Issue Limi- tation	Issue Price	Current Price
Amen Plates				
Festival Of Lights, Damascene*	1972	500	125.00	125.00 to 135.00

Amen, Festival Of Lights Plate

America House is a subsidiary of the Franklin Mint. Limited edition plates were first made in 1972.

Title	Date of Issue	Issue Limi- tation	Issue Price	Current Price
America House Plates				
Annual, Landing Of Columbus, Bronze	1972	1500	100.00	75.00 to 100.00
Annual, Landing Of Columbus, Sterling	1972	1000	250.00	175.00 to 250.00
America The Beautiful Plates				
U.S.Capitol, Red Carnival	1969	Year	20.00	25.00 to 30.00
Mount Rushmore, Green Carnival	1970	Year	20.00	15.00 to 20.00
Statue Of Liberty, Amber Carnival	1971	Year	20.00	15.00 to 20.00
American Archives, see International Silver				

American Commemorative Council,
Williamsburg Plate

American Commemorative Council, in conjunction with The National Historical Society, has issued a series of plates to commemorate the bicentennial. The plates are made by Gorham China Company. The first plate was issued in 1972.

Title	Date of Issue	Issue Limi- tation	Issue Price	Current Price
American Commemorative Council Plates				
Southern Landmark, Monticello	1973	9800	35.00	35.00
Southern Landmark, Williamsburg*	1973	9800	40.00	40.00
American Crystal Plates				
Astronaut	1969			45.00 to 55.00
Christmas	1970			40.00 to 60.00
Christmas	1971		25.00	20.00 to 40.00

American Historical, Aviation Plate,
Amelia Earhart

American Historical, Aviation Plate,
Charles Lindbergh

American Historical, Bicentennial Plate,
1972, Turning Point

American Historical, Bicentennial Plate,
1972, A New Dawn

Christmas	1972		30.00
Christmas	1973	20.00	20.00
Mother's Day	1972	2000	25.00	30.00 to 55.00
Mother's Day	1973		25.00	25.00

American Historical Plates, Ltd., of Mineola, New York, introduced limited editions in 1972. Their plates are produced by Castleton (Shenango) China.

American Historical Plates

Aviation, Amelia Earhart*	1972	3500	40.00	40.00
Aviation, Charles Lindbergh*	1972	3500	40.00	40.00
Bicentennial, A New Dawn**	1972	7600	60.00	45.00 to 60.00
Bicentennial, Turning Point*	1972	7600	60.00	45.00 to 60.00
Bicentennial, Silent Foe*	1973	7600	60.00	45.00 to 60.00
Bicentennial, The Declaration*	1973	7600	60.00	60.00
Bicentennial, The Star-Spangled Banner*	1973	7600	60.00	60.00
Bicentennial, USS Constitution*	1973	7600	60.00	60.00
Bicentennial, One Nation*	1974	7600	60.00	60.00
Bicentennial, Westward Ho**	1974	7600	60.00	60.00
Natural History, Painted Lady*	1973	1500	40.00	40.00
Natural History, Roseate Spoonbill*	1973	1500	40.00	40.00

Andrew Wyeth Plates

Kuerner Farm, Signed	1971	275	350.00	350.00
Kuerner Farm, Unsigned*	1971	12500	50.00	30.00 to 50.00

Anheuser Busch Plate

Americana, Clydesdale Horses, Silver*	1973	1000	15.00	150.00 to 200.00
Americana, The Brew House, Silver	1974	5000	15.00	150.00

Anri, an Italian manufacturer of hand-carved wooden limited edition plates, was founded by Anton Riffeser, Sr. in 1916. Anri entered the limited edition market with a Christmas plate in 1971. Mother's Day and Father's Day plates were added in 1972.

Anri, see also Ferrandiz

Anri Plates

Christmas, Jakob In Groden*	1971	10000	45.00	30.00 to 50.00
Christmas, Pipers At Alberobello*	1972	5500	45.00	30.00 to 45.00
Christmas	1973		45.00	45.00
Father's Day, Alpine Father & Children*	1972	2000	35.00	17.00 to 35.00
Father's Day*	1973	900	45.00	25.00 to 45.00
Mother's Day, Alpine Mother & Children*	1972	5000	35.00	15.00 to 35.00
Mother's Day*	1973		45.00	25.00 to 45.00

Antique Trader Weekly, a Dubuque, Iowa, publication, introduced its line of limited edition plates in 1971. Artist Ralph Anderson of Schiller Park, Illinois, designed the first set of holiday plates. The plates are manufactured by Taylor, Smith, and Taylor of East Liverpool, Ohio.

Antique Trader Plates

Bible, David & Goliath	1973	2000	10.75	10.75
Bible, Moses And The Golden Idol	1973	2000	10.75	10.75
Bible, Noah's Ark	1973	2000	10.75	10.75
Bible, Samson	1973	2000	10.75	10.75
Christmas	1971	1500	11.95	11.95
Christmas	1972	1000	11.95	11.95
Currier & Ives, Baseball		2000	10.00	10.00
Currier & Ives, Franklin Experiment		2000	10.00	10.00
Currier & Ives, Haying Time		2000	10.00	10.00
Currier & Ives, The Road-Winter		2000	10.00	10.00
Currier & Ives, Winter In The Country		2000	10.00	10.00
Easter	1971	1500	11.95	11.95
Easter	1972	1000	11.95	11.95
Father's Day	1971	1500	11.95	11.95
Father's Day	1972	1000	11.95	11.95
Mother's Day	1971	1500	11.95	11.95
Mother's Day	1972	1000	11.95	11.95
Russell, A Bad One		2000	11.95	11.95
Russell, Discovery Of Last Chance Gulch**		2000	11.95	11.95

American Historical, Bicentennial Plate,
1973, Silent Foe

American Historical, Natural History Plate,
Painted Lady

Andrew Wyeth, Kuerner Farm Plate

American Historical, Natural History Plate,
Roseate Spoonbill

American Historical, Bicentennial Plate,
1973, The Declaration

American Historical, Bicentennial Plate,
1974, One Nation

American Historical, Bicentennial Plate,
1973, The Star-Spangled Banner

Anri, Christmas Plate, 1971

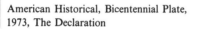

American Historical, Bicentennial Plate,
1974, Westward Ho

American Historical, Bicentennial Plate,
1973, U.S.S.Constitution

Anri, Christmas Plate, 1972

Antique Trader, Russell Plate,
Doubtful Visitor

Arta Enamel, Christmas Plate, 1973

Antique Trader,
Russell Plate, Innocent Allies

Anri, Father's Day, 1972

Anri, Father's Day, 1973

Antique Trader, Russell Plate,
Discovery Of Last Chance Gulch

Arta Enamel, Mother's Day Plate, 1973

Anri, Mother's Day, 1973

Anri, Mother's Day, 1972

Russell, Doubtful Visitor*		2000	11.95	11.95
Russell, Innocent Allies*		2000	11.95	11.95
Russell, Wagon Boss		2000	11.95	11.95
Thanksgiving	1971	1500	11.95	11.95
Thanksgiving	1972	1000	11.95	11.95

Arlington Mint Plates

Hands In Prayer, Sterling	1972		125.00	125.00

Aynsley,
1000th Year Of English Monarchy Plate

The Armstrong Bicentennial series was commissioned by David Armstrong and David Downs of Pomona, California. The bronze plates are made by the cire perdue (lost wax) method.

Armstrong Plates

Bicentennial, Calm Before The Storm	1971	250	300.00	Unknown
Bicentennial, Gaspee Incident	1972	175	250.00	250.00

Army plate, see Quality Systems

Arta Enamel Factory, located in Austria, introduced limited edition plates in 1973. The plates are hand-painted on white enamel.

Arta Enamel Plates

Christmas, Nativity*	1973	300	50.00	50.00
Mother's Day, Mother & Children*	1973	220	50.00	50.00

Arthur King, see King

Asta Stromberg, see Stromberg

Atelier D'Art Faure, see Poillerat

Audubon Bird plates, see Franklin Mint, Reed & Barton

Avon limited edition plates, distributed by the Avon Perfume Company, were first issued in 1972. The plates are made by Enoch Wedgwood of England, and are limited to the production of one year.

Avon Plates

Christmas	1972	Year	15.00	Unknown
Christmas	1973	Year	15.00	15.00
Commemorative, Betsy Ross	1974	Year	15.00	15.00
Mother's Day	1974	Year	15.00	15.00

Bareuther, Christmas Plate, 1970

Aynsley pottery has been made in the Staffordshire district since 1775. Fine decorated earthenware was produced in the early years. Bone china was introduced by founder John Aynsley's grandson in the mid-1800s.

Aynsley Plates

1000th Year Of English Monarchy*	1973	1000	30.00	Unknown

Bareuther & Co., a German porcelain factory, was founded in 1867 by the Ries family. In 1884, the factory was sold to Oskar Bareuther. The first limited edition Bareuther Christmas plate was issued in 1967 in honor of the factory's 100th Anniversary. Mother's Day and Father's Day plates followed in 1969.

Bareuther Bells

Christmas*	1973	Year	15.00	15.00
Christmas	1974	Year	17.00	17.00

Bareuther, Christmas Plate, 1971

Bareuther Eggs

Easter	1974	Year	13.50	13.50

Bareuther, Christmas Plate, 1972

Bareuther Plates

Christmas, Stifskirche*	1967	Year	10.00	60.00 to 75.00
Christmas, Kappelkirche*	1968	Year	10.00	9.00 to 25.00
Christmas, Christkindlemarkt*	1969	Year	10.00	7.00 to 15.00
Christmas, Chapel In Oberndorf*	1970	Year	12.50	6.00 to 15.00
Christmas, Toys For Sale*	1971	Year	14.50	9.00 to 15.00
Christmas, Christmas In Munich*	1972	Year	14.50	8.00 to 15.00
Christmas, Snow Scene*	1973	Year	15.00	15.00
Christmas, Church In The Black Forest*	1974	Year	19.00	19.00
Father's Day, Castle Neuschwanstein*	1969	Year	10.00	25.00 to 50.00
Father's Day, Castle Pfalz*	1970	Year	12.50	5.00 to 15.00
Father's Day, Castle Heidelberg*	1971	Year	12.50	8.00 to 13.00
Father's Day, Castle Hohenschwangau*	1972	Year	14.50	10.00 to 14.50
Father's Day, Castle Katz*	1973	Year	15.00	15.00

Bareuther, Christmas Plate, 1969

Bareuther, Christmas Plate, 1967

Bareuther, Christmas Plate, 1968

Bareuther, Christmas Bell, 1973

Bareuther, Father's Day Plate, 1970

Bareuther, Christmas Plate, 1973

Bareuther, Father's Day Plate, 1972

Bareuther, Mother's Day Plate, 1969

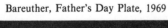

Bareuther, Father's Day Plate, 1969

Bareuther, Mother's Day Plate, 1970

Bareuther, Father's Day Plate, 1973

Father's Day	1974	Year	19.00	19.00
Mother's Day*	1969	Year	10.00	25.00 to 50.00
Mother's Day*	1970	Year	12.50	5.00 to 13.00
Mother's Day*	1971	Year	12.50	8.00 to 13.00
Mother's Day*	1972	Year	14.50	10.00 to 14.50
Mother's Day*	1973	Year	15.00	10.00 to 15.00
Mother's Day	1974	Year	19.00	19.00
Thanksgiving*	1971	Year	12.50	10.00 to 15.00
Thanksgiving*	1972	Year	14.50	13.00 to 15.00
Thanksgiving*	1973	Year	15.00	15.00
Thanksgiving	1974	Year	19.00	19.00

Bareuther, Father's Day Plate, 1971

Barrymore, Lionel, see Gorham

Bayel Crystal has been made in France since 1666. Limited edition crystal plates were first made in 1972.

Bayel Plates

Rose*	1972	300	50.00	50.00
Lilies	1973	300	50.00	50.00
Orchid	1973	300	50.00	50.00

Belleek Eggs

Easter	1972		25.00	25.00

Belleek Plates

Christmas, Castle Caldwell	1970	5000	25.00	75.00 to 105.00
Christmas, Celtic Cross	1971	5000	35.00	25.00 to 40.00
Christmas, Flight Of The Earls	1972	7500	35.00	25.00 to 35.00
Christmas	1973		39.00	39.00

Bareuther, Mother's Day Plate, 1972

Belleek Vase, see Lenox

The Bengough Collection of Canadiana was recently founded by Bomac Batten Ltd. of Canada. Its limited edition line, introduced in 1972, is silver and gold.

Bengough Plates

Christmas, Charles Dickens' Christmas Carol*	1972	490	125.00	125.00
Northwest Mounted Police, 1898 Dress Uniform*	1972	1000	140.00	140.00
Northwest Mounted Police, First Uniform*	1972	1000	140.00	140.00
Royal Canadian Police, Review Order Dress*	1972	1000	140.00	140.00

Berlin Design limited edition plates and mugs were first made in 1970 by the Kaiser Alboth Factory of Germany. The items are made exclusively for distribution by Schmid Brothers of Randolph, Massachusetts.

Berlin Bells

Christmas, Christmas Angel*	1972	5000	10.00	10.00
Christmas*	1973		15.00	11.00 to 15.00

Berlin Goblets

Composer, Beethoven*	1972	3000	37.50	35.00 to 37.50
Composer, Mozart*	1972	3000	37.50	35.00 to 37.50

Berlin Mugs

Christmas, Callenberg Castle	1971	700	40.00	30.00 to 50.00
Christmas, Heidelberg Castle*	1972	700	40.00	25.00 to 50.00
Christmas, Marienberg Castle*	1973	700	50.00	35.00 to 50.00

Bareuther, Mother's Day Plate, 1973

Bareuther, Mother's Day Plate, 1971

Berlin Plates

Christmas, Christmas In Bernkastel	1970	4000	14.50	25.00 to 39.00
Christmas, Christmas In Rothenburg*	1971	20000	14.50	7.00 to 15.00
Christmas, Christmas In Michelstadt*	1972	Year	15.00	8.00 to 15.00
Christmas, Christmas At Wendelstein*	1973	Year	20.00	15.00 to 20.00
Christmas	1974	Year	22.50	22.50
Father's Day, Brooklyn Bridge On Opening Day	1971	12000	14.50	5.00 to 15.00
Father's Day, Continent Spanned*	1972	3000	15.00	6.00 to 15.00
Father's Day, Landing Of Columbus*	1973	2000	18.00	9.00 to 18.00
Father's Day	1974		22.50	22.50
Mother's Day, Gray Poodles	1971	20000	14.50	10.00 to 25.00
Mother's Day, Fledglings*	1972	10000	15.00	5.00 to 15.00
Mother's Day, Ducks*	1973	5000	16.50	10.00 to 18.00
Mother's Day	1974		22.50	22.50

Bareuther, Thanksgiving Plate, 1971

Bareuther, Thanksgiving Plate, 1972

Bareuther, Thanksgiving Plate, 1973

Bengough, Christmas Plate, 1972

Bayel, Rose Plate, 1972

Bengough,
Northwest Mounted Police Plate,
First Uniform   1898 Dress Uniform

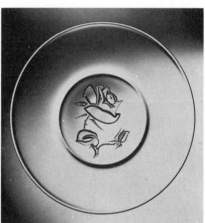

Bengough,
Royal Canadian Police Plate,
Review Order Dress

Berlin, Christmas Bell, 1973

Berlin, Christmas Bell, 1972

Berlin, Composer Goblet, Beethoven

Berlin, Christmas Mug, 1972

Berlin, Composer Goblet, Mozart

Berlin, Christmas Plate, 1973

Berlin, Christmas Plate, 1971

Berlin, Christmas Mug, 1973

Berlin, Mother's Day Plate, 1972

Berlin, Father's Day Plate, 1972

Berlin, Plate, Father's Day, 1973

Berlin, Mother's Day, 1973

Berlin, Vermeer Plate, The Geographer

Bing & Grondahl, Christmas Plate, 1895

Bing & Grondahl, Christmas Plate, 1896

Bing & Grondahl, Christmas Plate, 1897

Bing & Grondahl, Christmas Plate, 1898

Bing & Grondahl, Christmas Plate, 1899

Bing & Grondahl, Christmas Plate, 1900

Vermeer, The Geographer*	1973	3000	100.00	100.00
Vermeer, The Milkmaid	1973	3000	120.00	120.00

Berta Hummel, see Hummel Schmid

Betournes, see Jean-Paul Loup

Bicentennial Council Plates

Declaration Of Independence, Gold On Silver	1973	Year	175.00	175.00

*Bing & Grondahl, Danish pioneer in the field of limited edition
Christmas plates, was founded in 1853. The firm's famous cobalt underglaze
technique was introduced at the Paris World Exhibition in 1889.
Bing & Grondahl's first limited edition Christmas plate, issued in 1895,
was inspired by the Danish tradition of exchanging plates of cookies at
Christmastime. The Easter plaque was made between 1910 and 1935 only.
In 1915, the company introduced its first 5-year Jubilee plate. Mother's
Day plates were introduced in 1969. Each mold is destroyed at the end of
the year.*

Bing & Grondahl Bells

Annual	1974	Year	50.00	200.00 to 250.00

Bing & Grondahl Plates

Christmas, Behind The Frozen Window*	1895	Year	.50	2000.00 to 2800.00
Christmas, New Moon Over Snow-Covered Trees*	1896	Year		975.00 to 1300.00
Christmas, Christmas Meal Of The Sparrows*	1897	Year		625.00 to 780.00
Christmas, Roses And Christmas Star*	1898	Year		350.00 to 480.00
Christmas, Crows Enjoying Christmas*	1899	Year		600.00 to 795.00
Christmas, Church Bells Chiming In Christmas*	1900	Year		400.00 to 600.00
Christmas, Three Wise Men From The East*	1901	Year		218.00 to 250.00
Christmas, Interior Of A Gothic Church*	1902	Year		135.00 to 165.00
Christmas, Happy Expectation Of Children*	1903	Year		125.00 to 160.00
Christmas, View From Frederiksberg Hill*	1904	Year		70.00 to 90.00
Christmas, Anxiety Of The Coming Christmas*	1905	Year		50.00 to 90.00
Christmas, Sleighing On Christmas Eve*	1906	Year		51.00 to 65.00
Christmas, The Little Match Girl*	1907	Year		80.00 to 100.00
Christmas, St.Petri Church Of Copenhagen*	1908	Year		39.00 to 57.50
Christmas, Happiness Over The Yule Tree*	1909	Year		52.00 to 75.00
Christmas, The Old Organist*	1910	Year		48.00 to 65.00
Christmas, Sung By Angels To Shepherds*	1911	Year		48.00 to 60.00
Christmas, Going To Church On Christmas Eve*	1912	Year		48.00 to 65.00
Christmas, Bringing Home The Yule Tree*	1913	Year		48.00 to 65.00
Christmas, Castle Of Amalienborg, Copenhagen*	1914	Year		37.00 to 52.50
Christmas, Dog Getting Double Meal*	1915	Year		66.00 to 90.00
Christmas, Prayer Of The Sparrows*	1916	Year		39.00 to 60.00
Christmas, Arrival Of The Christmas Boat*	1917	Year		39.00 to 60.00
Christmas, Fishing Boat Returning Home*	1918	Year		39.00 to 55.00
Christmas, Outside The Lighted Window*	1919	Year		39.00 to 65.00
Christmas, Hare In The Snow*	1920	Year		36.00 to 52.00
Christmas, Pigeons In The Castle Court*	1921	Year		36.00 to 52.00
Christmas, Star Of Bethlehem*	1922	Year		35.00 to 50.00
Christmas, Royal Hunting Castle*	1923	Year		36.00 to 52.00
Christmas, Lighthouse In Danish Waters*	1924	Year		36.00 to 52.00
Christmas, The Child's Christmas*	1925	Year		36.00 to 52.00
Christmas, Churchgoers On Christmas Day*	1926	Year		36.00 to 52.00
Christmas, Skating Couple*	1927	Year		44.00 to 65.00
Christmas, Eskimos Looking At Village Church*	1928	Year		36.00 to 52.00
Christmas, Fox Outside Farm On Christmas Eve*	1929	Year		44.00 to 60.00
Christmas, Yule Tree In Town Hall Square*	1930	Year		51.00 to 70.00
Christmas, Arrival Of The Christmas Train*	1931	Year		41.00 to 60.00
Christmas, Lifeboat At Work*	1932	Year		40.00 to 65.00
Christmas, The Korsor Nyborg Ferry*	1933	Year		36.00 to 52.00
Christmas, Church Bell In Tower*	1934	Year		36.00 to 52.00
Christmas, Lillebelt Bridge*	1935	Year		36.00 to 52.00
Christmas, Royal Guard, Amalienborg Castle*	1936	Year		43.00 to 52.00
Christmas, Arrival Of Christmas Guests*	1937	Year		44.00 to 68.00
Christmas, Lighting The Candles*	1938	Year		65.00 to 90.00
Christmas, Old Lock-Eye, The Sandman*	1939	Year		85.00 to 125.00
Christmas, Delivering Christmas Letters*	1940	Year		95.00 to 125.00
Christmas, Horses Enjoying Christmas Meal*	1941	Year		175.00 to 240.00
Christmas, Danish Farm On Christmas Night*	1942	Year		95.00 to 135.00
Christmas, The Ribe Cathedral*	1943	Year		77.50 to 135.00

Bing & Grondahl, Christmas Plate, 1901

Bing & Grondahl, Christmas Plate, 1907

Bing & Grondahl, Christmas Plate, 1905

Bing & Grondahl, Christmas Plate, 1902

Bing & Grondahl, Christmas Plate, 1908

Bing & Grondahl, Christmas Plate, 1906

Bing & Grondahl, Christmas Plate, 1903

Bing & Grondahl, Christmas Plate, 1904

Bing & Grondahl, Christmas Plate, 1909

Bing & Grondahl, Christmas Plate, 1910

Bing & Grondahl, Christmas Plate, 1911

Bing & Grondahl, Christmas Plate, 1915

Bing & Grondahl, Christmas Plate, 1917

Bing & Grondahl, Christmas Plate, 1912

Bing & Grondahl, Christmas Plate, 1918

Bing & Grondahl, Christmas Plate, 1913

Bing & Grondahl, Christmas Plate, 1914

Bing & Grondahl, Christmas Plate, 1916

Bing & Grondahl, Christmas Plate, 1919

Bing & Grondahl, Christmas Plate, 1920

Bing & Grondahl, Christmas Plate, 1921

Bing & Grondahl, Christmas Plate, 1925

Bing & Grondahl, Christmas Plate, 1927

Bing & Grondahl, Christmas Plate, 1922

Bing & Grondahl, Christmas Plate, 1928

Bing & Grondahl, Christmas Plate, 1923

Bing & Grondahl, Christmas Plate, 1924

Bing & Grondahl, Christmas Plate, 1926

Bing & Grondahl, Christmas Plate, 1929

Bing & Grondahl, Christmas Plate, 1930

Bing & Grondahl, Christmas Plate, 1931

Bing & Grondahl, Christmas Plate, 1935

Bing & Grondahl, Christmas Plate, 1937

Bing & Grondahl, Christmas Plate, 1932

Bing & Grondahl, Christmas Plate, 1938

Bing & Grondahl, Christmas Plate, 1936

Bing & Grondahl, Christmas Plate, 1933

Bing & Grondahl, Christmas Plate, 1934

Bing & Grondahl, Christmas Plate, 1939

Bing & Grondahl, Christmas Plate, 1940

Christmas, Sorgenfri Castle*	1944	Year		65.00 to 120.00
Christmas, Old Water Mill*	1945	Year		65.00 to 120.00
Christmas, Commemoration Cross*	1946	Year		38.00 to 53.00
Christmas, Dybbol Mill*	1947	Year		47.00 to 80.00
Christmas, Watchman, Sculpture Of Town Hall*	1948	Year		36.50 to 62.00
Christmas, 19th Century Danish Soldier*	1949	Year		36.00 to 52.00
Christmas, Kronborg Castle At Elsinore*	1950	Year		49.00 to 68.00
Christmas, Jens Bang, New Passenger Boat*	1951	Year		39.00 to 55.00
Christmas, Copenhagen Canals At Wintertime*	1952	Year		39.00 to 55.00
Christmas, King's Boat In Greenland Waters*	1953	Year		36.00 to 60.00
Christmas, Birthplace Of H.C.Andersen*	1954	Year		57.00 to 60.00
Christmas, Kalundborg Church*	1955	Year		48.00 to 65.00
Christmas, Christmas In Copenhagen*	1956	Year		65.00 to 115.00
Christmas, Christmas Candles*	1957	Year		65.00 to 115.00
Christmas, Santa Claus*	1958	Year		58.00 to 82.00
Christmas, Christmas Eve*	1959	Year		85.00 to 110.00
Christmas, Danish Village Church*	1960	Year		80.00 to 125.00
Christmas, Winter Harmony*	1961	Year		60.00 to 85.00
Christmas, Winter Night*	1962	Year		32.50 to 45.00
Christmas, Christmas Elf*	1963	Year		66.00 to 95.00
Christmas, Fir Tree And Hare*	1964	Year		25.00 to 40.00
Christmas, Bringing Home The Christmas Tree*	1965	Year		25.00 to 40.00
Christmas, Home For Christmas*	1966	Year		20.00 to 33.00
Christmas, Sharing The Joy Of Christmas*	1967	Year		15.00 to 30.00
Christmas, Christmas In Church*	1968	Year		16.00 to 25.00
Christmas, Guests' Arrival*	1969	Year	15.00	13.00 to 22.00
Christmas, Pheasants In Snow*	1970	Year	15.00	9.00 to 20.00
Christmas, Girl At Piano*	1971	Year	15.00	8.00 to 17.00
Christmas, Dogsled*	1972	Year	16.00	7.00 to 16.00
Christmas, Gate*	1973	Year	19.50	11.00 to 20.00
Christmas	1974	Year	22.50	22.50
Commemorative, Greenland				8.00
Commemorative, May 4				20.00
Commemorative, Olympic*	1972			10.00 to 18.00
Commemorative, Rebild				8.00
Commemorative, 800th Birthday				12.00 to 18.00
Easter	1910	Year		40.00
Easter	1911	Year		40.00
Easter	1912	Year		40.00
Easter	1913	Year		40.00
Easter	1914	Year		40.00
Easter	1915	Year		40.00
Easter	1916	Year		40.00
Easter	1917	Year		40.00
Easter	1918	Year		40.00
Easter	1919	Year		40.00
Easter	1920	Year		40.00
Easter	1921	Year		40.00
Easter	1922	Year		40.00
Easter	1923	Year		40.00
Easter	1924	Year		40.00
Easter	1925	Year		40.00
Easter	1926	Year		42.50
Easter	1927	Year		50.00
Easter	1928	Year		50.00
Easter	1929	Year		50.00
Easter	1930	Year		100.00
Easter	1931	Year		100.00
Easter	1932	Year		100.00
Easter	1933	Year		100.00
Easter	1934	Year		300.00
Easter	1935	Year		500.00
Jubilee*	1915	Year		80.00 to 100.00
Jubilee*	1920	Year		75.00 to 80.00
Jubilee*	1925	Year		100.00
Jubilee*	1930	Year		150.00 to 200.00
Jubilee*	1935	Year		500.00 to 600.00
Jubilee*	1940	Year		1000.00 to 1200.00
Jubilee*	1945	Year		200.00 to 300.00
Jubilee*	1950	Year		130.00 to 150.00

Bing & Grondahl, Christmas Plate, 1941

Bing & Grondahl, Christmas Plate, 1942

Bing & Grondahl, Christmas Plate, 1943

Bing & Grondahl, Christmas Plate, 1944

Bing & Grondahl, Christmas Plate, 1945

Bing & Grondahl, Christmas Plate, 1951

Bing & Grondahl, Christmas Plate, 1949

Bing & Grondahl, Christmas Plate, 1946

Bing & Grondahl, Christmas Plate, 1952

Bing & Grondahl, Christmas Plate, 1950

Bing & Grondahl, Christmas Plate, 1947

Bing & Grondahl, Christmas Plate, 1948

Bing & Grondahl, Christmas Plate, 1953

Bing & Grondahl, Christmas Plate, 1954

Bing & Grondahl, Christmas Plate, 1955

Bing & Grondahl, Christmas Plate, 1959

Bing & Grondahl, Christmas Plate, 1961

Bing & Grondahl, Christmas Plate, 1956

Bing & Grondahl, Christmas Plate, 1962

Bing & Grondahl, Christmas Plate, 1960

Bing & Grondahl, Christmas Plate, 1957

Bing & Grondahl, Christmas Plate, 1963

Bing & Grondahl, Christmas Plate, 1958

Bing & Grondahl, Christmas Plate, 1964

Bing & Grondahl, Christmas Plate, 1965

Bing & Grondahl, Christmas Plate, 1969

Bing & Grondahl, Christmas Plate, 1970

Bing & Grondahl, Christmas Plate, 1966

Bing & Grondahl, Christmas Plate, 1971

Bing & Grondahl, Mother's Day Plate, 1974

Bing & Grondahl, Christmas Plate, 1967

Bing & Grondahl, Christmas Plate, 1968

Bing & Grondahl, Christmas Plate, 1972

Bing & Grondahl, Christmas Plate, 1973

Mallek, Christmas Game Bird Plate, 1972,
Gambel Quail

Mallek, Amish Harvest Plate, 1972

Mallek, Navajo Christmas Plate, 1971,
Indian Wise Men

Mallek, Easter Plaque, 1972, Chicks In The Nest

Mallek, Navajo Thanksgiving Plaque, 1972

Wheaton, Presidential Plate, Eisenhower

Wheaton, Presidential Plate, Kennedy

Wheaton, Presidential Plate, Lincoln

Wheaton, Presidential Plate, Hoover

Wheaton, Presidential Plate, F.D.Roosevelt

Wheaton, Presidential Plate, Monroe

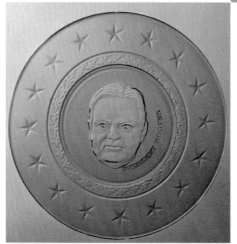

Poole, Medieval Calendar Plate, April

Poole, Medieval Calendar Plate, March

Fenton, Craftsmen Plate, 1972, Blacksmith

Fenton, Mother's Day Plate, 1974,
Carnival, Blue Satin, White Satin

Fenton, Craftsmen Plate, 1974, Cooper

Fenton, Christmas Plate, 1972, Blue Satin

Fenton, Craftsmen Plate, 1973, Shoemaker

Fenton, Mother's Day Plate, 1973, Carnival, Blue Satin, White Satin

Jean-Paul Loup, Six Crafts,
The Vinedresser

Jean-Paul Loup, Six Crafts,
The Butcher

Jean-Paul Loup, Six Crafts,
The Sower

Jean-Paul Loup, Six Crafts,
The Reaper

Jean-Paul Loup, Six Crafts,
The Plowman

Jean-Paul Loup, Six Crafts,
The Mower

Jean-Paul Loup, Christmas Plate, 1972

Jean-Paul Loup, Christmas Plate, 1973

Jean-Paul Loup, Mother's Day Plate, 1974

Wedgwood, Christmas Plate, 1973

Wedgwood, Calendar Plate, 1973

Wedgwood, Child's Day Plate, 1972

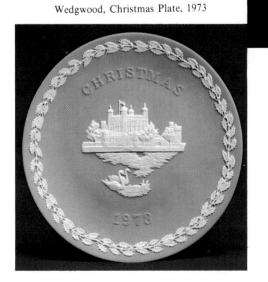

Wedgwood, Calendar Plate, 1974

Wedgwood, State Seal Compotier,
John Hancock & Massachusetts

Gustavsberg, 90th Anniversary Plate, Gustaf Adolph VI
Gustavsberg, Endangered Species Plate, Hedgehog
Gustavsberg, Accession Plate, Carl XVI Gustaf
Gustavsberg, Endangered Species Plate, Owl
Gustavsberg, Christmas Plate, 1973
Gustavsberg, Congratulations Plate, 1973

Wedgwood, State Seal Compotier,
Philip Livingston & New York

Wedgwood, Bicentennial Plate, 1973

Svend Jensen, Mother's Day Plate, 1974

Svend Jensen, Christmas Plate, 1974

Borsato, Tender Musings Plaque

Royal Crown Derby,
Derbyshire Landscape Dessert Plate,
Wolfscote Dale

Pickard, Lockhart Bird Plate, 1971, Mallard

Pickard, Lockhart Bird Plate, 1972,
Mockingbird

Borsato, Golden Years Plaque

Royal Worcester, Doris Lindner, American Saddle Horse

Royal Worcester, Doris Lindner,
Princess Anne On Doublet

Royal Worcester, Doris Lindner, Palomino

Royal Worcester, Doris Lindner, Suffolk Punch

Royal Worcester, Bernard Winskill, Duke Of Wellington

Royal Worcester, Bernard Winskill, Napoleon Bonaparte

Jubilee	1955	Year		125.00 to 140.00
Jubilee	1960	Year		100.00 to 110.00
Jubilee	1965	Year		100.00 to 110.00
Jubilee	1970	Year		12.00 to 25.00
Mother's Day, Dogs	1969	5000	8.00	150.00 to 300.00
Mother's Day, Bird & Chicks	1970	Year	9.00	12.50 to 30.00
Mother's Day, Cat & Kittens	1971	Year	10.00	5.00 to 11.00
Mother's Day, Mare & Foal	1972	Year	10.00	7.50 to 11.00
Mother's Day, Duck & Ducklings	1973	Year	13.00	8.00 to 13.00
Mother's Day, Polar Bears	1974	Year	13.00	13.00 to 16.50

Blue Delft, Christmas Plate, 1973

Blue Delft Co., whose Dutch name is Schoonhaven, issued its first Christmas tile in 1967. Matching plates and spoons were added in 1970. Mother's Day and Father's Day plates and spoons followed in 1971.

Blue Delft, see also Crown Delft, Royal Delft, Zenith

Blue Delft Mugs

Father's Day, Francesco Lana's Airship	1971	Year	10.00	9.00 to 10.00
Father's Day, Dr.Jonathan's Balloon	1972	Year	10.00	10.00

Blue Delft Plates

Christmas, Drawbridge Near Binnenhof	1970	Year	12.00	11.00 to 14.00
Christmas, St.Laurens Church	1971	Year	12.00	8.00 to 14.00
Christmas, Church At Bierkade Of Amsterdam	1972	Year	12.00	8.00 to 12.00
Christmas, St Jan's Church*	1973	Year	12.00	12.00
Christmas, Dongeradeel	1974	Year	13.00	13.00
Father's Day, Francesco Lana's Airship	1971	Year	12.00	7.00 to 12.00
Father's Day, Dr.Jonathan's Balloon	1972	Year	12.00	6.00 to 12.00
Mother's Day, Mother & Daughter Of 1600s	1971	Year	12.00	6.00 to 12.00
Mother's Day, Mother & Daughter, Isle Of Urk	1972	Year	12.00	6.00 to 12.00
Mother's Day, Rembrandt's Mother*	1973	Year	12.00	6.00 to 12.00

Blue Delft, Mother's Day Plate, 1973

Blue Delft Spoons

Christmas, Drawbridge Near Binnenhof	1970	Year	7.00	7.00 to 10.00
Christmas, St.Laurens Church	1971	Year	7.00	7.00 to 10.00
Christmas, Church At Bierkade Of Amsterdam	1972	Year	7.00	7.00 to 9.00
Christmas, St.Jan's Church*	1973	Year	7.00	7.00
Christmas, Dongeradeel	1974	Year	8.75	8.75

Blue Delft Tiles

Christmas, Winter Scene	1967	Year	5.00	15.00 to 25.00
Christmas, Admiring The Tree	1968	Year	5.00	12.50 to 20.00
Christmas, Windmill	1969	Year	5.00	7.50 to 10.00
Christmas, Drawbridge Near Binnenhof	1970	Year	5.00	5.00 to 7.50
Christmas, St.Laurens Church	1971	Year	5.00	5.00 to 6.50
Christmas, Church At Bierkade	1972	Year	5.00	5.00 to 6.00
Christmas, St.Jan's Church*	1973	Year	5.00	5.00
Christmas, Dongeradeel	1974	Year	6.00	6.00

Blue Delft, Christmas Tile,.1973

Boehm porcelains were first made by Edward Marshall Boehm in Trenton, New Jersey, in 1950. The Malvern Boehm studio of London was established after Mr. Boehm's death in 1969. Bone china Boehm figurines are made at the English factory. Hard paste porcelains are still made in New Jersey. Lenox China has also issued a limited edition plate series featuring Boehm birds.

See listing for Boehm in Figurine section

Boehm Bird plates, see also Lenox

Boehm Plates

Bird Of Peace*	1972	5000	150.00	350.00 to 500.00
Eaglet, Companion*	1973	6000	175.00	190.00 to 295.00

Blue Delft,
Christmas Spoon, 1973

Bonita limited edition plates are made by the Bonita Silver Company of Mexico. They were first issued in 1972.

Bonita Plates

Mother's Day, Mother With Baby, Silver	1972	4000	125.00	50.00 to 125.00

Borsato Porcelains have been made by Antonio Borsato of Milan, Italy, since 1937. Limited editions were first made in 1973.

See listing for Borsato in Figurine section

Boehm, Bird Of Peace Plate

Bonita, Mother's Day Plate, 1972

Borsato, Tender Musings Plaque

Buffalo Pottery, Christmas Plate, 1950

Boehm, Eaglet Plate

Buffalo Pottery, Christmas Plate, 1951

Buffalo Pottery, Christmas Plate, 1954

Buffalo Pottery, Christmas Plate, 1953

Buffalo Pottery, Christmas Plate, 1955

Buffalo Pottery, Christmas Plate, 1952

Borsato Plaques

Golden Years, 13 1/2 In.Diameter**	1973	700	1450.00	1450.00
Tender Musings, 13 1/2 In.Diameter*	1974	250	1650.00	1650.00

Paul Briant & Sons Silversmiths of Washington state entered the limited edition market in 1971. The plates are made of 24k gold plate over copper.

Briant Plates

Christmas, Fruits Of The Spirit	1971	350	125.00	125.00 to 150.00
Christmas, Labour Of Love, Gold Over Copper	1972	700	100.00	90.00 to 100.00
Christmas, Annunciation, Silver	1973		100.00	100.00
Easter, The Last Sacrifice, Gold Over Copper	1972	500	85.00	68.00 to 85.00

Buffalo Pottery was made in Buffalo, New York after 1902. The company was established by the Larkin Company, famous manufacturers of soap. Limited edition Christmas plates were made between 1950 and 1962.

Buffalo Pottery Plates

Christmas*	1950	1800	35.00 to 45.00
Christmas*	1951	1800	35.00 to 40.00
Christmas*	1952	1800	35.00 to 40.00
Christmas*	1953	1800	35.00 to 40.00
Christmas*	1954	1800	30.00 to 35.00
Christmas*	1955	1800	30.00 to 35.00
Christmas*	1956	1800	25.00 to 30.00
Christmas*	1957	1800	25.00 to 30.00
Christmas*	1958	1800	25.00 to 30.00
Christmas*	1959	1800	25.00 to 30.00
Christmas*	1960	1800	25.00 to 30.00
Christmas, Edged In Gold*	1962	900	125.00 to 150.00

Bygdo was organized in 1939 by Mr. Svend Knudsen. Christmas plates & mugs, first issued in 1969, are based on the fairy tales of Hans Christian Andersen. A number of other commemorative series have been introduced since 1970.

Bygdo Mugs

Christmas, Shepherdess & Chimney Sweep*	1969	1000	10.00	5.00 to 10.00
Christmas, Clumsy Hans*	1970	1000	10.00	5.00 to 10.00
Christmas, The Flying Trunk*	1971	1000	10.00	5.00 to 10.00
Christmas, Chinese Nightingale*	1972	1000	10.00	5.00 to 10.00

Bygdo Plates

Apollo 11, First Moon Landing*	1969		10.00	7.50 to 10.00
Christmas, The Shepherdess & Chimney Sweep	1969	5000	10.00	6.00 to 10.00
Christmas, Clumsy Hans*	1970	5000	10.00	6.00 to 10.00
Christmas, The Flying Trunk	1971	5000	10.00	6.00 to 10.00
Christmas, Chinese Nightingale	1972	5000	10.00	6.00 to 10.00
Christmas*	1973	5000	10.00	10.00
Church, Artemarks Kurka*	1973	5000	10.00	10.00
Commemorative, King Frederik IX*		40000	10.00	7.50 to 10.00
Commemorative, Mormon*	1974	10000		

Capo di Monte limited editions are made in Italy. Christmas plates were first made in 1972. Mother's Day plates followed in 1973.

Capo di Monte Bells

Christmas	1973	350	17.50	17.50

Capo di Monte Plates

Christmas, Cherubs*	1972	500	55.00	100.00 to 125.00
Christmas	1973	1000	55.00	55.00
Mother's Day	1973	500	55.00	60.00 to 95.00

The Caritas, or charity, plate was commissioned by Rose Kennedy for a charitable cause.

Caritas Plate

Rose Kennedy	1973		20.00	20.00 to 30.00

Carlo Monti limited edition plates are of enamel on copper. 1973 is the first year they were made.

Buffalo Pottery, Christmas Plate, 1956

Buffalo Pottery, Christmas Plate, 1957

Buffalo Pottery, Christmas Plate, 1958

Buffalo Pottery, Christmas Plate, 1959

Buffalo Pottery, Christmas Plate, 1960

Buffalo Pottery, Christmas Plate, 1962

Bygdo, Apollo Plate, 1969

Bygdo, Christmas Plate, 1970

Bygdo, Christmas Plate, 1973

Bygdo, Christmas Mug, 1970

Bygdo, Christmas Mug, 1972

Bygdo, Christmas Mug, 1971

Bygdo, Christmas Mug, 1969, Side View

Carlo Monti Plates

Mother's Day, Madonna & Child	1973	2000	35.00	35.00

Carte a Jouer plates, see Puiforcat

The Cartier Plate series is a collection of porcelain plates reproducing famous stained glass in French cathedrals. The plates are made in Limoges, France.

Cartier Plates

Chartres Cathedral	1972	12500	50.00	25.00 to 50.00
Chartres Cathedral, Millous	1974	500	130.00	130.00

The Chagall plate is part of a series issued by Georg Jensen of New York City.

Chagall Plate

The Lovers*	1972	12500	50.00	30.00 to 50.00

Chaim Gross, see Judaic Heritage Society

Charles Russell, see Antique Trader

Chateau, Inc., of Indianapolis, Indiana, entered the limited edition field in 1972. The plates are produced in Denmark by the Kesa factory.

Chateau Plates

Apollo 16	1973	1000	20.00	15.00 to 15.00
Auto, 1915 Model T Ford		1000	20.00	20.00
Auto, 1913 Rolls-Royce		1000	20.00	20.00
Bicentennial, First		2500	20.00	20.00
Bicentennial, Second		2500	20.00	20.00
City, Boston	1972	1000	15.00	15.00
City, Chicago	1972	1000	15.00	15.00
City, Indianapolis	1972	2000	15.00	15.00
City, New Orleans	1972	275	15.00	15.00
City, San Francisco	1972	1500	15.00	15.00
City, Washington, D.C.	1972	275	15.00	15.00
Dixie		2500	20.00	20.00
Famous American, Eisenhower, Crystal		2500	20.00	20.00
State, Alabama	1972	750	15.00	15.00
State, Alaska	1972	250	15.00	15.00
State, Arizona	1972	450	15.00	15.00
State, Arkansas	1972	450	15.00	15.00
State, California	1972	775	15.00	15.00
State, Colorado	1972	250	15.00	15.00
State, Connecticut	1972	250	15.00	15.00
State, Delaware	1972	250	15.00	15.00
State, Florida	1972	1000	15.00	15.00
State, Georgia	1972	1000	15.00	15.00
State, Hawaii	1972	500	15.00	15.00
State, Idaho	1972	250	15.00	15.00
State, Illinois	1972	1500	15.00	15.00
State, Indiana	1972	1500	15.00	15.00
State, Iowa	1972	1500	15.00	15.00
State, Kansas	1972	450	15.00	15.00
State, Kentucky	1972	1000	15.00	15.00
State, Louisiana	1972	650	15.00	15.00
State, Maine	1972	500	15.00	15.00
State, Maryland	1972	500	15.00	15.00
State, Massachusetts	1972	500	15.00	15.00
State, Michigan	1972	700	15.00	15.00
State, Minnesota	1972	1500	15.00	15.00
State, Mississippi	1972	400	15.00	15.00
State, Missouri	1972	1500	15.00	15.00
State, Montana	1972	225	15.00	15.00
State, Nebraska	1972	500	15.00	15.00
State, Nevada	1972	250	15.00	15.00
State, New Hampshire	1972	250	15.00	15.00
State, New Jersey	1972	500	15.00	15.00
State, New Mexico	1972	500	15.00	15.00
State, New York	1972	525	15.00	15.00
State, North Carolina	1972	750	15.00	15.00
State, North Dakota	1972	325	15.00	15.00

Bygdo, Commemorative Plate,
King Frederik IX

Bygdo, Commemorative Plate, Mormon

Bygdo, Church Plate, 1973

Capo di Monte, Christmas Plate, 1972

Chagall, The Lovers Plate

State, Ohio	1972	1425	15.00	15.00
State, Oklahoma	1972	1150	15.00	15.00
State, Oregon	1972	775	15.00	15.00
State, Pennsylvania	1972	500	15.00	15.00
State, Rhode Island	1972	250	15.00	15.00
State, South Carolina	1972	750	15.00	15.00
State, South Dakota	1972	250	15.00	15.00
State, Tennessee	1972	750	15.00	15.00
State, Texas	1972	2000	15.00	15.00
State, Utah	1972	250	15.00	15.00
State, Vermont	1972	340	15.00	15.00
State, Virginia	1972	525	15.00	15.00
State, Washington	1972	475	15.00	15.00
State, West Virginia	1972	525	15.00	15.00
State, Wisconsin	1972	825	15.00	15.00
State, Wyoming	1972	250	15.00	15.00
State, Alabama	1973	1500	15.00	15.00
State, Alaska	1973	250	15.00	15.00
State, Arizona	1973	500	15.00	15.00
State, Arkansas	1973	500	15.00	15.00
State, California	1973	2000	15.00	15.00
State, Colorado	1973	250	15.00	15.00
State, Connecticut	1973	500	15.00	15.00
State, Delaware	1973	250	15.00	15.00
State, Florida	1973	1000	15.00	15.00
State, Georgia	1973	1000	15.00	15.00
State, Hawaii	1973	500	15.00	15.00
State, Idaho	1973	250	15.00	15.00
State, Illinois	1973	2000	15.00	15.00
State, Indiana	1973	1500	15.00	15.00
State, Iowa	1973	1500	15.00	15.00
State, Kansas	1973	1000	15.00	15.00
State, Kentucky	1973	1000	15.00	15.00
State, Louisiana	1973	750	15.00	15.00
State, Maine	1973	500	15.00	15.00
State, Maryland	1973	500	15.00	15.00
State, Massachusetts	1973	1000	15.00	15.00
State, Michigan	1973	1000	15.00	15.00
State, Minnesota	1973	1500	15.00	15.00
State, Mississippi	1973	500	15.00	15.00
State, Missouri	1973	1500	15.00	15.00
State, Montana	1973	250	15.00	15.00
State, Nebraska	1973	1000	15.00	15.00
State, Nevada	1973	250	15.00	15.00
State, New Hampshire	1973	250	15.00	15.00
State, New Jersey	1973	1000	15.00	15.00
State, New Mexico	1973	500	15.00	15.00
State, New York	1973	2000	15.00	15.00
State, North Carolina	1973	750	15.00	15.00
State, North Dakota	1973	500	15.00	15.00
State, Ohio	1973	1500	15.00	15.00
State, Oklahoma	1973	1500	15.00	15.00
State, Oregon	1973	775	15.00	15.00
State, Pennsylvania	1973	1500	15.00	15.00
State, Rhode Island	1973	500	15.00	15.00
State, South Carolina	1973	750	15.00	15.00
State, South Dakota	1973	250	15.00	15.00
State, Tennessee	1973	1000	15.00	15.00
State, Texas	1973	2000	15.00	15.00
State, Utah	1973	500	15.00	15.00
State, Vermont	1973	350	15.00	15.00
State, Virginia	1973	750	15.00	15.00
State, Washington	1973	500	15.00	15.00
State, West Virginia	1973	525	15.00	15.00
State, Wisconsin	1973	1000	15.00	15.00
State, Wyoming	1973	250	15.00	15.00

Collector's Weekly, American Plate, 1972

Collector's Weekly, American Plate, 1973

Chief Wapello plate, see Wapello County

Church plate, see Danish Church

Churchill Mint Plaques

Mother's Day, Horse And Foal, Silver	1973	500	75.00	75.00

Churchill Mint Plates

Christmas, Mockingbird On Holly	1972	2000	150.00	150.00
Christmas, Scissor-Tailed Flycatcher	1973	2000	150.00	150.00

Churchill plate, see Silver Creations

Cleveland Mint Plates

Da Vinci, Last Supper, Silver	1972	5000	150.00	100.00 to 150.00

Cleveland Mint, Churchill plate, see Silver Creations

Coalport Plates

Indy 500	1972	2000	49.95	50.00

Collector Creations Plates

Alice In Wonderland, Damascene	1973	750	100.00	100.00
Christmas, Christmas By Thomas Nast, Damascene	1973	750	100.00	100.00

Cristal d'Albret, Four Seasons Plate, Autumn

Collector's Weekly, an antiques publication published in Kermit, Texas, introduced limited edition plates in 1971. The cobalt glass plates are made by the Big Pine Key Glass Works of Florida.

Collector's Weekly Plates

American, Miss Liberty, Carnival	1971	500	12.50	12.50
American, Miss Liberty, Carnival*	1972	900	12.50	12.50
American, Eagle, Carnival*	1973	900	9.75	9.75

Count Agazzi Plates

Apollo 11	1969	1000	17.00	18.00 to 20.00
Children's Hour, Owl	1970	2000	12.50	10.00 to 12.50
Children's Hour, Cat	1971	2000	12.50	10.00 to 12.50
Children's Hour, Panda	1973	2000	12.50	12.50
Christmas	1973	1000	19.50	19.50
Easter, Playing The Violin	1971	600	12.50	9.00 to 12.50
Easter, At Prayer	1972	600	12.50	9.00 to 12.50
Easter	1973	600	12.50	12.50
Famous Personalities	1968	600	8.00	25.00 to 35.00
Famous Personalities	1970	1000	12.50	12.50 to 15.00
Famous Personalities	1973	600	15.00	15.00
Father's Day	1972	144	35.00	30.00 to 40.00
Father's Day	1973	288	19.50	19.50
Mother's Day	1972	144	35.00	30.00 to 45.00
Mother's Day	1973	720	19.50	19.50
Peace				12.00 to 15.00

Cristal d'Albret, Four Seasons Plate, Spring

Creative World, Pearl Buck plate, see Pearl Buck

Creative World, see also Veneto Flair

Creative World Plates

Stained Glass, Madonna	1973	1500	95.00	95.00 to 100.00

Cristal d'Albret plates and paperweights are made at the glassworks of Vianne, France. Limited edition sulfide paperweights were first made in 1966. Limited edition crystal plates were introduced in 1972.

See listing for Cristal d'Albret in Paperweight section

Cristal d'Albret Plates

Bird Of Peace	1972	3700	88.00	100.00 to 190.00
Four Seasons, Summer	1972	1000	64.00	130.00 to 295.00
Four Seasons, Autumn*	1973	1000	64.00	64.00 to 75.00
Four Seasons, Spring*	1973	1000	64.00	64.00 to 75.00

Crown Delft Plates

Christmas, Man By The Fire	1969		10.00	10.00 to 20.00
Christmas, Two Sleigh Riders	1970		10.00	6.00 to 10.00
Christmas, Christmas Tree On Market Square	1971		10.00	6.00 to 10.00
Christmas, Baking For Christmas	1972		10.00	6.00 to 10.00
Father's Day	1970		10.00	6.00 to 10.00
Father's Day	1971		10.00	6.00 to 10.00
Father's Day	1972		10.00	6.00 to 10.00
Mother's Day, Sheep	1970		10.00	10.00 to 15.00
Mother's Day, Stork	1971		10.00	6.00 to 10.00
Mother's Day, Ducks	1972		10.00	6.00 to 10.00

Curry, Christmas Plaque, 1972

Danbury Mint, Bicentennial, 1973, The Boston Tea Party

Danbury Mint, Christmas Plate, 1972, Currier & Ives

Danbury Mint, Creation Of Adam Plate

Crown Delft Tiles

Christmas, Man By The Fire	1969	4.50	7.50 to 10.00
Christmas, Two Sleigh Riders	1970	4.50	5.00 to 9.00
Christmas, Christmas Tree On Market Square	1971	4.50	4.50 to 6.50
Christmas, Baking For Christmas	1972	4.50	4.50
Christmas	1973	5.00	5.00
Father's Day	1970	4.50	5.00 to 7.50
Father's Day	1971	4.50	4.50 to 6.00
Mother's Day, Sheep	1970	4.50	5.00 to 7.50
Mother's Day, Stork	1971	4.50	4.50

Crown Staffordshire Plates

Christmas	1972		25.00	25.00 to 30.00
Christmas	1973		27.50	27.50
Mother's Day	1973	10000	27.50	27.50 to 30.00

Currier & Ives plates, see Antique Trader, Danbury Mint, Reed & Barton

Bill Curry Productions of Chesapeake, Ohio first made limited edition tile plaques in 1972. The tiles are produced by Screencraft, U.S.A. of Massachusetts.

Curry Plaques

Christmas, Baby Santa Claus *	1972	1000	12.00	12.00
Christmas, Mistletoe Bird	1973	1000	12.00	12.00
Indian, Cheyenne Chief	1973	1000	10.00	10.00
Indian, Cheyenne Chief, Proof	1973	50	25.00	25.00
Indian, Chief Crazy Horse	1973	1000	10.00	10.00
Indian, Chief Crazy Horse, Proof	1973	50	25.00	25.00
Indian, Chief Gall, Sioux	1973	1000	10.00	10.00
Indian, Chief Gall, Sioux, Proof	1973	50	25.00	25.00
Indian, Chief Rain-In-The-Face, Sioux	1973	1000	10.00	10.00
Indian, Chief Rain-In-The-Face, Sioux, Proof	1973	50	25.00	25.00
Indian, Chief Red Fox, Sioux	1973	1000	10.00	10.00
Indian, Chief Red Fox, Sioux, Proof	1973	50	25.00	25.00
Indian, Chief Sitting Bull, Sioux	1973	1000	10.00	10.00
Indian, Chief Sitting Bull, Sioux, Proof	1973	50	25.00	25.00
Indian, Chief Yellow Hand, Cheyenne	1973	1000	10.00	10.00
Indian, Chief Yellow Hand, Cheyenne, Proof	1973	50	25.00	25.00
Indian, Comanche Chief	1973	1000	10.00	10.00
Indian, Comanche Chief, Proof	1973	50	25.00	25.00
Indian, Nez Perce Chief	1973	1000	10.00	10.00
Indian, Nez Perce Chief, Proof	1973	50	25.00	25.00
Indian, Shoshone Chief	1973	1000	10.00	10.00
Indian, Shoshone Chief, Proof	1973	50	25.00	25.00
Indian, Sioux Chief	1973	1000	10.00	10.00
Indian, Sioux Chief, Proof	1973	50	25.00	25.00
Indian, Yuma Chief	1973	1000	10.00	10.00
Indian, Yuma Chief, Proof	1973	50	25.00	25.00

d'Albret, see Cristal d'Albret

Da Vinci Last Supper plate, see Cleveland Mint

Dali, see Daum, Lincoln Mint, Puiforcat

Danbury Mint, a division of Glendinning Companies, Inc., creates and markets art medals and limited edition plates. All limited editions are struck for the Danbury Mint by other organizations. Limited edition plates were first introduced in 1972.

See listing for Danbury Mint in Bar & Ingot and Medal sections

Danbury Mint Plates

Bicentennial, Boston Tea Party, Gold & Silver*	1973	7500	125.00	125.00
Bicentennial, 1st Continental Congress, Silver	1974		125.00	125.00
Christmas, Currier & Ives, Sterling*	1972		125.00	75.00 to 150.00
Christmas, Currier & Ives, Sterling	1973		125.00	125.00
Creation Of Adam, Sterling*	1972	7500	150.00	125.00 to 150.00
The Pieta, Sterling*	1973	7500	150.00	150.00

Danish Church Plates

Christmas	1968	10.00	20.00 to 35.00
Christmas	1969	10.00	15.00 to 25.00
Christmas	1970	10.00	7.50 to 20.00

Christmas	1971		12.00	9.00 to 15.00
Christmas	1972		12.00	8.00 to 12.00
Christmas	1973		14.00	14.00

Danbury Mint, The Pieta Plate

Daum, the French firm noted for Daum Nancy cameo glass was founded in 1875 by Auguste and Antonin Daum. Crystal, a new medium for the company, was introduced following World War II. The first limited edition Four Seasons plate series was made by the pate de verre process in 1969. Daum also produces limited edition plates in crystal.

Daum Plates

Composer, Bach	1970	2000	60.00	35.00 to 60.00
Composer, Beethoven	1970	2000	60.00	35.00 to 60.00
Composer, Mozart	1971	2000	60.00	35.00 to 60.00
Composer, Wagner	1971	2000	60.00	35.00 to 60.00
Composer, Debussy	1972	2000	60.00	35.00 to 60.00
Composer, Gershwin	1972	2000	60.00	35.00 to 60.00
Dali, Pair	1971	2000	400.00	275.00 to 400.00
Four Seasons, Set Of 4 1969-	970	2000	600.00	350.00 to 600.00

Davis plates are sponsored by Mr. & Mrs. Vernon Davis of Hagerstown Maryland. They feature famous photographs taken by Mr. Davis during his career as a journalist.

Davis Plates

Camp David	1972	250	12.00	12.00
Last Trolley	1973	250	12.00	12.00

De Grazia Plates

Beautiful Burden		200	75.00	75.00
Bell Of Hope		200	75.00	75.00
Heavenly Blessing		200	75.00	75.00

Delft, see Blue Delft, Crown Delft, Royal Delft, Zenith

Denby, Queen's Handmaiden Plate

Denby Plates

Queen's Handmaid & King's Fisherman, Pair*	1973	5000	100.00	100.00

Detlefsen Plates

Americana, Memories	1973	4000	40.00	40.00
Americana, Coming Around The Mountain	1974		40.00	40.00

Devlin, Stuart, see Reco

Dorothy Doughty, see Royal Worcester

Dresden Plates

Christmas, Shepherd Scene	1971	3500	15.00	25.00 to 55.00
Christmas, Niklas Church	1972	8500	15.00	10.00 to 25.00
Christmas, Mountain Church	1973	6000	18.00	18.00
Mother's Day, Doe & Fawn	1972	8000	15.00	25.00 to 40.00
Mother's Day, Mare & Foal*	1973	6000	16.00	16.00
Mother's Day, Tiger & Cub*	1974	5000	20.00	20.00

Denby, King's Fisherman Plate

Dresden, Mother's Day Plate, 1973

Dudley Plates

Apollo Peace	1969	2000	13.50	13.50 to 15.00

Edward Warren Sawyer, see George Washington Mint

Egermann Decanters

Thanksgiving, Turkey & Basket	1970	50	35.00	75.00 to 95.00
Thanksgiving, Turkey & Basket	1971	360	35.00	35.00 to 55.00
Thanksgiving, Turkey & Cornucopia	1972	500	45.00	37.50 to 45.00
Thanksgiving, Vintage	1973	500	45.00	45.00

Egermann Plates

Christmas	1972	500	55.00	45.00 to 65.00
Christmas*	1973	1000	55.00	50.00 to 55.00

Eschenbach Plates

Christmas, Nuremberg	1971		13.00	5.00 to 13.00
Christmas, Church Maria Gern	1972		13.00	5.00 to 13.00

Ewings, see Scottish

Faure, see Poillerat

Fenton Art Glass Company, founded in 1905 in Martins Ferry, Ohio, by Frank L. Fenton, is now located in Williamstown, West Virginia.

Dresden, Mother's Day Plate, 1974

Egermann, Christmas Plate, 1973

Fenton, Christmas Plate, 1970, Carnival

Fenton, Christmas Plate, 1971, Carnival

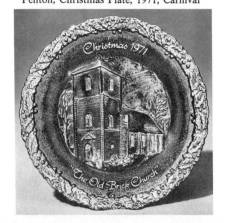

It is noted for early carnival glass, produced between 1907 and 1920. Fenton is still using carnival glass, as well as blue and white satin glass, for its limited edition commemorative plates, introduced in 1970. The company trademark is an early glassworker. Editions are limited to a six-month production period, with molds being destroyed at the end of that period.

Fenton Plates

Christmas, Little Brown Church, Blue Satin	1970	Year	12.50	7.50 to 12.50
Christmas, Little Brown Church, Carnival*	1970	Year	12.50	6.50 to 12.50
Christmas, Old Brick Church, Blue Satin	1971	Year	12.50	7.50 to 12.50
Christmas, Old Brick Church, Carnival*	1971	Year	12.50	7.50 to 12.50
Christmas, Two-Horned Church, Blue Satin**	1972	Year	12.50	12.50 to 15.00
Christmas, Two-Horned Church, Carnival*	1972	Year	12.50	12.00 to 14.00
Christmas, Two-Horned Church, White Satin*	1972	Year	12.50	12.50 to 15.00
Christmas, St.Mary's, Blue Satin*	1973	Year	12.50	12.50
Christmas, St.Mary's, Carnival*	1973	Year	12.50	12.50
Christmas, St.Mary's, White Satin*	1973	Year	12.50	12.50
Christmas, Blue Satin	1974	Year	13.50	13.50
Christmas, Carnival	1974	Year	13.50	13.50
Craftsmen, Glassblower, Carnival*	1970	Year	10.00	10.00 to 12.50
Craftsmen, Printer, Carnival*	1971	Year	10.00	10.00 to 12.50
Craftsmen, Blacksmith, Carnival**	1972	Year	10.00	10.00 to 12.50
Craftsmen, Shoemaker, Carnival**	1973	Year	10.00	10.00 to 12.50
Craftsmen, Cooper, Carnival**	1974	Year	11.00	11.00
Mother's Day, Madonna, Blue Satin*	1971	Year	12.50	7.50 to 12.50
Mother's Day, Madonna, Carnival*	1971	Year	12.50	7.50 to 15.00
Mother's Day, Madonna, Blue Satin*	1972	Year	12.50	7.50 to 12.50
Mother's Day, Madonna, Carnival*	1972	Year	12.50	7.50 to 12.50
Mother's Day, Madonna, White Satin*	1972	Year	12.50	12.50
Mother's Day, Cowper Madonna, Blue Satin**	1973	Year	12.50	12.50
Mother's Day, Cowper Madonna, Carnival**	1973	Year	12.50	12.50
Mother's Day, Cowper Madonna, White Satin**	1973	Year	12.50	12.50
Mother's Day, Madonna Of Grotto, Blue Satin**	1974	Year	12.50	12.50
Mother's Day, Madonna Of Grotto, Carnival**	1974	Year	12.50	12.50
Mother's Day, Madonna Of Grotto, White Satin**	1974	Year	12.50	12.50
Valentine's Day, Romeo & Juliet, Blue Satin	1972	Year	15.00	12.00 to 20.00
Valentine's Day, Romeo & Juliet, Carnival	1972	Year	15.00	12.00 to 20.00

Juan Ferrandiz, Spanish artist, is designer of many Anri limited editions. In 1972, he introduced his own series of wood and porcelain limited edition plates. The wooden plates are manufactured by Anri of Italy, and Hutschenreuther of West Germany produces the porcelain plates.

Christmas, Away In The Manger, Porcelain*	1972	5000	30.00	18.00 to 35.00
Christmas, Finishing The Cradle, Wood	1972	2500	35.00	30.00 to 40.00
Christmas, Porcelain	1973	3000	30.00	30.00
Christmas, Wood	1973	1500	40.00	40.00
Mother's Day, Wood*	1972	2500	35.00	22.50 to 35.00
Mother's Day, Wood	1973	1500	40.00	40.00

Festival of Lights plate, see Amen

Fischer Bells

Christmas, Crystal	1972	6025	10.00	10.00 to 15.00
Christmas, Crystal	1973	10000	12.00	12.00

Fontana Plates

Christmas, Couple & Dog*	1972	2000	35.00	30.00 to 65.00
Christmas, Sleighing*	1973	1000	35.00	30.00 to 37.50
Mother's Day, Mother & Child*	1973	2000	35.00	35.00

Fostoria Glass Company was founded in Fostoria, Ohio, in 1887, and moved to its present location in Moundsville, West Virginia, in 1891. The firm has made all types of glassware, tableware, bottles, and decorative glass through the years. Limited edition plates were introduced in 1971.

Fostoria Plates

History, Betsy Ross	1971	5000	12.50	12.00 to 16.00
History, Francis Scott Key*	1972	8000	12.50	12.00 to 13.00
History, Washington Crossing Delaware*	1973		12.50	12.50
History, Spirit Of '76	1974		13.00	13.00

Fenton, Craftsmen Plate, 1970, Glassblower

Fenton, Craftsmen Plate, 1972, Blacksmith

Fenton, Craftsmen Plate, 1971, Printer

Fenton, Mother's Day Plate,
1973, Carnival

Fenton, Mother's Day Plate,
1972, Carnival

Fenton, Mother's Day Plate,
1972, Blue Satin

Fenton, Mother's Day Plate,
1973, Blue Satin

Fenton, Mother's Day Plate,
1973, White Satin

Fenton, Mother's Day Plate,
1972, White Satin

Fenton, Christmas Plate,
1973, Carnival

Fenton, Christmas Plate,
1972, Carnival

Fenton, Christmas Plate,
1973, Blue Satin

Fenton, Christmas Plate,
1972, White Satin

Fenton, Christmas Plate,
1973, White Satin

Fenton, Christmas Plate,
1972, Blue Satin

Fenton, Craftsmen Plate, 1974, Cooper

Fenton, Mother's Day Plate,
1971, Carnival

Fenton, Mother's Day Plate,
1971, Blue Satin

Fenton, Craftsmen Plate, 1973, Shoemaker

Ferrandiz, Christmas Plate, 1972, Porcelain

Fontana, Christmas Plate, 1973

Ferrandiz, Mother's Day Plate, 1972

Fontana, Christmas Plate, 1972

Fontana, Mother's Day Plate, 1973

Fostoria, History Plate, 1972

Fostoria, State Plate, Massachusetts

Fostoria, History Plate, 1973

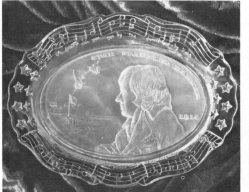

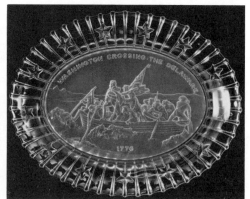

State, California*	1971	6000	12.50	12.50 to 14.00
State, New York*	1971	12000	12.50	12.50 to 14.00
State, Ohio*	1971	3000	12.50	12.50 to 14.00
State, Florida*	1972		12.50	12.50 to 14.00
State, Hawaii*	1972		12.50	12.50 to 14.00
State, Massachusetts*	1972		12.50	12.50 to 14.00
State, Pennsylvania	1972		12.50	12.50 to 14.00

Four Seasons, Rockwell, see Gorham

Franklin Mint was organized in the early 1960s by Joseph Segel and Gilroy Roberts, chief sculptor engraver for the U.S. Mint. It is located in Franklin Center, Pennsylvania. Franklin Mint introduced the first sterling silver collector's plate on the market in 1970.

See listing for Franklin Mint in Bar & Ingot and Medal sections

Franklin Mint Christmas Ornaments

Fostoria, State Plate, Florida

Partridge In A Pear Tree, Nickel Silver	1966	2251	1.25	Unknown
Two Turtle Doves, Nickel Silver	1966	2551	1.25	Unknown
Three French Hens, Nickel Silver	1966	2560	1.25	Unknown
Four Calling Birds, Nickel Silver	1966	2556	1.25	Unknown
Five Golden Rings, Nickel Silver	1966	2498	1.25	Unknown
Six Geese A-Laying, Nickel Silver	1966	2595	1.25	Unknown
Seven Swans A-Swimming, Nickel Silver	1966	2727	1.25	Unknown
Eight Maids A-Milking, Nickel Silver	1966	2554	1.25	Unknown
Nine Drummers Drumming, Nickel Silver	1966	2794	1.25	Unknown
Ten Pipers Piping, Nickel Silver	1966	2549	1.25	Unknown
Eleven Ladies Dancing, Nickel Silver	1966	2544	1.25	Unknown
Twelve Lords A-Leaping, Nickel Silver	1966	2547	1.25	Unknown
Partridge In A Pear Tree, Bronze	1970	6000	2.93	Unknown
Two Turtle Doves, Bronze	1970	6000	2.93	Unknown
Three French Hens, Bronze	1970	6000	2.93	Unknown
Four Calling Birds, Bronze	1970	6000	2.93	Unknown
Five Golden Rings, Bronze	1970	6000	2.93	Unknown
Six Geese A-Laying, Bronze	1970	6000	2.93	Unknown
Seven Swans A-Swimming, Bronze	1970	6000	2.93	Unknown
Eight Maids A-Milking, Bronze	1970	6000	2.93	Unknown
Nine Drummers Drumming, Bronze	1970	6000	2.93	Unknown
Ten Pipers Piping, Bronze	1970	6000	2.93	Unknown
Eleven Ladies Dancing, Bronze	1970	6000	2.93	Unknown
Twelve Lords A-Leaping, Bronze	1970	6000	2.93	Unknown
Partridge In A Pear Tree, Sterling	1970	1000	12.50	Unknown
Two Turtle Doves, Sterling	1970	1000	12.50	Unknown
Three French Hens, Sterling	1970	1000	12.50	Unknown
Four Calling Birds, Sterling	1970	1000	12.50	Unknown
Five Golden Rings, Sterling	1970	1000	12.50	Unknown
Six Geese A-Laying, Sterling	1970	1000	12.50	Unknown
Seven Swans A-Swimming, Sterling	1970	1000	12.50	Unknown
Eight Maids A-Milking, Sterling	1970	1000	12.50	Unknown
Nine Drummers Drumming, Sterling	1970	1000	12.50	Unknown
Ten Pipers Piping, Sterling	1970	1000	12.50	Unknown
Eleven Ladies Dancing, Sterling	1970	1000	12.50	Unknown
Twelve Lords A-Leaping, Sterling	1970	1000	12.50	Unknown

Fostoria, State Plate,
Ohio

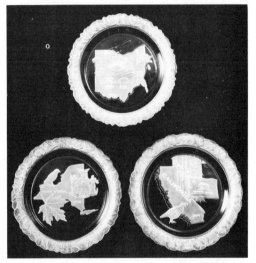

Fostoria, State Plate,   Fostoria, State Plate,
New York   California

Silent Night, Sterling	1971	14683	30.00	40.00 to 55.00
The First Noel, Sterling	1972		30.00	30.00 to 35.00
O Come All Ye Faithful, Sterling	1973		30.00	30.00

Franklin Mint Plaques

America, Sterling Silver	1970	150	750.00	Unknown
America, Bronze On Ebony	1970	400	250.00	Unknown
Danaides, Paul Vincze, Silver	1967	75	1250.00	Unknown
John F.Kennedy Memorial, Silver	1967	50	750.00	7500.00 to 10000.00
Horses, Roberts, Silver	1968	250	350.00	Unknown
Mayan Paradise, Sierra-Franco, Silver	1969	125	225.00	500.00
Mother & Child, Hromych, Silver	1968	200	175.00	Unknown
Children At Play, Parks, Silver	1969	200	375.00	Unknown
Kikabdanu, Sierra-Franco, Silver	1969	375	150.00	Unknown
Toreador & Bull, Romano, Silver	1969	225	250.00	Unknown
Wild Geese, Roberts, Silver	1969			Unknown
Zodiac, Aquarius, Bronze	1970	300	125.00	Unknown

Fostoria, State Plate, Hawaii

Franklin Mint, American West Plate,
Horizon's West, Silver

Franklin Mint, American West Plate,
Mountain Man, Silver

Franklin Mint, American West Plate,
Plains Hunter, Silver

Franklin Mint, American West Plate,
Prospector, Silver

Zodiac, Aquarius, Silver	1970	100	375.00	Unknown
Zodiac, Aries, Bronze	1970	300	125.00	Unknown
Zodiac, Aries, Silver	1970	100	375.00	Unknown
Zodiac, Cancer, Bronze	1970	300	125.00	Unknown
Zodiac, Cancer, Silver	1970	100	375.00	Unknown
Zodiac, Capricorn, Bronze	1970	300	125.00	Unknown
Zodiac, Capricorn, Silver	1970	100	375.00	Unknown
Zodiac, Gemini, Bronze	1970	300	125.00	Unknown
Zodiac, Gemini, Silver	1970	100	375.00	Unknown
Zodiac, Leo, Bronze	1970	300	125.00	Unknown
Zodiac, Leo, Silver	1970	100	375.00	Unknown
Zodiac, Libra, Bronze	1970	300	125.00	Unknown
Zodiac, Libra, Silver	1970	100	375.00	Unknown
Zodiac, Pisces, Bronze	1970	300	125.00	Unknown
Zodiac, Pisces, Silver	1970	100	375.00	Unknown
Zodiac, Sagittarius, Bronze	1970	300	125.00	Unknown
Zodiac, Sagittarius, Silver	1970	100	375.00	Unknown
Zodiac, Scorpio, Silver	1970	100	375.00	Unknown
Zodiac, Taurus, Bronze	1970	300	125.00	Unknown
Zodiac, Taurus, Silver	1970	100	375.00	Unknown
Zodiac, Virgo, Bronze	1970	300	125.00	Unknown
Zodiac, Virgo, Silver	1970	100	375.00	Unknown

Franklin Mint Plates

American West, Horizon's West, Gold	1972	67	2200.00	2200.00
American West, Horizon's West, Silver*	1972	5860	150.00	125.00 to 160.00
American West, Mountain Man, Gold	1973	67	2200.00	2200.00
American West, Mountain Man, Silver*	1973	5860	150.00	125.00 to 160.00
American West, Plains Hunter, Gold	1973	67	2200.00	2200.00
American West, Plains Hunter, Silver*	1973	5860	150.00	135.00 to 160.00
American West, Prospector, Gold	1973	67	2200.00	2200.00
American West, Prospector, Silver*	1973	5860	150.00	135.00 to 160.00
American West, Trapper To The West, Gold	1973	67	2200.00	2200.00
American West, Trapper To The West, Silver	1973	5860	150.00	145.00 to 160.00
Audubon Bird, Bald Eagle*	1972	13939	125.00	120.00 to 150.00
Audubon Bird, Bobwhite	1972	13939	125.00	100.00 to 150.00
Audubon Bird, Cardinal*	1972	13939	125.00	100.00 to 150.00
Audubon Bird, Mallards	1972	13939	125.00	87.50 to 150.00
Audubon Bird, Goldfinch	1973	13939	99.50	99.50
Christmas, Rockwell, Bringing Home The Tree*	1970	18321	100.00	350.00 to 450.00
Christmas, Rockwell, Under The Mistletoe	1971	24792	100.00	125.00 to 175.00
Christmas, Rockwell, The Carolers*	1972	29074	125.00	120.00 to 150.00
Easter, Resurrection, Silver*	1973	7116	175.00	175.00
James Wyeth, Brandywine*	1972	19670	125.00	120.00 to 150.00
James Wyeth, Winter Fox	1973		125.00	125.00
James Wyeth, Riding To The Hunt, Sterling	1974	Year	150.00	150.00
Mother's Day, Mother & Child	1972	21987	125.00	95.00 to 175.00
Mother's Day*	1973	Year	125.00	125.00 to 155.00
Mother's Day	1974	Year	150.00	150.00
President, Adams, John*	1972	10304	150.00	125.00 to 150.00
President, Jefferson, Thomas*	1972	10304	150.00	150.00
President, Washington, George*	1972	10304	150.00	125.00 to 150.00
President, Adams, John Quincy*	1973	10304	150.00	125.00 to 150.00
President, Jackson, Andrew*	1973	10304	150.00	150.00
President, Madison, James*	1973	10304	150.00	150.00
President, Monroe, James*	1973	10304	150.00	150.00
President, Van Buren, Martin*	1973	10304	150.00	150.00
Thanksgiving	1971	Year		100.00 to 150.00
Thanksgiving, First Thanksgiving	1972	10142	125.00	125.00 to 150.00
Thanksgiving, Wild Turkey	1973		125.00	125.00

Franklin Mint Spoons, Signature Edition

Apostle, Judas, Sterling	1973	Year	17.50	17.50
Apostle, St.Andrew, Sterling	1973	Year	17.50	17.50
Apostle, St.Bartholomew, Sterling	1973	Year	17.50	17.50
Apostle, St.James The Greater, Sterling	1973	Year	17.50	17.50
Apostle, St.James The Lesser, Sterling	1973	Year	17.50	17.50
Apostle, St.John, Sterling	1973	Year	17.50	17.50
Apostle, St.Matthew, Sterling	1973	Year	17.50	17.50
Apostle, St.Peter, Sterling	1973	Year	17.50	17.50
Apostle, St.Philip, Sterling	1973	Year	17.50	17.50
Apostle, St.Simon The Canaanite, Sterling	1973	Year	17.50	17.50

Franklin Mint, Audubon Bird Plate,
Eagle

Franklin Mint, Easter Plate, 1973

Franklin Mint, Christmas Plate, 1972

Franklin Mint,
James Wyeth Plate, 1972

Franklin Mint, Audubon Bird Plate,
Cardinal

Franklin Mint, Christmas Plate, 1970

Franklin Mint,
Mother's Day Plate, 1973

Franklin Mint, President Plate,
George Washington

Franklin Mint, President Plate,
James Madison

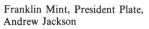

Franklin Mint, President Plate,
Andrew Jackson

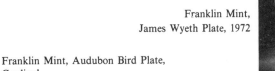

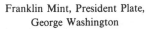

Franklin Mint, President Plate,
John Adams

Franklin Mint, President Plate,
Thomas Jefferson

Franklin Mint, President Plate,
Martin Van Buren

Franklin Mint, President Plate,
John Quincy Adams

Franklin Mint, Christmas Spoon, 1972,
Twelve Days Of Christmas

Franklin Mint, President Plate,
James Monroe

Frankoma, Bicentennial Plate, 1972

Frankoma, Bicentennial Plate, 1973

Frankoma, Christmas Plate, 1966

Frankoma, Christmas Plate, 1965

Apostle, St.Thaddeus, Sterling	1973	Year	17.50	17.50
Apostle, St.Thomas, Sterling	1973	Year	17.50	17.50
Christmas, Partridge, Gold Plate	1972	1018	16.25	16.25
Christmas, Two Turtle Doves, Gold Plate	1972	1018	16.25	16.25
Christmas, Three French Hens, Gold Plate	1972	1018	16.25	16.25
Christmas, Four Calling Birds, Gold Plate	1972	1018	16.25	16.25
Christmas, Five Golden Rings, Gold Plate	1972	1018	16.25	16.25
Christmas, Six Geese A-Laying, Gold Plate	1972	1018	16.25	16.25
Christmas, Seven Swans A-Swimming, Gold Plate	1972	1018	16.25	16.25
Christmas, Eight Maids A-Milking, Gold Plate	1972	1018	16.25	16.25
Christmas, Nine Pipers Piping, Gold Plate	1972	1018	16.25	16.25
Christmas, Ten Drummers Drumming, Gold Plate	1972	1018	16.25	16.25
Christmas, Eleven Ladies Dancing, Gold Plate	1972	1018	16.25	16.25
Christmas, Twelve Lords A-Leaping, Gold Plate	1972	1018	16.25	16.25
Christmas, Partridge, Sterling*	1972	3306	12.00	12.00
Christmas, Two Turtle Doves, Sterling*	1972	3306	12.00	12.00
Christmas, Three French Hens, Sterling*	1972	3306	12.00	12.00
Christmas, Four Calling Birds, Sterling*	1972	3306	12.00	12.00
Christmas, Five Golden Rings*	1972	3306	12.00	12.00
Christmas, Six Geese A-Laying, Sterling*	1972	3306	12.00	12.00
Christmas, Seven Swans A-Swimming, Sterling*	1972	3306	12.00	12.00
Christmas, Eight Maids A-Milking, Sterling*	1972	3306	12.00	12.00
Christmas, Nine Pipers Piping, Sterling*	1972	3306	12.00	12.00
Christmas, Ten Drummers Drumming, Sterling*	1972	3306	12.00	12.00
Christmas, Eleven Ladies Dancing, Sterling*	1972	3306	12.00	12.00
Christmas, Twelve Lords A-Leaping, Sterling*	1972	3306	12.00	12.00
Zodiac, Aquarius, Gold Plate	1972	1229	15.75	15.75
Zodiac, Aries, Gold Plate	1972	1229	15.75	15.75
Zodiac, Cancer, Gold Plate	1972	1229	15.75	15.75
Zodiac, Capricorn, Gold Plate	1972	1229	15.75	15.75
Zodiac, Gemini, Gold Plate	1972	1229	15.75	15.75
Zodiac, Leo, Gold Plate	1972	1229	15.75	15.75
Zodiac, Libra, Gold Plate	1972	1229	15.75	15.75
Zodiac, Pisces, Gold Plate	1972	1229	15.75	15.75
Zodiac, Sagittarius, Gold Plate	1972	1229	15.75	15.75
Zodiac, Scorpio, Gold Plate	1972	1229	15.75	15.75
Zodiac, Taurus, Gold Plate	1972	1229	15.75	15.75
Zodiac, Virgo, Gold Plate	1972	1229	15.75	15.75
Zodiac, Aquarius, Sterling	1972	5386	11.25	11.25
Zodiac, Aries, Sterling	1972	5386	11.25	11.25
Zodiac, Cancer, Sterling	1972	5386	11.25	11.25
Zodiac, Capricorn, Sterling	1972	5386	11.25	11.25
Zodiac, Gemini, Sterling	1972	5386	11.25	11.25
Zodiac, Leo, Sterling	1972	5386	11.25	11.25
Zodiac, Libra, Sterling	1972	5386	11.25	11.25
Zodiac, Pisces, Sterling	1972	5386	11.25	11.25
Zodiac, Sagittarius, Sterling	1972	5386	11.25	11.25
Zodiac, Scorpio, Sterling	1972	5386	11.25	11.25
Zodiac, Taurus, Sterling	1972	5386	11.25	11.25
Zodiac, Virgo, Sterling	1972	5386	11.25	11.25

Frankoma, Christmas Plate, 1967

Frankoma, Christmas Plate, 1968

Frankoma, Christmas Plate, 1969

Frankoma, Christmas Plate, 1970

Frankoma Pottery was the first U.S. firm to introduce Christmas plates in 1965. It was originally known as The Frank Potteries when John F. Frank opened shop in 1933. The factory is now located in Sapulpa, Oklahoma. Their limited edition plates are of a semitranslucent 'Della Robbia' white glaze over a colored body.

Frankoma Mugs

GOP, White	1968	Year	3.00	20.00 to 25.00
GOP, Red	1969	Year	3.00	5.00 to 10.00
GOP, Blue	1970	Year	3.00	4.00 to 7.00
GOP, Black	1971	Year	3.00	3.00 to 6.00
GOP, Green And White	1972	Year	3.00	3.00 to 4.50

Frankoma Plates

Bicentennial, Provocations*	1972	Year	6.00	5.00 to 7.50
Bicentennial, Patriots And Leaders*	1973	Year	6.00	5.00 to 60.00
Christmas, Goodwill Towards Men*	1965	Year	5.00	150.00 to 180.00
Christmas, Bethlehem Shepherds*	1966	Year	5.00	55.00 to 75.00
Christmas, Gifts For The Christ Child*	1967	Year	5.00	35.00 to 60.00

Frankoma, Christmas Plate, 1971

Frankoma, Christmas Plate, 1972

Frankoma, Christmas Plate, 1973

Furstenberg, Christmas Plate, 1973

Christmas, Flight Into Egypt*	1968	Year	5.00	8.00 to 15.00
Christmas, Laid In A Manger*	1969	Year	5.00	5.00 to 8.00
Christmas, King Of Kings*	1970	Year	5.00	5.00 to 7.50
Christmas, No Room In The Inn*	1971	Year	5.00	5.00 to 8.00
Christmas, Seeking The Christ Child*	1972	Year	5.00	5.00 to 7.50
Christmas, The Annunciation*	1973	Year	5.00	5.00
Teenagers Of The Bible	1973		5.00	5.00

Frederick Remington, see George Washington Mint, Gorham

Fujihara Plates

Chinese Lunar Calendar, Year Of The Rat	1972	1710	20.00	20.00
Chinese Lunar Calendar, Year Of The Ox	1973	1710	20.00	20.00

Furstenberg Porcelain Factory, the oldest in the German Federal Republic, was founded in 1747 by King Carl I. Limited editions, introduced in 1971, include plates and Christmas ornaments. The company mark is a blue F surmounted by a crown.

Furstenberg Ornaments

Christmas, Angel	1973	2000	25.00	25.00
Easter Egg*	1973	3000	15.00	15.00 to 20.00
Easter Egg*	1974	2000	18.50	18.50

Furstenberg Plates

Christmas, Rabbits	1971	7500	14.00	12.00 to 20.00
Christmas	1972	6000	15.00	12.50 to 15.00
Christmas*	1973	5000	18.00	18.00
Christmas	1974	4000	20.00	20.00
Deluxe Christmas, Wise Men	1971	1500	45.00	50.00 to 90.00
Deluxe Christmas, Holy Family	1972	2000	45.00	30.00 to 50.00
Deluxe Christmas*	1973	2000	60.00	50.00 to 60.00
Easter, Sheep	1971	3500	15.00	35.00 to 85.00
Easter, Chicks	1972	6000	15.00	8.50 to 20.00
Easter, Bunnies*	1973	4000	16.00	10.00 to 20.00
Easter, Pussywillow*	1974	4000	20.00	20.00
Mother's Day	1972	5000	15.00	12.00 to 20.00
Mother's Day*	1973	5000	16.00	10.00 to 20.00
Mother's Day*	1974	4000	20.00	20.00
Olympic	1972	5000	20.00	40.00 to 70.00

Gainsborough, see Gorham

Georg Jensen of Denmark, the famous Danish silver company entered the limited edition market in 1971 with the introduction of an annual Christmas spoon. The spoons are made of gold-plated silver. Each spoon is made until October 1 of the year, when the mold is destroyed. Georg Jensen of Denmark should not be confused with Georg Jenson of New York.

Georg Jensen Spoons

Christmas, Cherry Blossom**	1971	Year	25.00	45.00 to 55.00
Christmas, Cornflower**	1972	Year	25.00	35.00 to 400.00
Christmas, Corn Marigold**	1973	Year	25.00	25.00 to 30.00
Christmas	1974	Year	25.00	25.00

Georg Jensen of New York is a division of Kenton Wholesale, Inc. Limited edition plates, which include the Andrew Wyeth, Cartier, and Chagall plates, were first made in 1971.

Georg Jensen, see also Andrew Wyeth, Cartier, Chagall

Georg Jensen Plates

Christmas, Doves	1972	Year	15.00	12.00 to 15.00
Christmas*	1973	Year	15.00	15.00
Mother's Day, Mother & Child*	1973	10000	15.00	15.00
Mother's Day	1974		17.50	17.50

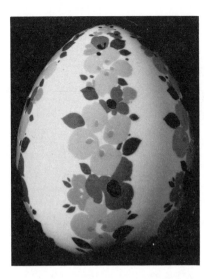

Furstenberg, Easter Egg, 1973

Fuerstenberg, Easter Egg, 1974

Furstenberg, Deluxe Christmas Plate,
1973

Fuerstenberg, Easter Plate, 1974

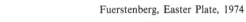

Furstenberg, Easter Plate, 1973

Furstenberg, Mother's Day Plate, 1973

Fuerstenberg, Mother's Day Plate, 1974

Georg Jensen,
Christmas Spoon, 1972

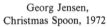

Georg Jensen, Christmas Spoon, 1971

Georg Jensen, Christmas Spoon, 1973

Georg Jensen, Christmas Plate, 1973

Georg Jensen, Mother's Day Plate, 1973

Georg Jensen,
Christmas Spoon, 1974

George Washington Mint, Remington Plate,
The Rattlesnake, Sterling

George Washington Mint,
Mother's Day Plate, 1972, Sterling

George Washington Mint,
N.C. Wyeth Plate,
Uncle Sam's America, Sterling

George Washington Mint,
Sawyer Plate, American Indian,
Curley, Sterling

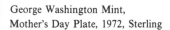

Gorham, Sons Of Liberty Bowl

Gorham, Barrymore Plate, Quiet Waters

George Washington Mint, Picasso Plate,
Don Quixote De La Mancha, Sterling

George Washington Mint of New York City was founded in 1971.
Limited edition gold, silver, and proof plates were introduced in 1972.
The plates are made by the Medallic Art Company. George Washington
Mint went out of business in 1973. The Picasso, Remington, and
Mother's Day series are being continued by the Medallic Art Company.

George Washington Mint, see also Washington Mint

George Washington Mint Plates

Israel Anniversary, The Struggle	1973	10000	300.00	250.00 to 300.00
Mother's Day, Whistler's Mother, Gold	1972	100	2000.00	Unknown
Mother's Day, Whistler's Mother, Proof	1972	100	1000.00	Unknown
Mother's Day, Whistler's Mother, Sterling*	1972	9800	150.00	75.00 to 150.00
Mother's Day, Motherhood, Sterling	1974	2500	175.00	175.00
N.C.Wyeth, Uncle Sam's America, Gold	1972	100	2000.00	Unknown
N.C.Wyeth, Uncle Sam's America, Proof	1972	100	1000.00	Unknown
N.C.Wyeth, Uncle Sam's America, Sterling*	1972	9800	150.00	75.00 to 150.00
N.C.Wyeth, Massed Flags, Gold	1973	100	2000.00	2000.00
N.C.Wyeth, Massed Flags, Proof	1973	100	1000.00	1000.00
N.C.Wyeth, Massed Flags, Sterling	1973	2300	150.00	100.00 to 150.00
Picasso, Don Quixote De La Mancha, Gold	1972	100	2000.00	2000.00
Picasso, Don Quixote De La Mancha, Proof	1972	100	1000.00	Unknown
Picasso, Don Quixote De La Mancha, Sterling*	1972	9800	125.00	75.00 to 150.00
Picasso, The Rites Of Spring, Sterling	1974	9800	150.00	150.00
Remington, The Rattlesnake, Gold	1972	100	2000.00	Unknown
Remington, The Rattlesnake, Proof	1972	100	1000.00	Unknown
Remington, The Rattlesnake, Sterling*	1972	9800	250.00	195.00 to 250.00
Remington, Coming Through The Rye, Sterling	1974	2500	300.00	300.00
Sawyer, American Indian, Curley, Gold	1972	100	2000.00	2000.00
Sawyer, American Indian, Curley, Proof	1972	100	1000.00	Unknown
Sawyer, American Indian, Curley, Sterling*	1972	7300	150.00	90.00 to 150.00
Sawyer, American Indian, Two Moons, Gold	1973	100	2000.00	2000.00
Sawyer, American Indian, Two Moons, Proof	1973	100	1000.00	Unknown
Sawyer, American Indian, Two Moons, Sterling	1973	7300	150.00	100.00 to 150.00

Gibson Girl Plates

Gibson Girl, Set Of 24	1971	100	150.00	150.00

Gilbert Poillerat, see Cristal d'Albret, Poillerat

Goebel Hummel, see Hummel Goebel

Gorham Silver Co., of Providence, Rhode Island, was founded in
1831. Crystal and China were added in 1970. The first limited edition
item, a silver Christmas ornament, was introduced in 1970. Limited edition
porcelain plates were issued in 1971.

See listing for Gorham in Figurine, Bar & Ingot, and Medal sections

Gorham Bowl

Sons Of Liberty, Paul Revere, Sterling*	1972	250	1250.00	1250.00

Gorham Ornaments

Christmas, Snowflake, Sterling	1970	Year	10.00	15.00 to 25.00
Christmas, Snowflake, Sterling	1971	Year	10.00	10.00 to 20.00
Christmas, Snowflake, Sterling	1972	Year	10.00	9.00 to 12.50
Christmas, Snowflake, Sterling	1973	Year	10.95	11.00

Gorham Plates

Barrymore, Quiet Waters, Porcelain*	1971	15000	25.00	20.00 to 25.00
Barrymore, San Pedro, Porcelain	1972	15000	25.00	20.00 to 25.00
Barrymore, Little Boatyard, Silver Plate	1972	1000	100.00	60.00 to 100.00
Barrymore, Nantucket, Silver Plate	1973	1000	100.00	60.00 to 100.00
Bicentennial, Burning Of The Gaspee, Pewter	1972	5000	35.00	17.50 to 35.00
Bicentennial, Burning Of The Gaspee, Silver	1972	750	500.00	500.00
Bicentennial, 1776, Silver*	1972	500	500.00	500.00
Bicentennial, 1776, Vermeil	1972	250	750.00	750.00
Bicentennial, Boston Tea Party, Pewter	1973	5000	35.00	17.50 to 35.00
Bicentennial, Boston Tea Party, Silver	1973	750	550.00	500.00 to 550.00
Christmas, Moppets	1973	Year	12.50	12.50 to 15.00
Gainsborough, The Honorable Mrs.Graham*	1973	7500	50.00	35.00 to 50.00
Kentucky Derby, The Big Three, Rockwell	1974	10000	17.50	17.50
Mother's Day, Moppets	1973	Year	12.50	12.50 to 15.00
Mother's Day, Moppets	1974	Year	10.00	10.00
Rembrandt, Man In Gilt Helmet, Porcelain	1971	10000	50.00	40.00 to 50.00
Rembrandt, Self-Portrait With Saskia	1972	10000	50.00	35.00 to 50.00

Gorham, Bicentennial Plate, 1776, Silver

Gorham, Gainsborough Plate,
The Honorable Mrs.Graham

Gorham, Remington Plate,
A New Year On The Cimarron

Gorham, Remington Plate, Aiding A Comrade

Gorham, Rockwell Plate, Four Seasons, 1973, Set Of 4

Remington, A New Year On The Cimarron*	1973	Year	25.00	20.00 to 25.00
Remington, Aiding A Comrade*	1973	Year	25.00	20.00 to 25.00
Remington, The Fight For The Waterhole*	1973	Year	25.00	20.00 to 25.00
Remington, The Flight*	1973	Year	25.00	20.00 to 25.00
Rockwell, Butter Girl	1974		15.00	15.00 to 20.00
Rockwell, Four Seasons, Boy & Dog, Set Of 4	1971	Year	60.00	100.00 to 175.00
Rockwell, Four Seasons, Young Love, Set Of 4	1972	Year	60.00	50.00 to 75.00
Rockwell, Four Seasons, Seasons Of Love, 4*	1973	Year	60.00	60.00
Rockwell, Four Seasons, Grandpa & Me, Set Of 4	1974	Year	60.00	60.00

Gorham Spoons

Christmas, Star Of Bethlehem	1971	Year	10.00	10.00 to 15.00
Christmas, Musical Instruments	1972	Year	10.00	10.00
Christmas, Bells*	1973	Year	10.95	10.95
Christmas, Demispoon*	1973	Year	5.50	5.50

Gorham Tea Caddy

Bicentennial, Boston Tea Party	1973	10000	17.73	13.00 to 25.00

Grandma Moses Plates

First Set Of 4		80.00	50.00 to 80.00
Second Set Of 4		80.00	50.00 to 80.00

See listing for Granget in Figurine section

Granget Plates

Spring, Kildeer, American	1973	5000	75.00	69.00 to 88.00
Winter, Sparrows, American	1972	5000	50.00	75.00 to 105.00
Winter, Sparrows, European	1972	5000	35.00	20.00 to 35.00
Winter, Squirrel, American	1973	5000	75.00	70.00 to 75.00
Winter, Squirrel, European	1973	5000	45.00	30.00 to 45.00
Winter, Partridge, American	1974	5000	75.00	75.00

Greenaway, see Kate Greenaway

Greentree Pottery of Audubon, Iowa, was established in 1968 by Judy Sutcliffe. The pottery produces many privately commissioned plates. All plates are handmade.

Greentree Plates

Grant Wood's Studio	1971	2000	10.00	15.00
Grant Wood's Antioch School	1972	2000	10.00	12.00
Grant Wood At Stone City	1973	2000	10.00	10.00
Kennedy, Center For The Performing Arts	1972	2000	20.00	20.00
Kennedy, Birthplace, Brookline Mass.	1973	2000	12.00	12.00
Mississippi River, Delta Queen	1973	2000	10.00	10.00
Mississippi River, Tri-Centennial	1973	2000	10.00	10.00
Motorcar, 1929 Packard Dietrich Convertible	1972	2000	20.00	20.00
Motorcar, Model A Ford	1973	2000	20.00	20.00

Gregory, Mary, see Mary Gregory

Gross, Chaim, see Judiaic Heritage Society

Gunther Granget, see Granget

Gustavsberg limited editions were first introduced into the United States in 1971. The plates are made at the Gustavsberg factory in Stockholm, Sweden.

Gustavsberg Plates

Accession, Karl Gustaf XVI**	1973	Year	9.00	9.00
Christmas*	1971	Year	12.50	15.00 to 20.00
Christmas*	1972	Year	12.50	12.50 to 150.00
Christmas**	1973	Year	12.50	12.50
Congratulations	1972	Year	12.50	12.50
Congratulations**	1973	Year	12.50	12.50
Endangered Species, Hedgehog**		Year	24.00	24.00
Endangered Species, Owl**		Year	24.00	24.00
United Nations*	1972	Year	12.50	12.50
90th Anniversary, Gustaf Adolf VI**	1972	Year	9.00	9.00

Hamilton Mint of Arlington Heights, Illinois, is a private mint. Limited edition gold and silver plates, medals, and ingots were introduced in 1972. Editions are serially numbered on the back. When an edition is completed, the die is destroyed.

Gorham, Remington Plate,
The Fight For The Waterhole

Gorham, Christmas Demispoon, 1973

Gorham, Remington Plate,
The Flight

Gustavsberg, Christmas Plate, 1971

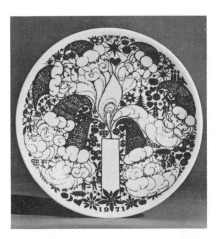

Hammersley, Bicentennial Bell, 1973

Gustavsberg, Christmas Plate, 1973

Gustavsberg, Christmas Plate, 1972

Gustavsberg, 90th Anniversary
Gustaf VI Adolf Plate

Gustavsberg, United Nations Plate

Haviland, Christmas Ornament, 1971

Haviland, Christmas Ornament, 1972

Haviland, Christmas Ornament, 1973

Haviland, Presidential Cup & Saucer, Lincoln

See listing for Hamilton Mint in Bar & Ingot and Medal sections

Hamilton Mint Plates

John F.Kennedy Memorial, Gold On Pewter	1974	Year	40.00	40.00
John F.Kennedy Memorial, Pewter	1974	Year	25.00	25.00
Mother's Day, Generations Of Love, Gold	1973	25	1750.00	1750.00
Mother's Day, Generations Of Love, Sterling	1973	1000	125.00	125.00
Picasso, Le Gourmet, Sterling	1972	5000	125.00	95.00 to 155.00
Picasso, Tragedy	1972	5000	125.00	95.00 to 195.00
Picasso, The Lovers, Sterling	1973	5000	125.00	95.00 to 125.00
St.Patrick's Day, Silver	1973	Year	75.00	75.00

Hammersley China Company of Stoke-on-Trent, England, produces items exclusively for distribution by Schmid Brothers in the United States. Hammersley limited editions were first made in 1973.

Hammersley Bells

Bicentennial, The Sound Of Liberty*	1973	15000	25.00	25.00 to 30.00

Hammersley Bell, see also Spode

Hans Christian Andersen Plates, see Bygdo

Harm Bird plates, see Spode

Haviland & Co. was founded in Limoges, France in 1893 by David Haviland, an American. Limited editions were introduced in 1970.

Haviland Ornaments

Birds Of Peace & Love, Pair	1973	15000	17.50	17.50
Christmas, Dancing Angels*	1971	30000	8.95	10.00 to 13.00
Christmas, Horse*	1972	30000	9.95	9.95
Christmas, Ringing Bells*	1973	30000	9.95	9.00 to 10.50
Christmas	1974	30000	10.95	10.95

Haviland Plates

Bicentennial, Burning Of The Gaspee	1972	10000	39.95	30.00 to 45.00
Bicentennial, Boston Tea Party*	1973	10000	39.95	35.00 to 40.00
Christmas, Partridge In A Pear Tree*	1970	30000	25.00	75.00 to 130.00
Bicentennial, First Continental Congress	1974	10000	39.95	39.95
Christmas, Two Turtle Doves*	1971	30000	25.00	27.50 to 45.00
Christmas, Three French Hens*	1972	30000	27.50	25.00 to 35.00
Christmas, Four Colly Birds*	1973	30000	28.50	25.00 to 30.00
Christmas, Five Golden Rings	1974		30.00	30.00
Mother's Day, Breakfast	1973	10000	29.95	25.00 to 30.00
Mother's Day	1974	10000	29.95	29.95
Presidential, Grant*	1970	3000	100.00	75.00 to 100.00
Presidential, Hayes*	1972	2500	110.00	100.00 to 110.00
Presidential, Lincoln Cup & Saucer*	1972	2500	80.00	75.00 to 80.00
Presidential, Lincoln*	1969	2500	100.00	
Signed				200.00 to 250.0
Unsigned				125.00 to 175.00
Presidential, Washington*	1968	2500	35.00	
Signed				85.00 to 105.00
Unsigned				50.00 to 70.00

Haviland & Parlon Plates

Christmas, Madonna	1972	5000	35.00	30.00 to 50.00
Christmas	1973	5000	35.00	150.00
Unicorn Tapestry, Start Of The Hunt*	1971	12000	35.00	75.00 to 125.00
Unicorn Tapestry, Captivity*	1972	12000	35.00	35.00 to 45.00
Unicorn Tapestry, Fountain*	1973	12000	35.00	35.00
Unicorn Tapestry	1974	12000	37.50	37.50

Heritage Society Plates

Mayflower Crossing	1970	375	40.00	30.00 to 40.00
Bicentennial, Pair	1972	5000	120.00	100.00 to 120.00

Historic Mint Plates

Christmas, Adoration Of The Magi, Silver	1972	1200	130.00	100.00 to 130.00
Christmas, Christmas In New England, Silver	1972	1200	130.00	100.00 to 130.00
Endangered Species, Crocodile	1972	220	32.50	30.00 to 35.00
Endangered Species, Galapagos Tortoise	1972	220	32.50	30.00 to 35.00
Endangered Species, Indian Rhinoceros	1972	220	32.50	30.00 to 35.00
Endangered Species, Ivory-Billed Woodpecker	1972	220	32.50	30.00 to 35.00
Endangered Species, Malayan Tapir	1972	220	32.50	30.00 to 35.00

Haviland, Bicentennial Plate, 1973

Haviland, Christmas Plate, 1972

Haviland, Christmas Plate, 1971

Haviland, Presidential Plate, Lincoln

Haviland, Christmas Plate, 1970

Haviland, Presidential Plate, Hayes

Haviland, Christmas Plate, 1973

Haviland, Presidential Plate, Grant

Haviland, Presidential Plate, Washington

Haviland, Presidential Plate,
Hayes, Reverse

Haviland & Parlon,
Unicorn Tapestry Plate, 1971

Haviland & Parlon,
Unicorn Tapestry Plate, 1972

Haviland & Parlon,
Unicorn Tapestry Plate, 1973

Hummell Goebel, Olympic Plate, 1972

Endangered Species, Monkey-Eating Eagle	1972	220	32.50	30.00 to 35.00
Endangered Species, Orang-Utang	1972	220	32.50	30.00 to 35.00
Endangered Species, Peregrine Falcon	1972	220	32.50	30.00 to 35.00
Endangered Species, Polar Bear	1972	220	32.50	30.00 to 35.00
Endangered Species, Siberian Tiger	1972	220	32.50	30.00 to 35.00
Endangered Species, Snow Leopard	1972	220	32.50	30.00 to 35.00
Endangered Species, White-Tailed Gnu	1972	220	32.50	30.00 to 35.00
Endangered Species, Set Of 12, Crystal	1972	460	350.00	325.00 to 375.00

Historic Norway, see Nidaros

The Historic Plate Company is a division of Jerald Sulky Co. of Waterloo, Iowa. The limited edition series, featuring great harness racing horses, was introduced in 1972.

Historic Plates

Hambletonian 10**	1972	2000	20.00	15.00 to 20.00

Historical Heritage Gold & Silver Items

Cook Bi-Centenary Tankard, Gold	1970	50	4250.00	4250.00
Cook Bi-Centenary Tankard, Silver	1970	750	425.00	425.00
Mayflower Cream Jug, Gold	1972	50	2000.00	2000.00
Mayflower Cream Jug, Silver	1972	2000	400.00	400.00
Moon Landing Beaker, Gold	1969	250	2500.00	2500.00
Moon Landing Beaker, Silver	1969	1500	250.00	250.00
Prince Of Wales Investiture Goblet, Gold	1969	250	2500.00	2500.00
Prince Of Wales Investiture Goblet, Silver	1969	1000	250.00	250.00
Queen's Tray, Gold	1972	250	2500.00	2500.00
Queen's Tray, Silver*	1972	3500	250.00	250.00
Roman Bowl And Spoon, Gold	1972	50	2000.00	2000.00
Roman Bowl And Spoon, Silver	1972	1500	250.00	250.00

Holmegaard Glassworks of Copenhagen, Denmark, was established in 1825 by the Danneskiold-Samsoe family. In 1965, it merged with the large Kastrup glassworks to become the Kastrup and Holmegaard Glass Company. Limited editions, called 'unique pieces' in Denmark, were first introduced into the United States in 1974. Kylle Svanlund is designer of the series.

Holmegaard Glass Series

Kylle Svanlund Centerpiece Bowl, Purple**	1974	50
Kylle Svanlund Deep Bowl, Crystal**	1974	50
Kylle Svanlund Oblong Glass Sculpture**	1974	50
Kylle Svanlund Glass Sculptures, Pair**	1974	50

Hummel limited edition plates, made by W. Goebel Porzellanfabrik of Oeslau, Germany, are based on the sketches of Berta Hummel. The F. W. Goebel factory was founded in 1871 by Franz and William Goebel. In 1934, under the trade name of Hummelwerk, the Germany factory, in collaboration with Berta Hummel, produced the first Hummel figurines. Limited edition plates were introduced in 1971. A series of limited edition figurines commemorating the American Bicentennial was issued in 1974.

See listing for Goebel in Figurine section

Hummel Goebel Plates

Annual	1971	Year	25.00	75.00 to 225.00
Annual*	1972	Year	30.00	30.00 to 40.00
Annual*	1973	Year	32.50	32.50
Annual, Goosegirl	1974	Year	40.00	40.00
Mother's Day	1974	Year	40.00	40.00
Olympic*	1972	Year	16.00	15.00 to 16.00

Hummel Schmid limited editions are made in West Germany for exclusive distribution by Schmid Brothers in the United States. Permission to reproduce the works of Berta Hummel on limited edition items was granted to Schmid Brothers by Victoria Hummel, mother of the artist, in 1971.

Hummel Schmid Bells

Christmas, Angel With Flute	1972	20000	15.00	20.00 to 25.00
Christmas, Silent Night*	1973		15.00	15.00
Christmas	1974		17.50	17.50

Hummel Goebel, Annual Plate, 1973

Hummel Goebel, Annual Plate, 1972

Hummel Schmid,
Christmas Bell, 1973

Hummel Schmid, Mother's Day Plate, 1972

Hummel Schmid, Christmas Plate, 1973

Hummel Schmid, Christmas Plate, 1972

Hummel Schmid, Christmas Cup, 1973

Hutschenreuther, Ruthven Bird Plates, 1972

Hutschenreuther, Ruthven Bird Plates, 1973

Imperial, Christmas Plate, 1970, Carnival

Imperial, Christmas Plate, 1971, Crystal

Imperial, Christmas Plate, 1972, Crystal

Imperial, Christmas Plate, 1973, Crystal

Hummel Schmid Cups

Child's*	1973	Year	10.00	9.50 to 12.50
Child's	1974	Year	12.00	12.00

Hummel Schmid Plates

Christmas, Angel In Christmas Setting	1971	Year	15.00	20.00 to 25.00
Christmas, Angel With Flute*	1972	20000	15.00	10.00 to 20.00
Christmas, Silent Night*	1973	Year	15.00	15.00
Christmas	1974	Year	18.50	18.50
Mother's Day, Playing Hooky*	1972	Year	15.00	15.00 to 20.00
Mother's Day, Fishing	1973	Year	15.00	15.00
Mother's Day	1974	Year	18.50	18.50

Hutschenreuther Porcelain Company of Selb, Germany, was established in 1856. Limited edition plates were first made in 1970.

Hutschenreuther Plates

Ruthven Birds, Bluebird & Goldfinch*	1972	5000	100.00	75.00 to 150.00
Ruthven Birds, Mockingbird & Robin*	1973	5000	100.00	85.00 to 125.00

Imperial Glass Corporation was founded in Bellaire, Ohio, in 1902. In 1940, Imperial bought out Central Glass Works of Wheeling, West Virginia. In 1958, they purchased all the molds, trademarks, etc., of the Heisey Co. of Newark, Ohio. The production facilities of Cambridge Glass Company were acquired in 1960. Imperial's limited editions were introduced in 1970 and are available in crystal or carnival.

Imperial Plates

Christmas, Partridge, Blue Carnival*	1970	Year	12.00	9.00 to 12.50
Christmas, Partridge, Crystal	1970	Year	15.00	12.00 to 18.50
Christmas, Two Turtledoves, Green Carnival	1971	Year	12.00	11.00 to 12.50
Christmas, Two Turtledoves, Crystal*	1971	Year	16.50	15.00 to 17.00
Christmas, Three French Hens, Amber Carnival	1972	Year	12.00	12.00 to 12.50
Christmas, Three French Hens, Crystal*	1972	Year	16.50	15.00 to 16.50
Christmas, Four Colly Birds, White Carnival	1973	Year	12.00	12.00
Christmas, Four Colly Birds, Crystal*	1973	Year	16.50	16.50
Christmas, Five Golden Rings, Carnival	1974	Year	15.00	15.00
Christmas, Five Golden Rings, Crystal	1974	Year	18.50	18.50
Coin, 1964 Kennedy Half Dollar*	1971		15.00	10.00 to 15.00
Coin, Eisenhower*	1972		15.00	11.00 to 15.00

Indian Art Eggs

Easter	1972	5000	12.00	15.00 to 20.00
Easter	1973		13.00	13.00 to 16.00

Indianapolis 500 plate, see Coalport

International Silver Company of Meriden, Connecticut, was incorporated by a group of New England silversmiths in 1898. The company makes a large variety of silver and silver-plated wares. Limited edition pewter and silver plates were first made in 1972.

See listing for International Silver in Bar & Ingot section

International Silver Plates

Bicentennial, We Are One, Pewter*	1972	7500	40.00	40.00
Bicentennial, Paul Revere, Pewter*	1973	7500	40.00	40.00
Bicentennial, Stand At Concord Bridge, Pewter*	1973	7500	40.00	40.00
Bicentennial, Crossing The Delaware, Pewter*	1974	7500	40.00	40.00
Bicentennial, Surrender Of Cornwallis, Pewter*	1974	7500	40.00	40.00
Bicentennial, Valley Forge, Pewter*	1974	7500	40.00	40.00
Christmas, Christmas Rose, Gold & Silver*	1972	2500	100.00	90.00 to 115.00

Interpace, see Modgliani, Quality Systems, Shenango

The Ispanky plate was designed by Lazlo Ispanky, noted porcelain sculptor. Medallic Art Company of Danbury, Connecticut, produced the plate.

See listing for Ispanky in Figurine section

Ispanky Plate

Panda, Sterling*	1973	3500	150.00	150.00 to 175.00

Imperial, Coin Plate, 1971

Imperial, Coin Plate, 1972

International Silver, Bicentennial Plate,
1972, We Are One

International Silver, Bicentennial Plate,
1974, Surrender Of Cornwallis

International Silver, Bicentennial Plate,
1974, Crossing The Delaware

International Silver, Bicentennial Plate,
1973, Paul Revere

International Silver,
Christmas Plate, 1972

International Silver, Bicentennial Plate,
1973, Stand At Concord Bridge

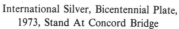

Ispanky, Panda Plate, 1973

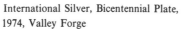

International Silver, Bicentennial Plate,
1974, Valley Forge

Jean-Paul Loup, Christmas Plate, 1971

Jean-Paul Loup, Christmas Plate, 1972

Jean-Paul Loup, Christmas Plate, 1973

Judaic Heritage, Chanukah Plate, Silver

Israel Creations, Inc. commissioned the Naaman Works of Israel to produce the first Passover plate in the 1960s. In 1967, the Annual Israel Commemorative plate series was started.

Israel Creations Plates

Tower Of David	1967	5000	7.50	7.50 to 12.50
Wailing Wall	1967	5000	7.50	15.00 to 25.00
Masada	1968	5000	7.50	7.50 to 12.50
Rachel's Tomb	1969	5000	7.50	7.50 to 12.50
Tiberias	1970	5000	8.00	7.00 to 12.00
Nazareth	1971	5000	8.00	7.00 to 11.00
Beersheba	1972	5000	9.00	7.00 to 9.00

Jackson, A. Y., see Wellings Mint

James Wyeth, see Franklin Mint

Jean-Paul Loup, the editor of Art of Chicago, joined the Betournes Studio of Limoges, France, to issue their first limited edition plates in 1971. The plates and porcelain paintings are hand-applied enamel on copper. Each plate is signed by both Michel Betourne and Jean-Paul Loup.

See listing for Jean-Paul Loup in Figurine section

Jean-Paul Loup/Betournes Plates

Christmas*	1971	300	125.00	800.00 to 1000.00
Christmas**	1972	500	150.00	325.00 to 375.00
Christmas**	1973	500	175.00	175.00 to 200.00
Mother's Day**	1974	500	250.00	250.00

Jefferson Mint of Amador City, California, introduced limited edition silver plates and bars in 1972. Medals in bronze and silver were added in 1973.

Jefferson Mint Plates

Christmas, Silver	1972	Year	125.00	100.00 to 125.00
Christmas, Silver	1973	Year	125.00	125.00

Jensen, Georg, see Georg Jensen

Jensen, Svend, see Svend Jensen

John Ruthven Bird plates, see Hutschenreuther

Josair Plates

Bicentennial, American Eagle, Crystal	1972	400	250.00	250.00
Bicentennial, American Flag, Crystal	1973	400	250.00	250.00

Juan Ferrandiz, see Anri, Ferrandiz

The Judaic Heritage Society first made medals commemorating Jewish traditions in 1969. Limited edition plates were introduced in 1972.

See listing for Judaic Heritage Society in Medal section

Judaic Heritage Society Cups

Cup Of Fulfillment, Gold	1973	25	3000.00	3000.00
Cup Of Fulfillment, Silver	1973	999	325.00	325.00

Judaic Heritage Society Plates

Chanukah, Gold	1972	100	1900.00	1900.00
Chanukah, Silver*	1972	2000	150.00	150.00
Pesach, Silver	1972	5000	150.00	150.00
Purim, Silver	1974	1000	175.00	175.00

Kaiser Porcelain Manufactory was founded in 1872 by August Alboth in Colburg, Germany. The plant was moved to Steffelstein, Bavaria, in 1953. Their first limited edition plate was made in 1970. That year, the company's mark was changed from AK and a crown to 'Kaiser Porcelain.'

See listing for Kaiser in Figurine section

Kaiser Plaques

Birds, Cardinal & Blue Titmouse, Pair	1973	2000	200.00	200.00

Kaiser Plates

Anniversary, Doves In The Park	1972	12000	16.50	13.50 to 16.50
Anniversary	1973	7000	16.50	16.50 to 18.00
Christmas, Waiting For Santa	1970	Year	12.50	20.00 to 35.00

Christmas, Silent Night	1971	Year	13.50	12.00 to 16.50
Christmas, Welcome Home	1972	10000	16.50	11.00 to 16.50
Christmas	1973	8000	18.00	18.00
Christmas	1974		20.00	20.00
Little Critters, Set Of 6	1973	5000	100.00	100.00
Mother's Day, Mare & Foal	1971	Year	13.00	20.00 to 35.00
Mother's Day, Flowers For Mother	1972	8000	16.50	12.00 to 19.00
Mother's Day	1973	7000	17.00	12.00 to 17.00
Mother's Day, Fox & Cubs		1974	22.00	22.00
Passion Play	1970			17.50 to 22.50
Toronto Horse Show	1973	1000	29.00	22.50 to 30.00
Yacht, Cetonia	1972	1000	50.00	45.00 to 50.00
Yacht, Westward	1972	1000	50.00	45.00 to 50.00

King's Porcelain, Christmas Plate, 1973

Kate Greenaway, who was a famous illustrator of children's books, drew pictures of children in high-waisted empire dresses. She lived from 1846 to 1901. The current limited edition Kate Greenaway plates are made by Meakin pottery of England.

Kate Greenaway Plates

Mother's Day	1971	14.95	15.00 to 20.00
Mother's Day	1972	14.95	15.00 to 20.00
Mother's Day	1973	16.95	16.95

Kay Mallek, see Mallek

Keller & George, jewelers from Charlottesville, Virginia, commissioned Reed & Barton to produce a series of Bicentennial plates in damascene. The series was begun in 1972 and will be issued through 1976.

Keller & George Plates

Bicentennial, Monticello, Damascene	1972	1000	75.00	75.00
Bicentennial, Monticello, Silver Plate	1972	200	200.00	200.00
Bicentennial, Mt.Vernon, Damascene	1973		75.00	75.00

King's Porcelain,
Flowers Of America Plate, 1973

Kera Mugs

Christmas, Kobenhavn	1967	Year	6.00	6.00
Christmas, Forste	1968	Year	6.00	6.00
Christmas, Andersen's House	1969	Year	6.00	6.00
Christmas, PA Langelinie	1970	Year	6.00	6.00
Christmas, Lille Peter	1971	Year	6.00	6.00

Kera Plates

Christmas, Kobenhavn	1967	Year	6.00	12.00 to 24.00
Christmas, Forste	1968	Year	6.00	10.00 to 20.00
Christmas, Andersen's House	1969	Year	6.00	8.00 to 16.00
Christmas, PA Langelinie	1970	Year	6.00	6.00 to 16.00
Christmas, Lille Peter	1971	Year	6.00	6.00 to 10.00
Moon, Apollo 11	1969		6.00	6.00 to 10.00
Moon, Apollo 13	1970		6.00	6.00 to 10.00
Mother's Day	1970	Year	6.00	6.00 to 10.00
Mother's Day	1971	Year	6.00	6.00 to 10.00

King's Porcelain,
Flowers Of America Plate, Roses

Arthur King, New York City jeweler, designs and creates his own series of limited edition plates. The hammered style silver plates are 4 inches in diameter.

King Plates

Christmas	1972	750	325.00	325.00
Gold Reserve Act	1973	750	400.00	400.00

King's Porcelain Factory is located in Italy. Their limited edition plates, introduced in 1973, are high bas relief and hand-painted. Limited edition figurines were first made in 1974.

See listing for King's Porcelain in Figurine section

King's Porcelain Plates

Christmas, Nativity*	1973	1500	150.00	150.00
Flowers Of America, Carnation*	1973	1000	85.00	85.00
Flowers Of America, Roses*	1974	1000	100.00	100.00
Mother's Day, The Dancing Girl*	1973	1500	100.00	100.00 to 120.00
Mother's Day, The Dancing Boy*	1974	1500	115.00	115.00

King's Porcelain, Mother's Day Plate, 1973

King's Porcelain, Mother's Day Plate, 1974

Kingsbridge, Wild Ducks Decanter
3/4 Liter   1/2 Liter   2/3 Liter

Kingsbridge,   Kingsbridge,
Wild Ducks Vase, Footed   Wild Ducks Vase, Ball

Kingsbridge,
Wild Ducks Plate

Kosta, Annual Plate, 1973

Kingsbridge crystal limited editions are made in Bavaria, West Germany. Each piece is hand engraved, numbered, and signed.

Kingsbridge Decanters

Wild Ducks, 1/2 Liter*		300	50.00	55.00 to 65.00
Wild Ducks, 2/3 Liter*		300	60.00	65.00 to 70.00
Wild Ducks, 3/4 Liter*		300	70.00	70.00

Kingsbridge Plates

Wild Ducks		300	100.00	100.00 to 115.00

Kingsbridge Vases

Wild Ducks, Ball*		300	50.00	55.00 to 60.00
Wild Ducks, Footed*		300	60.00	55.00 to 65.00

Kirk limited editions are made by Samuel Kirk and Sons, Inc. The firm was started in Baltimore, Maryland, in 1815. The company is well known for both antique and modern silver wares. Limited edition plates and spoons were first made in 1972.

See listing for Kirk in Figurine Section

Kirk Plates

Bicentennial, Washington, Silver	1972	5000	75.00	55.00 to 75.00
Christmas, Flight Into Egypt, Silver	1972	3500	150.00	100.00 to 150.00
Mother's Day, Mother & Child, Silver	1972	3500	75.00	95.00 to 135.00
Mother's Day, Silver	1973	2500	80.00	80.00
Thanksgiving, Thanksgiving Ways And Means	1972	3500	150.00	100.00 to 150.00
U.S.S. Constellation	1972	825	75.00	75.00

Kirk Spoons

Christmas, Snowflake, Gold	1972	81	125.00	95.00 to 145.00
Christmas, Snowflake, Silver	1972	6000	12.50	12.50 to 15.0

Kosta Glassworks of Sweden was founded in 1742 by King Charles II. The limited edition line, introduced in 1970, includes paperweights, plates, and mugs.

See listing for Kosta in Paperweight section

Kosta Mugs

Annual, Heraldic Lion	1971	Year		25.00 to 300.00
Annual, Owl	1972	Year		22.50 to 27.50
Annual, Eagle*	1973	Year	40.00	40.00

Kosta Plates

Annual, Madonna & Child	1971	Year	30.00	20.00 to 30.00
Annual, St.George & The Dragon	1972	Year	30.00	25.00 to 35.00
Annual, Ship*	1973	Year	40.00	40.00

KPM Eggs

Easter	1972	600	60.00	70.00 to 90.00
Easter*	1973	500	60.00	60.00 to 65.00
Easter*	1974	350	80.00	80.00

KPM Plaques

Olympic	1972	8000		12.00 to 18.00

Kurz Bells

Christmas	1973	500	50.00	50.00

Kurz Plates

Christmas	1972	500	60.00	50.00 to 75.00
Christmas	1973	500	70.00	70.00
Mother's Day	1973	500	65.00	60.00 to 65.00

Kurz Tankards

Christmas	1973	500	55.00	55.00

Kylle Svanlund, see Holmegaard

Lalique & Cie was established in 1909 by Rene Lalique in Paris. The glass was famous internationally. The present factory, located in Alsace, was opened in 1920. Limited edition annual plates were first issued in 1965. The production of the plates has been increased each year, with a range between 2,000 in 1965 to 7,500 in 1973.

Lalique Plates

Annual, Two Birds	1965	2000	25.00	900.00 to 1100.00
Annual, Dreamrose	1966	5000	25.00	140.00 to 250.00
Annual, Fish*	1967		30.00	90.00 to 150.00
Annual, Antelope*	1968		30.00	50.00 to 100.00
Annual, Butterfly*	1969		30.00	50.00 to 85.00
Annual, Peacock*	1970		35.00	50.00 to 75.00
Annual, Owl*	1971		35.00	40.00 to 75.00
Annual, Shell*	1972		40.00	40.00 to 55.00
Annual	1973	7500	42.50	42.50
Annual	1974		45.00	45.00

Kosta, Annual Mug, 1973

La Monnaie de Paris, see Puiforcat

Lenox pottery was founded in Trenton, New Jersey, in 1889 by Walter Scott Lenox. It was later moved to its present site in Pomona, New Jersey. Lenox entered the limited edition market in 1970 with the introduction of the Edward Marshall Boehm Bird series. The Boehm Bird of Peace and Eaglet plates, commissioned by Boehm Studios, are not part of the Lenox series.

Lenox, Boehm Birds, see also Boehm plates

Lenox Plates

Boehm Birds, Wood Thrush*	1970		35.00	190.00 to 250.00
Boehm Birds, Goldfinch*	1971		35.00	90.00 to 125.00
Boehm Birds, Mountain Bluebird**	1972		37.50	60.00 to 90.00
Boehm Birds, Meadowlark	1973		37.50	40.00 to 50.00
Boehm Wildlife, Raccoons**	1973		50.00	75.00 to 110.00
Boehm Wildlife, Foxes	1974		52.00	52.00
States Of Confederacy, Set Of 10	1972	2500	900.00	950.00 to 1500.00

KPM, Easter Egg, 1973

Lenox Vases

Belleek		5000	250.00	250.00 to 275.00

Lihs Lindner limited editions are designed by Mr. Helmut H. Lihs of Long Beach, California, and manufactured by the Lindner Company of Kueps Bavaria, Germany.

Lihs Lindner Bells

Christmas, Drummer Boy	1973	3000	25.00	25.00

Lihs Lindner Plates

Christmas, Little Drummer Boy*	1972	6000	20.00	20.00 to 30.00
Christmas, We Wish You A Merry Christmas*	1973	6000	25.00	25.00
Easter, Bunnies*	1973	1500	22.00	30.00 to 35.00
Easter	1974		25.00	25.00
Flag*	1973	3000	60.00	60.00
Mother's Day*	1972	1000	20.00	65.00 to 90.00
Mother's Day*	1973	2000	24.00	24.00
Mother's Day	1974		25.00	25.00
Union Pacific Railroad	1972	1500	22.00	20.00 to 25.00
Union Pacific Railroad, Big Boy	1973	1500	25.00	25.00

Lihs Lindner Vases

Christmas, Poinsettia*	1972	500	85.00	85.00

KPM, Easter Egg, 1974

Limoges, see Royal Limoges

Limoges, Dali plates, see Puiforcat

The Lincoln Mint of Chicago, Illinois, entered the limited edition field in 1971. Gold, silver, and vermeil plates, medals, and ingots are made. Lincoln Mint has produced official state bicentennial and governors medals for a number of states. Although many of the medal series were officially announced as an edition of 5,000, the complete 5,000 were never issued in most cases.

See listing for Lincoln Mint in Bar & Ingot and Medal sections

Lalique, Annual Plate, 1967

Lincoln Mint Bells

Alice In Daliland, Sterling*	1972	5000	200.00	200.00

Lincoln Mint Plates

Christmas, Madonna Della Seggiola, Gold Plate	1972	125	150.00	150.00
Christmas, Madonna Della Seggiola, Silver*	1972	3000	125.00	100.00 to 125.00

Lalique, Annual Plate, 1968

Lenox, Boehm Bird Plate, 1971

Lalique, Annual Plate, 1972

Lenox, Boehm Bird Plate, 1972

Lalique, Annual Plate, 1969

Lalique, Annual Plate, 1970

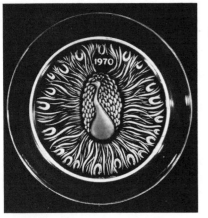

Lenox, Boehm Bird Plate, 1970

Lihs Lindner, Christmas Plate, 1973

Lihs Lindner, Christmas Plate, 1972

Lalique, Annual Plate, 1971

Lihs Lindner, Easter Plate, 1973

Lihs Lindner, Mother's Day Plate, 1972

Lihs Lindner, Christmas Vase,
1972

Lihs Lindner, Mother's Day Plate, 1973

Lihs Lindner, Flag Plate, 1973

Lincoln Mint, Christmas Plate,
1972, Silver

Lincoln Mint, Dali Plate, 1972,
Dyonisiaque Et Pallas Athena, Silver

Lincoln Mint,
Alice In Daliland Bell, 1972

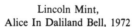

Lladro, Christmas Plate, 1972

Lincoln Mint, Dali Easter Plate,
1974

Lladro, Christmas Plate, 1971

Lladro, Mother's Day Plate, 1971

Lladro, Mother's Day Plate, 1972

Lladro, Mother's Day Plate, 1973

Dali, Unicorn Dyonisiaque, Gold	1971	100	1500.00	1500.00
Dali, Unicorn Dyonisiaque, Silver	1971	5000	100.00	75.00 to 125.00
Dali, Dyonisiaque Et Pallas Athena, Gold	1972	300	2000.00	2000.00
Dali, Dyonisiaque Et Pallas Athena, Gold Plate	1972	2500	150.00	100.00 to 150.00
Dali, Dyonisiaque Et Pallas Athena, Silver*	1972	7500	125.00	85.00 to 125.00
Dali, Easter Christ, Gold Plate	1972	10000	200.00	150.00 to 200.00
Dali, Easter Christ, Silver*	1972	20000	150.00	75.00 to 150.00
Dali, Easter Christ, Pewter	1974		45.00	45.00
Mother's Day, Collies, Silver	1972		125.00	50.00 to 125.00

Lindner Lihs, see Lihs Lindner

Lionel Barrymore, see Gorham

Little Critters plate, see Kaiser

Lladro Porcelain factory of Tabernes Blanques, Spain, produced its first limited edition Mother's Day plate in 1971. The plates are a combination of bas-relief white bisque with an underglaze blue border. Lladro also produces a large line of limited and nonlimited edition sculptures.

See listing for Lladro in Figurine Section

Lladro Plates

Christmas, Caroling*	1971		27.50	17.50 to 35.00
Christmas, Umbrella*	1972		35.00	17.50 to 35.00
Christmas	1973		45.00	45.00
Mother's Day, Kiss Of The Child*	1971		27.50	65.00 to 110.00
Mother's Day, Bird & Chicks*	1972	3500	27.50	20.00 to 35.00
Mother's Day*	1973	2000	45.00	35.00 to 45.00

Lockhart Bird plates, see Pickard

Long's Peak Plate Company of Westminster, Colorado, was formed in 1972 by Gil and Fran Nation. Each plate is hand painted by artist Kenneth V. Williams of Colorado Springs.

Long's Peak Plate Company Plates

Father's Day	1972	150	65.00	65.00
Wild Animal	1972	150	65.00	65.00
Wild Bird	1972	150	65.00	65.00
Western Scenery	1972	150	65.00	65.00

Lori Bells

Christmas	1973	1000	17.50	17.50

Loup, Jean-Paul, see Jean-Paul Loup

Lourioux Plate

Chateau, Fontainebleau	1971		12.50	5.00 to 12.50

Lund & Clausen Plates

Astronaut, Moon Landing	1969			8.00 to 13.50
Astronaut	1971			9.00 to 14.00
Christmas, Deer Park	1971		13.50	7.00 to 13.50
Christmas, Stave Church	1972		13.50	8.00 to 13.50
Mother's Day, Rose	1970			7.00 to 15.00
Mother's Day, Forget-Me-Nots	1971			10.00 to 14.50
Mother's Day, Bluebell	1972			12.50 to 14.50
Mother's Day, Lilies-Of-The-Valley	1973		16.00	16.00

The first Kay Mallek Navajo Christmas plate was made in 1971. The limited edition plaques and plates are designed by contemporary Arizona artists and marketed through Kay Mallek Creations of Tucson, Arizona.

Mallek Plaques

Bunnies*	1972	500	60.00	60.00
Easter, Chicks In The Nest**	1972	500	60.00	60.00
Navajo Thanksgiving**	1972	500	60.00	60.00

Mallek Plates

Amish Harvest Plate**	1972	1000	17.00	17.00 to 22.00
Chinese Lunar Calendar, Year Of The Rat*	1972	1000	15.00	15.00 to 20.00
Chinese Lunar Calendar, Year Of The Ox*	1973	1000	15.00	15.00 to 17.50
Christmas, Game Bird, Gambel Quail**	1972	1500	15.00	15.00 to 20.00
Christmas, Game Bird*	1973	1500	15.00	15.00 to 17.00
Christmas, Navidad En Mexico*	1972	500	15.00	15.00 to 20.00

Mallek, Amish Harvest Plate, 1972

Mallek, Navajo Christmas Plate, 1971

Mallek, Christmas Plate, 1972,
Navidad En Mexico

Mallek, Navajo Christmas Plate, 1972

Mallek,
Chinese Lunar Calendar Plate, 1972

Mallek, Christmas Plate, 1973, Game Bird

Mallek, Navajo Christmas Plate, 1973

Mallek, Christmas Plate, 1972, Game Bird

Mallek,
Navajo Thanksgiving Plaque,
1972

Mallek, Bunnies Plaque, 1972

Mallek, Chinese Lunar Calendar Plate, 1973

Mark Twain, Huck Finn Plate, 1973

Mark Twain, Tom Sawyer Plate, 1973

Marmot, Christmas Plate, 1972

Navajo Christmas, Indian Wise Men**	1971	1000	15.00	50.00 to 125.00
Navajo Christmas, On The Reservation*	1972	2000	17.00	15.00 to 20.00
Navajo Christmas*	1973	2000	17.00	17.00

Manjundo Company of Kyoto, Japan, was founded in 1772.

Manjundo Plates

Chinese Lunar Calendar, Year Of The Rat	1972	5000	15.00	15.00
Chinese Lunar Calendar, Year Of The Ox	1973	5000	15.00	15.00

Marc Chagall plate, see Chagall

The Mark Twain plate series is made by Ridgewood China Co. of Burbank, California.

Mark Twain Plates

Tom & Huck, Pair*	1973	45.00	45.00

Marmot Plates

Christmas, Polar Bear	1970	5000	13.00	10.00 to 24.00
Christmas, Buffalo	1971	6000	14.00	9.00 to 14.00
Christmas, Boy & Grandfather*	1972	5000	16.00	12.00 to 16.00
Christmas, Snowman*	1973	2000	20.00	20.00
Father's Day, Stag	1970	3500	12.00	10.00 to 22.50
Father's Day, Horse*	1971	3500	12.50	9.00 to 12.50
Mother's Day, Seal*	1972	6000	16.00	16.00 to 25.00
Mother's Day, Polar Bear*	1973	2000	20.00	18.50 to 24.00
Mother's Day, Penguins*	1974	2000	24.00	24.00
President, George Washington*	1971	1500	25.00	25.00 to 30.00
President, Thomas Jefferson*	1972	1500	25.00	20.00 to 30.00
President, John Adams*	1973	1500	25.00	25.00

The term Mary Gregory glass refers to any glass decorated with a special type of white silhouette figure. Antique Mary Gregory glass was made between 1870 and 1910. The modern limited edition type, introduced in 1973, is made in Czechoslovakia.

Mary Gregory Bells

Christmas	1973	1000	17.50	17.50

Mary Gregory Plates

Christmas	1973	1000	55.00	55.00 to 70.00
Mother's Day	1973	500	55.00	70.00 to 100.00

Meissen Plates

Christmas	1940	60.00 to 70.00
Christmas	1941	60.00 to 70.00
Christmas	1942	60.00 to 70.00
Christmas	1943	60.00 to 70.00
Christmas	1944	60.00 to 70.00
Christmas	1945	60.00 to 70.00
Christmas	1946	60.00 to 70.00
Christmas	1947	60.00 to 70.00
Christmas	1948	60.00 to 70.00
Christmas	1949	60.00 to 70.00
Christmas	1950	60.00 to 70.00
Christmas	1951	60.00 to 70.00
Christmas	1952	60.00 to 70.00
Christmas	1953	60.00 to 70.00
Christmas	1954	60.00 to 70.00
Christmas	1955	60.00 to 70.00
Christmas	1956	60.00 to 70.00
Christmas	1957	60.00 to 70.00
Christmas	1958	60.00 to 70.00
Christmas	1959	60.00 to 70.00
Christmas	1960	60.00 to 70.00
Christmas	1961	60.00 to 70.00
Christmas	1962	60.00 to 70.00
Christmas	1963	60.00 to 70.00
Christmas	1964	60.00 to 70.00
Christmas	1965	60.00 to 70.00
Christmas	1966	60.00 to 70.00
Christmas	1967	60.00 to 70.00

Marmot, Christmas Plate, 1973

Marmot, Mother's Day Plate, 1974

Marmot, Father's Day Plate, 1971

Marmot, President Plate, 1971

Marmot, President Plate, 1972

Marmot, Mother's Day Plate, 1972

Marmot, President Plate, 1973

Marmot, Mother's Day Plate, 1973

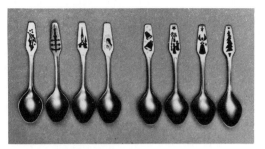

Meka, Christmas Spoon, 1966 - 1973

Meka, Mother's Day Spoon,
1970 - 1974

Metawa, Christmas Plate, 1973

Michelsen,
Christmas Fork And Spoon,
1969

Christmas	1968			60.00 to 70.00
Christmas	1969			55.00 to 60.00
Christmas	1970			45.00 to 55.00
Christmas	1971			40.00 to 50.00
Christmas	1972			35.00 to 45.00

Meissen, Kate Greenaway, see Kate Greenaway

The Meka Company of Copenhagen, Denmark, was started in 1940 by Mr. Kage Meyer. The company produces tableware, jewelry, and trophies. Limited edition spoons were first made in 1966. The spoons are limited to the production of one year.

Meka Spoons

Christmas**	1966	Year	5.00	10.00 to 15.00
Christmas**	1967	Year	5.00	7.50 to 10.00
Christmas**	1968	Year	5.00	6.00 to 7.00
Christmas**	1969	Year	5.00	5.00
Christmas**	1970	Year	6.00	6.00 to 7.00
Christmas**	1971	Year	6.00	6.00
Christmas**	1972	Year	6.00	6.00
Christmas**	1973	Year	6.00	6.00
Christmas**	1974	Year	6.00	6.00
Mother's Day**	1970	5000	5.00	15.00 to 20.00
Mother's Day**	1971	5000	5.00	9.00 to 12.00
Mother's Day**	1972	5000	5.00	8.00 to 10.00
Mother's Day**	1973	5000	7.50	7.50
Mother's Day**	1974	5000	7.50	7.50

Metawa pewter limited editions are made by the N. V. Metawa Company of Tiel, Holland. Each limited edition piece is marked with the 'Water Gate' hallmark, a symbol used on Dutch pewter since 1647. Limited editions were first made in 1972.

Metawa Plates

Christmas, Ice Skaters	1972	3000	30.00	25.00 to 30.00
Christmas, One-Horse Open Sleigh*	1973	1500	30.00	30.00

A. Michelsen Silversmiths of Copenhagen, Denmark, was established in 1841. Annual Christmas spoons and forks were introduced in 1910. Although the spoons and forks were not originally limited, the old issues from 1910 to 1960 are no longer available, and production of the 1960 - 1973 series will be discontinued next year. Thereafter only the spoon and fork of the year will be available. The spoons and forks are made of enamel and gold plate on sterling silver.

Michelsen Forks

Christmas, Star Of Bethlehem	1910	125.00 to 185.00
Christmas, The Infant Christ	1911	125.00 to 185.00
Christmas, Christmas Bells	1912	125.00 to 185.00
Christmas, Christmas Scenery	1913	125.00 to 185.00
Christmas, Christmas Angel	1914	125.00 to 185.00
Christmas, Three Kings Of Cologne	1915	125.00 to 185.00
Christmas, The Madonna	1916	125.00 to 1850.0
Christmas, Epiphany	1917	125.00 to 185.00
Christmas, Mistletoe	1918	125.00 to 185.00
Christmas, Peace On Earth	1919	125.00 to 185.00
Christmas, The Mill Of Dybbol	1920	36.00 to 52.00
Christmas, Christmas Boat	1921	36.00 to 52.00
Christmas, Holly	1922	36.00 to 52.00
Christmas, Cathedral In Copenhagen	1923	36.00 to 52.00
Christmas, Sheaf Of Grain	1924	36.00 to 52.00
Christmas, Poinsettia	1925	36.00 to 52.00
Christmas, Organ Pipes	1926	36.00 to 52.00
Christmas, Spire Of Famous Church, Copenhagen	1927	36.00 to 52.00
Christmas, Epiphyllum	1928	36.00 to 52.00
Christmas, Christmas Rose	1929	36.00 to 52.00
Christmas, Christmas In Port	1930	36.00 to 46.00
Christmas, Star Of Bethlehem	1931	36.00 to 46.00
Christmas, Children Around Christmas Tree	1932	36.00 to 46.00
Christmas, Little Match Girl	1933	36.00 to 46.00
Christmas, Holy Night	1934	36.00 to 46.00

Christmas, Kneeling Shepherd	1935		36.00 to 46.00
Christmas, Christmas Candle	1936		36.00 to 46.00
Christmas, Birds In The Christmas Sheaf	1937		36.00 to 46.00
Christmas, Snowberries	1938		36.00 to 46.00
Christmas, Gift-Laden Christmas Tree	1939		36.00 to 46.00
Christmas, Star Of Bethlehem	1940		33.00 to 38.00
Christmas, Mistletoe	1941		33.00 to 38.00
Christmas, Madonna And Child	1942		33.00 to 38.00
Christmas, Dove Of Peace	1943		33.00 to 38.00
Christmas, Hearty Holiday Spirit	1944		33.00 to 38.00
Christmas, Snow Crystals	1945		33.00 to 38.00
Christmas, Holly	1946		33.00 to 38.00
Christmas, Falling Snowflakes	1947		33.00 to 38.00
Christmas, Christmas Ram	1948		33.00 to 38.00
Christmas, Candles Of Advent	1949		33.00 to 38.00
Christmas, Winter Forest	1950		30.00 to 32.00
Christmas, Colorful Christmas	1951		30.00 to 32.00
Christmas, Santa And The Reindeer	1952		30.00 to 32.00
Christmas, The Herald Angels	1953		30.00 to 32.00
Christmas, Coronets	1954		30.00 to 32.00
Christmas, Poinsettia	1955		30.00 to 32.00
Christmas, Snow Flowers	1956		30.00 to 32.00
Christmas, Danish Yule-Nisses	1957		30.00 to 32.00
Christmas, The Wise Men From The East	1958		30.00 to 32.00
Christmas, The Lucia Bride	1959		30.00 to 32.00
Christmas, Winter Solstice	1960		28.50 to 30.00
Christmas, Organ Pipes	1961		28.50 to 30.00
Christmas, Madonna And Child	1962		28.50 to 30.00
Christmas, Santa's Village	1963		28.50 to 30.00
Christmas, Orion	1964		28.50 to 30.00
Christmas, The Christmas Tree	1965		28.50 to 30.00
Christmas, Flight Into Egypt	1966		28.50 to 30.00
Christmas, Splendor Of Yule	1967		28.50 to 30.00
Christmas, A Mother's Heart	1968		28.50 to 30.00
Christmas, Greenlander*	1969		28.50 to 30.00
Christmas, Mr Snowman's Christmas Tree**	1970		28.50 to 30.00
Christmas, Golden Universe*	1971		26.00 to 28.50
Christmas, Herald**	1972		27.00
Christmas, Solstice And Family**	1973	36.00	36.00

Michelsen Spoons

Christmas, Star Of Bethelhem**	1910	75.00 to 110.00
Christmas, The Infant Christ**	1911	75.00 to 110.00
Christmas, Christmas Bells**	1912	75.00 to 110.00
Christmas, Christmas Scenery**	1913	75.00 to 110.00
Christmas, Christmas Angel**	1914	75.00 to 110.00
Christmas, Three Kings Of Cologne**	1915	75.00 to 110.00
Christmas, The Madonna**	1916	75.00 to 110.00
Christmas, Epiphany**	1917	75.00 to 110.00
Christmas, Mistletoe**	1918	75.00 to 110.00
Christmas, Peace On Earth**	1919	75.00 to 110.00
Christmas, The Mill Of Dybbol**	1920	36.00 to 52.00
Christmas, Christmas Boat**	1921	36.00 to 52.00
Christmas, Holly**	1922	36.00 to 52.00
Christmas, Cathedral In Copenhagen**	1923	36.00 to 52.00
Christmas, Sheaf Of Grain**	1924	36.00 to 52.00
Christmas, Poinsettia**	1925	36.00 to 52.00
Christmas, Organ Pipes**	1926	36.00 to 52.00
Christmas, Spire Of Famous Church**	1927	36.00 to 52.00
Christmas, Epiphyllum**	1928	36.00 to 52.00
Christmas, Christmas Rose**	1929	36.00 to 52.00
Christmas, Christmas In Port**	1930	36.00 to 46.00
Christmas, Star Of Bethlehem**	1931	36.00 to 46.00
Christmas, Children Around Christmas Tree**	1932	36.00 to 46.00
Christmas, Little Match Girl**	1933	36.00 to 46.00
Christmas, Holy Night**	1934	36.00 to 46.00
Christmas, Kneeling Shepherd**	1935	36.00 to 46.00
Christmas, Christmas Candle**	1936	36.00 to 46.00
Christmas, Birds In The Christmas Sheaf**	1937	36.00 to 46.00
Christmas, Snowberries**	1938	36.00 to 46.00
Christmas, Gift-Laden Christmas Tree**	1939	36.00 to 46.00

Michelsen,
Christmas Fork And Spoon,
1970

Michelsen,
Christmas Fork And Spoon,
1971

Michelsen,
Christmas Fork And Spoon,
1972

Michelsen,
Christmas Fork And Spoon,
1973

Michelsen, Christmas Spoons, 1920 - 1929

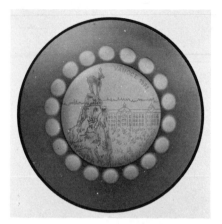

Moser, Annual Plate, 1973

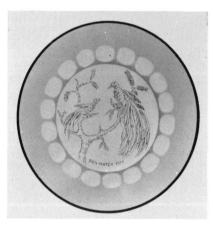

Moser, Mother's Day Plate, 1971

Moser, Mother's Day Plate, 1973

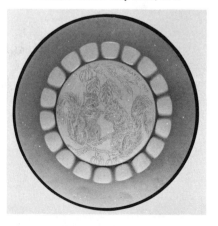

Christmas, Star Of Bethlehem**	1940		33.00 to 38.00
Christmas, Mistletoe**	1941		33.00 to 38.00
Christmas, Madonna And Child**	1942		33.00 to 38.00
Christmas, Dove Of Peace**	1943		33.00 to 38.00
Christmas, Hearty Holiday Spirit**	1944		33.00 to 38.00
Christmas, Snow Crystals**	1945		33.00 to 38.00
Christmas, Holly**	1946		33.00 to 38.00
Christmas, Falling Snowflakes**	1947		33.00 to 38.00
Christmas, Christmas Ram**	1948		33.00 to 38.00
Christmas, Candles Of Advent**	1949		33.00 to 38.00
Christmas, Winter Forest**	1950		30.00 to 32.00
Christmas, Colorful Christmas**	1951		30.00 to 32.00
Christmas, Santa And The Reindeer**	1952		30.00 to 32.00
Christmas, The Herald Angels**	1953		30.00 to 32.00
Christmas, Coronets**	1954		30.00 to 32.00
Christmas, Poinsettia**	1955		30.00 to 32.00
Christmas, Snow Flowers**	1956		30.00 to 32.00
Christmas, Danish Yule-Nisses**	1957		30.00 to 32.00
Christmas, Wise Men From The East**	1958		30.00 to 32.00
Christmas, The Lucia Bride**	1959		30.00 to 32.00
Christmas, Winter Solstice**	1960		28.50 to 30.00
Christmas, Organ Pipes**	1961		28.50 to 30.00
Christmas, Madonna And Child**	1962		28.50 to 30.00
Christmas, Santa's Village**	1963		28.50 to 30.00
Christmas, Orion**	1964		28.50 to 30.00
Christmas, The Christmas Tree**	1965		28.50 to 30.00
Christmas, Flight Into Egypt**	1966		28.50 to 30.00
Christmas, Splendor Of Yule**	1967		28.50 to 30.00
Christmas, A Mother's Heart**	1968		28.50 to 30.00
Christmas, Greenlander**	1969		28.50 to 30.00
Christmas, Mr.Snowman's Christmas Tree*	1970		28.50 to 30.00
Christmas, Golden Universe**	1971		26.00 to 28.50
Christmas, Herald**	1972		27.00
Christmas, Solstice And Family**	1973	36.00	36.00

Mickey Mouse, see Walt Disney

Millous, Pierre, see Cartier

The Modigliani plate was made and distributed by Interpace Corporation of New Castle, Pennsylvania.

Modigliani Plates

Caryatid	1972	10000	60.00	35.00 to 60.00

Montana Historical Society Plates

Free Trapper, Damascene	1972	2500	65.00	65.00 to 75.00

Moppets, see Gorham

Mormon Plates

125th Anniversary, Mormons, Damascene	1972	1000	75.00	75.00

Mormon plate, see also Bygdo

Moser, now known as Karlovy Vary Glassworks-Moser-of Czechoslovakia, was founded by Kolomon Moser in 1857 at Karlsbad, Czechoslovakia. Moser became famous for enameled art nouveau glass around the turn of the century. Limited edition plates, introduced in 1970, are of copper wheel cut crystal.

Moser Plates

Annual, Hradcany Castle, Lavender	1970	400	75.00	200.00 to 300.00
Annual, Karlstein Castle, Pale Green	1971	1365	75.00	70.00 to 80.00
Annual, Old Town Hall	1972	1000	85.00	60.00 to 90.00
Annual, Capricorn*	1973	300	90.00	90.00
Mother's Day, Peacocks, Pale Green*	1971	350	75.00	200.00 to 300.00
Mother's Day, Butterflies, Cobalt Blue	1972	750	85.00	60.00 to 95.00
Mother's Day, Squirrels*	1973	200	90.00	90.00

Mueller Plates

Christmas, Christmas In The Tyrol	1971		6.50 to 15.00
Christmas, Christmas Messenger	1972		12.50 to 17.50

Mueller Steins

Christmas, Christmas In The Tyrol	1971		20.00	17.50 to 22.50

Christmas, Christmas Messenger	1972		20.00	17.50 to 22.50

Museum of Sporting Heritage Plates

Fight Of The Century, Ali & Frazier, Gold	1974	100	4500.00	4500.00
Fight Of The Century, Ali & Frazier, Silver	1974	1500	275.00	275.00

N. C. Wyeth, see George Washington Mint

National Historical Society, see American Commemorative Council

Navajo Christmas plate, see Mallek

New World, see Seven Seas

Noritake, Mother's Day Cup, 1973

Nidaros plates, also called Historic Norway or Norsk, are made in Norway. They are made in blue, green, or red aluminum.

Nidaros Bells

Christmas	1973	Year	29.50	29.50

Nidaros Plates

Christmas, Nidaros Cathedral	1970		12.50	12.50 to 15.00
Christmas, Stave Church	1971		12.50	11.00 to 15.00
Christmas, Gokstad Viking Ship	1972		13.00	13.00 to 15.00

Noritake marked porcelain was first made in Japan after 1904. Noritake limited editions were introduced in 1971.

Noritake Bells

Christmas, Holly	1972		15.00	12.50 to 15.00
Christmas	1973		15.00	12.50 to 15.00
Christmas**	1974			

Noritake Cups

Mother's Day*	1973		15.00	15.00
Mother's Day**	1974	4000	17.50	17.50

Noritake, Easter Egg, 1973

Noritake Eggs

Easter, Bunnies	1971	Year	10.00	45.00 to 55.00
Easter, Flowers	1972	Year	10.00	15.00 to 20.00
Easter, Mother Hen & Chicks*	1973	Year	10.00	10.00 to 15.00
Easter**	1974	Year	11.00	11.00

Noritake Hearts

Valentine's Day	1973	10000	20.00	15.00 to 20.00
Valentine's Day**	1974	5000	15.00	15.00

Noritake Mugs

Father's Day	1972		20.00	25.00 to 35.00
Father's Day*	1973	9000	20.00	20.00
Father's Day**	1974	2500	17.50	17.50

Noritake Ornaments

Mother's Day, Doe & Fawn**	1974	2800	40.00	40.00

Norman Rockwell, see Franklin Mint, Gorham

Norsk Plate, see Nidaros

Oberammergau plate, see Kaiser, Passion Play plate

OMA Plates

Western Series, Bronco Buster	1972	500	100.00	Unknown
Western Series, Chuck Wagon	1972	500	100.00	Unknown
Western Series, Round-Up	1972	500	100.00	Unknown
Wildlife Series, Eagle	1973	500	100.00	Unknown

Noritake, Father's Day Mug, 1973

Orrefors, Christmas Plate, 1973

Orrefors Glassworks, located in the Swedish province of Smaland, was established in 1916. Collector's plates were introduced in 1970.

Orrefors Plates

Annual, Notre Dame Cathedral	1970	Year	45.00	35.00 to 50.00
Annual, Westminister Abbey	1971	Year	50.00	35.00 to 50.00
Annual, Basilica Di San Marco	1972	Year	50.00	35.00 to 50.00
Annual, Cologne Cathedral*	1973	Year	50.00	50.00
Annual, Rue De La Victoire	1974	Year	60.00	60.00
Christmas*	1973	6000	35.00	35.00 to 45.00
Mother's Day, Flowers For Mother	1971	Year	45.00	45.00 to 52.50
Mother's Day, Mother With Children	1972	Year	45.00	35.00 to 45.00
Mother's Day*	1973	Year	45.00	35.00 to 45.00

Michelsen, Christmas Spoons, 1940 - 1949

Michelsen, Christmas Spoons, 1950 - 1959

Michelsen, Christmas Spoons, 1960 - 1969

Pairpoint, Bicentennial Bowl, 1973

Pairpoint, Bicentennial Mug, 1973

Orrefors, Annual Plate, 1973

KÖLNER DOM

Orrefors, Mother's Day Plate, 1973

Pairpoint, Peachblow Bell, 1973

Pairpoint limited editions are made by the Pairpoint Glass Company of Sagamore, Massachusetts. Artisans in Glass, Inc. of New York is the distributor of Pairpoint limited editions.

See listing for Pairpoint in Paperweight section

Pairpoint Bells

Peachblow, Decorated**	1973	1000	125.00	125.00

Pairpoint Bowls

Bicentennial, Paul Revere*	1973	500	200.00	200.00

Pairpoint Cups

New Bedford, Crystal*	1973	50	700.00	700.00

Pairpoint Goblets

Bicentennial*	1973	500	200.00	200.00

Pairpoint, New Bedford Cup, 1973

Pairpoint Mugs

Bicentennial*	1973	500	75.00	75.00

Pairpoint Ornaments

Elephant On Bubble Ball*	1973	500	80.00	80.00

Pairpoint Urns

Bicentennial*	1973	500	250.00	250.00

Palazzo Vecchio Plates

Annual, Byzantine Madonna	1973	504	75.00	75.00

Palisander plates are made in Denmark. They are made of rosewood with silver inlay.

Palisander Plates

Bicentennial	1973	250	50.00	50.00
Christmas, Red Robin On Holly	1971	1200	50.00	40.00 to 50.00
Christmas, Flying Geese	1972	1200	50.00	40.00 to 55.00
Presidential, George Washington	1971	1000	50.00	45.00 to 55.00
Presidential, Thomas Jefferson	1972	1000	50.00	50.00
Presidential, John Adams	1973	1000	50.00	50.00

Pairpoint, Bicentennial Goblet, 1973

Papal plates, see Royal Tettau

Paul Briant, see Briant

Peanuts Plates

Christmas, Woodstock Pulling Snoopy's Sled*	1972	20000	10.00	7.00 to 15.00
Christmas, Snoopy*	1973		10.00	10.00
Mother's Day, Linus With Rose*	1972	15000	10.00	7.00 to 15.00
Mother's Day, Snoopy & Woodstock*	1973	8000	10.00	10.00
Mother's Day	1974		10.00	10.00

Pearl Buck Plates

The Good Earth	1973	10000	37.50	30.00 to 37.50

Picasso Plates, see George Washington Mint, Hamilton Mint

Pickard China Studio was established in Chicago by Wilder Austin Pickard in 1898. In 1935, the company opened a china factory in Antioch, Illinois. The current trademark, a lion with fleur-de-lis, was adopted in 1938. The first limited edition plates by Pickard were made in 1970.

Pickard Plates

Lockhart Birds, Woodcock & Ruffed Grouse*	1970	2000	150.00	210.00 to 235.00
Lockhart Birds, Green-Winged Teal & Mallard*	1971	2000	150.00	165.00 to 175.00
Lockhart Birds, Mockingbird & Cardinal*	1972	2000	150.00	160.00 to 170.00
Lockhart Birds, Wild Turkey & Pheasant*	1973	2000	165.00	165.00
Lockhart Birds, Bald Eagle	1974	2000	150.00	150.00
President, Harry S.Truman*	1972	3000	35.00	45.00 to 75.00
President, Abraham Lincoln*	1973	5000	35.00	35.00 to 50.00

Pairpoint, Bicentennial Urn, 1973

Pierre Millous, see Cartier

The Poillerat Christmas plates, designed by French artist Gilbert Poillerat, are produced by the Atelier d'Art Faure of Limoges, France. The plates are enamel on copper. Poillerat also designs crystal plates and paperweights for Cristal d'Albret.

Poillerat Bird of Peace and Four Seasons plate, see Cristal d'Albret

Pairpoint, Elephant On Bubble Ball Ornament, 1973

Peanuts, Christmas Plate, 1972

Peanuts, Christmas Plate, 1973

Peanuts, Mother's Day Plate, 1972

Peanuts, Mother's Day Plate, 1973

Pickard, Lockhart Bird Plate, 1970,
Woodcock

Pickard, Lockhart Bird Plate, 1971,
Green-Winged Teal

Pickard, Lockhart Bird Plate, 1972,
Cardinal

Pickard, Lockhart Bird Plate, 1971,
Mallard

Pickard, Lockhart Bird Plate, 1973,
Pheasant

Pickard, Lockhart Bird Plate, 1972,
Mockingbird

Pickard, Lockhart Bird Plate, 1973,
Wild Turkey

Pickard, President Plate, 1972

Poillerat Plates

Christmas, Three Kings*	1972	500	350.00	350.00
Christmas, Rose	1973	250	350.00	350.00

Pickard, President Plate, 1973

The Poole Pottery of Poole, Dorset, England, has produced pottery since 1873. Limited edition plates, which were first made in 1972, are handmade to resemble stained glass windows. A limited edition porcelain line featuring game birds was introduced in 1973.

See listing for Poole in Figurine section

Poole Plates

Cathedral, Chartres*	1973	1000	125.00	125.00
Medieval Calendar Series, January*	1972	1000	100.00	100.00 to 125.00
Medieval Calendar Series, February*	1972	1000	100.00	100.00 to 125.00
Medieval Calendar Series, March**	1973	1000	125.00	125.00
Medieval Calendar Series, April**	1973	1000	125.00	125.00

Porcelaine de Paris Plates

Lao Tse, Set Of 4	1973	300	175.00	160.00 to 175.00

Poillerat, Christmas Plate, 1972

Porcelana Granada plates are made in Colombia, South America. The limited edition Christmas series, begun in 1971, is based on the life of Christ.

Porcelana Granada Plates

Christmas, The Annunciation	1971	10000	12.00	10.00 to 12.00
Christmas, Mary & Elizabeth	1972	6000	13.00	10.00 to 13.00
Christmas, Road To Bethlehem	1973	5000	14.00	14.00

Porsgrund, Norway's only porcelain factory, was started in 1887 by Johan Jermiassen. Porsgrund made one of the world's first Christmas plates in 1909 only. The contemporary Christmas plate series was begun in 1968. Mugs were added in 1970.

Porsgrund Mugs

Christmas, Road To Bethlehem	1970	Year	20.00	13.00 to 20.00
Christmas, A Child Is Born	1971	Year	20.00	10.00 to 15.00
Christmas, Hark The Herald Angels	1972	Year	20.00	12.50 to 20.00
Christmas, Promise Of The Saviour*	1973	Year	20.00	20.00
Christmas	1974	Year	20.00	20.00
Father's Day, Cookout	1972	Year	11.00	7.50 to 11.00
Father's Day, Sledding*	1973	Year	11.00	11.00

Poole, Cathedral Plate, 1973

Poole, Medieval Calendar Plate, 1972
January February

Porsgrund Plates

Christmas, Christmas Flowers	1909			400.00 to 475.00
Christmas, Church Scene	1968	Year	7.50	55.00 to 75.00
Christmas, Three Kings	1969	Year	10.00	12.50 to 25.00
Christmas, Road To Bethlehem	1970	Year	10.00	10.00 to 15.00
Christmas, A Child Is Born	1971	Year	12.00	8.00 to 15.00
Christmas, Hark The Herald Angels	1972	Year	12.00	9.00 to 12.00
Christmas, Promise Of The Saviour*	1973	Year	12.00	12.00
Christmas	1974	Year	15.00	15.00
Deluxe Christmas, Road To Bethlehem*	1970	3000	50.00	20.00 to 50.00
Deluxe Christmas, A Child Is Born	1971	3000	50.00	35.00 to 50.00
Deluxe Christmas, Hark The Herald Angels	1972	3000	50.00	35.00 to 50.00
Deluxe Christmas, Promise Of The Saviour*	1973	3000	50.00	50.00
Easter, Ducks	1972	Year	12.00	12.00 to 20.00
Easter, Birds*	1973	Year	12.00	12.00
Father's Day, Father & Son Fishing	1971	Year	7.50	4.00 to 10.00
Father's Day, Cookout	1972	Year	8.00	4.00 to 12.00
Father's Day, Sledding*	1973	Year	8.00	8.00
Father's Day, Wheelbarrow	1974	Year	10.00	10.00
Jubilee, Femboringer	1970		25.00	12.00 to 25.00
Mother's Day, Mare & Foal*	1970	Year	7.50	7.50 to 17.50
Mother's Day, Boy & Geese	1971	Year	7.50	4.00 to 10.00
Mother's Day, Doe & Fawn	1972	Year	8.00	4.00 to 10.00
Mother's Day, Cat & Kittens*	1973	Year	12.00	12.00
Mother's Day, Boy & Goat	1974	Year	10.00	10.00

The Puiforcat Exodus plate was made by La Monnaie de Paris, the official French government mint. Puiforcat porcelain limited editions are made in Limoges, France.

Poole, Medieval Calendar Plate, 1973, March

Poole, Medieval Calendar Plate, 1973, April

Porsgrund, Easter Plate, 1973

Puiforcat, Dali Carte A Jouer Plates, 1972

Porsgrund, Deluxe Christmas Plate, 1970

Porsgrund, Christmas Plate, 1973

Porsgrund, Deluxe Christmas Plate, 1973

Porsgrund, Christmas Mug, 1973

Porsgrund, Father's Day Mug, 1973

Puiforcat Plates

Dali, Carte A Jouer, Set Of 5*	1972	2000	300.00	250.00 to 350.00
Exodus, Silver*	1973	2000	200.00	200.00

Quality Systems plates are manufactured by Interpace Corporation of New Castle, Pennsylvania.

Quality Systems Plates

Air Force	1972	1200	20.00	20.00
Army	1972	1200	20.00	20.00

Porsgrund, Mother's Day Plate, 1970

Ram limited editions are manufactured by the Ram China Plate Company of Minneapolis, Minnesota.

Ram Plates

Christmas, Boston 500 Series	1973	500	30.00	30.00
Easter, Boston 500 Series*	1973	500	30.00	30.00
Father's Day, Boston 500 Series	1973	500	30.00	30.00
Great Bird Heroes, Cher Ami*	1973	1000	7.95	7.95
Great Bird Heroes, The Mocker*	1973	1000	7.95	7.95
Mother's Day, Boston 500 Series*	1973	500	30.00	30.00

Ray Harm Bird plates, see Spode

Reco Plates

Americana, Gaspee, Stuart Devlin, Silver	1972	1000	200.00	200.00
Four Seasons, Fall	1973	2500	50.00	50.00
Four Seasons, Spring*	1973	2500	50.00	50.00
Four Seasons, Summer	1973	2500	50.00	50.00
Four Seasons, Winter	1973	2500	50.00	50.00
Western, The Mountain Man*	1974	1000	165.00	165.00

Porsgrund, Mother's Day Plate, 1973

Reed & Barton Silversmiths of Taunton, Massachusetts, was established in 1824. Limited edition plates of Damascene silver (a combination of copper, bronze, and silver) were first made in 1970.

Reed & Barton Ornaments

Christmas, Silver Cross	1971	10.00	10.00 to 15.00
Christmas, Silver Cross	1972	10.00	10.00 to 15.00
Christmas, Silver Cross	1973	10.00	10.00

Reed & Barton Plates

Audubon Birds, Pine Siskin*	1971	5000	60.00	65.00 to 90.00
Audubon Birds, Red-Shouldered Hawk*	1971	5000	60.00	40.00 to 60.00
Audubon Birds, Red Cardinal*	1972	5000	60.00	40.00 to 60.00
Audubon Birds, Stilt Sandpiper*	1972	5000	60.00	40.00 to 60.00
Chicago Fire			60.00	65.00 to 70.00
Christmas, Partridge*	1970	2500	60.00	175.00 to 200.00
Christmas, We Three Kings*	1971	7500	60.00	50.00 to 75.00
Christmas, Hark The Herald Angels*	1972	7500	60.00	60.00
Christmas, Adoration Of The King*	1973	7500	60.00	60.00
Currier & Ives, Village Blacksmith	1972	1500	85.00	85.00 to 100.00
Currier & Ives, Western Migration	1972	1500		90.00 to 125.00
Currier & Ives, Oaken Bucket	1973	1500	85.00	85.00
Currier & Ives, Winter In The Country	1973	1500		90.00 to 110.00
Delta Queen	1972		75.00	40.00 to 75.00
Kentucky Derby	1972	1000	75.00	75.00
Mission, San Diego	1971		75.00	75.00 to 100.00
Mission, Caramel	1972		75.00	60.00 to 75.00
Riva Ridge	1973	1000	75.00	75.00
Zodiac	1970			85.00 to 100.00

Puiforcat, Exodus Plate, 1973

Ram, Great Bird Hero Plate, 1973, Cher Ami

Rembrandt, see Gorham

Remington Plates

Apache Scout, Carnival	1972	750	12.50	12.50
Sioux Chief, Carnival*	1973	750	9.50	9.50 to 12.50

Remington, see also George Washington Mint, Gorham

Rexxford crystal limited editions are made in Bavaria, West Germany.

Rexxford Bowls

Fleur De Lis, Oval*		300	500.00	500.00
Fleur De Lis, Round*		250	500.00	250.00 to 500.00
Russian*		300	250.00	250.00

Ram, Great Bird Hero Plate, 1973, The Mocker

Reed & Barton, Audubon Bird Plate,
1971, Red-Shouldered Hawk

Ram, Easter Plate,
1973

Ram, Mother's Day Plate,
1973

Reed & Barton, Audubon Bird Plate,
1972, Stilt Sandpiper

Reco, Four Seasons Plate, 1973, Spring

Reed & Barton, Christmas Plate, 1970

Reco, Western Plate, The Mountain Man,
1974

Reed & Barton, Audubon Bird Plate,
1972, Red Cardinal

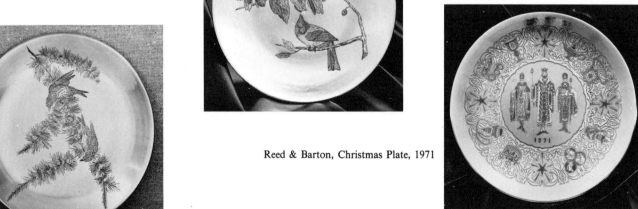

Reed & Barton, Christmas Plate, 1971

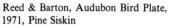

Reed & Barton, Audubon Bird Plate,
1971, Pine Siskin

Rorstrand, Christmas Plate, 1973

Reed & Barton, Christmas Plate, 1972

Rexxford, Fleur De Lis Bowl, Round

Rorstrand, Father's Day Plate, 1973

Reed & Barton, Christmas Plate, 1973

Rexxford, Fleur De Lis Bowl, Oval

Rorstrand, Mother's Day Plate, 1973

Remington, Sioux Chief Plate, 1973

Rexxford, Russian Bowl

Rosenthal, Christmas Plate, 1964

Rosenthal, Christmas Plate,
1965

Rosenthal, Christmas Plate, 1967

Rosenthal, Christmas Plate, 1968

Rockwell, see Franklin Mint, Gorham

Rorstrand, founded in Sweden in 1726, is the oldest porcelain factory in Scandinavia and the second oldest in all of Europe. Rorstrand entered the limited edition market in 1968 with its Christmas plates. Mother's and Father's Day plates were introduced in 1971.

Rorstrand Plates

Christmas, Bringing Home The Tree	1968	Year	10.00	75.00 to 125.00
Christmas, Fisherman Sailing Home	1969	Year	10.00	12.00 to 15.00
Christmas, Nils With His Geese	1970	Year	10.00	8.00 to 15.00
Christmas, Nils In Lapland	1971	Year	13.50	10.00 to 16.00
Christmas, Dalecarlian Fiddler	1972	Year	16.00	10.00 to 16.00
Christmas*	1973	Year	16.00	16.00
Christmas	1974	Year	19.00	19.00
Father's Day, Father & Child	1971	Year	10.00	10.00 to 15.00
Father's Day, A Meal At Home	1972	Year	10.00	10.00 to 15.00
Father's Day*	1973	Year	15.00	15.00
Mother's Day, Mother & Child	1971	Year	10.00	7.00 to 15.00
Mother's Day, Shelling Peas	1972	Year	15.00	10.00 to 15.00
Mother's Day*	1973	Year	15.00	15.00

Rose Kennedy plate, see Caritas

Rosenthal Company of West Germany was founded by Philip Rosenthal, Sr., in 1880. The company made open-stock Christmas plates from 1910 through 1970. All of these molds were destroyed in 1970. Limited edition Christmas plates were initiated in 1971.

Rosenthal Plates

Annual, Tapio Wirkkala, Finland	1971	3000	100.00	100.00 to 120.00
Annual, Natale, Sapone, Italy	1972	3000	100.00	100.00 to 120.00
Christmas*	1910			45.00 to 55.00
Christmas*	1911			45.00 to 55.00
Christmas*	1912			45.00 to 55.00
Christmas*	1913			45.00 to 55.00
Christmas*	1914			45.00 to 55.00
Christmas*	1915			45.00 to 55.00
Christmas*	1916			45.00 to 55.00
Christmas*	1917			45.00 to 55.00
Christmas*	1918			45.00 to 55.00
Christmas*	1919			45.00 to 55.00
Christmas*	1920			45.00 to 55.00
Christmas*	1921			45.00 to 55.00
Christmas*	1922			45.00 to 55.00
Christmas*	1923			45.00 to 55.00
Christmas*	1924			45.00 to 55.00
Christmas*	1925			45.00 to 55.00
Christmas*	1926			45.00 to 55.00
Christmas*	1927			45.00 to 55.00
Christmas*	1928			45.00 to 55.00
Christmas*	1929			45.00 to 55.00
Christmas*	1930			45.00 to 55.00
Christmas*	1931			45.00 to 55.00
Christmas*	1932			45.00 to 55.00
Christmas*	1933			45.00 to 55.00
Christmas	1934			45.00 to 55.00
Christmas	1935			45.00 to 55.00
Christmas	1936			45.00 to 55.00
Christmas	1937			45.00 to 55.00
Christmas	1938			45.00 to 55.00
Christmas	1939			45.00 to 55.00
Christmas	1940			45.00 to 55.00
Christmas	1941			45.00 to 55.00
Christmas	1942			45.00 to 55.00
Christmas	1943			45.00 to 55.00
Christmas	1944			45.00 to 55.00
Christmas	1945			45.00 to 55.00
Christmas*	1946			45.00 to 55.00
Christmas*	1947			45.00 to 55.00
Christmas*	1948			45.00 to 55.00
Christmas*	1949			45.00 to 55.00

Rosenthal, Christmas Plate, 1969

Rosenthal, Deluxe Christmas Plate, 1972

Rosenthal, Christmas Plate, 1970

Rosenthal, Christmas Plates

1910	1911	1912
1913	1914	1915

Rosenthal, Christmas Plates

Rosenthal, Christmas Plates

1916	1917	1918
1919	1920	1921

Rosenthal, Christmas Plates

Rosenthal, Christmas Plates

1922	1923	1924

1925	1926	1927

Rosenthal, Christmas Plates

Rosenthal, Christmas Plate, 1971

Rosenthal, Christmas Plate, 1972

Royal Bavarian, Christmas Plate, 1973

Christmas*	1950			45.00 to 55.00
Christmas*	1951			45.00 to 55.00
Christmas*	1952			45.00 to 55.00
Christmas*	1953			45.00 to 55.00
Christmas*	1954			45.00 to 55.00
Christmas*	1955			45.00 to 55.00
Christmas*	1956			45.00 to 55.00
Christmas*	1957			45.00 to 55.00
Christmas*	1958			45.00 to 55.00
Christmas*	1959			45.00 to 55.00
Christmas*	1960			45.00 to 55.00
Christmas*	1961			45.00 to 55.00
Christmas*	1962			45.00 to 55.00
Christmas*	1963			45.00 to 55.00
Christmas*	1964			45.00 to 55.00
Christmas*	1965			45.00 to 55.00
Christmas	1966			45.00 to 55.00
Christmas*	1967			45.00 to 55.00
Christmas*	1968			45.00 to 55.00
Christmas*	1969			45.00 to 55.00
Christmas*	1970			45.00 to 55.00
Christmas*	1971	1500	42.00	40.00 to 55.00
Christmas*	1972	1500	50.00	50.00 to 60.00
Christmas	1973	1500	77.00	77.00
Deluxe Christmas, Winblad	1971	4000	95.00	95.00 to 120.00
Deluxe Christmas, Winblad*	1972	4000	100.00	100.00 to 120.00
Deluxe Christmas, Winblad**	1973	4000	120.00	120.00

Roskilde, see Danish Church

Royal Bavarian Plates

Christmas, The Three Wise Men*	1973	8.00	8.00

Royal Bayreuth Porcelain has been made in Germany since the late nineteenth century. Limited editions were first made in 1972. The popular Sunbonnet Babies plates, made by the factory during the early twentieth century, have been reissued in a limited edition.

Royal Bayreuth Plaques

European Songbirds, Set Of 6	2000	210.00	200.00 to 225.00

Royal Bayreuth Plates

Christmas, Carriage In The Village*	1972	4000	15.00	15.00 to 20.00
Christmas**	1973	5000	16.50	16.50
Mother's Day, Consolation*	1973	4000	16.50	16.50 to 20.00
Mother's Day, Young Americans	1974	4000	25.00	25.00
Sunbonnet Babies, Set Of 7**	1973		120.00	120.00

Royal Berlin, see KPM

Royal Canadian Mounted Police, see Bengough

Royal Copenhagen Porcelain Manufactory, Ltd., of Copenhagen, Denmark, was established in 1755. The first commemorative plate was made in 1888. Christmas plates were introduced in 1908, and the first Mother's Day plate was made in 1971. Royal Copenhagen has also produced many special commemorative plates in limited edition over the years.

Royal Copenhagen Mugs

Year, Large*	1967	Year	50.00 to 65.00
Year, Small*	1967	Year	15.00 to 30.00
Year, Large*	1968	Year	35.00 to 45.00
Year, Small*	1968	Year	15.00 to 22.00
Year, Large*	1969	Year	30.00 to 35.00
Year, Small*	1969	Year	15.00 to 18.00
Year, Large*	1970	Year	28.00 to 35.00
Year, Small*	1970	Year	12.50 to 15.00
Year, Large*	1971	Year	27.50 to 35.00
Year, Small*	1971	Year	10.00 to 14.50
Year, Large*	1972	Year	30.00 to 35.00
Year, Small*	1972	Year	10.00 to 14.50
Year, Large**	1973	Year	35.00	35.00
Year, Small**	1973	Year	14.50	14.50

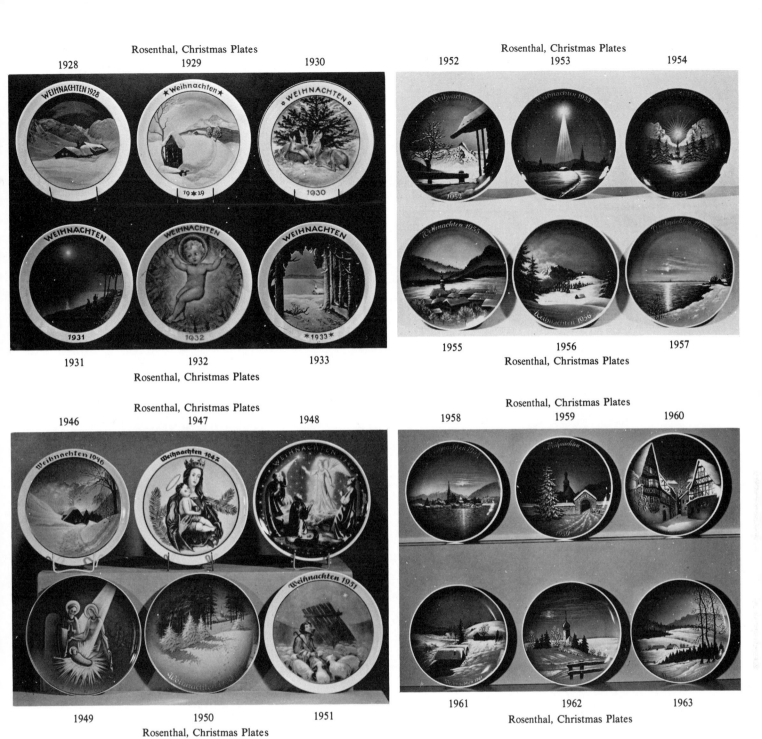

Rosenthal, Christmas Plates

1928 1929 1930

1931 1932 1933

Rosenthal, Christmas Plates

Rosenthal, Christmas Plates

1952 1953 1954

1955 1956 1957

Rosenthal, Christmas Plates

Rosenthal, Christmas Plates

1946 1947 1948

1949 1950 1951

Rosenthal, Christmas Plates

Rosenthal, Christmas Plates

1958 1959 1960

1961 1962 1963

Rosenthal, Christmas Plates

Royal Bayreuth, Christmas Plate, 1972

Royal Bayreuth, Mother's Day Plate, 1973

Royal Copenhagen, Year Mug,
1967, Large, Small

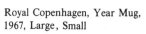

Royal Copenhagen, Year Mug,
1969, Large, Small

Royal Copenhagen, Year Mug, 1973, Large, Small

Royal Copenhagen, Year Mug,
1970, Large, Small

Royal Copenhagen, Year Mug,
1968, Large, Small

Royal Copenhagen,
Christmas Plate, 1908

Royal Copenhagen, Year Mug,
1971, Large, Small

Royal Copenhagen, Christmas Plate, 1910

Royal Copenhagen,
Christmas Plate, 1909

Royal Copenhagen, Year Mug,
1972, Large, Small

Royal Copenhagen Plates

Christmas, Madonna & Child*	1908	Year		850.00 to 1000.00
Christmas, Danish Landscape*	1909	Year		65.00 to 100.00
Christmas, Adoration Of The Magi*	1910	Year		60.00 to 95.00
Christmas, Danish Landscape, Sheaf Of Corn*	1911	Year		65.00 to 110.00
Christmas, Danish Landscape, Small	1911			2000.00
Christmas, Elderly Couple By Christmas Tree*	1912	Year		81.00 to 110.00
Christmas, Spire Of Frederik Church*	1913	Year		80.00 to 105.00
Christmas, Sparrows In Tree*	1914	Year		73.00 to 90.00
Christmas, Snow-Covered Landscape*	1915	Year		63.00 to 90.00
Christmas, Angel And Shepherd	1916	Year		48.00 to 65.00
Christmas, Tower Of Our Saviour's Church	1917	Year		48.00 to 65.00
Christmas, The Shepherds*	1918	Year		48.00 to 65.00
Christmas, Shepherds In The Field, Large*	1918	49		Unknown
Christmas, In The Park*	1919	Year		48.00 to 65.00
Christmas, Mary With Child Jesus	1920	Year		40.00 to 60.00
Christmas, Marketplace In Aabenraa*	1921	Year		36.50 to 52.50
Christmas, Three Singing Angels*	1922	Year		36.50 to 52.50
Christmas, Danish Landscape*	1923	Year		50.00 to 65.00
Christmas, Christmas Star Over The Sea	1924	Year		50.00 to 60.00
Christmas, Street Scene From Christianshavn*	1925	Year		50.00 to 60.00
Christmas, View From Christianshavn Canal	1926	Year		50.00 to 55.00
Christmas, Ship's Boy At The Tiller*	1927	Year		65.00 to 80.00
Christmas, Vicar's Family On Way To Church*	1928	Year		45.00 to 65.00
Christmas, Grundtvig Church, Copenhagen*	1929	Year		45.00 to 60.00
Christmas, Fishing Boats*	1930	Year		45.00 to 60.00
Christmas, Mother & Child*	1931	Year		47.50 to 65.00
Christmas, Frederiksberg Gardens With Statue	1932	Year		47.00 to 65.00
Christmas, Ferry & The Great Belt	1933	Year		65.00 to 80.00
Christmas, Hermitage Castle*	1934	Year		65.00 to 80.00
Christmas, Fishing Boat Off Kronborg Castle	1935	Year		75.00 to 87.00
Christmas, Roskilde Cathedral*	1936	Year		77.00 to 100.00
Christmas, Christmas Scene In Main Street*	1937	Year		85.00 to 100.00
Christmas, Round Church In Osterlars*	1938	Year		150.00 to 215.00
Christmas, Expeditionary Ship In Greenland*	1939	Year		150.00 to 215.00
Christmas, The Good Shepherd*	1940	Year		250.00 to 300.00
Christmas, Danish Village Church*	1941	Year		175.00 to 275.00
Christmas, Bell Tower Of Old Church*	1942	Year		225.00 to 300.00
Christmas, Flight Of Holy Family To Egypt*	1943	Year		300.00 to 450.00
Christmas, Typical Danish Winter Scene*	1944	Year		90.00 to 125.00
Christmas, A Peaceful Motif*	1945	Year		225.00 to 325.00
Christmas, Zealand Village Church*	1946	Year		90.00 to 120.00
Christmas, The Good Shepherd*	1947	Year		100.00 to 150.00
Christmas, Noddebo Church At Christmastime	1948	Year		65.00 to 95.00
Christmas, Church Of Our Lady*	1949	Year		75.00 to 115.00
Christmas, Boeslunde Church, Zealand*	1950	Year		70.00 to 110.00
Christmas, Christmas Angel*	1951	Year		175.00 to 220.00
Christmas, Christmas In The Forest	1952	Year		50.00 to 70.00
Christmas, Frederiksborg Castle	1953	Year		50.00 to 70.00
Christmas, Amalienborg Palace, Copengagen*	1954	Year		75.00 to 105.00
Christmas, Fano Girl*	1955	Year		100.00 to 195.00
Christmas, Rosenborg Castle*	1956	Year		65.00 to 105.00
Christmas, The Good Shepherd*	1957	Year		60.00 to 75.00
Christmas, Sunshine Over Greenland*	1958	Year		65.00 to 80.00
Christmas, Christmas Night*	1959	Year		75.00 to 100.00
Christmas, The Stag*	1960	Year		75.00 to 100.00
Christmas, Training Ship*	1961	Year		80.00 to 100.00
Christmas, Little Mermaid At Wintertime	1962	Year		120.00 to 130.00
Christmas, Hojsager Mill	1963	Year		37.50 to 50.00
Christmas, Fetching The Christmas Tree*	1964	Year		35.00 to 40.00
Christmas, Little Skaters*	1965	Year		35.00 to 45.00
Christmas, Blackbird At Christmastime	1966	Year		30.00 to 36.00
Christmas, The Royal Oak	1967	Year		22.00 to 29.00
Christmas, The Last Umiak*	1968	Year		20.00 to 25.00
Christmas, Geese On Farm	1969	Year	15.00	15.00 to 20.00
Christmas, Cat & Rose*	1970	Year	15.00	12.50 to 18.50
Christmas, Rabbit In Snow*	1971	Year	16.00	10.00 to 16.00
Christmas, Desert	1972	Year	16.00	10.00 to 16.00
Christmas, Going Home For Christmas*	1973	Year	22.00	22.00
Christmas	1974	Year	22.00	22.00

Royal Copenhagen, Christmas Plate, 1911

Royal Copenhagen, Christmas Plate, 1911,
Small

Royal Copenhagen, Christmas Plate, 1912

Royal Copenhagen, Christmas Plate, 1913

Royal Copenhagen, Christmas Plate, 1914

Royal Copenhagen, Christmas Plate, 1922

Royal Copenhagen, Christmas Plate, 1919

Royal Copenhagen, Christmas Plate, 1923

Royal Copenhagen, Christmas Plate, 1915

Royal Copenhagen, Christmas Plate, 1918

Royal Copenhagen, Christmas Plate, 1925

Royal Copenhagen, Christmas Plate, 1921

Royal Copenhagen, Christmas Plate, 1927

Royal Copenhagen, Christmas Plate, 1918,
Large

Royal Copenhagen, Christmas Plate, 1931

Royal Copenhagen, Christmas Plate, 1940

Royal Copenhagen, Christmas Plate, 1938

Royal Copenhagen, Christmas Plate, 1941

Royal Copenhagen, Christmas Plate, 1933

Royal Copenhagen, Christmas Plate, 1936

Royal Copenhagen, Christmas Plate, 1942

Royal Copenhagen, Christmas Plate, 1939

Royal Copenhagen, Christmas Plate, 1943

Royal Copenhagen, Christmas Plate, 1937

Royal Copenhagen, Christmas Plate, 1944

Royal Copenhagen, Christmas Plate, 1951

Royal Copenhagen, Christmas Plate, 1949

Royal Copenhagen, Christmas Plate, 1954

Royal Copenhagen, Christmas Plate, 1945

Royal Copenhagen, Christmas Plate, 1946

Royal Copenhagen, Christmas Plate, 1955

Royal Copenhagen, Christmas Plate, 1950

Royal Copenhagen, Christmas Plate, 1956

Royal Copenhagen, Christmas Plate, 1947

Royal Copenhagen, Christmas Plate, 1957

Royal Copenhagen, Christmas Plate, 1965

Royal Copenhagen, Christmas Plate, 1961

Royal Copenhagen, Christmas Plate, 1968

Royal Copenhagen, Christmas Plate, 1958

Royal Copenhagen, Christmas Plate, 1959

Royal Copenhagen, Christmas Plate, 1970

Royal Copenhagen, Christmas Plate, 1964

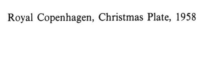

Royal Copenhagen, Christmas Plate, 1971

Royal Copenhagen, Christmas Plate, 1960

Royal Copenhagen, Christmas Plate, 1973

Royal Copenhagen, Mother's Day Plate, 1971

Royal Copenhagen, Mother's Day Plate, 1972

Royal Copenhagen, Mother's Day Plate, 1973

Mother's Day*	1971	Year	13.00	35.00 to 55.00
Mother's Day*	1972	Year	13.00	10.00 to 16.00
Mother's Day*	1973	Year	16.00	9.00 to 16.00
Mother's Day	1974	Year	15.00	15.00

Royal Copenhagen Special Commemorative Plates

Scandinavian Exhibition In Copenhagen*	1888	1200	Unknown
Golden Wedding, Christian IX & Louise*	1892	1200	Unknown
Silver Wedding, Prince Frederik & Louise*	1894	1200	Unknown
Diploma Of Honor, Women's Exhibition*	1895	13	Unknown
Women's Exhibition In Copenhagen*	1895	1200	Unknown
Wedding, Prince Carl To Princess Maud*	1896	1200	Unknown
Wedding, Princess Louise To Friederich*	1896	1200	Unknown
Art And Industry Exhibition In Stockholm*	1897	1200	Unknown
Jutland Farmers Association Exhibition*	1897	1200	Unknown
Odd Fellows Hospital, Dragon & Rapier*	1897	1500	Unknown
Odd Fellows Hospital, St.George & Dragon*	1897	100	Unknown
Stockholm Exhibition, Royal Crown Of Sweden*	1897	100	Unknown
Stockholm Exhibition, Three Wavy Lines*	1897	100	Unknown
Wedding, Princess Ingeborg To Prince Carl*	1897	1200	Unknown
Women's Building In Copenhagen*	1897	1200	Unknown
80th Birthday, Queen Louise*	1897	1200	Unknown
Art Society Of 18th November*	1898	300	Unknown
Industrial Exhibition In Naskov*	1898	500	Unknown
Odd Fellows Hospital, Icelandic Falcon*	1898	2500	Unknown
The Cenotaph On Skamlingsbanken*	1898	1200	Unknown
Tourist Association Of Denmark*	1898	800	Unknown
Wedding, Prince Christian & Alexandrine*	1898	2500	Unknown
25th Anniversary, Wine Merchants*	1898	600	Unknown
50th Anniversary, Slesvig-Holstein War*	1898	850	Unknown
80th Birthday, King Christian IX*	1898	1200	Unknown
Freemason Lodge, Armed Mason*	1899	600	Unknown
Freemason Lodge, Masonic Insignia*	1899	800	Unknown
Odd Fellows, I.O.O.F.*	1899	500	Unknown
Odd Fellows Hospital, Geyser & Dragon*	1899	200	Unknown
Odd Fellows Hospital, Icelandic Volcano*	1899	200	Unknown
Odd Fellows Hospital, Polar Bear	1899	1900	Unknown
Odd Fellows Hospital, Skogafos Waterfall*	1899	200	Unknown
25th Anniversary, Copenhagen Students*	1899	100	Unknown
25th Anniversary, Royal Theatre, Copenhagen*	1899	35	Unknown
50th Anniversary, Battle Of Fredericia*	1899	200	Unknown
50th Anniversary, Olaf Rye*	1899	1000	Unknown
Danish-Norwegian Friendship Association*	1900	50	Unknown
Danish Participation In World Exhibition*	1900	600	Unknown
Glasgow Exhibition*	1901	262	Unknown
Turn Of The Century*	1901	500	Unknown
Vordingborg Exhibition*	1901	455	Unknown
Coronation, King Edward VII Of England*	1902	1000	Unknown
May Day Festival*	1903	500	Unknown
Odd Fellows, 25th Anniversary, Hourglass*	1903	250	Unknown
St.Louis Exhibition*	1903	500	Unknown
Town Hall Of Gentofte*	1903	225	Unknown
40th Anniversary, Christian IX, Closed Edge*	1903	1200	Unknown
40th Anniversary, Christian IX, Open Edge	1903	40	Unknown
Foundation Of Journalists' Association*	1904	300	Unknown
Restoration, Ribe Cathedral*	1904	200	Unknown
25th Anniversary, Danish Teetotallers' Club*	1904	1000	Unknown
750th Anniversary, Bulow Family*	1904	700	Unknown
Copenhagen Agricultural Exhibition*	1905	454	Unknown
Fishery Association*	1905	666	Unknown
Odd Fellows Hospital, Frigate*	1905	300	Unknown
100th Anniversary, Hans Christian Andersen*	1905	800	Unknown
Accession To Throne, King Frederik VIII*	1906	1500	Unknown
Completion Of Frescoes, Viborg Cathedral*	1906	243	Unknown
Coronation, Haakon VII & Maud*	1906	1500	Unknown
Danish Virgin Islands' Church Fund*	1906	300	Unknown
Danish Virgin Islands' Nursing Home*	1906	300	Unknown
Freemason Lodge, 50th Anniversary*	1906	800	Unknown
King Christian IX, Commemorative*	1906	1500	Unknown
40th Anniversary Danish Commercial Travel*	1906	1000	Unknown
Centenary, Fire Of Koldinghus Castle*	1907	600	Unknown

Royal Copenhagen,
Scandinavian Exhibition In Copenhagen,
1888

Royal Copenhagen, Wedding,
Princess Louise To Friederich, 1896

Royal Copenhagen,
Women's Exhibition In Copenhagen, 1895

Royal Copenhagen,
Art And Industry Exhibition In Stockholm,
1897

Royal Copenhagen,
Golden Wedding,
Christian IX & Louise, 1892

Royal Copenhagen,
Silver Wedding,
Prince Frederik & Louise, 1894

Royal Copenhagen,
Jutland Farmers Association Exhibition,
1897

Royal Copenhagen, Wedding,
Prince Carl To Princess Maud, 1896

Royal Copenhagen,
Diploma Of Honor,
Women's Exhibition, 1895

Royal Copenhagen,
Odd Fellows Hospital,
Dragon & Rapier, 1897

Royal Copenhagen, Odd Fellows Hospital,
St.George & Dragon, 1897

Royal Copenhagen,
Art Society Of 18th November, 1898

Royal Copenhagen,
Women's Building In Copenhagen, 1897

Royal Copenhagen,
Industrial Exhibition In Naskov, 1898

Royal Copenhagen, Stockholm Exhibition,
Royal Crown Of Sweden, 1897

Royal Copenhagen, Stockholm Exhibition,
Three Wavy Lines, 1897

Royal Copenhagen,
Odd Fellows Hospital,
Icelandic Falcon, 1898

Royal Copenhagen,
80th Birthday, Queen Louise, 1897

Royal Copenhagen,
The Cenotaph On Skamlingsbanken,
1898

Royal Copenhagen, Wedding,
Princess Ingeborg To Prince Carl,
1897

Cybis, Unicorn

Royal Worcester, Doris Lindner,
Prince's Grace & Foal

Royal Worcester, Dorothy Doughty, Redstarts & Gorse

Royal Worcester, Dorothy Doughty, Wrens & Burnet Rose

Royal Worcester, Dorothy Doughty, Gray Wagtail

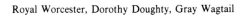

Royal Worcester, Ronald Van Ruyckevelt,
Rainbow Parrot Fish

Royal Worcester,
Ronald Van Ruyckevelt, Felicity

Royal Worcester,
Ronald Van Ruyckevelt, Elaine

Royal Worcester, Ronald Van Ruyckevelt,
Green-Winged Teal

Royal Worcester, Ronald Van Ruyckevelt,
Charlotte & Jane

Royal Worcester, Doris Lindner, Charolais Bull

Royal Worcester, Ronald Van Ruyckevelt, Dolphin

Moussalli, Tufted Titmouse

Moussalli, Redbreasted Grosbeak

Moussalli, Indigo Bunting

Moussalli, Say's Phoebe

Moussalli, Snow Bunting

Royal Worcester, Ronald Van Ruyckevelt, Languedoc

Moussalli, Black-Capped Chickadee

Burgues, White-Breasted Nuthatches, Male & Female

Burgues, Veiltail Goldfish

Burgues, King Penguins

Burgues, Bighorn Sheep

Burgues, Daffodil Manco

Burgues, Ruby-Throated Hummingbird

Burgues, Chipmunk With Fly Amanita

Cybis, Shoshone, Sacajawea

Cybis, Autumn Dogwood With Chickadees

Cybis, Clematis With House Wren

Cybis, Blackfeet, Beaverhead, Medicine Man

Cybis, Carousel Horse

Royal Doulton, Christmas Plate, 1973

Royal Doulton, Prince Charles Bust

Granget, Woodcarving, Eagle

Royal Doulton, Cello   Royal Doulton, Virginals   St. Louis, Red Flower Faceted

St.Louis, Pinwheel, Blue & White Swirl   St.Louis, Pinwheel, 5-Color Swirl

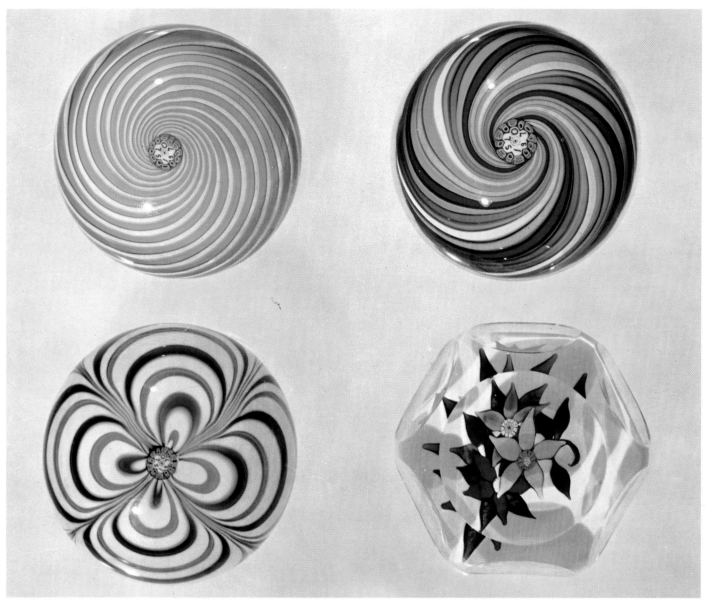

St.Louis, Marbrie, Blue, Yellow, & White   St.Louis, Flat Bouquet On Opaque White Ground

Cristal d'Albret, Paul Revere, Overlay   Cristal d'Albret, Leonardo da Vinci, Overlay

Noritake, Mother's Day Cup, 1974   Noritake, Father's Day Mug, 1974   Noritake, Christmas Bell, 1974

Noritake, Valentine's Day Heart, 1974   Noritake, Easter Egg, 1974   Noritake, Mother's Day Ornament, 1974,
Doe & Fawn

Cristal d'Albret, John & Jackie Kennedy Overlay

Royal Crown Derby,
British Birds Cup & Saucer, Dipper

Royal Copenhagen,
Tourist Association Of Denmark, 1898

Royal Copenhagen, Freemason Lodge,
Masonic Insignia, 1899

Royal Copenhagen, 80th Birthday,
King Christian IX, 1898

Royal Copenhagen, Odd Fellows,
I.O.O.F., 1899

Royal Copenhagen, Wedding,
Prince Christian & Alexandrine, 1898

Royal Copenhagen, 25th Anniversary,
Wine Merchants, 1898

Royal Copenhagen, Odd Fellows Hospital,
Geyser & Dragon, 1899

Royal Copenhagen, Freemason Lodge,
Armed Mason, 1899

Royal Copenhagen, Odd Fellows Hospital,
Icelandic Volcano, 1899

Royal Copenhagen, 50th Anniversary,
Slesvig-Holstein War, 1898

Royal Copenhagen,
Odd Fellows Hospital,
Skogafos Waterfall, 1899

Royal Copenhagen,
Danish Participation In World Exhibition,
1900

Royal Copenhagen, 50th Anniversary,
Olaf Rye, 1899

Royal Copenhagen,
Glasgow Exhibition, 1901

Royal Copenhagen, 25th Anniversary,
Copenhagen Students, 1899

Royal Copenhagen, 25th Anniversary,
Royal Theatre, Copenhagen, 1899

Royal Copenhagen,
Turn Of The Century, 1901

Royal Copenhagen,
Danish-Norwegian Friendship Association,
1900

Royal Copenhagen,
Vordingborg Exhibition, 1901

Royal Copenhagen, 50th Anniversary,
Battle Of Fredericia, 1899

Royal Copenhagen, Coronation,
King Edward VII Of England, 1902

Royal Copenhagen,
Foundation Of Journalists' Association,
1904

Royal Copenhagen,
Town Hall Of Gentofte, 1903

Royal Copenhagen, Restoration,
Ribe Cathedral, 1904

Royal Copenhagen,
May Day Festival, 1903

Royal Copenhagen, Odd Fellows,
25th Anniversary, Hourglass, 1903

Royal Copenhagen, 25th Anniversary,
Danish Teetotallers' Club, 1904

Royal Copenhagen, 40th Anniversary,
Christian IX, Open Edge, 1903

Royal Copenhagen, 750th Anniversary,
Bulow Family, 1904

Royal Copenhagen,
St.Louis Exhibition, 1903

Royal Copenhagen,
Copenhagen Agricultural Exhibition,
1905

Royal Copenhagen, Coronation,
Haakon VII & Maud, 1906

Royal Copenhagen, Accession To Throne,
King Frederik VIII, 1906

Royal Copenhagen,
Danish Virgin Islands' Church Fund,
1906

Royal Copenhagen,
Fishery Association, 1905

Royal Copenhagen,
Odd Fellows Hospital,
Frigate, 1905

Royal Copenhagen,
Danish Virgin Islands' Nursing Home,
1906

Royal Copenhagen, Completion Of Frescoes,
Viborg Cathedral, 1906

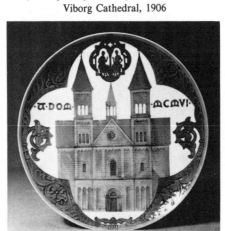

Royal Copenhagen, Freemason Lodge,
50th Anniversary, 1906

Royal Copenhagen, 100th Anniversary,
Hans Christian Andersen, 1905

Royal Copenhagen, King Christian IX,
Commemorative, 1906

Royal Copenhagen,
Hotel And Restaurant Association,
1907

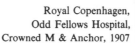

Royal Copenhagen,
Danish Virgin Islands' Day Nursery, 1907

Royal Copenhagen,
Odd Fellows Hospital,
Crowned M & Anchor, 1907

Royal Copenhagen,
40th Anniversary Danish Commercial Travel,
1906

Royal Copenhagen, Centenary,
Fire Of Koldinghus Castle, 1907

Royal Copenhagen,
Philatelist Club Stamp Exhibition,
1907

Royal Copenhagen,
Fano Commemorative, 1907

Royal Copenhagen,
Saint Canute Cathedral,
Odense, 1907

Royal Copenhagen,
Danish Virgin Islands' Church Fund,
Cross, 1907

Royal Copenhagen, 10th Anniversary,
Aarhus Commercial Travel, 1907

Royal Copenhagen, 30th Anniversary,
Red Cross Society, 1907

Royal Copenhagen, 50th Anniversary,
Agricultural Show, 1907

Royal Copenhagen, 250th Anniversary,
Battalion, 1907

Danish Virgin Islands' Church Fund, Cross*	1907	250	Unknown
Danish Virgin Islands' Day Nursery*	1907	36	Unknown
Fano Commemorative *	1907	215	Unknown
Hotel And Restaurant Association*	1907	372	Unknown
Odd Fellows Hospital, Crowned M & Anchor*	1907	430	Unknown
Philatelist Club Stamp Exhibition*	1907	457	Unknown
Saint Canute Cathedral, Odense*	1907	212	Unknown
10th Anniversary, Aarhus Commercial Travel*	1907	300	Unknown
30th Anniversary Red Cross Society*	1907	300	Unknown
50th Anniversary, Agricultural Show*	1907	208	Unknown
250th Anniversary, Battalion*	1907	650	Unknown
250th Anniversary, Royal Lifeguard Regiment*	1907	825	Unknown
Freemason Lodge, St.Clemens*	1908	331	Unknown
Freemason Lodge, St.Clemens, Lamb On Rock*	1908	29	Unknown
Journalists' Association, Ballet Dancer*	1908	250	Unknown
American Exhibition In Aarhus*	1909	396	Unknown
Congress For Raw Material Testing*	1909	25	Unknown
Danish Expedition To Greenland, Dogsleds*	1909	341	Unknown
Danish Expedition To Greenland, Eskimo*	1909	315	Unknown
Danish Expedition To Greenland, Two Men*	1909	5	Unknown
Danish Expedition To Northeast Greenland*	1909	642	Unknown
Danish Relief Mission To Messina*	1909	1107	Unknown
Freemason Lodge, St.Andrew*	1909	127	Unknown
Freemason Lodge, St.Andrew, Oval*	1909	28	Unknown
Mutual Aid Society Of Maribo County*	1909	238	Unknown
National Exhibition, Aarhus*	1909	1460	Unknown
Preservation Of Frigate Jylland, Large*	1909	18	Unknown
Preservation Of Frigate Jylland, Small*	1909	496	Unknown
Princess Marie Commemorative*	1909	2756	Unknown
Wedding, Prince Harald & Helena*	1909	1653	Unknown
Zoological Garden, Copenhagen*	1909	392	Unknown
Danish Women's Club, Defense Of Denmark*	1910	2423	Unknown
First Flight From Copenhagen To Malmo*	1910	251	Unknown
Welfare, Duchess Of Hessen*	1910	480	Unknown
West Indian Church And Kindergarten Fund*	1910	251	Unknown
Bishop Thomas Skat Rordam Commemorative*	1911	205	Unknown
Carlsberg Research Laboratories*	1911	200	Unknown
Castle Ruin Lindos On Rhodos Island*	1911	143	Unknown
Centenary, Carlsberg Brewery*	1911	575	Unknown
Coronation, King George V Of England*	1911	1936	75.00
Danish Commercial Travelers' Building	1911	812	Unknown
Granary Of Carlsberg	1911	135	Unknown
Neptune Fountain, Frederiksborg Castle	1911	158	Unknown
Palmhouse, Botanical Gardens In Copenhagen	1911	137	Unknown
Peristyle At Carlsberg	1911	161	Unknown
Racing Boat Club, Copenhagen	1911	174	Unknown
Restoration Of Frederiksborg Castle	1911	194	Unknown
Royal Danish Society Of Sciences & Letters	1911	125	Unknown
200th Anniversary Danish Postal Service	1911	492	Unknown
1000th Anniversary, Conquest Of Normandy	1911	131	Unknown
Castle Of Kalmar, Sweden	1912	125	Unknown
Copenhagen Fishery Exhibition*	1912	291	Unknown
Copenhagen Rifle Corps*	1912	375	Unknown
Coronation, King Christian X & Alexandrine*	1912	2179	100.00
Danish Virgin Islands' Charity*	1912	424	Unknown
Danish Women's Club, Defense Of Denmark*	1912	1677	Unknown
Granting Of Municipal Charter, Herning*	1912	285	Unknown
King Frederik VIII Commemoration*	1912	1975	Unknown
Saint Canute Cathedral, Swans*	1912	490	Unknown
Scene From The Beach At The Skaw*	1912	139	Unknown
50th Anniversary Old People's Home*	1912	399	Unknown
150th Anniversary Royal Hussar Regiment*	1912	359	Unknown
Cathedral Of Our Lady, Copenhagen*	1913	163	Unknown
25th Anniversary, Danish Tourist Association*	1913	573	Unknown
70th Anniversary, Tivoli Gardens*	1913	626	Unknown
500th Anniversary, Landskrona, Sweden*	1913	120	Unknown
Baltic Exhibition*	1914	265	Unknown
Charity, Queen's Christmas Fund*	1914	599	Unknown
Scene Of Frankfurt Am Main*	1914	1107	Unknown
50th Anniversary, Battle Of Dybbol*	1914	2814	Unknown

Royal Copenhagen, 250th Anniversary,
Royal Lifeguard Regiment, 1907

Royal Copenhagen,
Danish Expedition To Greenland,
Dogsleds, 1909

Royal Copenhagen,
American Exhibition In Aarhus, 1909

Royal Copenhagen,
Danish Expedition To Greenland,
Eskimo, 1909

Royal Copenhagen,
Freemason Lodge, St.Clemens, 1908

Royal Copenhagen,
Freemason Lodge, St.Clemens,
Lamb On Rock, 1908

Royal Copenhagen, Danish Expedition
To Northeast Greenland, 1909

Royal Copenhagen,
Congress For Raw Material Testing, 1909

Royal Copenhagen,
Danish Expedition To Greenland,
Two Men, 1909

Royal Copenhagen,
Journalists' Association,
Ballet Dancer, 1908

Royal Copenhagen,
Danish Relief Mission To Messina,
1909

Royal Copenhagen,
Preservation Of Frigate Jylland,
Small, 1909

Royal Copenhagen, Freemason Lodge,
St.Andrew, Oval, 1909

Royal Copenhagen,
Princess Marie Commemorative, 1909

Royal Copenhagen, Freemason Lodge,
St.Andrew, 1909

Royal Copenhagen,
Mutual Aid Society Of Maribo County,
1909

Royal Copenhagen, Wedding,
Prince Harald & Helena, 1909

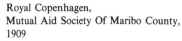

Royal Copenhagen,
Preservation Of Frigate Jylland,
Large, 1909

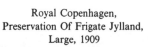

Royal Copenhagen, Zoological Garden,
Copenhagen, 1909

Royal Copenhagen,
National Exhibition, Aarhus, 1909

Royal Copenhagen,
Danish Women's Club,
Defense Of Denmark, 1910

Royal Copenhagen,
Bishop Thomas Skat Rordam
Commemorative, 1911

Royal Copenhagen, Carlsberg Brewery, 1911

Royal Copenhagen, Coronation,
King George V Of England,
1911

Royal Copenhagen, First Flight
From Copenhagen To Malmo,
1910

Royal Copenhagen, Welfare,
Duchess Of Hessen, 1910

Royal Copenhagen,
Danish Commercial Travelers' Building,
1911

Royal Copenhagen,
Castle Ruin Lindos On Rhodos Island,
1911

Royal Copenhagen,
Carlsberg Research Laboratories, 1911

Royal Copenhagen, West Indian Church
And Kindergarten Fund, 1910

Royal Copenhagen,
Copenhagen Fishery Exhibition, 1912

Royal Copenhagen,
King Frederik VIII Commemoration,
1912

Royal Copenhagen, Danish Women's Club,
Defense Of Denmark, 1912

Royal Copenhagen,
Saint Canute Cathedral, Swans, 1912

Royal Copenhagen,
Copenhagen Rifle Corps, 1912

Royal Copenhagen,
Coronation, King Christian X & Alexandrine,
1912

Royal Copenhagen,
Scene From The Beach At The Skaw,
1912

Royal Copenhagen,
Granting Of Municipal Charter, Herning, 1912

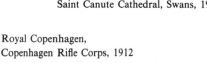

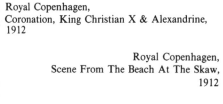

Royal Copenhagen,
50th Anniversary Old People's Home,
1912

Royal Copenhagen,
Danish Virgin Islands' Charity, 1912

Royal Copenhagen,
150th Anniversary Royal Hussar Regiment,
1912

Royal Copenhagen, Charity,
Queen's Christmas Fund, 1914

Royal Copenhagen, 500th Anniversary,
Landskrona, Sweden, 1913

Royal Copenhagen,
Scene Of Frankfurt Am Main, 1914

Royal Copenhagen,
Cathedral Of Our Lady,
Copenhagen, 1913

Royal Copenhagen, 25th Anniversary,
Danish Tourist Association, 1913

Royal Copenhagen, 50th Anniversary,
Battle Of Dybbol, 1914

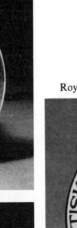

Royal Copenhagen, Baltic Exhibition, 1914

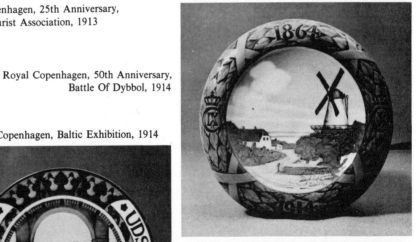

Royal Copenhagen, 50th Anniversary,
Victory At Helgoland, 1914

Royal Copenhagen, 70th Anniversary,
Tivoli Gardens, 1913

Royal Copenhagen, 70th Birthday,
Queen Alexandra Of England, 1914

Royal Copenhagen, Charity,
World War I, St.George & Dragon, 1915

Royal Copenhagen,
Meeting Of Scandinavian Kings In Malmo, 1915

Royal Copenhagen, San Francisco Exhibition, 1915

50th Anniversary, Victory At Helgoland*	1914	1761		Unknown
70th Birthday, Queen Alexandra Of England*	1914	929		Unknown
Charity, World War I, St.George & Dragon*	1915	2123		Unknown
Meeting Of Scandinavian Kings In Malmo*	1915	3610		Unknown
San Francisco Exhibition*	1915	557		Unknown
San Francisco Exhibition, California*	1915	179		Unknown
San Francisco Exhibition, Landscape*	1915	1197		Unknown
25th Anniversary, Haand I Haand Insurance*	1915	421		Unknown
100th Anniversary, Army Cadet Academy*	1915	683		Unknown
Denmark Association, Landscape*	1916	1044		Unknown
Odd Fellows, Good Samaritan*	1916	890		Unknown
Actors' Association, Olaf Poulsen*	1917	765		Unknown
Coast Artillery Association, Fortress*	1917	511		Unknown
Danish Commercial Travelers, Zealand*	1917	174		Unknown
Odd Fellows, Men Greeting Each Other*	1917	587		Unknown
Red Cross Society, Denmark, Nurse*	1917	360		Unknown
70th Birthday, Empress Dagmar Of Russia*	1917	2359		Unknown
Corporation Of Publicans, Copenhagen*	1918	600		Unknown
Founding Of Mercantile Navy Museum, Kronborg*	1918	1435		Unknown
Odd Fellows Foundling Home, Moses*	1918	1325		Unknown
Odd Fellows, 25th Anniversary Roskilde Lodge*	1918	352		Unknown
Odd Fellows, 40th Anniversary*	1918	1570		Unknown
40th Anniversary, Army Supply Corps*	1918	603		Unknown
50th Anniversary, City Of Esbjerg	1918	417		Unknown
100th Anniversary, Birth Of Christian IX*	1918	3063		Unknown
Odd Fellows, Centenary, Blacksmith*	1919	1500		Unknown
Peace Plate*	1919	3488		Unknown
Reunification With Slesvig, Landscape*	1919	5054		Unknown
Reunification With Slesvig, Queen Thyra*	1919	4411		Unknown
40th Anniversary, Danish Teetotallers' Club*	1919	157		Unknown
Memorial, Scandinavian Soldiers, World War I*	1920	802		Unknown
Odd Fellows, 25th Anniversary Ansgar Lodge*	1920	592		Unknown
35th Anniversary, Aarhus Fire Brigade*	1920	367		Unknown
50th Birthday, King Christian X*	1920	2601		Unknown
100th Anniversary, Copenhagen Students' Club*	1920	1229		Unknown
Silver Wedding, Haakon VII & Maud*	1921	606		Unknown
Wedding, Princess Margrethe & Rene*	1921	1124		Unknown
Charity, Home For Children, Bethlehem*	1922	866		Unknown
Civic Association Of Frederiksberg*	1922	634		Unknown
Freemason Lodge, St.John, Iceland, Harbor*	1922	300		Unknown
200th Anniversary, Danish Theatre*	1922	577		Unknown
25th Anniversary, Portland Cement Works*	1923	368		Unknown
40th Anniversary, Home For Children*	1923	397		Unknown
Odd Fellows, 25th Anniversary, Lighthouse*	1924	337		Unknown
First Flight, Copenhagen To Tokyo*	1926	212		Unknown
Frigate Jylland*	1926	1903		Unknown
25th Anniversary, Royal Danish Auto Club*	1926	670		Unknown
50th Anniversary, Artisans' Guild, Hjorring*	1926	443		Unknown
600th Anniversary, Municipal Charter, Skive*	1926	617		Unknown
200th Anniversary, Nibe's Municipal Charter	1927	114		Unknown
B & W Shipbuilding Company, Copenhagen*	1928	158		Unknown
Christiansborg Castle, Copenhagen*	1928	121		Unknown
Prince Valdemar & Marie's Benevolent Fund*	1928	232		Unknown
50th Anniversary, Botanical Gardens*	1928	1214		Unknown
20th Anniversary, Copenhagen Rifle Corps*	1929	169		Unknown
150th Anniversary, Royal Copenhagen*	1929	216		Unknown
150th Anniversary, Royal Copenhagen, Seascape*	1929	1815		Unknown
Freemasons Lodge, Copenhagen*	1930	324		Unknown
10th Anniversary, Reunification Of Slesvig*	1930	1175		Unknown
50th Anniversary, Order Of Good Templar*	1930	304		Unknown
Silver Wedding, Frederik IX & Ingrid*	1960			Unknown
200th Anniversary, Royal Hussar	1962		10.00	40.00 to 55.00
Virgin Islands Commemorative	1967		12.00	25.00 to 35.00
Frankfurt Am Main	1968			25.00 to 35.00
150th Anniversary, City Of Frederikshavn*	1968			Unknown
Apollo 11	1969		15.00	20.00 to 30.00
Danish Flag*	1969			20.00 to 30.00
Mill Dybbol	1970			20.00 to 25.00
King Frederik IX	1972		22.00	20.00 to 22.00
Olympics	1972		25.00	25.00 to 30.00

Royal Copenhagen, 100th Anniversary,
Army Cadet Academy, 1915

Royal Copenhagen, Actors' Association,
Olaf Poulsen, 1917

Royal Copenhagen,
Denmark Association, Landscape, 1916

Royal Copenhagen,
Coast Artillery Association, Fortress,
1917

Royal Copenhagen,
San Francisco Exhibition, Landscape,
1915

Royal Copenhagen, 25th Anniversary,
Haand I Haand Insurance, 1915

Royal Copenhagen,
Danish Commercial Travelers,
Zealand, 1917

Royal Copenhagen, Odd Fellows,
Good Samaritan, 1916

Royal Copenhagen, Odd Fellows,
Men Greeting Each Other, 1917

Royal Copenhagen,
San Francisco Exhibition, California, 1915

Royal Copenhagen, Red Cross Society,
Denmark, Nurse, 1917

Royal Copenhagen, 40th Anniversary,
Army Supply Corps, 1918

Royal Copenhagen,
Odd Fellows Foundling Home, Moses, 1918

Royal Copenhagen, 100th Anniversary,
Birth Of Christian IX, 1918

Royal Copenhagen, 70th Birthday,
Empress Dagmar Of Russia, 1917

Royal Copenhagen,
Founding Of Mercantile Navy Museum,
Kronborg, 1918

Royal Copenhagen, Odd Fellows,
25th Anniversary Roskilde Lodge, 1918

Royal Copenhagen, Odd Fellows,
40th Anniversary, 1918

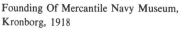

Royal Copenhagen, Odd Fellows,
Centenary, Blacksmith, 1919

Royal Copenhagen,
Corporation Of Publicans,
Copenhagen, 1918

Royal Copenhagen,
Peace Plate, 1919

Royal Copenhagen, 35th Anniversary,
Aarhus Fire Brigade, 1920

Royal Copenhagen, Memorial,
Scandianavian Soldiers,
World War I, 1920

Royal Copenhagen, 50th Birthday,
King Christian X, 1920

Royal Copenhagen,
Reunification With Slesvig,
Landscape, 1919

Royal Copenhagen, 40th Anniversary,
Danish Teetotallers' Club, 1919

Royal Copenhagen, 100th Anniversary,
Copenhagen Students' Club, 1920

Royal Copenhagen, Odd Fellows,
25th Anniversary Ansgar Lodge, 1920

Royal Copenhagen, Silver Wedding,
Haakon VII & Maud, 1921

Royal Copenhagen,
Reunification With Slesvig,
Queen Thyra, 1919

Royal Copenhagen,
Wedding Princess Margrethe & Rene,
1921

Royal Copenhagen, 40th Anniversary,
Home For Children, 1923

Royal Copenhagen, 200th Anniversary,
Danish Theatre, 1922

Royal Copenhagen, 25th Anniversary,
Lighthouse, 1924

Royal Copenhagen, Charity,
Home For Children, Bethlehem, 1922

Royal Copenhagen,
Civic Association Of Frederiksberg,
1922

Royal Copenhagen, First Flight,
Copenhagen To Tokyo, 1926

Royal Copenhagen, 25th Anniversary,
Portland Cement Works, 1923

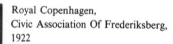

Royal Copenhagen,
Frigate Jylland, 1926

Royal Copenhagen, Freemason Lodge,
St.John, Iceland, Harbor, 1922

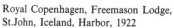

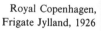

Royal Copenhagen, 50th Anniversary,
Artisans' Guild, Hjorring, 1926

Royal Copenhagen, 50th Anniversary,
Botanical Gardens, 1928

Royal Copenhagen,
B & W Shipbuilding Company,
Copenhagen, 1928

Royal Copenhagen, 25th Anniversary,
Royal Danish Auto Club, 1926

Royal Copenhagen,
Christiansborg Castle, Copenhagen, 1928

Royal Copenhagen, 600th Anniversary,
Municipal Charter, Skive, 1926

Royal Copenhagen, 20th Anniversary,
Copenhagen Rifle Corps, 1929

Royal Copenhagen,
Prince Valdemar & Marie's
Benevolent Fund, 1928

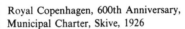

Royal Copenhagen, 150th Anniversary,
Royal Copenhagen, 1929

Royal Copenhagen, 200th Anniversary,
Nibe's Municipal Charter, 1927

Royal Copenhagen, 150th Anniversary,
Royal Copenhagen, Seascape, 1929

Royal Copenhagen, Silver Wedding,
Frederik IX & Ingrid, 1960

Royal Copenhagen, Freemasons' Lodge,
Copenhagen, 1930

Royal Copenhagen, 50th Anniversary,
Order Of Good Templar, 1930

Royal Copenhagen, 150th Anniversary,
City Of Frederikshavn, 1968

Royal Copenhagen, 10th Anniversary,
Reunification Of Slesvig, 1930

Royal Copenhagen, Dannebrog,
Danish Flag, 1969

Royal Crown Derby of England was established as the Derby factory in 1750. The name Royal Crown Derby was used after 1890. Current limited editons were introduced in 1969.

See listing for Royal Crown Derby in Figurine Section

Royal Crown Derby,
Investiture Of The Prince Of Wales Bell, 1969

Royal Crown Derby Bells

Investiture Of The Prince Of Wales*	1969	500	45.00	45.00

Royal Crown Derby Cup & Saucers

British Birds, Common Sandpiper	1972	50	150.00	150.00
British Birds, Dipper**	1972	50	150.00	150.00
British Birds, Lapwing	1972	50	150.00	150.00
British Birds, Mallard	1972	50	150.00	150.00
British Birds, Oystercatcher	1972	50	150.00	150.00
British Birds, Tufted Duck	1972	50	150.00	150.00

Royal Crown Derby Dessert Plates

Derbyshire Landscapes, Beeley Brook	1972	50	225.00	225.00
Derbyshire Landscapes, Dove Holes	1972	50	225.00	225.00
Derbyshire Landscapes, Dovedale	1972	50	225.00	225.00
Derbyshire Landscapes, Edale Head	1972	50	225.00	225.00
Derbyshire Landscapes, Edenser	1972	50	225.00	225.00
Derbyshire Landscapes, Haddon Hall	1972	50	225.00	225.00
Derbyshire Landscapes, Lathkil Dale	1972	50	225.00	225.00
Derbyshire Landscapes, Milldale	1972	50	225.00	225.00
Derbyshire Landscapes, Nether Bridge	1972	50	225.00	225.00
Derbyshire Landscapes, Stanton Moor	1972	50	225.00	225.00
Derbyshire Landscapes, Stoney Middleton	1972	50	225.00	225.00
Derbyshire Landscapes, Wolfscote Dale**	1972	50	225.00	225.00

Royal Crown Derby Vases

Kendleston Vase	1973	125	290.00	290.00

Royal Danish, Christmas Bell, 1973

Royal Danish Bells

Christmas*	1973		8.00	8.00 to 10.00

Royal Delft, Christmas Plate, 1973
10 Inch   7 Inch

Royal Delft of Holland, also known as De Porceleyne Fles, has been making delftware for over 300 years. Christmas plates were introduced in 1915. No plates were made between the years 1942 and 1954. Contemporary limited editions were started in 1968.

Royal Delft,
Ambassador Plate, 1973

Royal Delft Mugs

Ambassador*	1973	4500	45.00	45.00

Royal Delft Plates

Ambassador*	1973	4500	75.00	75.00
Apollo 11				15.00 to 17.50
Christmas	1915	Year		60.00 to 70.00
Christmas	1916	Year		55.00 to 60.00
Christmas	1917	Year		55.00 to 60.00
Christmas	1918	Year		55.00 to 60.00
Christmas	1919	Year		55.00 to 6.00
Christmas	1920	Year		55.00 to 65.00
Christmas	1921	Year		55.00 to 65.00
Christmas	1922	Year		55.00 to 65.00
Christmas	1923	Year		55.00 to 65.00
Christmas	1924	Year		55.00 to 65.00
Christmas	1925	Year		55.00 to 65.00
Christmas	1926	Year		55.00 to 65.00
Christmas	1927	Year		55.00 to 65.00
Christmas	1928	Year		55.00 to 65.00
Christmas	1929	Year		55.00 to 65.00
Christmas	1930	Year		60.00 to 70.00
Christmas	1931	Year		60.00 to 70.00
Christmas	1932	Year		60.00 to 70.00
Christmas	1933	Year		55.00 to 65.00
Christmas	1934	Year		55.00 to 65.00
Christmas	1935	Year		55.00 to 65.00
Christmas	1936	Year		55.00 to 65.00
Christmas	1937	Year		55.00 to 65.00
Christmas	1938	Year		55.00 to 65.00
Christmas	1939	Year		55.00 to 65.00
Christmas	1940	Year		60.00 to 70.00

Royal Delft,
Ambassador Mug, 1973

Royal Delft, Easter Plate, 1973

Royal Delft, Father's Day Plate, 1973

Royal Delft, Mother's Day Plate, 1973

Royal Delft, Valentine's Day Plate, 1973

Christmas	1941	Year		70.00 to 75.00
Christmas	1955	Year		70.00 to 80.00
Christmas	1956	Year		70.00 to 75.00
Christmas	1957	Year		55.00 to 65.00
Christmas	1958	Year		55.00 to 65.00
Christmas	1959	Year		55.00 to 65.00
Christmas	1960	Year		55.00 to 65.00
Christmas	1961	Year		55.00 to 65.00
Christmas	1962	Year		55.00 to 65.00
Christmas	1963	Year		75.00 to 85.00
Christmas	1964	Year		55.00 to 65.00
Christmas	1965	Year		55.00 to 65.00
Christmas	1966	Year		55.00 to 65.00
Christmas	1967	Year		55.00 to 65.00
Christmas, Walmolen Mill, 7 Inch	1968	Year		25.00 to 35.00
Christmas, Schreierstoren, 10 Inch	1968	Year		40.00 to 45.00
Christmas, Mill Near Gorkum, 7 Inch	1969	Year		35.00 to 40.00
Christmas, Old Church In Dordrecht, 10 Inch	1969	Year		40.00 to 45.00
Christmas, Mill Near Haarlem, 7 Inch	1970	Year		30.00 to 40.00
Christmas, Cathedral In Veere, 10 Inch	1970	Year		48.00 to 60.00
Christmas, Towngate Of Zierkee, 7 Inch	1971	1500	40.00	30.00 to 45.00
Christmas, Canal Scene In Utrecht, 10 Inch	1971	550	60.00	50.00 to 65.0
Christmas, Towngate At Elburg, 7 Inch	1972	3500	40.00	30.00 to 40.00
Christmas, Church Of Edam, 10 Inch	1972	1500	70.00	60.00 to 70.00
Christmas, Towngate Of Amersfoort, 7 Inch*	1973	4500	50.00	50.00
Christmas, Weigh Office In Alkmaar, 10 Inch*	1973	1500	75.00	75.00
Easter, Dutch Palm Sunday Cross*	1973	3500	75.00	75.00
Father's Day, Fisherman & Son Of Volendam	1972	1500	40.00	35.00 to 50.00
Father's Day, Looking At The Zuider Zee*	1973	2000	50.00	45.00 to 50.00
Mother's Day, Mother & Daughter Of Volendam	1971		35.00	50.00 to 90.00
Mother's Day, Women Of Hindeloopen	1972	2500	40.00	30.00 to 50.00
Mother's Day, Marken Villagers*	1973	3000	50.00	50.00
Olympic	1972			35.00 to 40.00
Pilgrim Fathers	1970			20.00 to 25.00
Valentine's Day*	1973	1500	75.00	75.00

The Doulton Porcelain factory was founded in 1815. Royal Doulton is the name used on pottery made after 1902. A series of limited edition commemorative and special wares was made during the 1930s. Modern limited edition Christmas plates and mugs were first made in 1971. Royal Doulton also makes a line of limited edition porcelains.

See listing for Royal Doulton in Figurine section

Royal Doulton Plaques

Christmas, Christmas Carol	1972	13000	37.50	35.00 to 40.00
Christmas	1973		37.50	37.50

Royal Doulton Plates

Christmas, Christmas In England	1972	11000	35.00	35.00 to 40.00
Christmas	1973	15000	37.50	37.50
Christmas, Christmas In Bulgaria	1974	15000	40.00	40.00
Harlequin, LeRoy Neiman	1973	15000	50.00	50.00
Mother's Day, Colette & Child	1973	15000	40.00	40.00
Mother's Day, Sayuri & Child	1974		40.00	40.00

Royal Doulton Tankards

Christmas, Cratchit & Scrooge	1971	13000	35.00	35.00 to 45.00
Christmas, Carolers	1972	15000	37.50	37.50 to 40.00
Christmas	1973	15000	40.00	40.00

Royal Doulton Commemorative & Special Wares

Regency Coach Jug*	1931	500	250.00 to 300.00
George Washington Jug*	1932	1000	225.00 to 275.00
Captain Cook Jug*	1933	350	Unknown
Drake Jug*	1933	500	Unknown
John Peel Loving Cup	1933	500	Unknown
Shakespeare Jug*	1933	1000	250.00 to 300.00
Tower Of London Jug	1933	500	250.00 to 300.00
Apothecary Loving Cup	1934	600	Unknown
Guy Fawkes Jug	1934	600	225.00 to 275.00
Pied Piper Jug	1934	600	275.00 to 325.00
Treasure Island Jug*	1934	600	300.00

Royal Doulton, Regency Coach Jug, 1931

Royal Doulton, Drake Jug, 1933

Royal Doulton, George Washington Jug, 1932
(side views)

Royal Doulton, George Washington Jug, 1932
(front view)

Royal Doulton, Shakespeare Jug, 1933

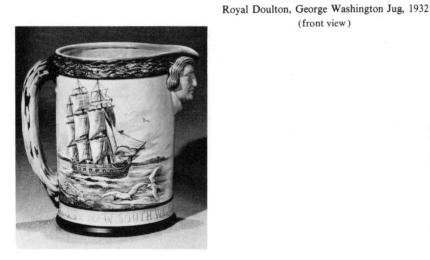

Royal Doulton, Treasure Island Jug, 1934

Royal Doulton, Captain Cook Jug, 1933

Royal Doulton, Three Musketeers Loving Cup, 1936

Royal Doulton, Dickens Jug, 1936

Royal Doulton, Elizabeth II Coronation Loving Cup, 1953

Royal Doulton,
Edward VIII Coronation Loving Cup, Small, 1937

Royal Doulton, Village Blacksmith Jug, 1936

Royal Doulton,
Edward VIII Coronation Loving Cup, Large, 1937

Royale, Easter Ornament, 1973

Royal Doulton,
George VI Coronation Loving Cup, 1937

Royal Doulton, Mayflower Loving Cup, 1970

King George & Mary Silver Wedding Loving Cup	1935	1000		Unknown
Nelson Loving Cup	1935	600		Unknown
Dickens Jug*	1936	1000		275.00 to 300.00
Three Musketeers Loving Cup*	1936	600		250.00 to 300.00
Village Blacksmith Jug*	1936	590		Unknown
Edward VIII Coronation Loving Cup, Large	1937	2000		Unknown
Edward VIII Coronation Loving Cup, Small	1937	2000		Unknown
George VI Coronation Loving Cup*	1937	2000		Unknown
Elizabeth II Coronation Loving Cup*	1953	2000		Unknown
Charles Dickens Loving Cup	1970	500	285.00	285.00
Mayflower Loving Cup*	1970	500	285.00	285.00

Royal Tettau,   Royal Tettau,
Papal Plate, 1972   Papal Plate, 1973

Royal Tettau,
Papal Plate, 1971

Royal Irish Plates

Eamon De Valera, Silver	1973	2500	175.00	175.00

Royal Limoges Plates

Christmas, Les Santons De Noel	1972	5000	25.00	20.00 to 25.00
Christmas, Three Wise Men	1973	5000	25.00	25.00

Royal Netherland Plates

Bald Eagle, Crystal*	1973	3500	75.00	75.00

Royal Princess Plates

Christmas, Three Wise Men	1973		10.00	10.00

Royal Rockwood Plates

Christmas	1970			30.00 to 60.00
Christmas	1971			20.00 to 35.00
Christmas	1972	2500		12.00 to 20.00
Father's Day	1970			20.00 to 25.00
Father's Day	1971			15.00 to 20.00
Father's Day	1972			15.00 to 25.00
Father's Day	1973		15.00	15.00

Royal Tettau was established in Germany in 1794. It is parent company to Royal Bayreuth. Limited editions were first made in 1971.

Royal Tettau Plates

Christmas, Carriage In The Village	1972		12.50	12.50 to 15.00
Papal, Pope Paul VI*	1971	5000	100.00	75.00 to 100.00
Papal, Pope John XXIII*	1972	5000	100.00	75.00 to 100.00
Papal, Pope Pius XII*	1973	5000	100.00	100.00

Royal Netherland, Bald Eagle Plate, 1973

The Royal Worcester Porcelain Factory, of Worcester, England, was founded under the name of Worcester, in 1751. The name was changed to Royal Worcester in 1862. Limited edition plates, in both pewter and porcelain, were first introduced in 1972. Limited edition porcelains have been made since the 1930s.

See listing for Royal Worcester in Figurine section

Royal Worcester Plates

Bicentennial, Boston Tea Party, Pewter*	1972	10000	45.00	30.00 to 45.00
Bicentennial, Paul Revere, Pewter*	1973	10000	45.00	45.00
Bicentennial, Incident At Concord Bridge	1974	10000	50.00	50.00
Dorothy Doughty, Redstarts & Beech*	1972	2500	150.00	195.00 to 365.00
Dorothy Doughty, Myrtle Warbler & Cherry	1973	3000	150.00	175.00 to 310.00

Royal Worcester Spoons

Annual*	1965	Year	27.50	35.00 to 45.00
Annual*	1966	Year	27.50	35.00 to 45.00
Annual*	1967	Year	27.50	35.00 to 34.00
Annual*	1968	Year	27.50	35.00 to 45.00
Annual*	1969	Year	27.50	35.00 to 45.00
Annual*	1970	Year	27.50	35.00 to 45.00
Annual*	1971	Year	27.50	35.00 to 45.00

Royal Worcester, Bicentennial Plate, 1972

Royale Ornaments

Easter Rabbit, Decorated	1972	200	85.00	85.00 to 100.00
Easter Rabbit, White	1972	2500	20.00	20.00 to 30.00
Easter Rabbit, Decorated	1973	200	85.00	85.00
Easter Rabbit, White*	1973	2000	20.00	20.00

Royale Plaques

Baltimore Orioles	1972	350	200.00	200.00 to 225.00

Royal Worcester, Bicentennial Plate, 1973

Royal Worcester, Dorothy Doughty Plate, 1972

Royal Worcester, Christmas Spoon, 1966 - 1972

Royale Worcester, Dorothy Doughty Plate, 1973

Royale, Christmas Plate, 1969

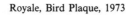

Royale, Game Plate, 1973

Royale, Christmas Plate, 1973

Royale, Bird Plaque, 1973

Royale, Mother's Day Plate, 1970

Royale, Father's Day Plate, 1974

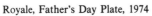

Royale, Mother's Day Plate, 1973

Scarlet Tanagers*	1973	350	200.00	200.00

Royale Plates

Apollo, Landing On The Moon	1969	2000	30.00	65.00 to 80.00
Christmas, Christmas Fair*	1969	6000	12.00	35.00 to 65.00
Christmas, Mass At Kalundborg Church	1970	10000	13.00	9.00 to 14.00
Christmas, Snow On Rooftops	1971	8000	15.00	10.00 to 16.00
Christmas, Elks In Winter	1972	8000	16.00	10.00 to 16.00
Christmas*	1973	6000	18.00	18.00
Christmas	1974	5000	22.00	22.00
Father's Day, Sailing Ship	1970	5000	13.00	10.00 to 18.00
Father's Day, Man Fishing	1971	5000	13.00	9.00 to 15.00
Father's Day, Mountain Climber	1972	5000	16.00	10.00 to 16.00
Father's Day	1973	4000	18.00	18.00
Father's Day, American Bald Eagle*	1974	2500	22.00	22.00
Game, Setters Pointing Quail	1972	500	180.00	180.00 to 220.00
Game, Fox*	1973	500	200.00	200.00
Mother's Day, Swan & Brood*	1970	6000	12.00	25.00 to 40.00
Mother's Day, Deer	1971	9000	13.00	10.00 to 15.00
Mother's Day, Rabbits	1972	9000	16.00	10.00 to 16.00
Mother's Day, Owl*	1973	6000	18.00	18.00
Mother's Day, Duck & Ducklings*	1974	5000	22.00	22.00

See listing for Royale Germania Crystal in Paperweight section

Royale Germania Crystal Goblets

Annual, Green	1972	500	160.00	160.00 to 190.00
Annual, Blue*	1973	300	180.00	180.00
Annual, Topaz*	1974	300	200.00	200.00

Royale, Mother's Day Plate, 1974

Royale Germania Crystal Plates

Annual, Orchid, Blue*	1970	600	200.00	275.00 to 400.00
Annual, Cyclamen, Red	1971	1000	200.00	150.00 to 225.00
Annual, Silver Thistle, Green	1972	1000	250.00	150.00 to 250.00
Annual, Tulip, Lilac*	1973	600	275.00	275.00
Annual, Sunflowers, Topaz*	1974	500	300.00	300.00
Mother's Day, Roses, Red	1971	250	180.00	250.00 to 375.00
Mother's Day, Elephant, Green	1972	750	180.00	160.00 to 220.00
Mother's Day, Koala Bear, Lilac*	1973	600	200.00	200.00
Mother's Day, Squirrels, Topaz*	1974	500	240.00	240.00

Russell, Charles, see Antique Trader

Ruthven Bird plates, see Hutschenreuther

Royale Germania,
Annual Goblet,
1973

Sabino Plates

Annual, King Henry IV & Maria De Medici	1970	1500		70.00 to 100.00
Annual, Milo And The Beasts	1971	1500		50.00 to 75.00
Annual	1972			80.00 to 120.00

Salvador Dali, see Daum, Lincoln Mint, Puiforcat

Santa Clara Plates

Christmas, The Christmas Message	1970	10000	12.00	12.00 to 15.00
Christmas, Three Wise Men	1971	10000	12.00	10.00 to 12.00
Christmas, Children In The Woods	1972	10000	12.00	12.00 to 15.00
Christmas	1973	2500	25.00	25.00
Mother's Day, Mother & Child	1971	10000	12.00	10.00 to 12.00
Mother's Day	1972	12000	12.00	10.00 to 12.00

Sawyer plate, see George Washington Mint

Schmid, see Berlin, Hummel, Peanuts, Walt Disney

Schumann Plates

Christmas, Snow Scene*	1971	10000	12.00	7.00 to 10.00
Christmas, Deer In Snow*	1972	15000	12.00	10.00 to 12.00
Christmas*	1973	5000	12.00	12.00
Composer, Beethoven				10.00 to 13.00
Composer, Mozart				10.00 to 13.00

Royale Germania,
Annual Goblet,
1974

Scottish Plates

Annual, Edinburgh*	1972	2500	25.00	25.00

Sebring Heritage Plates

Father's Day	1971	Year	12.50	5.00 to 12.50
Father's Day	1972	Year	12.50	5.00 to 12.50
Fourth Of July	1971	Year	12.50	5.00 to 12.50

Royale Germania, Annual Plate, 1970

Schumann, Christmas Plate, 1971

Royale Germania,
Mother's Day Plate, 1974

Schumann, Christmas Plate, 1972

Royale Germania, Annual Plate, 1973

Royale Germania, Annual Plate, 1974

Schumann, Christmas Plate, 1973

Scottish, Annual Plate, 1972

Selandia, Christmas Plate, 1972

Royale Germania, Mother's Day Plate, 1973

Mother's Day	1971	Year	12.50	5.00 to 12.50
Mother's Day	1972	Year	12.50	5.00 to 12.50

Selandia Pewter Company of Norway, makers of domestic pewter ware, introduced its first limited edition pewter plate in 1972. The first 200 plates of each series are signed by the artist.

Selandia Plates

Christmas, On The Way To Bethlehem, Signed	1972	250	100.00	100.00
Christmas, On The Way To Bethlehem, Unsigned*	1972	4750	30.00	30.00 to 35.00
Christmas, Three Wise Men, Signed	1973	200	100.00	100.00
Christmas, Three Wise Men, Unsigned*	1973	4750	35.00	35.00

Seven Seas Plates

Christmas, New World, Holy Family*	1970	3500	15.00	10.00 to 15.00
Christmas, Traditional, I Heard The Bells*	1970	4000	15.00	10.00 to 15.00
Christmas, New World, Three Wise Men*	1971	1500	15.00	10.00 to 15.00
Christmas, Traditional, Oh Tannenbaum*	1971	4000	15.00	10.00 to 15.00
Christmas, New World, And Shepherds Watched*	1972	1500	18.00	15.00 to 18.00
Christmas, Traditional, Deck The Halls*	1972	1500	18.00	15.00 to 18.00
Christmas, O Holy Night*	1973	2000	18.00	18.00
History, Landing On The Moon, No Flag	1969	2000	13.50	20.00 to 35.00
History, Landing On The Moon, With Flag*	1969	2000	13.50	10.00 to 15.00
History, Year Of Crisis*	1970	4000	15.00	15.00 to 25.00
History, First Vehicular Travel*	1971	3000	15.00	15.00 to 25.00
History, Man's Final Trip To The Moon	1972	2000	15.00	15.00 to 20.00
History, Peace*	1973	3000	15.00	15.00 to 20.00
Mother's Day, Girl Of All Nations*	1970	5000	15.00	10.00 to 15.00
Mother's Day, Sharing Confidences	1971	1400	15.00	15.00 to 20.00
Mother's Day, Scandinavian Girl*	1972	1600	15.00	15.00 to 20.00
Mother's Day, All American Girl*	1973	1500	15.00	15.00
Passion Play*	1970	2500	18.00	10.00 to 25.00

Seville Plates

Christmas, Madonna From Spain	1971		15.00 to 30.00
Christmas, Ancient Spanish Church	1972		15.00 to 25.00

Shenango China Company, of New Castle, Pennsylvania, was founded in 1905. It is presently a division of Interpace Corporation. Two series of limited edition Christmas plates were made to be given away as premiums to customers. The first was based on Dickens' Christmas Carol and was made from 1949 through 1961. No plate was made in 1951. The second series, based on Twelve Days of Christmas, was started in 1964 and will continue until 1975. The plates were free so there is no issue price information. In 1937, a series of 12 limited edition American Legion Auxiliary plates was produced to raise funds for the Indianapolis branch of the American Legion. The edition numbers of these plates are not known.

Shenango Plates

Christmas, Dickens	1949	Year	20.00 to 27.50
Christmas, Dickens	1950	Year	20.00 to 27.50
Christmas, Dickens	1952	Year	20.00 to 27.50
Christmas, Dickens	1953	Year	20.00 to 27.50
Christmas, Dickens	1954	Year	20.00 to 25.00
Christmas, Dickens	1955	Year	20.00 to 25.00
Christmas, Dickens	1956	Year	20.00 to 25.00
Christmas, Dickens	1957	Year	20.00 to 25.00
Christmas, Dickens	1958	Year	20.00 to 25.00
Christmas, Dickens	1959	Year	20.00 to 25.00
Christmas, Dickens	1960	Year	20.00 to 25.00
Christmas, Dickens	1961	Year	20.00 to 25.00
Christmas, Twelve Days	1964	Year	Unknown
Christmas, Twelve Days	1965	Year	Unknown
Christmas, Twelve Days	1966	Year	Unknown
Christmas, Twelve Days	1967	Year	Unknown
Christmas, Twelve Days	1968	Year	Unknown
Christmas, Twelve Days	1969	Year	Unknown
Christmas, Twelve Days	1970	Year	Unknown
Christmas, Twelve Days	1971	Year	Unknown
Christmas, Twelve Days	1972	Year	Unknown
Christmas, Twelve Days	1973	Year	Unknown

Selandia, Christmas Plate, 1973

Seven Seas, Christmas Plate, New World, 1970

Seven Seas, Christmas Plate, Traditional, 1970

Seven Seas, Christmas Plate, New World, 1971

Seven Seas, Christmas Plate,
Traditional, 1971

Seven Seas, History Plate, 1969

Seven Seas, Mother's Day Plate, 1971

Seven Seas, History Plate, 1970

Seven Seas, Christmas Plate,
Traditional, 1972

Seven Seas, Christmas Plate,
New World, 1972

Seven Seas, History Plate, 1971

Seven Seas, Mother's Day, 1972

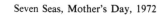

Seven Seas, History Plate, 1973

Seven Seas, Christmas Plate, 1973

Shuler, see Kurz

Silver City Plates

Christmas, Winter Scene	1969		10.00 to 20.00
Christmas, Water Mill	1970		12.50 to 17.50
Christmas, Skating Scene	1971		12.50 to 17.50
Christmas, Logging In Winter	1972		15.00 to 20.00
Christmas	1973		25.00
Independence Hall	1972	13.50	10.00 to 15.00

Seven Seas, Mother's Day Plate, 1973

See listing for Silver Creations in Figurine & Bar & Ingot sections

Silver Creations Plates

Churchillian Heritage, Proof	1972	550.00	375.00 to 550.00
Churchillian Heritage, Silver	1972	150.00	95.00 to 150.00

L. E. Smith Glass Company of Mt. Pleasant, Pennsylvania, was founded in the early 1900s. Limited edition carnival glass plates were first made in 1971. A series of pewter and silver plates is made by Wendell August Forge for the Smith Glass Company.

Smith Glass, see also Wendell August Forge

Smith Glass Plates

Coin, Morgan Silver Dollar	1971	5000	10.00	7.50 to 10.00
Kennedy, Carnival*	1971	2500	10.00	10.00 to 20.00
Lincoln, Carnival*	1971	2500	10.00	10.00 to 20.00
Jefferson Davis, Carnival	1972	5000	11.00	7.50 to 12.50
Robert E.Lee, Carnival	1972	5000	11.00	7.50 to 12.50

Seven Seas, Passion Play Plate, 1970

Southern Landmark plate, see American Commemorative Council

Spode Works, located in England's Staffordshire district, was founded in 1776 by Josiah Spode. Spode formed a partnership with William Copeland whose descendants now manage the Spode factory. Limited edition Christmas plates were introduced in 1970.

Spode Bells

Christmas, Hammersley*	1971	Year	25.00	25.00
Christmas, Hammersley*	1972	Year	25.00	25.00

Spode Loving Cups

European Community	1972	500	245.00	245.00

Spode Plates

Christmas, Partridge In A Pear Tree	1970	Year	35.00	20.00 to 35.00
Christmas, In Heaven The Angels Singing*	1971	Year	35.00	20.00 to 35.00
Christmas, We Saw 3 Ships A-Sailing*	1972	Year	35.00	20.00 to 35.00
Christmas	1973	Year	35.00	20.00 to 35.00
Christmas*	1974	Year	35.00	35.00
European Community	1973	5000	59.00	50.00 to 60.00
Imperial Plate Of Persia*	1971	10000	125.00	75.00 to 125.00
Lowestoft	1970			15.00 to 25.00
Ray Harm Birds, Set Of 12	1972		350.00	550.00 to 650.00

Smith Glass, Kennedy Plate, 1971

St.Amand, a French faience factory, was founded in 1707. Their products were introduced to the U.S.A. in 1968. St.Amand's first limited edition Annual plate was issued in 1970.

St. Amand Plates

Christmas	1970	10000	7.00	4.50 to 8.50
Christmas, Two Deer	1971	Year	7.50	4.00 to 7.50
Christmas	1972	Year	7.50	4.00 to 7.50

Smith Glass, Lincoln Plate, 1971

St. Louis Gateway Arch plate, see Stix, Baer & Fuller

Stanek Plates

Moon Landing*	1969			600.00 to 1000.00
Mayflower*	1972	60		600.00
Santa Maria*	1972	60		600.00
Eagle	1973	400	250.00	250.00

Sterling America limited editions, introduced in 1970, are made of sterling on crystal. Two Christmas plate series are made.

Sterling America Plates

Christmas, Customs, Yule Log*	1970	2500	18.00	18.00 to 25.00

Spode, Hammersley Bell, 1971

Spode, Hammersley Bell, 1972

Spode, Christmas Plate, 1972

Stanek, Moon Landing Plate, 1969

Spode, Christmas Plate, 1971

Spode, Christmas Plate, 1973, Reverse

Stanek, Mayflower Plate

Spode, Imperial Plate Of Persia, Reverse

Stanek, Santa Maria Plate

Spode, Imperial Plate Of Persia, 1971

Sterling America,
Christmas Plate, Customs, 1970

Sterling America,
Christmas Plate, Customs, 1971

Sterling America,
Christmas Plate, Customs, 1972

Sterling America,
Christmas Plate, 12 Days, 1970

Sterling America,
Christmas Plate, 12 Days, 1971

Sterling America,
Christmas Plate, 12 Days, 1972

Sterling America, Mother's Day Plate, 1971

Sterling America, Mother's Day Plate, 1973

Stromberg, Crystal State Flower Plate

Sterling America, Mother's Day Plate, 1972

Svend Jensen, Christmas Plate, 1971

Svend Jensen, Christmas Plate, 1972

Svend Jensen, Christmas Plate, 1974

Svend Jensen, Mother's Day Plate, 1971

Christmas, 12 Days, Partridge*	1970	2500	18.00	18.00 to 25.00
Christmas, Customs, Stroovland-Holland*	1971	2500	18.00	18.00 to 20.00
Christmas, 12 Days, Turtledoves*	1971	2500	18.00	16.00 to 20.00
Christmas, Customs, Norway*	1972	2500	18.00	16.00 to 20.00
Christmas, 12 Days, Three French Hens*	1972	2500	18.00	16.00 to 20.00
Christmas	1973	2500	20.00	20.00
Mother's Day*	1971	2500	18.00	18.00 to 25.00
Mother's Day*	1972	2500	18.00	18.00 to 20.00
Mother's Day*	1973	2500	20.00	20.00
Mother's Day	1974	2500	20.00	20.00

Stieff limited edition pewter plates are made by Stieff Silversmiths of Baltimore, Maryland.

Stieff Plates

Bicentennial, Declaration Of Independence	1972	10000	50.00	25.00 to 50.00

The St. Louis Gateway Arch plate was produced for Stix, Baer & Fuller, a St. Louis department store, by Reed & Barton. The plate is made of damascene silver.

Stix, Baer & Fuller Plates

St.Louis Gateway Arch	1972	1000	75.00	75.00

Stromberg Glassworks of Sweden was founded in 1876. Limited edition plates and mugs are hand blown and cut.

Stromberg Mugs

Annual, Aztec	1968			40.00 to 60.00
Annual, Moon Craft	1969			30.00 to 50.00
Annual, Jingo Ji	1970			20.00 to 30.00
Annual, Freden	1971			20.00 to 30.00
Annual, Olympiad	1972			20.00 to 30.00
Annual, Brotherhood	1973		30.00	30.00

Stromberg Plates

Crystal State Flower, Each*		250	35.00	25.00 to 40.00

Stuart Devlin, see Reco

Stumar Plates

Christmas, The Old Canal	1971			6.00 to 12.50
Christmas, Countryside	1972			7.50 to 10.00
Mother's Day, Amish Mother & Daughter	1971		8.00	8.00 to 10.00
Mother's Day, Children	1972		8.00	8.00 to 10.00
Mother's Day	1973		10.00	10.00

Stupell Plates

Mother's Day	1973		250.00	250.00

Svend Jensen of Denmark entered the limited edition field with Christmas and Mother's Day plates in 1970. The plates are limited to the year of production. Desiree Porcelain Company of Denmark produces the plates.

Svend Jensen Plates

Christmas, Hans Christian Andersen's House*	1970	20136	14.00	20.00 to 30.00
Christmas, The Little Match Girl*	1971	Year	15.00	12.00 to 17.00
Christmas, Little Mermaid*	1972	22122	16.50	12.00 to 16.50
Christmas, The Fir Tree*	1973	Year	20.00	18.00 to 22.00
Christmas, Chimney Sweep**	1974	Year	22.00	22.00
Mother's Day, A Bouquet For Mother	1970	13740	14.00	15.00 to 30.00
Mother's Day, Mother's Love*	1971	14310	15.00	12.50 to 20.00
Mother's Day, Child In Arms*	1972	11018	16.50	12.50 to 20.00
Mother's Day, Flowers For Mother*	1973	Year	20.00	18.00 to 20.00
Mother's Day, Child With Flowers**	1974	Year	22.00	22.00

Tapestry plate, see Haviland & Parlon

Texas Ranger, see WNW Mint

Tirschenreuth limited edition plates, introduced in 1969, are made by the Porzellanfabrik Tirschenreuth of Germany. The factory was founded in 1856.

Tirschenreuth Plates

Christmas, Homestead*	1969	3500	12.00	12.00 to 24.00

Christmas, Church	1970	3500	12.00	10.00 to 15.00
Christmas, Star Of Bethlehem	1971	3500	12.00	10.00 to 15.00
Christmas, Elk Silhouette	1972	3500	13.00	10.00 to 16.00
Christmas	1973		14.00	14.00

Toronto Horse Show plate, see Kaiser

Towle Silversmiths of Newburyport, Massachusetts, was established by William Moulton in 1664. Towle limited editon ornaments were first issued in 1971. Plates followed in 1972.

See listing for Towle in Figurine Section

Towle Ornaments

Christmas, Medallion	1971		10.00	10.00 to 15.00
Christmas, Medallion	1972		10.00	10.00
Christmas, Medallion	1973		10.00	10.00

Towle Plates

Christmas, Wise Men, Sterling*	1972	2500	250.00	250.00
Valentine's Day, Silver Plate, 6 1/2 In.	1972		10.00	10.00
Valentine's Day, Silver Plate, 6 1/2 In.	1973		10.00	10.00

U. S. Bicentennial Society Plates

Bicentennial, Double Eagle*	1973	5000	125.00	125.00
Inaugural	1973	1500	50.00	50.00
Patriot, John & Polly Marshall, Pair*	1973	2500	250.00	250.00
Winslow Homer, Set Of 6*	1973	2500	525.00	525.00

Ukrainian Easter eggs are designed by Ukrainian artist Ostap Kobycia. They are made of wood.

Ukrainian Eggs

Easter	1974	500	12.50	12.50

Ulmer Keramic Plates

Christmas, Peace On Earth	1971		15.00	12.50 to 17.50
Christmas, Let Us Adore Him	1972		15.00	12.00 to 15.00

Unicorn plate, see Haviland & Parlon

Val St.Lambert Cristalleries of Belgium was founded by Messieurs Kemlin and Lelievre in 1825. Limited editions were introduced in 1968.

Val St. Lambert Plates

American Heritage, Pilgrim Fathers*	1969	500	200.00	200.00
American Heritage, Paul Revere's Ride*	1970	500	200.00	200.00
American Heritage, Washington On Delaware*	1971	500	225.00	225.00
Old Masters, Rubens & Rembrandt*	1968	5000	50.00	60.00 to 80.00
Old Masters, Van Dyck & Van Gogh*	1969	5000	50.00	30.00 to 50.00
Old Masters, Da Vinci & Michelangelo	1970	5000	50.00	30.00 to 50.00
Old Masters, El Greco & Goya*	1971	5000	50.00	30.00 to 50.00
Old Masters, Reynolds & Gainsborough*	1972	5000	50.00	30.00 to 50.00
Rembrandt	1970		25.00	20.00 to 30.00

Veneto Flair plates are designed and manufactured by Vincente Tiziano in Northern Italy. Creative World is the U. S. distributor for Veneto Flair. The first limited edition faience plate was produced in 1970.

Veneto Flair, see also Carlo Monte, Creative World, Fontana, Pearl Buck

Veneto Flair Bells

Christmas	1973	1000	25.00	25.00 to 30.00

Veneto Flair Plates

Bellini Madonna	1970	500	45.00	395.00 to 500.00
Bird, Owl	1972	2000	37.50	55.00 to 85.00
Bird, Falcon	1973	2000	37.50	40.00 to 60.00
Cat, Persian	1974	2000	40.00	40.00
Christmas, Three Kings	1971	1500	35.00	125.00 to 195.00
Christmas, Three Shepherds*	1972	2000	45.00	50.00 to 75.00
Christmas, Holy Family	1973	2000	55.00	55.00
Dog, German Shepherd*	1972	2000	37.50	50.00 to 80.00
Dog, Poodle	1973	2000	37.50	40.00 to 65.00
Easter	1973	2000	50.00	65.00 to 95.00

Svend Jensen, Mother's Day Plate, 1972

Svend Jensen, Mother's Day Plate, 1973

Tirschenreuth, Christmas Plate, 1969

Towle, Christmas Plate, 1972

U.S.Bicentennial Society, Winslow Homer Plates, 1973

U.S.Bicentennial Society, Bicentennial Plate, 1973, Double Eagle

U.S.Bicentennial Society, Patriot Plates, 1973

Val St.Lambert, American Heritage Plate, 1969

Val St.Lambert, American Heritage Plate, 1970

Val St.Lambert, Old Masters Plates, 1968

Val St.Lambert, Old Masters Plates, 1969

Val St.Lambert, Old Masters Plates, 1971

Val St.Lambert, Old Masters Plates, 1972

Veneto Flair, Christmas Plate, 1972

Vernonware, Christmas Plate, 1971

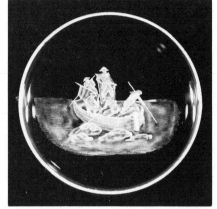

Val St.Lambert, American Heritage Plate, 1971

Vernonware, Christmas Plate, 1972

Veneto Flair, Four Seasons Plate, 1973, Winter

Veneto Flair, Last Supper Plate, Scene 1

Veneto Flair, Dog Plate, 1972

Vernonware, Christmas Plate, 1973

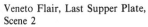

Veneto, Wildlife Plate, 1973

Veneto Flair, Last Supper Plate, Scene 2

Easter	1974	2000	50.00	50.00
Four Seasons, Spring, Sterling	1972	2000	125.00	75.00 to 125.00
Four Seasons, Fall, Sterling	1972	2000	125.00	75.00 to 125.00
Four Seasons, Winter, Sterling	1973	250	125.00	125.00
Four Seasons, Winter, Silver Plate*	1973	2000	75.00	75.00
Goddess Of Pomona	1973	500	75.00	75.00
Last Supper, First Scene*	1972	2000	100.00	65.00 to 100.00
Last Supper, Second Scene*	1973	2000	70.00	60.00 to 70.00
Mosaic, Justine	1973	500	50.00	85.00 to 135.00
Mosaic, Pelican	1974	2000	50.00	50.00
Mother's Day	1972	2000	45.00	95.00 to 145.00
Mother's Day	1973	2000	55.00	55.00 to 85.00
Mother's Day	1974		55.00	55.00
Valentine's Day, Silver	1973		135.00	85.00 to 135.00
Wildlife, Deer (stag)	1971	500	45.00	300.00 to 450.00
Wildlife, Elephant	1971	1000	37.50	120.00 to 150.00
Wildlife, Puma	1972	2000	37.50	45.00 to 95.00
Wildlife, Tiger*	1973	2000	37.50	40.00 to 60.00
Wildlife, Lion	1974	500	35.00	35.00

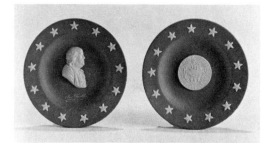

Wedgwood, State Seal Compotier,
Benjamin Franklin & Pennsylvania, 1972

Vernonware is a division of Metlox Potteries of Manhattan Beach, California. The limited edition plates, introduced in 1971, are hand-painted bas-relief with a Della Robbia border.

Vernonware Plates

Christmas, Partridge In A Pear Tree*	1971	10000	15.00	25.00 to 35.00
Christmas, Jingle Bells*	1972	12000	17.50	15.00 to 20.00
Christmas, Silent Night*	1973	10000	20.00	20.00

Viletta Plates

Christmas, Joy To The World	1970	10.00	5.00 to 10.00
Christmas, Hark The Herald Angels Sing	1971	10.00	5.00 to 10.00
Christmas, Silent Night	1972	10.00	5.00 to 10.00
Christmas, Shepherds Watch	1973	10.00	10.00

Wallace Silversmiths Ornaments

Christmas, Peace Doves	1971	Year	12.50	15.00 to 17.50
Christmas, Peace Doves	1972	Year	12.50	7.50 to 12.50
Christmas, Peace Doves	1973	Year	14.00	14.00

Wedgwood, State Seal Compotier,
Thomas Jefferson & Virginia

Walt Disney Plates

Christmas, Mickey Mouse	1973	10.00	10.00
Christmas	1974	10.00	10.00
Mother's Day	1974	10.00	10.00

Wanick Plates

Christmas, The Carders, Pewter	1972	2000	50.00	35.00 to 50.00

Wapello County Plates

Chief Wapello	1972	15.00	15.00

The Washington Mint of Beachwood, Ohio, was organized in 1970. Limited edition silver bars were first issued in 1971 and silver plates followed in 1972.

See listing for Washington Mint in Bar & Ingot section

Washington Mint, see also George Washington Mint

Washington Mint Plates

Last Supper, Sterling	1972	125.00	100.00 to 125.00

Waterflord Vases

Magi	1971	250	1200.00	1200.00
Ten Commandments	1972	250	1400.00	1400.00

Wedgwood, State Seal Compotier,
John Hancock & Massachusetts

Wedgwood, State Seal Compotier,
Philip Livingston & New York

Wedgwood was established in Etruria, England, by Josiah Wedgwood in 1759. The factory was moved to Barlaston in 1940. Wedgwood is famous for its Jasperware, Basalt, and Queensware, all produced in the eighteenth century. These wares are still used by Wedgwood for its limited editions, introduced in 1969.

See listing for Wedgwood in Figurine section

Wedgwood Compotiers

State Seal, Benjamin Franklin & Pennsylvania*	1972	5000	20.00	15.00 to 20.00

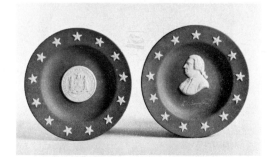

Wedgwood, Calendar Plate, 1971

Wedgwood, Calendar Plate, 1972

Wedgwood, Calendar Plate, 1973

Wedgwood, Child's Day Plate, 1971

State Seal, Thomas Jefferson & Virginia, Pair*	1972	5000	20.00	15.00 to 20.00
State Seal, John Hancock & Massachusetts**	1973	5000	20.00	15.00 to 20.00
State Seal, Philip Livingston & New York**	1973	5000	20.00	15.00 to 20.00

Wedgwood Mugs

Christmas	1971	Year		20.00 to 35.00
Christmas	1972	Year		20.00 to 30.00
Christmas	1973	Year	25.00	25.00

Wedgwood Plates

Apollo	1969		30.00	20.00 to 30.00
Bicentennial, Boston Tea Party	1972	5000	30.00	30.00 to 40.00
Bicentennial, Battle Of Concord	1973	5000	30.00	30.00
Bicentennial, Paul Revere**	1973	5000	30.00	30.00
Calendar*	1971	Year	12.00	8.00 to 12.00
Calendar*	1972	Year	12.00	10.00 to 12.00
Calendar**	1973	Year	12.00	12.00
Calendar**	1974	YEA	12.00	12.00
Child's Day, American, The Sandman*	1971	Year	7.95	8.00 to 10.00
Child's Day, The Tinder Box**	1972	Year	7.95	8.00 to 10.00
Christmas, Windsor Castle*	1969	Year	25.00	100.00 to 180.00
Christmas, Trafalgar Square*	1970	Year	25.00	25.00 to 40.00
Christmas, Picadilly Circus*	1971	Year	30.00	20.00 to 35.00
Christmas, St.Paul's Cathedral*	1972	Year	35.00	25.00 to 35.00
Christmas, Tower Of London**	1973	Year	40.00	40.00
Indian, Chief Black Hawk, Black Basalt	1972	500	275.00	275.00
Mother's Day, Mother's Little Angel*	1971	Year	20.00	15.00 to 25.00
Mother's Day, Seamstress*	1972	Year	20.00	12.00 to 20.00
Mother's Day, Baptism Of Achilles	1973	Year	25.00	25.00
Mother's Day, Domestic Employment	1974	Year	30.00	30.00
Olympics	1972			18.00 to 25.00

Wellings Mint Plates

Annual, A.Y.Jackson, St.Urbain, Gold	1971	1000.00		850.00 to 1000.00
Annual, A.Y.Jackson, St.Urbain, Sterling	1971	100.00		45.00 to 100.00
Annual, A.Y.Jackson, On The River, Sterling	1972	125.00		50.00 to 125.00
Mother's Day, Sterling	1972	125.00		60.00 to 125.00

Wendell August Forge produces silver and pewter limited edition plates for the L. E. Smith Glass Company of Mount Pleasant, Pennsylvania.

Wendell August Forge Plates

Great Americans, JFK, Pewter	1971	5000	40.00	25.00 to 40.00
Great Americans, JFK, Silver*	1971	500	200.00	200.00
Great Americans, Lincoln, Pewter	1972	5000	40.00	25.00 to 40.00
Great Americans, Lincoln, Silver*	1972	500	2000.0	
Great Moments, Landing Of Pilgrims, Pewter	1972	3000	40.00	25.00 to 40.00
Great Moments, Landing Of Pilgrims, Silver*	1972	250	200.00	200.00
Great Moments, First Thanksgiving, Pewter*	1973	3000	40.00	40.00
Great Moments, First Thanksgiving, Silver	1973	500	200.00	200.00
Peace, Doves, Silver*	1973	2500	250.00	250.00
Wings Of Man, Columbus' Ships, Pewter	1971	5000	40.00	25.00 to 40.00
Wings Of Man, Columbus' Ships, Silver*	1971	500	200.00	200.00
Wings Of Man, Conestoga Wagon, Pewter*	1972	5000	40.00	25.00 to 40.00
Wings Of Man, Conestoga Wagon, Silver	1972	500	200.00	200.00

Westmoreland Glass Company of Grapeville, Pennsylvania, was established in 1889. Limited edition plates, introduced in 1972, are hand-painted in gold on black glass.

Westmoreland Plates

Christmas, Holy Birth*	1972	2500	35.00	35.00 to 40.00
Christmas, Manger Scene*	1973	3500	35.00	30.00 to 35.00

Wheaton Industries of Millville, New Jersey, was established in 1888. The firm made hand-blown and pressed glassware. Wheaton now makes all types of containers for industry, as well as many collectors' bottles. Limited edition plates were first made in 1971.

Wheaton Commemorative Plates

Presidential, Adams	1971	9648	5.00	5.00 to 7.00
Presidential, Eisenhower**	1971	8856	5.00	5.00 to 7.00
Presidential, Hoover**	1971	10152	5.00	5.00 to 7.00

Wedgwood, Child's Day Plate, 1972

Wedgwood, Mother's Day Plate, 1972

Wedgwood, Christmas Plate, 1972

Wendell August Forge,
Great Americans Plate, 1971, Silver

Wedgwood, Christmas Plate, 1969

Wedgwood, Christmas Plate, 1970

Wendell August Forge,
Great Americans Plate, 1972, Silver

Wedgwood, Mother's Day Plate, 1971

Wendell August Forge,
Great Moments Plate, 1972, Silver

Wedgwood, Christmas Plate, 1971

Wendell August Forge,
Great Moments Plate, 1973, Pewter

WNW Mint, Bicentennial Plate, 1972

Wendell August Forge, Peace Plate, 1973

WNW Mint, Texas Ranger Plate, 1973

Wendell August Forge,
Wings Of Man Plate, 1971, Silver

Westmoreland, Christmas Plate, 1972

Wendell August Forge,
Wings Of Man Plate, 1972, Pewter

Westmoreland,
Christmas Plate, 1973

Zenith, Easter Egg, 1972

Presidential, Kennedy**	1971	11160	5.00	5.00 to 7.00
Presidential, Lincoln**	1971	9648	5.00	5.00 to 7.00
Presidential, Madison	1971	9504	5.00	5.00 to 7.00
Presidential, Monroe**	1971	9792	5.00	5.00 to 7.00
Presidential, Roosevelt, F.D.**	1971	9432	5.00	5.00 to 7.00
Presidential, Taft	1971	9648	5.00	5.00 to 7.00
Presidential, Van Buren	1971	9576	5.00	5.00 to 7.00
Presidential, Washington**	1971	10800	5.00	5.00 to 7.00
Presidential, Wilson	1971	8712	5.00	5.00 to 7.00

Whistler's Mother plate, see George Washington Mint

White House of the Confederacy limited edition plates were commissioned by the Trustees of the White House of the Confederacy. The plates are made by Lenox.

White House of the Confederacy Plates

Confederacy Collection, Set Of 10	1972	1000	900.00	900.00 to 1000.00

Wittig Bells

New Year's, Cranberry	1972	Year	25.00	25.00 to 35.00
New Year's, Amber	1973	Year	25.00	25.00 to 30.00

Winblad Plate, see Rosenthal

Winslow Homer plates, see U.S. Bicentennial Society

See listing for WNW Mint in Medal section

WNW Mint Industries of Amarillo, Texas, introduced limited edition silver plates in 1972. Limited edition medals in bronze and silver were first issued in 1971.

WNW Mint Plates

Bicentennial, Liberty Bell, Sterling*	1972	15000	125.00	125.00 to 200.00
Texas Rangers' Sesquicentennial, Silver*	1973	506	125.00	125.00 to 175.00

Worcester, see Royal Worcester

Wyeth, Andrew, see Andrew Wyeth

Wyeth, James, see Franklin Mint

Wyeth, N. C., see George Washington Mint

Yacht plate, see Kaiser

Zenith, located in Gouda, Holland, is one of the original delft potteries. Limited editions are produced in both blue and green delft. Fourteen different birthday plates are made each year, representing each day of the week, for both boys and girls.

Zenith Eggs

Easter, Blue Delft*	1972	750		60.00 to 70.00
Easter, Green Delft	1973	750	60.00	60.00 to 65.00

Zenith Plates

Anniversary, Autumn	1973	500	45.00	45.00
Anniversary, Spring	1973	500	45.00	45.00
Anniversary, Summer	1973	500	45.00	45.00
Anniversary, Winter	1973	500	45.00	45.00
Annual Greetje, Gretel Tending Geese, Green*	1973	750	60.00	60.00 to 80.00
Birthday, Boy*	1973	3000	15.00	15.00
Birthday, Girl*	1973	3000	15.00	15.00
Hans Brinker, Green Delft*	1972	500	60.00	100.00 to 125.00
Hans Brinker, Green Delft	1973	750	60.00	60.00 to 80.00

Zenith, Birthday Plate, 1973, Girl

Zenith, Birthday Plate, 1973, Boy

Zenith, Hans Brinker Plate, 1972

Zenith, Annual Greetje Plate, 1973

4

Medals

American Revolution Bicentennial Commission,
California

American Revolution Bicentennial Commission,
Connecticut

American Revolution Bicentennial Commission,
Illinois

Title	Date of Issue	Issue Limi- tation	Issue Price	Current Price
American Revolution Bicentennial Commission Medals, Official				
Alabama, Bronze	1973	Year	3.50	3.50
Alabama, Sterling	1973	Year	12.50	12.50
California, Bronze	1973	Year	3.50	3.50
California, Sterling*	1973	Year	12.50	12.50
Connecticut, Silver, 39mm.	1973		12.50	12.50
Connecticut State, Silver, 63mm.*	1973	2500	45.00	45.00
Danbury, Connecticut, Silver, 39mm.	1973		10.00	10.00
Greater Cleveland, Silver, 39mm.	1973	200	10.00	10.00
Illinois, Bronze	1973	Year	3.50	3.50
Illinois, Sterling*	1973	Year	12.50	12.50
Indiana, Silver, 63mm.*		2500	45.00	45.00
Louisiana, Bronze	1973	Year	3.50	3.50
Louisiana, Sterling*	1973	Year	12.50	12.50
New York City, Silver, 39mm.	1972		10.00	10.00
New York City, Silver, 63mm.*	1972		40.00	40.00
New York State, Silver, 39mm.	1973	20000	12.00	12.00
New York State, Silver, 63mm.*	1973	10000	40.00	40.00
Oklahoma, Bronze	1973	Year	3.50	3.50
Oklahoma, Sterling*	1973	Year	12.50	12.50
Saratoga County, Bronze, 39mm.	1973	6000	2.50	2.50
Saratoga County, Silver, 39mm.	1973	2500	12.50	12.50
South Dakota, Bronze	1973	Year	3.50	3.50
South Dakota, Sterling	1973	Year	12.50	12.50

Apollo Series, see Continental Mint Medals; Franklin Mint
Medals, Project Apollo Series; Presidential Art Medals, Inc.,
Apollo

Aviation Hall of Fame Series, see Presidential Art Medals, Inc.,
Aviation

Bicentennial Medals, see American Revolution Bicentennial
Commission, Official

Boy Scout Oath Series, see Wittnauer Mint Medals

Title	Date of Issue	Issue Limi- tation	Issue Price	Current Price
Captive Nations Medals				
Eisenhower, Dwight D., Bronze & Silver Set	1969	2000	15.00	Unknown
Eisenhower, Dwight D., Silver, 39mm.*	1969	10000	10.00	Unknown
Chase Commemorative Society Medals				
Astronauts, Silver	1968	1933		Unknown
Bunker Hill, Silver	1967	1933		Unknown
Churchill, Winston, Silver	1965	1933		Unknown

Columbus, Christopher, Silver	1968	1933		Unknown
Edison, Thomas, Silver	1966	1933		Unknown
Gold Rush, Silver	1967	1933		Unknown
Iwo Jima, Silver	1968	1200		Unknown
Jones, John Paul, Silver	1967	1933		Unknown
Kennedy, John F., Silver	1967	1933		Unknown
King, Martin Luther, Bronze	1968			Unknown
King, Martin Luther, Silver	1968	1200		Unknown
Lincoln, Abraham, Silver	1966	1933		Unknown
MacArthur, Douglas, Silver	1967	1933		Unknown
Rogers, Will, Silver	1967	1933		Unknown
Roosevelt, Theodore, Silver	1966	1933		Unknown
Stevenson, Adlai, Silver	1966	1933		Unknown
Twain, Mark, Silver	1967	1933		Unknown
U.S.Capitol, Silver	1966	1933		Unknown
Unknown Soldiers, Silver	1966	1933		Unknown
Washington, George, Silver	1966	1933		Unknown
Wright Brothers, Silver	1968	1200		Unknown

Chicago Historical Society Medals

Great Chicago Fire, Bronze, Large	1971	2500	6.00	Unknown
Great Chicago Fire, Bronze, Small	1971	10000	1.00	Unknown
Great Chicago Fire, Silver, Large	1971	2500	35.00	Unknown
Great Chicago Fire, Silver, Small	1971	500	10.00	Unknown

Circle of the Friends of the Medallion Medals

Abdul Baha, Persian Reformer, 76mm.	1912		Unknown
Centennial U.S.-British Peace, 70mm.	1914		Unknown
Dickens, Charles, 70mm.	1912		Unknown
Fremont, John, 76mm.	1913		Unknown
Hudson-Fulton, 70mm.	1909		Unknown
Joan Of Arc, 70mm.	1915		Unknown
Lafayette, 77mm.	1911		Unknown
Motherhood, 70mm.	1911		Unknown
New Netherland 250th Anniversary, 70mm.	1914		Unknown
Saint Brendan, 70mm.	1911		Unknown
The Ocean, 70mm.	1913		Unknown
Wanderer Returns Home, 70mm.	1910		Unknown

City and State Medals, Official

Alabama Sesquicentennial, Bronze	1969	10000		Unknown
Alabama Sesquicentennial, Silver	1969	2500		Unknown
Alaska Centennial, Bronze	1966	10000		Unknown
Alaska Centennial, Silver	1966	10000		Unknown
Alaska Purchase Centennial, Bronze	1965	15015	1.00	2.00
Alaska Purchase Centennial, Silver	1965	2500		10.00
Alaska Statehood, Bronze	1959	23600	4.00	Unknown
Alaska Statehood, Gold	1959	100		Unknown
Alaska Statehood, Silver	1959	990	33.00	Unknown
Albany, New York, 200th Anniversary, Silver	1953	1250		Unknown
Albany, New York, 200th Anniversary, Bronze	1953	1250		Unknown
California Bicentennial, Bronze, 39mm. Unimedal	1969	203940	2.00	Unknown
California Bicentennial, Bronze, 63mm.	1969	41515	5.00	Unknown
California Bicentennial, Silver, 39mm. Unimedal	1969	90945	10.00	Unknown
California Bicentennial, Silver, 63mm.*	1969	20000	35.00	Unknown
Colorado Bicentennial, Silver	1959	10000		Unknown
Connecticut Tercentenary, Bronze, 33mm.	1935	200		Unknown
Connecticut Tercentenary, Bronze, 76mm.	1935	2500		Unknown
Connecticut Tercentenary, Silver	1935	1		Unknown
Delaware Colony, Bronze	1938	2000		Unknown
Delaware Colony, Silver	1938	104		Unknown
Hawaii Statehood, Bronze *	1959	29599	4.00	9.50
Hawaii Statehood, Silver	1959	3154	30.00	Unknown
Idaho Territorial Centennial, Bronze, 45mm.	1963	100		Unknown
Idaho Territorial Centennial, Bronze, 64mm.	1963	6000		Unknown
Idaho Territorial Centennial, Silver, 64mm.	1963	6		Unknown
Illinois Sesquicentennial, Bronze, 38mm.	1968	250761		Unknown
Illinois Sesquicentennial, Bronze, 63mm.	1968	14146		Unknown
Illinois Sesquicentennial, Silver, 38mm.	1968	11000		Unknown
Illinois Sesquicentennial, Silver, 63mm.	1968	12500		Unknown
Indiana Centennial, Bronze	1916			Unknown
Indiana Sesquicentennial, Bronze, 38mm.	1966	30079	1.00	Unknown

American Revolution Bicentennial Commission,
Indiana

American Revolution Bicentennial Commission,
Louisiana

American Revolution Bicentennial Commission,
New York City

American Revolution Bicentennial Commission,
New York State

American Revolution Bicentennial Commission,
Oklahoma

Captive Nations Medal, Dwight D.Eisenhower

City & State Medals, California Bicentennial, Silver

City & State Medals, Hawaii Statehood

City & State Medals, New Mexico Statehood

City & State Medals, San Juan, 450th Anniversary

Indiana Sesquicentennial, Bronze, 63mm.	1966	7190	4.00	Unknown
Indiana Sesquicentennial, Silver, 44mm.	1966	6000	10.00	Unknown
Indiana Sesquicentennial, Silver, 63mm.	1966	2000	24.00	Unknown
Kansas Centennial, Silver	1960	20000		Unknown
Maine Sesquicentennial, Bronze, 38mm.	1970	12350		Unknown
Maine Sesquicentennial, Bronze, 63mm.	1970	4350		Unknown
Maine Sesquicentennial, Silver, 38mm.	1970	4359		Unknown
Maine Sesquicentennial, Silver, 63mm.	1970	1120		Unknown
Memphis Sesquicentennial, Bronze	1968	40000		Unknown
Memphis Sesquicentennial, Silver	1968	15000		Unknown
Missouri Sesquicentennial, Bronze, 39mm.	1970	75600		Unknown
Missouri Sesquicentennial, Bronze, 39mm.	1971	29100		Unknown
Missouri Sesquicentennial, Bronze, 64mm.	1971	2002		Unknown
Missouri Sesquicentennial, Silver, 39mm.	1970	8100		Unknown
Missouri Sesquicentennial, Silver, 39mm.	1971	10100		Unknown
Missouri Sesquicentennial, Silver, 64mm.	1971	1000		Unknown
Montana Territorial Centennial, Bronze, 63mm.	1964	2500		Unknown
Montana Territorial Centennial, Silver, 41mm.	1964	1500		Unknown
Montana Territorial Centennial, Silver, 63mm.	1964	900		Unknown
Nebraska Centennial, Bronze, 33mm.	1967	49300	1.25	Unknown
Nebraska Centennial, Bronze, 44mm.	1967	5000	3.75	Unknown
Nebraska Centennial, Bronze Proof, 44mm.	1967	500		Unknown
Nebraska Centennial, Bronze, 70mm.	1967	3500	5.50	Unknown
Nebraska Centennial, Silver Proof, 44mm.	1967	500	11.00	Unknown
Nebraska Centennial, Silver, 44mm.	1967	10000		Unknown
Nevada Centennial, Silver, 1 15/16 In.	1963	20000		Unknown
New Jersey, 300th Anniversary, Bronze	1964			3.00
New Jersey, 300th Anniversary, Silver	1964			Unknown
New Mexico, 50th Anniversary, Bronze	1962	3000	4.00	Unknown
New Mexico, 50th Anniversary, Silver*	1962	1080	30.00	35.00
Ohio Sesquicentennial, Bronze, 70mm.	1953	10010		Unknown
Oklahoma Statehood, 50th Anniversary, Bronze	1957	1100		Unknown
Oklahoma Statehood, 50th Anniversary, Silver	1957			Unknown
Redding, Connecticut, 200th Anniversary, Bronze	1967	1000	3.50	Unknown
San Diego 200th Anniversary, Bronze, 1 15/16	1967	54200		Unknown
San Diego, 200th Anniversary, Bronze, 3 In.	1967	29500		Unknown
San Diego 200th Anniversary, Silver, 1 15/16	1967	55000		Unknown
San Diego 200th Anniversary, Silver, 3 In.	1967	1250		Unknown
San Juan, 450th Anniversary, Bronze, 39mm.	1971	12500	1.00	Unknown
San Juan, 450th Anniversary, Bronze, 63mm.	1971	1250	5.00	Unknown
San Juan, 450th Anniversary, Silver, 39mm.	1971	1250	10.00	Unknown
San Juan, 450th Anniversary, Silver, 63mm.*	1971	272	35.00	40.00
Santa Fe, 350th Anniversary, Bronze	1960	11000	4.00	4.00
Santa Fe, 350th Anniversary, Silver*	1960	2500	30.00	35.00
South Carolina Tricentennial, Bronze, 1 9/16	1969	20000		Unknown
South Carolina Tricentennial, Bronze, 3 In.	1969	3000		Unknown
South Carolina Tricentennial, Silver, 1 9/16	1969	3000		Unknown
South Carolina Tricentennial, Silver, 3 In.	1969	300		Unknown
St.Augustine Quadricentennial, Bronze, 64mm.	1965	3300		Unknown
St.Augustine Quadricentennial, Silver, 44mm.	1965	1487		Unknown
St.Louis Bicentennial, Bronze	1964	15000		Unknown
St.Louis Bicentennial, Silver	1964	10000		Unknown
Texas Declaration Of Independence, Bronze	1955	2000		Unknown
Vermont Colony, Bronze	1927	1250		Unknown
Vermont Colony, Silver	1927	6		Unknown
Vermont Statehood, 150th Anniversary, Bronze	1941			Unknown
Vermont Statehood, 150th Anniversary, Silver	1941			Unknown
Washington, D.C., Bronze	1950			17.50 to 19.50
West Virginia Centennial, Bronze	1962	20000	2.00	2.00
West Virginia Centennial, Silver	1962	6000	12.50	12.50 to 15.00
Wichita Centennial, Bronze	1969	9000		Unknown
Wichita Centennial, Silver	1969	3500		Unknown
Wyoming, Buffalo Bill, Bronze	1967	200		Unknown
Wyoming, Buffalo Bill, Silver	1967	3000	12.00	Unknown
Wyoming, Esther Morris, Bronze	1967	400		Unknown
Wyoming, Esther Morris, Silver	1967	2000	12.00	Unknown

Commemorative Arts Medals

Churchill Memorial, Bronze	1965	1000		Unknown
Churchill Memorial, Goldine	1965	1000		Unknown
Churchill Memorial, Silver	1965	200		Unknown

The Continental Mint of Panorama City, California, has made limited edition medals since the 1960s. Silver bars were first made in 1972.

See listing for Continental Mint in Bar & Ingot section

Continental Mint Medals

Apollo XI, Bronze*		25	7.50	7.00 to 15.00
Apollo XI, Silver, P		150	75.00	55.00 to 75.00
Apollo XII, Bronze		1000	7.50	6.50 to 7.50
Apollo XII, Silver, A*		500	39.00	35.00 to 39.00
Apollo XII, Silver, P		25	125.00	75.00 to 125.00
Apollo XIII, Bronze		200	7.50	6.50 to 7.50
Apollo XIII, Silver, A*		200	35.00	35.00 to 39.00
Apollo XIII, Silver, P		250	75.00	60.00 to 75.00
Apollo XIV, Bronze		350	7.50	6.50 to 7.50
Apollo XIV, Silver, A		200	39.00	35.00 to 39.00
Apollo XIV, Silver, P*		250	75.00	60.00 to 75.00
Apollo XV, Bronze		350	7.50	6.50 to 7.50
Apollo XV, Silver, A*		200	39.00	37.50 to 39.00
Apollo XV, Silver, P		150	75.00	60.00 to 75.00
Apollo XVI, Bronze		350	7.50	6.50 to 7.50
Apollo XVI, Silver, A		200	39.00	37.50 to 39.00
Apollo XVI, Silver, P*		150	75.00	60.00 to 75.00
Apollo XVII, Bronze		350	7.00	6.50 to 7.00
Apollo XVII, Silver, A*		200	39.00	37.50 to 39.00
Apollo XVII, Silver, P		150	75.00	60.00 to 75.00
Lawson Aviation, Bronze	1973	250	7.50	7.50
Lawson Aviation, Silver	1973	200	30.00	30.00
Mexico Soccer Games, Silver	1970	250	18.00	Unknown
Mexico Soccer Games, Bronze	1970	250	6.00	Unknown
Pittsburgh Pirate Baseball, Bronze	1971	250	6.00	Unknown
Pittsburgh Pirate Baseball, Silver	1971	300	18.00	Unknown

Danbury Mint, a division of Glendinning Companies, Inc., creates and markets art medals and limited edition plates. All limited editions are struck for the Danbury Mint by other organizations. Limited editions were first introduced in 1972.

See listing for Danbury Mint in Plate and Bar & Ingot sections

Danbury Mint Medals

Kennedy, John, Bronze, Cover	1973	15.00	15.00
Kennedy, John, Sterling, Cover	1973	25.00	25.00
Nixon, Peace Journey, Sterling	1972		22.50
Truman, Harry, Bronze, Set	1973		11.50
Truman, Harry, Sterling, Set	1973		19.50

Danbury Mint, Ducks Unlimited Series

Ducks Unlimited, Set Of 20, Silver, Each	1973	1000	28.50	28.50

Danbury Mint Medals, Life of Christ, 45mm.

Life Of Christ, Gold On Silver, Set Of 24, Each	1973	10000	15.00	20.00
Life Of Christ, Silver, Set Of 24, Each	1973	10000	12.00	15.00

Dentistry Series, see Medical Heritage Society Medals

Federal Brand Enterprise Medals

Churchill Memorial, Bronze	1965	7500	Unknown
Churchill Memorial, Silver	1965	1000	Unknown

Franklin Mint was organized in the early 1960s by Joseph Segel and Gilroy Roberts, chief sculptor engraver for the U.S. Mint. It is located in Franklin Center, Pennsylvania. Franklin Mint introduced the first sterling silver collector's plate on the market in 1970. Medals have been made since the 1960s. The official Franklin Mint code is used to describe the composition of the medals. The code is translated as follows:A-Platinum, B-Gold, C-Fine Silver .999, D-Sterling Silver .925, F-Gold on Sterling, J-Franklin Bronze, N-commercial bronze. Letters A, M, P, or Pl following the first code letter refer to Antique, Mint, Proof, or Proof-like finish. There are 25.4 Mm. to an inch.

See listing for Franklin Mint in Plate and Bar & Ingot sections

Franklin Mint, African Wild Life Series, see Franklin Mint

Medals, East African Wild Life Society

City & State Medals, Santa Fe, 350th Anniversary

Continental Mint, Apollo XI

Continental Mint, Apollo XII

Continental Mint, Apollo XIII

Continental Mint, Apollo XIV

Franklin Mint Medals, America in Space

Apollo 7, Schroeder, D, P	1970-1971	20377	7.50	10.00
Apollo 8, Nemeth, D, P	1970-1971	20377	7.50	10.00
Apollo 9, Stanton, D, P	1970-1971	20377	7.50	10.00
Apollo 10, Miller, D, P	1970-1971	20377	7.50	10.00
Apollo 11, Jones, D, P	1970-1971	20377	7.50	10.00
Explorer 1, Stanton, D, P	1970-1971	20377	7.50	10.00
Faith 7, Stanton, D, P	1970-1971	20377	7.50	10.00
Freedom 7, Lauser, D, P	1970-1971	20377	7.50	10.00
Friendship 7, Jones, D, P	1970-1971	20377	7.50	10.00
Gemini 3, Nemeth, D, P	1970-1971	20377	7.50	10.00
Gemini 4, Rufo, D, P	1970-1971	20377	7.50	10.00
Gemini 7/6, Park, D, P	1970-1971	20377	7.50	10.00
Gemini 8, Nathan, D, P	1970-1971	20377	7.50	10.00
Lunar Orbiter I, Blaker, D, P	1970-1971	20377	7.50	10.00
Mariner II, Ferrell, D, P	1970-1971	20377	7.50	10.00
Mariner IV, Bush, D, P	1970-1971	20377	7.50	10.00
Pioneer V, Rufo, D, P	1970-1971	20377	7.50	10.00
Ranger VII, Miller, D, P	1970-1971	20377	7.50	10.00
Relay I, Faulkner, D, P	1970-1971	20377	7.50	10.00
Surveyor I, Jones, D, P	1970-1971	20377	7.50	10.00
Syncom II, Stanton, D, P	1970-1971	20377	7.50	10.00
Telstar, Jones, D, P	1970-1971	20377	7.50	10.00
The Goddard Rocket, Stanton, D, P	1970-1971	20377	7.50	10.00
Tiros I, Park, D, P	1970-1971	20377	7.50	10.00
Apollo 7, Schroeder, J, P	1970-1971	7303	3.25	Unknown
Apollo 8, Nemeth, J, P	1970-1971	7303	3.25	Unknown
Apollo 9, Stanton, J, P	1970-1971	7303	3.25	Unknown
Apollo 10, Miller, J, P	1970-1971	7303	3.25	Unknown
Apollo 11, Jones, J, P	1970-1971	7303	3.25	Unknown
Explorer 1, Stanton, J, P	1970-1971	7303	3.25	Unknown
Faith 7, Stanton, J, P	1970-1971	7303	3.25	Unknown
Freedom 7, Lauser, J, P	1970-1971	7303	3.25	Unknown
Friendship 7, Jones, J, P	1970-1971	7303	3.25	Unknown
Gemini 3, Nemeth, J, P	1970-1971	7303	3.25	Unknown
Gemini 4, Rufo, J, P	1970-1971	7303	3.25	Unknown
Gemini 7/6, Park, J, P	1970-1971	7303	3.25	Unknown
Gemini 8, Nathan, J, P	1970-1971	7303	3.25	Unknown
Lunar Orbiter I, Blaker, J, P	1970-1971	7303	3.25	Unknown
Mariner II, Ferrell, J, P	1970-1971	7303	3.25	Unknown
Mariner IV, Bush, J, P	1970-1971	7303	3.25	Unknown
Pioneer V, Rufo, J, P	1970-1971	7303	3.25	Unknown
Ranger VII, Miller, J, P	1970-1971	7303	3.25	Unknown
Relay I, Faulkner, J, P	1970-1971	7303	3.25	Unknown
Surveyor I, Jones, J, P	1970-1971	7303	3.25	Unknown
Syncom II, Stanton, J, P	1970-1971	7303	3.25	Unknown
Telstar, Jones, J, P	1970-1971	7303	3.25	Unknown
The Goddard Rocket, Stanton, J, P	1970-1971	7303	3.25	Unknown
Tiros I, Park, J, P	1970-1971	7303	3.25	Unknown

**Franklin Mint, American Express Presidential Series, see Franklin
Mint Medals, Presidential Series, American Express**

**Franklin Mint Medals, American Heritage Medallic Treasury
of American History**

1492-Columbus Lands, 39mm., D, P	1971-1972	3134	9.50	Unknown
1607-Settlement At Jamestown, 39mm., D, P	1971-1972	3134	9.50	Unknown
1775-Paul Revere Sounds Alert, 39mm., D, P	1971-1972	3134	9.50	Unknown
1776-Independence Declared, 39mm., D, P	1971-1972	3134	9.50	Unknown
1789-Washington Takes Office, 39mm., D, P	1971-1972	3134	9.50	Unknown
1804-Lewis & Clark Go West, 39mm., D, P	1971-1972	3134	9.50	Unknown
1815-Jackson At New Orleans, 39mm., D, P	1971-1972	3134	9.50	Unknown
1836-Defense Of Alamo, 39mm., D, P	1971-1972	3134	9.50	Unknown
1849-California Gold Rush, 39mm., D, P	1971-1972	3134	9.50	Unknown
1863-Gettysburg Address, 39mm., D, P	1971-1972	3134	9.50	Unknown
1869-Golden Spike, 39mm., D, P	1971-1972	3134	9.50	Unknown
1903-Orville & Wilbur Wright, 39mm., D, P	1971-1972	3134	9.50	Unknown
1914-Opening Of Panama Canal, 39mm., D, P	1971-1972	3134	9.50	Unknown
1918-Armistice Brings Peace, 39mm., D, P	1971-1972	3134	9.50	Unknown
1927-Lindbergh Solos To Paris, 39mm., D, P	1971-1972	3134	9.50	Unknown

Continental Mint, Apollo XV

Continental Mint, Apollo XVI

Continental Mint, Apollo XVII

1939-Television, 39mm., D, P	1971-1972	3134	9.50	Unknown
1942-Nuclear Chain Reaction, 39mm., D, P	1971-1972	3134	9.50	Unknown
1944-D-Day, Invasion Of Europe, 39mm., D, P	1971-1972	3134	9.50	Unknown
1945-United Nations Charter, 39mm., D, P	1971-1972	3134	9.50	Unknown
1969-Americans Land On Moon, 39mm., D, P	1971-1972	3134	9.50	Unknown
1492-Columbus Lands, 39mm., D, Pl	1971-1972	151	9.50	Unknown
1607-Settlement At Jamestown, 39mm., D, Pl	1971-1972	151	9.50	Unknown
1775-Revere Sounds Alert, 39mm., D, Pl	1971-1972	151	9.50	Unknown
1776-Independence Declared, 39mm., D, Pl	1971-1972	151	9.50	Unknown
1789-Washington Takes Office, 39mm., D, Pl	1971-1972	151	9.50	Unknown
1804-Lewis & Clark Go West, 39mm., D, Pl	1971-1972	151	9.50	Unknown
1815-Jackson At New Orleans, 39mm., D, Pl	1971-1972	151	9.50	Unknown
1836-Defense Of Alamo, 39mm., D, Pl	1971-1972	151	9.50	Unknown
1849-California Gold Rush, 39mm., D, Pl	1971-1972	151	9.50	Unknown
1863-Gettysburg Address, 39mm., D, Pl	1971-1972	151	9.50	Unknown
1869-Golden Spike, 39mm., D, Pl	1971-1972	151	9.50	Unknown
1903-Orville & Wilbur Wright, 39mm., D, Pl	1971-1972	151	9.50	Unknown
1914-Opening Of Panama Canal, 39mm., D, Pl	1971-1972	151	9.50	Unknown
1918-Armistice Brings Peace, 39mm., D, Pl	1971-1972	151	9.50	Unknown
1927-Lindbergh Solos, Paris, 39mm., D, Pl	1971-1972	151	9.50	Unknown
1939-Television, 39mm., D, Pl	1971-1972	151	9.50	Unknown
1942-Nuclear Chain Reaction, 39mm., D, Pl	1971-1972	151	9.50	Unknown
1944-D-Day, 39mm., D, Pl	1971-1972	151	9.50	Unknown
1945-United Nations Charter, 39mm., D, Pl	1971-1972	151	9.50	Unknown
1969-Americans Land On Moon, 39mm., D, Pl	1971-1972	151	9.50	Unknown
1492-Columbus Lands, 39mm., F, P	1971-1972	931	14.50	Unknown
1607-Settlement At Jamestown, 39mm., F, P	1971-1972	931	14.50	Unknown
1775-Paul Revere Sounds Alert, 39mm., F, P	1971-1972	931	14.50	Unknown
1776-Independence Declared, 39mm., F, P	1971-1972	931	14.50	Unknown
1789-Washington Takes Office, 39mm., F, P	1971-1972	931	14.50	Unknown
1804-Lewis & Clark Go West, 39mm., F, P	1971-1972	931	14.50	Unknown
1815-Jackson At New Orleans, 39mm., F, P	1971-1972	931	14.50	Unknown
1836-Defense Of Alamo, 39mm., F, P	1971-1972	931	14.50	Unknown
1849-California Gold Rush, 39mm., F, P	1971-1972	931	14.50	Unknown
1863-Gettysburg Address, 39mm., F, P	1971-1972	931	14.50	Unknown
1869-Golden Spike, 39mm., F, P	1971-1972	931	14.50	Unknown
1903-Orville & Wilbur Wright, 39mm., F, P	1971-1972	931	14.50	Unknown
1914-Opening Of Panama Canal, 39mm., F, P	1971-1972	931	14.50	Unknown
1918-Armistice Brings Peace, 39mm., F, P	1971-1972	931	14.50	Unknown
1927-Lindbergh Solos To Paris, 39mm., F, P	1971-1972	931	14.50	Unknown
1939-Television, 39mm., F, P	1971-1972	931	14.50	Unknown
1942-Nuclear Chain Reaction, 39mm., F, P	1971-1972	931	14.50	Unknown
1944-D-Day, Invasion Of Europe, 39mm., F, P	1971-1972	931	14.50	Unknown
1945-United Nations Charter, 39mm., F, P	1971-1972	931	14.50	Unknown
1969-Americans Land On Moon, 39mm., F, P	1971-1972	931	14.50	Unknown
1492-Columbus Lands, 39mm., F, Pl	1971-1972	159	14.50	Unknown
1607-Settlement At Jamestown, 39mm., F, Pl	1971-1972	159	14.50	Unknown
1775-Revere Sounds Alert, 39mm., F, Pl	1971-1972	159	14.50	Unknown
1776-Independence Declared, 39mm., F, Pl	1971-1972	159	14.50	Unknown
1789-Washington Takes Office, 39mm., F, Pl	1971-1972	159	14.50	Unknown
1804-Lewis & Clark Go West, 39mm., F, Pl	1971-1972	159	14.50	Unknown
1815-Jackson At New Orleans, 39mm., F, Pl	1971-1972	159	14.50	Unknown
1836-Defense Of Alamo, 39mm., F, Pl	1971-1972	159	14.50	Unknown
1849-California Gold Rush, 39mm., F, Pl	1971-1972	159	14.50	Unknown
1863-Gettysburg Address, 39mm., F, Pl	1971-1972	159	14.50	Unknown
1869-Golden Spike, 39mm., F, Pl	1971-1972	159	14.50	Unknown
1903-Orville & Wilbur Wright, 39mm., F, Pl	1971-1972	159	14.50	Unknown
1914-Opening Of Panama Canal, 39mm., F, Pl	1971-1972	159	14.50	Unknown
1918-Armistice Brings Peace, 39mm., F, Pl	1971-1972	159	14.50	Unknown
1927-Lindbergh Solo, Paris, 39mm., F, Pl	1971-1972	159	14.50	Unknown
1939-Television, 39mm., F, Pl	1971-1972	159	14.50	Unknown
1942-Nuclear Chain Reaction, 39mm., F, Pl	1971-1972	159	14.50	Unknown
1944-D-Day, 39mm., F, Pl	1971-1972	159	14.50	Unknown
1945-United Nations Charter, 39mm., F, Pl	1971-1972	159	14.50	Unknown
1969-Americans Land On Moon, 39mm., F, Pl	1971-1972	159	14.50	Unknown

**Franklin Mint, American Landmarks Series, see Franklin Mint
Medals, Great American Landmarks**

Franklin Mint Medals, American Legion Treasury of Great American Victories

Concord, 1775, 39mm., D, P	1971-1972	1017	9.50	Unknown
Trenton, 1776, 39mm., D, P	1971-1972	1017	9.50	Unknown
Saratoga, 1777, 39mm., D, P	1971-1972	1017	9.50	Unknown
Flamborough Head, 1779, 39mm., D, P	1971-1972	1017	9.50	Unknown
Yorktown, 1781, 39mm., D, P	1971-1972	1017	9.50	Unknown
Lake Erie, 1813, 39mm., D, P	1971-1972	1017	9.50	Unknown
New Orleans, 1875, 39mm., D, P	1971-1972	1017	9.50	Unknown
Monterrey, 1846, 39mm., D, P	1971-1972	1017	9.50	Unknown
Buena Vista, 1847, 39mm., D, P	1971-1972	1017	9.50	Unknown
Manila Bay, 1898, 39mm., D, P	1971-1972	1017	9.50	Unknown
St. Mihiel, 1918, 39mm., D, P	1971-1972	1017	9.50	Unknown
Chateau-Thierry, 1918, 39mm., D, P	1971-1972	1017	9.50	Unknown
Belleau Wood, 1918, 39mm., D, P	1971-1972	1017	9.50	Unknown
Meuse Argonne, 1918, 39mm., D, P	1971-1972	1017	9.50	Unknown
Midway, 1942, 39mm., D, P	1971-1972	1017	9.50	Unknown
Guadalcanal, 1942, 39mm., D, P	1971-1972	1017	9.50	Unknown
Salerno, 1943, 39mm., D, P	1971-1972	1017	9.50	Unknown
The Marianas, 1944, 39mm., D, P	1971-1972	1017	9.50	Unknown
St. Lo, 1944, 39mm., D, P	1971-1972	1017	9.50	Unknown
Leyte Gulf, 1944, 39mm., D, P	1971-1972	1017	9.50	Unknown
Iwo Jima, 1945, 39mm., D, P	1971-1972	1017	9.50	Unknown
Remagen Bridge, 1945, 39mm., D, P	1971-1972	1017	9.50	Unknown
The Ruhr Pocket, 1945, 39mm., D, P	1971-1972	1017	9.50	Unknown
Okinawa, 1945, 39mm., D, P	1971-1972	1017	9.50	Unknown
Concord, 1775, 39mm., D, Pl	1972	1314	9.50	Unknown
Trenton, 1776, 39mm., D, Pl	1972	1314	9.50	Unknown
Saratoga, 1777, 39mm., D, Pl	1972	1314	9.50	Unknown
Flamborough Head, 1779, 39mm., D, Pl	1972	1314	9.50	Unknown
Yorktown, 1781, 39mm., D, Pl	1972	1314	9.50	Unknown
Lake Erie, 1813, 39mm., D, Pl	1972	1314	9.50	Unknown
New Orleans, 1875, 39mm., D, Pl	1972	1314	9.50	Unknown
Monterrey, 1846, 39mm., D, Pl	1972	1314	9.50	Unknown
Buena Vista, 1847, 39mm., D, Pl	1972	1314	9.50	Unknown
Manila Bay, 1898, 39mm., D, Pl	1972	1314	9.50	Unknown
Chateau-Thierry, 1918, 39mm., D, Pl	1972	1314	9.50	Unknown
Belleau Wood, 1918, 39mm., D, Pl	1972	1314	9.50	Unknown
St. Mihiel, 1918, 39mm., D, Pl	1972	1314	9.50	Unknown
Meuse Argonne, 1918, 39mm., D, Pl	1972	1314	9.50	Unknown
Midway, 1942, 39mm., D, Pl	1972	1314	9.50	Unknown
Guadalcanal, 1942, 39mm., D, Pl	1972	1314	9.50	Unknown
Salerno, 1943, 39mm., D, Pl	1972	1314	9.50	Unknown
The Marianas, 1944, 39mm., D, Pl	1972	1314	9.50	Unknown
St. Lo, 1944, 39mm., D, Pl	1972	1314	9.50	Unknown
Leyte Gulf, 1944, 39mm., D, Pl	1972	1314	9.50	Unknown
Iwo Jima, 1945, 39mm., D, Pl	1972	1314	9.50	Unknown
Remagen Bridge, 1945, 39mm., D, Pl	1972	1314	9.50	Unknown
The Ruhr Pocket, 1945, 39mm., D, Pl	1972	1314	9.50	Unknown
Okinawa, 1945, 39mm., D, Pl	1972	1314	9.50	Unknown
Concord, 1775, 39mm., J, P	1971-1972	462	4.00	Unknown
Trenton, 1776, 39mm., J, P	1971-1972	462	4.00	Unknown
Saratoga, 1777, 39mm., J, P	1971-1972	462	4.00	Unknown
Flamborough Head, 1779, 39mm., J, P	1971-1972	462	4.00	Unknown
Yorktown, 1781, 39mm., J, P	1971-1972	462	4.00	Unknown
Lake Erie, 1813, 39mm., J, P	1971-1972	462	4.00	Unknown
New Orleans, 1875, 39mm., J, P	1971-1972	462	4.00	Unknown
Monterrey, 1846, 39mm., J, P	1971-1972	462	4.00	Unknown
Buena Vista, 1847, 39mm., J, P	1971-1972	462	4.00	Unknown
Manila Bay, 1898, 39mm., J, P	1971-1972	462	4.00	Unknown
Chateau-Thierry, 1918, 39mm., J, P	1971-1972	462	4.00	Unknown
Belleau Wood, 1918, 39mm., J, P	1971-1972	462	4.00	Unknown
St. Mihiel, 1918, 38mm., J, P	1971-1972	462	4.00	Unknown
Meuse Argonne, 1918, 39mm., J, P	1971-1972	462	4.00	Unknown
Midway, 1942, 39mm., J, P	1971-1972	462	4.00	Unknown
Guadalcanal, 1942, 39mm., J, P	1971-1972	462	4.00	Unknown
Salerno, 1943, 39mm., J, P	1971-1972	462	4.00	Unknown
The Marianas, 1944, 39mm., J, P	1971-1972	462	4.00	Unknown

St. Lo, 1944, 39mm., J, P	1971-1972	462	4.00	Unknown
Leyte Gulf, 1944, 39mm., J, P	1971-1972	462	4.00	Unknown
Iwo Jima, 1945, 39mm., J, P	1971-1972	462	4.00	Unknown
Remagen Bridge, 1945, 39mm., J, P	1971-1972	462	4.00	Unknown
The Ruhr Pocket, 1945, 39mm., J, P	1971-1972	462	4.00	Unknown
Okinawa, 1945, 39mm., J, P	1971-1972	462	4.00	Unknown
Concord, 1775, 39mm., J, Pl	1972	878	4.00	Unknown
Trenton, 1776, 39mm., J, Pl	1972	878	4.00	Unknown
Saratoga, 1777, 39mm., J, Pl	1972	878	4.00	Unknown
Flamborough Head, 1779, 39mm., J, Pl	1972	878	4.00	Unknown
Yorktown, 1781, 39mm., J, Pl	1972	878	4.00	Unknown
Lake Erie, 1813, 39mm., J, Pl	1972	878	4.00	Unknown
New Orleans, 1875, 39mm., J, Pl	1972	878	4.00	Unknown
Monterrey, 1846, 39mm., J, Pl	1972	878	4.00	Unknown
Buena Vista, 1847, 39mm., J, Pl	1972	878	4.00	Unknown
Manila Bay, 1898, 39mm., J, Pl	1972	878	4.00	Unknown
Chateau-Thierry, 1918, 39mm., J, Pl	1972	878	4.00	Unknown
Belleau Wood, 1918, 39mm., J, Pl	1972	878	4.00	Unknown
St. Mihiel, 1918, 39mm., J, Pl	1972	878	4.00	Unknown
Meuse Argonne, 1918, 39mm., J, Pl	1972	878	4.00	Unknown
Midway, 1942, 39mm., J, Pl	1972	878	4.00	Unknown
Guadalcanal, 1942, 39mm., J, Pl	1972	878	4.00	Unknown
Salerno, 1943, 39mm., J, Pl	1972	878	4.00	Unknown
The Marianas, 1944, 39mm., J, Pl	1972	878	4.00	Unknown
St. Lo, 1944, 39mm., J, Pl	1972	878	4.00	Unknown
Leyte Gulf, 1944, 39mm., J, Pl	1972	878	4.00	Unknown
Iwo Jima, 1945, 39mm., J, Pl	1972	878	4.00	Unknown
Remagen Bridge, 1945, 39mm., J, Pl	1972	878	4.00	Unknown
The Ruhr Pocket, 1945, 39mm., J, Pl	1972	878	4.00	Unknown
Okinawa, 1945, 39mm., J, Pl	1972	878	4.00	Unknown

Franklin Mint, American Revolution Series, see Franklin Mint Medals, History of the American Revolution

Franklin Mint, Apollo Series, see Franklin Mint Medals, Project Apollo

Franklin Mint, Bible Series, see Franklin Mint Medals, Thomason Medallic Bible

Franklin Mint, Bicentennial Series, see Franklin Mint Medals, Fifty-State Bicentennial

Franklin Mint, Birds Series, see Franklin Mint Medals, Roberts' Bird Series

Franklin Mint, Builders of our Nation, see Franklin Mint Medals, Patriots Hall of Fame Series

Franklin Mint, Businessmen Series, see Franklin Mint Medals, Ten Greatest Men of American Business

Franklin Mint Medals, Calendar

Benjamin Franklin, Roberts, J	1966	625	3.00	Unknown
Benjamin Franklin, Roberts, J	1967	2267	4.50	Unknown
Benjamin Franklin, Roberts, D	1971	1656	50.00	Unknown
Benjamin Franklin, Roberts, J	1971	4406	10.00	Unknown
Zodiac Signs, D	1974	Year	60.00	49.50 to 73.50
Zodiac Signs, J	1974	Year	12.00	12.00

Franklin Mint Medals, Chiamata Degli Apostoli

Saint Andrew, 57mm., D, A	1972	1225	24.00	Unknown
Saint Bartholomew, 57mm., D, A	1972	1225	24.00	Unknown
Saint Matthew, 57mm., D, A	1972	1225	24.00	Unknown
Saint Matthias, 57mm., D, A	1972	1225	24.00	Unknown
Saint Peter, 57mm., D, A	1972	1225	24.00	Unknown
Saint Simon, 57mm., D, A	1972	1225	24.00	Unknown
Saint Thomas, 57mm., D, A	1972	1225	24.00	Unknown
Saint Andrew, 57mm., N, A	1972	626	9.00	Unknown
Saint Bartholomew, 57mm., N, A	1972	626	9.00	Unknown
Saint Matthew, 57mm., N, A	1972	626	9.00	Unknown
Saint Matthias, 57mm., N, A	1972	626	9.00	Unknown
Saint Peter, 57mm., Na,	1972	626	9.00	Unknown
Saint Simon, 57mm., N, A	1972	626	9.00	Unknown
Saint Thomas, 57mm., N, A	1972	626	9.00	Unknown

**Franklin Mint, Defenders of Freedom, see Franklin Mint Medals,
Patriots Hall of Fame**

**Franklin Mint, Division and Reunion Series, see Franklin Mint
Medals, Patriots Hall of Fame Series**

Franklin Mint Medals, East African Wild Life Society

African Buffalo, 51mm., D, P	1971-1972	3208	20.00	25.00 to 30.00
Black Rhinoceros, 51mm., D, P	1971-1972	3208	20.00	25.00 to 30.00
Cheetah, 51mm., D, P	1971-1972	3208	20.00	25.00 to 30.00
Eland, 51mm., D, P	1971-1972	3208	20.00	25.00 to 30.00
Elephant, 51mm., D, P	1971-1972	3208	20.00	25.00 to 30.00
Gerenuk, 51mm., D, P	1971-1972	3208	20.00	25.00 to 30.00
Gorilla, 51mm., D, P	1971-1972	3208	20.00	25.00 to 30.00
Grevy's Zebra, 51mm., D, P	1971-1972	3208	20.00	25.00 to 30.00
Hippopotamus, 51mm., D, P	1971-1972	3208	20.00	25.00 to 30.00
Impala, 51mm., D, P	1971-1972	3208	20.00	25.00 to 30.00
Klipspringer, 51mm., D, P	1971-1972	3208	20.00	25.00 to 30.00
Kongoni Hartebeest, 51mm., D, P	1971-1972	3208	20.00	25.00 to 30.00
Leopard, 51mm., D, P	1971-1972	3208	20.00	25.00 to 30.00
Lion, 51mm., D, P	1971-1972	3208	20.00	25.00 to 30.00
Reticulated Giraffe, 51mm., D, P	1971-1972	3208	20.00	25.00 to 30.00
Roan Antelope, 51mm., D, P	1971-1972	3208	20.00	25.00 to 30.00
Sable Antelope, 51mm., D, P	1971-1972	3208	20.00	25.00 to 30.00
Thomson's Gazelle, 51mm., D, P	1971-1972	3208	20.00	25.00 to 30.00
Warthog, 51mm., D, P	1971-1972	3208	20.00	25.00 to 30.00
Wildebeest, 51mm., D, P	1971-1972	3208	20.00	25.00 to 30.00
African Buffalo, 51mm., F, P	1971-1972	2687	25.00	30.00 to 35.00
Black Rhinoceros, 51mm., F, P	1971-1972	2687	25.00	30.00 to 35.00
Cheetah, 51mm., F, P	1971-1972	2687	25.00	30.00 to 35.00
Eland, 51mm., F, P	1971-1972	2687	25.00	30.00 to 35.00
Elephant, 51mm., F, P	1971-1972	2687	25.00	30.00 to 35.00
Gerenuk, 51mm., F, P	1971-1972	2687	25.00	30.00 to 35.00
Gorilla, 51mm., F, P	1971-1972	2687	25.00	30.00 to 35.00
Grevy's Zebra, 51mm., F, P	1971-1972	2687	25.00	30.00 to 35.00
Hippopotamus, 51mm., F, P	1971-1972	2687	25.00	30.00 to 35.00
Impala, 51mm., F, P	1971-1972	2687	25.00	30.00 to 35.00
Klipspringer, 51mm., F, P	1971-1972	2687	25.00	30.00 to 35.00
Kongoni Hartebeest, 51mm., F, P	1971-1972	2687	25.00	30.00 to 35.00
Leopard, 51mm., F, P	1971-1972	2687	25.00	30.00 to 35.00
Lion, 51mm., F, P	1971-1972	2687	25.00	30.00 to 35.00
Reticulated Giraffe, 51mm., F, P	1971-1972	2687	25.00	30.00 to 35.00
Roan Antelope, 51mm., F, P	1971-1972	2687	25.00	30.00 to 35.00
Sable Antelope, 51mm., F, P	1971-1972	2687	25.00	30.00 to 35.00
Thomson's Gazelle, 51mm., F, P	1971-1972	2687	25.00	30.00 to 35.00
Warthog, 51mm., F, P	1971-1972	2687	25.00	30.00 to 35.00
Wildebeest, 51mm., F, P	1971-1972	2687	25.00	30.00 to 35.00
African Buffalo, 51mm., J, P	1971-1972	2329	8.00	10.00
Black Rhinoceros, 51mm., J, P	1971-1972	2329	8.00	10.00
Cheetah, 51mm., J, P	1971-1972	2329	8.00	10.00
Eland, 51mm., J, P	1971-1972	2329	8.00	10.00
Elephant, 51mm., J, P	1971-1972	2329	8.00	10.00
Gerenuk, 51mm., J, P	1971-1972	2329	8.00	10.00
Gorilla, 51mm., J, P	1971-1972	2329	8.00	10.00
Grevy's Zebra, 51mm., J, P	1971-1972	2329	8.00	10.00
Hippopotamus, 51mm., J, P	1971-1972	2329	8.00	10.00
Impala, 51mm., J, P	1971-1972	2329	8.00	10.00
Klipspringer, 51mm., J, P	1971-1972	2329	8.00	10.00
Kongoni Hartebeest, 51mm., J, P	1971-1972	2329	8.00	10.00
Leopard, 51mm., J, P	1971-1972	2329	8.00	10.00
Lion, 51mm., J, P	1971-1972	2329	8.00	10.00
Reticulated Giraffe, 51mm., J, P	1971-1972	2329	8.00	10.00
Roan Antelope, 51mm., J, P	1971-1972	2329	8.00	10.00
Sable Antelope, 51mm., J, P	1971-1972	2329	8.00	10.00
Thomson's Gazelle, 51mm., J, P	1971-1972	2329	8.00	10.00
Warthog, 51mm., J, P	1971-1972	2329	8.00	10.00
Wildebeest, 51mm., J, P	1971-1972	2329	8.00	10.00
African Buffalo, J	1973	Year	9.00	9.00

Black Rhinoceros, J	1973	Year	9.00	9.00
Cheetahs, J	1973	Year	9.00	9.00
Eland, J	1973	Year	9.00	9.00
Elephants, J	1973	Year	9.00	9.00
Gerenuks, J	1973	Year	9.00	9.00
Gorillas, J	1973	Year	9.00	9.00
Grevy's Zebras, J	1973	Year	9.00	9.00
Hippopotami, J	1973	Year	9.00	9.00
Impalas, J	1973	Year	9.00	9.00
Klipspringers, J	1973	Year	9.00	9.00
Kongoni Hartebeests, J	1973	Year	9.00	9.00
Leopard, J	1973	Year	9.00	9.00
Lions, J	1973	Year	9.00	9.00
Reticulated Giraffes, J	1973	Year	9.00	9.00
Roan Antelopes, J	1973	Year	9.00	9.00
Sable Antelopes, J	1973	Year	9.00	9.00
Thomson's Gazelles, J	1973	Year	9.00	9.00
Warthogs, J	1973	Year	9.00	9.00
Wildebeests, J	1973	Year	9.00	9.00

Franklin Mint Medals, Eyewitness Commemorative Issues

First Step On The Moon, A, M	1969	10800	20.00	30.00
First Step On The Moon, A, P	1969	69	750.00	1000.00
First Step On The Moon, D, M	1969	120382	7.50	35.00
First Step On The Moon, S, P	1969	329		Unknown
Apollo 15, 39mm., D, Pl	1971	31851	12.50	Unknown
Presidential Journey To China, 45mm., D, P	1972	28098	15.00	28.75
Presidential Journey To China, 45mm., F, P	1972	14624	20.00	Unknown
Presidential Journey To Russia, 45mm., D, P	1972	16334	15.00	27.50
Presidential Journey To Russia, 45mm., F, P	1972	7258	20.00	Unknown
Apollo 17, D, P	1973	30126	12.50	12.50
Skylab, D, P	1973	Year	15.00	22.50
Viet-Nam Peace Agreement, 45mm., D, P	1973	12357	15.00	22.50
Viet-Nam Peace Agreement, 45mm., F, P	1973	3302	20.00	20.00
Comet Kohoutek, 45mm, D, P	1973-1974	Year	17.50	17.50
Comet Kohoutek, 45mm, F, P	1973-1974	Year	22.50	22.50

Franklin Mint Medals, Fifty-State Bicentennial

Alabama, Beck, 39mm., D, P	1972-1976	20340	12.50	15.00 to 17.00
Alaska, Kirschbaum, 39mm., D, P	1972-1976	20340	12.50	15.00 to 17.00
Arizona, Robertson, 39mm., D, P	1972-1976	20340	12.50	15.00 to 17.00
Arkansas, Heflin, 39mm., D, P	1972-1976	20340	12.50	15.00 to 17.00
California, Knight, Jr., 39mm., D, P	1972-1976	20340	12.50	15.00 to 17.00
Colorado, Hughey, 39mm., D, P	1972-1976	20340	12.50	15.00 to 17.00
Connecticut, Lettick, 39mm., D, P	1972-1976	20340	12.50	15.00 to 17.00
Delaware, Martin, 39mm., D, P	1972-1976	20340	12.50	15.00 to 17.00
Florida, Butler, 39mm., D, P	1972-1976	20340	12.50	15.00 to 17.00
Georgia, Orr, Jr., 39mm., D, P	1972-1976	20340	12.50	15.00 to 17.00
Hawaii, Hakasone, 39mm., D, P	1972-1976	20340	12.50	15.00 to 17.00
Idaho, Evans, 39mm., D, P	1972-1976	20340	12.50	15.00 to 17.00
Illinois, Burnside, 3.Mm., D, P	1972-1976	20340	12.50	15.00 to 17.00
Indiana, Miller, 39mm., D, P	1972-1976	20340	12.50	15.00 to 17.00
Iowa, Kreye-Janowski, 39mm., D, P	1972-1976	20340	12.50	15.00 to 17.00
Kansas, Daves, 39mm., D, P	1972-1976	20340	12.50	15.00 to 17.00
Kentucky, Ventreese, Jr., 39mm., D, P	1972-1976	20340	12.50	15.00 to 17.00
Louisiana, Stracener, 39mm., D, P	1972-1976	20340	12.50	15.00 to 17.00
Maine, Dyer, 39mm., D, P	1972-1976	20340	12.50	15.00 to 17.00
Maryland, Lee, 39mm., D, P	1972-1976	20340	12.50	15.00 to 17.00
Massachusetts, Provest, 39mm., D, P	1972-1976	20340	12.50	15.00 to 17.00
Michigan, Junak, 39mm., D, P	1972-1976	20340	12.50	15.00 to 17.00
Minnesota, Hussung, 39mm., D, P	1972-1976	20340	12.50	15.00 to 17.00
Mississippi, Whittington, 39mm., D, P	1972-1976	20340	12.50	15.00 to 17.00
Missouri, Johnson, 39mm., D, P	1972-1976	20340	12.50	15.00 to 17.00
Montana, Mccall, Jr., 39mm., D, P	1972-1976	20340	12.50	15.00 to 17.00
Nebraska, Nelson, 39mm., D, P	1972-1976	20340	12.50	15.00 to 17.00
Nevada, Lesnick, 39mm., D, P	1972-1976	20340	12.50	15.00 to 17.00
New Hampshire, Lemire, 39mm., D, P	1972-1976	20340	12.50	15.00 to 17.00
New Jersey, Petruccelli, 39mm., D, P	1972-1976	20340	12.50	15.00 to 17.00
New Mexico, Vasquez, 39mm., D, P	1972-1976	20340	12.50	15.00 to 17.00
New York, Barton, 39mm., D, P	1972-1976	20340	12.50	15.00 to 17.00
North Carolina, Ferree, Jr., 39mm., D, P	1972-1976	20340	12.50	15.00 to 17.00

North Dakota, Hetland, 39mm., D, P	1972-1976	20340	12.50	15.00 to 17.00
Ohio, Young, 39mm., D, P	1972-1976	20340	12.50	15.00 to 17.00
Oklahoma, Taylor, 39mm., D, P	1972-1976	20340	12.50	15.00 to 17.00
Oregon, Erceg, 39mm., D, P	1972-1976	20340	12.50	15.00 to 17.00
Pennsylvania, Barnett, 39mm., D, P	1972-1976	20340	12.50	15.00 to 17.00
Rhode Island, Benson, 39mm., D, P	1972-1976	20340	12.50	15.00 to 17.00
South Carolina, Haynsworth, 39mm., D, P	1972-1976	20340	12.50	15.00 to 17.00
South Dakota, Inberg, 39mm., D, P	1972-1976	20340	12.50	15.00 to 17.00
Tennessee, Zimmerman, 39mm., D, P	1972-1976	20340	12.50	15.00 to 17.00
Texas, Campbell, 39mm., D, P	1972-1976	20340	12.50	15.00 to 17.00
Utah, Huler, 39mm., D, P	1972-1976	20340	12.50	15.00 to 17.00
Vermont, Kennedy, 39mm., D, P	1972-1976	20340	12.50	15.00 to 17.00
Virginia, Greenwell, 39mm., D, P	1972-1976	20340	12.50	15.00 to 17.00
Washington, Hall, 39mm., D, P	1972-1976	20340	12.50	15.00 to 17.00
West Virginia, Blevins, 39mm., D, P	1972-1976	20340	12.50	15.00 to 17.00
Wisconsin, Burkert, 39mm., D, P	1972-1976	20340	12.50	15.00 to 17.00
Wyoming, Deaderick, 39mm., D, P	1972-1976	20340	12.50	15.00 to 17.00

Franklin Mint Medals, First Ladies of the United States

Adams, Abigail, 1797-1801, 39mm., D, P	1971-1972	7373	9.50	10.00 to 11.00
Adams, Louisa, 1825-1829, 39mm., D, P	1971-1972	7373	9.50	10.00 to 11.00
Cleveland, Frances, 1885-1889, 39mm., D, P	1971-1972	7373	9.50	10.00 to 11.00
Coolidge, Grace, 1923-1929, 39mm., D, P	1971-1972	7373	9.50	10.00 to 11.00
Donelson, Emily, 1829-1836, 39mm., D, P	1971-1972	7373	9.50	10.00 to 11.00
Eisenhower, Mamie, 1953-1961, 39mm., D, P	1971-1972	7373	9.50	10.00 to 11.00
Fillmore, Abigail, 1850-1853, 39mm., D, P	1971-1972	7373	9.50	10.00 to 11.00
Garfield, Lucretia, 1881-1881, 39mm., D, P	1971-1972	7373	9.50	10.00 to 11.00
Grant, Julia, 1869-1877, 39mm., D, P	1971-1972	7373	9.50	10.00 to 11.00
Harding, Florence, 1921-1923, 39mm., D, P	1971-1972	7373	9.50	10.00 to 11.00
Harrison, Anna, 1841-1841, 39mm., D, P	1971-1972	7373	9.50	10.00 to 11.00
Harrison, Caroline, 1889-1892, 39mm., D, P	1971-1972	7373	9.50	10.00 to 11.00
Hayes, Lucy, 1877-1881, 39mm., D, P	1971-1972	7373	9.50	10.00 to 11.00
Hoover, Lou, 1929-1933, 39mm., D, P	1971-1972	7373	9.50	10.00 to 11.00
Jackson, Sarah, 1836-1837, 39mm., D, P	1971-1972	7373	9.50	10.00 to 11.00
Johnson, Eliza, 1865-1869, 39mm., D, P	1971-1972	7373	9.50	10.00 to 11.00
Johnson, Lady Bird, 1963-1969, 39mm., D, P	1971-1972	7373	9.50	10.00 to 11.00
Kennedy, Jacqueline, 1961-1963, 39mm., D, P	1971-1972	7373	9.50	10.00 to 11.00
Lane, Harriet, 1857-1861, 39mm., D, P	1971-1972	7373	9.50	10.00 to 11.00
Lincoln, Mary, 1861-1865, 39mm., D, P	1971-1972	7373	9.50	10.00 to 11.00
Madison, Dolley, 1809-1817, 39mm., D, P	1971-1972	7373	9.50	10.00 to 11.00
McElroy, Mary, 1881-1885, 39mm., D, P	1971-1972	7373	9.50	10.00 to 11.00
McKee, Mary, 1892-1893, 39mm., D, P	1971-1972	7373	9.50	10.00 to 11.00
McKinley, Ida, 1897-1901, 39mm., D, P	1971-1972	7373	9.50	10.00 to 11.00
Monroe, Elizabeth, 1817-1825, 39mm., D, P	1971-1972	7373	9.50	10.00 to 11.00
Nixon, Patricia, 1969-, 39mm., D, P	1971-1972	7373	9.50	10.00 to 11.00
Pierce, Jane, 1853-1857, 39mm., D, P	1971-1972	7373	9.50	10.00 to 11.00
Polk, Sarah, 1845-1849, 39mm., D, P	1971-1972	7373	9.50	10.00 to 11.00
Randolph, Martha, 1801-1809, 39mm., D, P	1971-1972	7373	9.50	10.00 to 11.00
Roosevelt, Edith, 1901-1909, 39mm., D, P	1971-1972	7373	9.50	10.00 to 11.00
Roosevelt, Eleanor, 1933-1945, 39mm., D, P	1971-1972	7373	9.50	10.00 to 11.00
Taft, Helen, 1909-1913, 39mm., D, P	1971-1972	7373	9.50	10.00 to 11.00
Taylor, Margaret, 1849-1850, 39mm., D, P	1971-1972	7373	9.50	10.00 to 11.00
Truman, Bess, 1945-1953, 39mm., D, P	1971-1972	7373	9.50	10.00 to 11.00
Tyler, Julia, 1844-1845, 39mm., D, P	1971-1972	7373	9.50	10.00 to 11.00
Tyler, Letitia, 1841-1842, 39mm., D, P	1971-1972	7373	9.50	10.00 to 11.00
Van Buren, Angelica, 1837-1841, 39mm., D, P	1971-1972	7373	9.50	10.00 to 11.00
Washington, Martha, 1789-1797, 39mm., D, P	1971-1972	7373	9.50	10.00 to 11.00
Wilson, Edith, 1915-1921, 39mm., D, P	1971-1972	7373	9.50	10.00 to 11.00
Wilson, Ellen, 1913-1914, 39mm., D, P	1971-1972	7373	9.50	10.00 to 11.00
Adams, Abigail, 1797-1801, 39mm., D, Pl	1972	2913	9.50	10.00 to 11.00
Adams, Louisa, 1825-1829, 39mm., D, Pl	1972	2913	9.50	10.00 to 11.00
Cleveland, Frances, 1885-1889, 39mm., D, Pl	1972	2913	9.50	10.00 to 11.00
Coolidge, Grace, 1923-1929, 39mm., D, Pl	1972	2913	9.50	10.00 to 11.00
Donelson, Emily, 1829-1836, 39mm., D, Pl	1972	2913	.95	10.00 to 11.00
Fillmore, Abigail, 1850-1853, 39mm., D, Pl	1972	2913	9.50	10.00 to 11.00
Eisenhower, Mamie, 1953-1961, 39mm., D, Pl	1972	2913	9.50	10.00 to 11.00
Garfield, Lucretia, 1881-1881, 39mm., D, Pl	1972	2913	9.50	10.00 to 11.00
Grant, Julia, 1869-1877, 39mm., D, Pl	1972	2913	9.50	10.00 to 11.00
Harding, Florence, 1921-1923, 39mm., D, Pl	1972	2913	9.50	10.00 to 11.00
Harrison, Anna, 1841-1841, 39mm., D, Pl	1972	2913	9.50	10.00 to 11.00

Harrison, Caroline, 1889-1892, 39mm., D, Pl	1972	2913	9.50	10.00 to 11.00
Hayes, Lucy, 1877-1881, 39mm., D, Pl	1972	2913	9.50	10.00 to 11.00
Hoover, Lou, 1929-1933, 39mm., D, Pl	1972	2913	9.50	10.00 to 11.00
Jackson, Sarah, 1836-1837, 39mm., D, Pl	1972	2913	9.50	10.00 to 11.00
Johnson, Eliza, 1865-1869, 39mm., D, Pl	1972	2913	9.50	10.00 to 11.00
Johnson, Lady Bird, 1963-1969, 39mm., D, Pl	1972	2913	9.50	10.00 to 11.00
Kennedy, Jacqueline, 1961-1963, 39mm., D, Pl	1972	2913	9.50	10.00 to 11.00
Lane, Harriet, 1857-1861, 39mm., D, Pl	1972	2913	9.50	10.00 to 11.00
Lincoln, Mary, 1861-1865, 39mm., D, Pl	1972	2913	9.50	10.00 to 11.00
Madison, Dolley, 1809-1817, 39mm., D, Pl	1972	2913	9.50	10.00 to 11.00
McElroy, Mary, 1881-1885, 39mm., D, Pl	1972	2913	9.50	10.00 to 11.00
McKee, Mary, 1892-1893, 39mm., D, Pl	1972	2913	9.50	10.00 to 11.00
McKinley, Ida, 1897-1901, 39mm., D, Pl	1972	2913	9.50	10.00 to 11.00
Monroe, Elizabeth, 1817-1825, 39mm., D, Pl	1972	2913	9.50	10.00 to 11.00
Nixon, Patricia, 1969-, 39mm., D, Pl	1972	2913	9.50	10.00 to 11.00
Pierce, Jane, 1853-1857, 39mm., D, Pl	1972	2913	9.50	10.00 to 11.00
Polk, Sarah, 1845-1849, 39mm., D, Pl	1972	2913	9.50	10.00 to 11.00
Randolph, Martha, 1801-1809, 39mm., D, Pi	1972	2913	9.50	10.00 to 11.00
Roosevelt, Edith, 1901-1909, 39mm., D, Pl	1972	2913	9.50	10.00 to 11.00
Roosevelt, Eleanor, 1933-1945, 39mm., D, Pl	1972	2913	9.50	10.00 to 11.00
Taft, Helen, 1909-1913, 39mm., D, Pl	1972	2913	9.50	10.00 to 11.00
Taylor, Margaret, 1849-1850, 39mm., D, Pl	1972	2913	9.50	10.00 to 11.00
Truman, Bess, 1945-1953, 39mm., D, Pl	1972	2913	9.50	10.00 to 11.00
Tyler, Julia, 1844-1845, 39mm., D, Pl	1972	2913	9.50	10.00 to 11.00
Tyler, Letitia, 1841-1842, 39mm., D, Pl	1972	2913	9.50	10.00 to 11.00
Van Buren, Angelica, 1837-1841, 39mm., D, Pl	1972	2913	9.50	10.00 to 11.00
Washington, Martha, 1789-1797, 39mm., D, Pl	1972	2913	9.50	10.00 to 11.00
Wilson, Edith, 1915-1921, 39mm., D, Pl	1972	2913	9.50	10.00 to 11.00
Wilson, Ellen, 1913-1914, 39mm., D, Pl	1972	2913	9.50	10.00 to 11.00

Franklin Mint, Football Series, see Franklin Mint Medals, Pro

Football's Immortals

Franklin Mint Medals, Gallery of Great Americans

Addams, Jane, Baldwin, 39mm., D, P	1970	8575	8.75	Unknown
Audubon, John J., Lauser, 39mm., D, P	1970	8575	8.75	Unknown
Boone, Daniel, Jones, 39mm., D, P	1970	8575	8.75	Unknown
Clemens, Samuel, Schroeder, 39mm., D, P	1970	8575	8.75	Unknown
Edison, Thomas A., Baldwin, 39mm., D, P	1970	8575	8.75	Unknown
Einstein, Albert, Rufo, 39mm., D, P	1970	8575	8.75	Unknown
Ford, Henry, Strailey, 39mm., D, P	1970	8575	8.75	Unknown
Pershing, John J., Lauser, 39mm., D, P	1970	8575	8.75	Unknown
Rogers, Will, Ferrell, 39mm., D, P	1970	8575	8.75	Unknown
Thorpe, Jim, Faulkner, 39mm., D, P	1970	8575	8.75	Unknown
Washington, Booker T., Rufo, 39mm., D, P	1970	8575	8.75	Unknown
Washington, George, Faulkner, 39mm., D, P	1970	8575	8.75	Unknown
Addams, Jane, Baldwin, 39mm., J, P	1970	4866	3.50	Unknown
Audubon, John J., Lauser, 39mm., J, P	1970	4866	3.50	Unknown
Boone, Daniel, Jones, 39mm., J, P	1970	4866	3.50	Unknown
Clemens, Samuel, Schroeder, 39mm., J, P	1970	4866	3.50	Unknown
Edison, Thomas A., Baldwin, 39mm., J, P	1970	4866	3.50	Unknown
Einstein, Albert, Rufo, 39mm., J, P	1970	4866	3.50	Unknown
Ford, Henry, Strailey, 39mm., J, P	1970	4866	3.50	Unknown
Pershing, John, Lauser, 39mm., J, P	1970	4866	3.50	Unknown
Rogers, Will, Ferrell, 39mm., J, P	1970	4866	3.50	Unknown
Thorpe, Jim, Faulkner, 39mm., J, P	1970	4866	3.50	Unknown
Washington, Booker T., Rufo, 39mm., J, P	1970	4866	3.50	Unknown
Washington, George, Faulkner, 39mm., J, P	1970	4866	3.50	Unknown
Bell, Alexander Graham, Ferrell, 39mm., D, P	1971	8578	8.75	Unknown
Byrd, Richard E., Park, 39mm., D, P	1971	8578	8.75	Unknown
Carnegie, Andrew, Blaker, 39mm., D, P	1971	8578	8.75	Unknown
Fields, W.C., Park, 39mm., D, P	1971	8578	8.75	Unknown
Franklin, Benjamin, Jones, 39mm., D, P	1971	8578	8.75	Unknown
Gershwin, George, Ferrell, 39mm., D, P	1971	8578	8.75	Unknown
Holmes, Oliver Wendell, Baldwin, 39mm., D, P	1971	8578	8.75	Unknown
Keller, Helen, Blaker, 39mm., D, P	1971	8578	8.75	Unknown
MacArthur, Douglas, Nemeth, 39mm., D, P	1971	8578	8.75	Unknown
Poe, Edgar Allan, Nemeth, 39mm., D, P	1971	8578	8.75	Unknown
Reed, Walter, Schroeder, 39mm., D, P	1971	8578	8.75	Unknown
Ruth, George 'Babe,' Ferrell, 39mm., D, P	1971	8578	8.75	Unknown

Bell, Alexander Graham, Ferrell, 39mm., J, P	1971	4866	3.50	Unknown
Byrd, Richard E., Park, 39mm., J, P	1971	4866	3.50	Unknown
Carnegie, Andrew, Blaker, 39mm., J, P	1971	4866	3.50	Unknown
Fields, W.C., Park, 39mm., J, P	1971	4866	3.50	Unknown
Franklin, Benjamin, Jones, 39mm., J, P	1971	4866	3.50	Unknown
Gershwin, George, Ferrell, 39mm., J, P	1971	4866	3.50	Unknown
Holmes, Oliver Wendell, Baldwin, 39mm., J, P	1971	4866	3.50	Unknown
Keller, Helen, Blaker, 39mm., J, P	1971	4866	3.50	Unknown
MacArthur, Douglas, Nemeth, 39mm., J, P	1971	4866	3.50	Unknown
Poe, Edgar Allan, Nemeth, 39mm., J, P	1971	4866	3.50	Unknown
Reed, Walter, Schroeder, 39mm., J, P	1971	4866	3.50	Unknown
Ruth, George 'Babe', Ferrell, 39mm., J, P	1971	4866	3.50	Unknown
Anthony, Susan B., Ferrell, 39mm., D, P	1972	2226	8.75	Unknown
Carver, George Washington, Faulkner, 39mm., D, P	1972	2226	8.75	Unknown
Cooper, Gary, Baldwin, 39mm., D, P	1972	2226	8.75	Unknown
Disney, Walt, Miller, 39mm., D, P	1972	2226	8.75	Unknown
Eisenhower, Dwight D., Faulkner, 39mm., D, P	1972	2226	8.75	Unknown
Gehrig, Lou, Ponter, 39mm., D, P	1972	2226	8.75	Unknown
Lewis & Clark, Ponter, 39mm., D, P	1972	2226	8.75	Unknown
Lincoln, Abraham, Baldwin, 39mm., D, P	1972	2226	8.75	Unknown
Longfellow, Henry Wadsworth, 39mm., D, P	1972	2226	8.75	Unknown
Mann, Horace, Park, 39mm., D, P	1972	2226	8.75	Unknown
Rockefeller, John D., Sr., Caimi, 39mm., D, P	1972	2226	8.75	Unknown
Wright, Wilbur & Orville, Faulkner, 39mm., D, P	1972	2226	8.75	Unknown
Anthony, Susan B., Ferrell, 39mm., J, P	1972	1338	3.50	Unknown
Carver, George Washington, Faulkner, 39mm., J, P	1972	1338	3.50	Unknown
Cooper, Gary, Baldwin, 39mm., J, P	1972	1338	3.50	Unknown
Disney, Walt, Miller, 39mm., J, P	1972	1338	3.50	Unknown
Eisenhower, Dwight D., Faulkner, 39mm., J, P	1972	1338	3.50	Unknown
Gehrig, Lou, Ponter, 39mm., J, P	1972	1338	3.50	Unknown
Lewis & Clark, Ponter, 39mm., J, P	1972	1338	3.50	Unknown
Lincoln, Abraham, Baldwin, 39mm., J, P	1972	1338	3.50	Unknown
Longfellow, Henry Wadsworth, 39mm., J, P	1972	1338	3.50	Unknown
Mann, Horace, Park, 39mm., J, P	1972	1338	3.50	Unknown
Rockefeller, John D., Sr., Caimi, 39mm., J, P	1972	1338	3.50	Unknown
Wright, Wilbur & Orville, Faulkner, 39mm., J, P	1972	1338	3.50	Unknown

Franklin Mint Medals, Genius of Michelangelo

Angel Supporting The Cross, D, P	1970-1972	19412	10.00	Unknown
Battle Of The Centaurs, D, P	1970-1972	19412	10.00	Unknown
Charon's Boat, D, P	1970-1972	19412	10.00	Unknown
Christ, The Judge With Mary, D, P	1970-1972	19412	10.00	Unknown
Creation Of The Sun & Moon, D, P	1970-1972	19412	10.00	Unknown
Crucifixion Of St.Peter, D, P	1970-1972	19412	10.00	Unknown
David, D, P	1970-1972	19412	10.00	Unknown
David & Goliath, D, P	1970-1972	19412	10.00	Unknown
Dawn, D, P	1970-1972	19412	10.00	Unknown
Ignudo, D, P	1970-1972	19412	10.00	Unknown
Judith & Holofernes, D, P	1970-1972	19412	10.00	Unknown
Mask Of Night, D, P	1970-1972	19412	10.00	Unknown
Noah's Sacrifice, D, P	1970-1972	19412	10.00	Unknown
St.Bartholomew, D, P	1970-1972	19412	10.00	Unknown
The Creation Of Adam, D, P	1970-1972	19412	10.00	Unknown
The Creation Of Eve, D, P	1970-1972	19412	10.00	Unknown
The Cumaean Sibyl, D, P	1970-1972	19412	10.00	Unknown
The Dammed Man, D, P	1970-1972	19412	10.00	Unknown
The Death Of Haman, D, P	1970-1972	19412	10.00	Unknown
The Delphic Sibyl, D, P	1970-1972	19412	10.00	Unknown
The Doni Tondo, D, P	1970-1972	19412	10.00	Unknown
The Expulsion, D, P	1970-1972	19412	10.00	Unknown
The Fall Of Phaeton, D, P	1970-1972	19412	10.00	Unknown
The Forefathers Of Christ, D, P	1970-1972	19412	10.00	Unknown
The Gathering Of The Waters, D, P	1970-1972	19412	10.00	Unknown
The Head Of God, D, P*	1970-1972	19412	10.00	Unknown
The Libyan Sibyl, D, P	1970-1972	19412	10.00	Unknown
The Prophet Isaiah, D, P	1970-1972	19412	10.00	Unknown
The Prophet Jeremiah, D, P	1970-1972	19412	10.00	Unknown
The Prophet Jonah, D, P	1970-1972	19412	10.00	Unknown
The Resurrection, D, P	1970-1972	19412	10.00	Unknown

Franklin Mint, Genius Of Michelangelo,
The Head Of God, 1970-1972

The Temptation, D, P	1970-1972	19412	10.00	Unknown
The Universal Flood, D, P	1970-1972	19412	10.00	Unknown
Tityus, D, P	1970-1972	19412	10.00	Unknown
David-Apollo, D, P	1973	19412	10.00	10.00
Day, D, P	1973	19412	10.00	10.00
Kneeling Angel, D, P	1973	19412	10.00	10.00
Little Satyr Of Bacchus, D, P	1973	19412	10.00	10.00
Lorenzo De Medici, D, P	1973	19412	10.00	10.00
Moses, D, P	1973	19412	10.00	10.00
Rachel, D, P	1973	19412	10.00	10.00
St, Paul, D, P	1973	19412	10.00	10.00
St.Petronius, D, P	1973	19412	10.00	10.00
The Bearded Prisoner, D, P	1973	19412	10.00	10.00
The Dying Slave, D, P	1973	19412	10.00	10.00
Brutus, D, P	1974	19412	10.00	10.00
Giuliano De Medici, D, P	1974	19412	10.00	10.00
Head Of Bruges Madonna, D, P	1974	19412	10.00	10.00
Head Of Child From Bruges Madonna, D, P	1974	19412	10.00	10.00
Leah, D, P	1974	19412	10.00	10.00
Madonna Of The Stairs, D, P	1974	19412	10.00	10.00
St.Matthew, D, P	1974	19412	10.00	10.00
St.Peter, D, P	1974	19412	10.00	10.00
Taddei Tondo, D, P	1974	19412	10.00	10.00
The Medici Madonna, D, P	1974	19412	10.00	10.00
The Pieta Of St.Peter's, D, P	1974	19412	10.00	10.00
The Risen Christ, D, P	1974	19412	10.00	10.00

Franklin Mint Medals, Genius of Rembrandt

Anatomy Lesson Of Doctor Tulp, 51mm., D, P	1972	5442	17.00	29.50
Aristotle & Bust Of Homer, 51mm., D, P	1972	5442	17.00	29.50
Jacob Blessing The Sons Of Joseph, 51mm., D, P	1972	5442	17.00	29.50
Jacob Wrestling With The Angel, 51mm., D, P	1972	5442	17.00	29.50
Jeremiah Lamenting, 51mm., D, P	1972	5442	17.00	29.50
Prophetess Hannah, 51mm., D, P	1972	5442	17.00	29.50
Portrait Of Saskia, 51mm., D, P	1972	5442	17.00	29.50
Bathsheba With King David's Letter, 51mm., D, P	1973	5442	17.00	17.00
Militia Co.Of Frans Banning Cocq, 51mm., D, P	1973	5442	17.00	17.00
Portrait Of Hendrickje Stoffels, 51mm., D, P	1973	5442	17.00	17.00
Portrait Of Jan Uytenbogaert, 51mm., D, P	1973	5442	17.00	17.00
Rembrandt's Son Titus At His Desk, 51mm., D, P	1973	5442	17.00	17.00
St.Jerome Reading, 51mm., D, P	1973	5442	17.00	17.00
The Money-Changer, 51mm., D, P	1973	5442	17.00	17.00
The Noble Slave, 51mm., D, P	1973	5442	17.00	17.00
The Polish Rider, 51mm., D, P	1973	5442	17.00	17.00
The Prodigal Son In The Tavern, 51mm., D, P	1973	5442	17.00	17.00
The Wedding Feast Of Samson, 51mm., D, P	1973	5442	17.00	17.00
Tobit & Anna With The Kid, 51mm., D, P	1973	5442	17.00	17.00
Boy In Fanciful Dress, 51mm., D, P	1974	5442	17.00	17.00
Christ Healing The Sick, 51mm., D, P	1974	5442	17.00	17.00
Christ In Storm On Sea Of Galilee, 51mm., D, P	1974	5442	17.00	17.00
Portrait Of Agatha Bas, 51mm., D, P	1974	5442	17.00	17.00
Portrait Of Jan Six, 51mm., D, P	1974	5442	17.00	17.00
Sampling Officials, Drapers' Guild, 51mm., D, P	1974	5442	17.00	17.00
Self-Portrait, 51mm., D, P	1974	5442	17.00	17.00
The Flight Into Egypt, 51mm., D, P	1974	5442	17.00	17.00
The Good Samaritan, 51mm., D, P	1974	5442	17.00	17.00
The Presentation At The Temple, 51mm., D, P	1974	5442	17.00	17.00
The Shipbuilder & His Wife, 51mm., D, P	1974	5442	17.00	17.00
The Three Trees, 51mm., D, P	1974	5442	17.00	17.00
Anatomy Lesson Of Doctor Tulp, 51mm., D, Pl	1972		17.00	Unknown
Aristotle & Bust Of Homer, 51mm., D, Pl	1972		17.00	Unknown
Jacob Blessing Sons Of Joseph, 51mm., D, Pl	1972		17.00	Unknown
Jacob Wrestling With The Angel, 51mm., D, Pl	1972		17.00	Unknown
Jeremiah Lamenting, 51mm., D, Pl	1972		17.00	Unknown
Portrait Of Saskia, 51mm., D, Pl	1972		17.00	Unknown
Prophetess Hannah, 51mm., D, Pl	1972		17.00	Unknown

Bathsheba With David's Letter, 51mm., D, Pl	1973	17.00	17.00
Militia Co.Of Frans Banning Cocq, 51mm., D, Pl	1973	17.00	17.00
Portrait Of Hendrickje Stoffels, 51mm., D, Pl	1973	17.00	17.00
Portrait Of Jan Uytenbogaert, 51mm., D, Pl	1973	17.00	17.00
Rembrandt's Son Titus At His Desk, 51mm., D, Pl	1973	17.00	17.00
St.Jerome Reading, 51mm., D, Pl	1973	17.00	17.00
The Money-Changer, 51mm., D, Pl	1973	17.00	17.00
The Noble Slave, 51mm., D, Pl	1973	17.00	17.00
The Polish Rider, 51mm., D, Pl	1973	17.00	17.00
The Prodigal Son In The Tavern, 51mm., D, Pl	1973	17.00	17.00
The Wedding Feast Of Samson, 51mm., D, Pl	1973	17.00	17.00
Tobit & Anna With The Kid, 51mm., D, Pl	1973	17.00	17.00
Boy In Fanciful Dress, 51mm., D, Pl	1974	17.00	17.00
Christ Healing The Sick, 51mm., D, Pl	1974	17.00	17.00
Christ In Storm On Sea Of Galilee, 51mm., D, Pl	1974	17.00	17.00
Portrait Of Agatha Bas, 51mm., D, Pl	1974	17.00	17.00
Portrait Of Jan Six, 51mm., D, Pl	1974	17.00	17.00
Sampling Officials, Drapers' Guild, 51mm., D, Pl	1974	17.00	17.00
Self-Portrait, 51mm., D, Pl	1974	17.00	17.00
The Flight Into Egypt, 51mm., D, Pl	1974	17.00	17.00
The Good Samaritan, 51mm., D, Pl	1974	17.00	17.00
The Presentation At The Temple, 51mm., D, Pl	1974	17.00	17.00
The Shipbuilder & His Wife, 51mm., D, Pl	1974	17.00	17.00
The Three Trees, 51mm., D, Pl	1974	17.00	17.00

Franklin Mint Medals, Governors' Edition

Alabama, Rufo, D, Pl	1970-1972	6249	8.75	Unknown
Alaska, Cornell, D, Pl	1970-1972	5399	8.75	Unknown
Arizona, Cornell, D, Pl	1970-1972	3749	8.75	Unknown
Arkansas, Stanton, D, Pl	1970-1972	3749	8.75	Unknown
California, Rufo, D, Pl	1970-1972	2899	8.75	Unknown
Colorado, Rufo, D, Pl	1970-1972	3749	8.75	Unknown
Connecticut, Cornell, D, Pl	1970-1972	2899	8.75	Unknown
Delaware, Jones, D, Pl	1970-1972	2899	8.75	Unknown
Florida, Cornell, D, Pl	1970-1972	866	8.75	Unknown
Georgia, Rufo, D, Pl	1970-1972	866	8.75	Unknown
Hawaii, Nathan, D, Pl	1970-1972	866	8.75	Unknown
Idaho, Jones, D, Pl	1970-1972	866	8.75	Unknown
Illinois, Nathan, D, Pl	1970-1972	866	8.75	Unknown
Indiana, Stanton, D, Pl	1970-1972	866	8.75	Unknown
Iowa, Rufo, D, Pl	1970-1972	866	8.75	Unknown
Kansas, Cornell, D, Pl	1970-1972	866	8.75	Unknown
Kentucky, Cornell, D, Pl	1970-1972	866	8.75	Unknown
Louisiana, Stanton, D, Pl	1970-1972	866	8.75	Unknown
Maine, Stanton, D, Pl	1970-1972	866	8.75	Unknown
Maryland, Rufo, D, Pl	1970-1972	866	8.75	Unknown
Massachusetts, Stanton, D, Pl	1970-1972	866	8.75	Unknown
Michigan, Cornell, D, Pl	1970-1972	866	8.75	Unknown
Minnesota, Rufo, D, Pl	1970-1972	866	8.75	Unknown
Mississippi, Rufo, D, Pl	1970-1972	866	8.75	Unknown
Missouri, Stanton, D, Pl	1970-1972	866	8.75	Unknown
Montana, Cornell, D, Pl	1970-1972	866	8.75	Unknown
Nebraska, Cornell, D, Pl	1970-1972	866	8.75	Unknown
Nevada, Cornell, D, Pl	1970-1972	866	8.75	Unknown
New Hampshire, Nathan, D, Pl	1970-1972	866	8.75	Unknown
New Jersey, Cornell, D, Pl	1970-1972	866	8.75	Unknown
New Mexico, Rufo, D, Pl	1970-1972	866	8.75	Unknown
New York, Stanton, D, Pl	1970-1972	866	8.75	Unknown
North Carolina, Rufo, D, Pl	1970-1972	866	8.75	Unknown
North Dakota, Stanton, D, Pl	1970-1972	866	8.75	Unknown
Ohio, Rufo, D, Pl	1970-1972	866	8.75	Unknown
Oklahoma, Rufo, D, Pl	1970-1972	866	8.75	Unknown
Oregon, Cornell, D, Pl	1970-1972	866	8.75	Unknown
Pennsylvania, Cornell, D, Pl	1970-1972	866	8.75	Unknown
Rhode Island, Cornell, D, Pl	1970-1972	866	8.75	Unknown
South Carolina, Stanton, D, Pl	1970-1972	869	8.75	Unknown
South Dakota, Stanton, D, Pl	1970-1972	866	8.75	Unknown
Tennessee, Stanton, D, Pl	1970-1972	866	8.75	Unknown
Texas, Cornell, D, Pl	1970-1972	866	8.75	Unknown
Utah, Rufo, D, Pl	1970-1972	866	8.75	Unknown

Vermont, Nathan, D, Pl	1970-1972	866	8.75	Unknown
Virginia, Stanton, D, Pl	1970-1972	866	8.75	Unknown
Washington, Rufo, D, Pl	1970-1972	866	8.75	Unknown
West Virginia, Cornell, D, Pl	1970-1972	866	8.75	Unknown
Wisconsin, Cornell, D, Pl	1970-1972	866	8.75	Unknown
Wyoming, Cornell, D, Pl	1970-1972	866	8.75	Unknown
Alabama, Rufo, F, Pl	1970-1972	9723	14.50	14.50 to 20.00
Alaska, Cornell, F, Pl	1970-1972	9723	14.50	14.50 to 20.00
Arizona, Cornell, F, Pl	1970-1972	6523	14.50	14.50 to 20.00
Arkansas, Stanton, F, Pl	1970-1972	6523	14.50	14.50 to 20.00
California, Rufo, F, Pl	1970-1972	6523	14.50	14.50 to 20.00
Colorado, Rufo, F, Pl	1970-1972	6523	14.50	14.50 to 20.00
Connecticut, Cornell, F, Pl	1970-1972	5084	14.50	14.50 to 20.00
Delaware, Jones, F, Pl	1970-1972	5084	14.50	14.50 to 20.00
Florida, Cornell, F, Pl	1970-1972	1303	14.50	14.50 to 20.00
Georgia, Rufo, F, Pl	1970-1972	1303	14.50	14.50 to 20.00
Hawaii, Nathan, F, Pl	1970-1972	1303	14.50	14.50 to 20.00
Idaho, Jones, F, Pl	1970-1972	1303	14.50	14.50 to 20.00
Illinois, Nathan, F, Pl	1970-1972	1303	14.50	14.50 to 20.00
Indiana, Stanton, F, Pl	1970-1972	1303	14.50	14.50 to 20.00
Iowa, Rufo, F, Pl	1970-1972	1303	14.50	14.50 to 20.00
Kansas, Cornell, F, Pl	1970-1972	1303	14.50	14.50 to 20.00
Kentucky, Cornell, F, Pl	1970-1972	1303	14.50	14.50 to 20.00
Louisiana, Stanton, F, Pl	1970-1972	1303	14.50	14.50 to 20.00
Maine, Stanton, F, Pl	1970-1972	1303	14.50	14.50 to 20.00
Maryland, Rufo, F, Pl	1970-1972	1303	14.50	14.50 to 20.00
Massachusetts, Stanton, F, Pl	1970-1972	1303	14.50	14.50 to 20.00
Michigan, Cornell, F, Pl	1970-1972	1303	14.50	14.50 to 20.00
Minnesota, Rufo, F, Pl	1970-1972	1303	14.50	14.50 to 20.00
Mississippi, Rufo, F, Pl	1970-1972	1303	14.50	14.50 to 20.00
Missouri, Stanton, F, Pl	1970-1972	1303	14.50	14.50 to 20.00
Montana, Cornell, F, Pl	1970-1972	1303	14.50	14.50 to 20.00
Nebraska, Cornell, F, Pl	1970-1972	1303	14.50	14.50 to 20.00
Nevada, Cornell, F, Pl	1970-1972	1303	14.50	14.50 to 20.00
New Hampshire, Nathan, F, Pl	1970-1972	1303	14.50	14.50 to 20.00
New Jersey, Cornell, F, Pl	1970-1972	1303	14.50	14.50 to 20.00
New Mexico, Rufo, F, Pl	1970-1972	1303	14.50	14.50 to 20.00
New York, Stanton, F, Pl	1970-1972	1303	14.50	14.50 to 20.00
North Carolina, Rufo, F, Pl	1970-1972	1303	14.50	14.50 to 20.00
North Dakota, Stanton, F, Pl	1970-1972	1303	14.50	14.50 to 20.00
Ohio, Rufo, F, Pl	1970-1972	1303	14.50	14.50 to 20.00
Oklahoma, Rufo, F, Pl	1970-1972	1303	14.50	14.50 to 20.00
Oregon, Cornell, F, Pl	1970-1972	1303	14.50	14.50 to 20.00
Pennsylvania, Cornell, F, Pl	1970-1972	1303	14.50	14.50 to 20.00
Rhode Island, Cornell, F, Pl	1970-1972	1303	14.50	14.50 to 20.00
South Carolina, Stanton, F, Pl	1970-1972	1303	14.50	14.50 to 20.00
South Dakota, Stanton, F, Pl	1970-1972	1303	14.50	14.50 to 20.00
Tennessee, Stanton, F, Pl	1970-1972	1303	14.50	14.50 to 20.00
Texas, Cornell, F, Pl	1970-1972	1303	14.50	14.50 to 20.00
Utah, Rufo, F, Pl	1970-1972	1303	14.50	14.50 to 20.00
Vermont, Nathan, F, Pl	1970-1972	1303	14.50	14.50 to 20.00
Virginia, Stanton, F, Pl	1970-1972	1303	14.50	14.50 to 20.00
Washington, Rufo, F, Pl	1970-1972	1303	14.50	14.50 to 20.00
West Virginia, Cornell, F, Pl	1970-1972	1303	14.50	14.50 to 20.00
Wisconsin, Cornell, F, Pl	1970-1972	1303	14.50	14.50 to 20.00
Wyoming, Cornell, F, Pl	1970-1972	1303	14.50	14.50 to 20.00
Alabama, Rufo, J, Pl	1970-1972	1371	3.50	Unknown
Alaska, Cornell, J, Pl	1970-1972	1266	3.50	Unknown
Arizona, Cornell, J, Pl	1970-1972	1266	3.50	Unknown
Arkansas, Stanton, J, Pl	1970-1972	1266	3.50	Unknown
California, Rufo, J, Pl	1970-1972	1161	3.50	Unknown
Colorado, Rufo, J, Pl	1970-1972	1266	3.50	Unknown
Connecticut, Cornell, J, Pl	1970-1972	1161	3.50	Unknown
Delaware, Jones, J, Pl	1970-1972	1161	3.50	Unknown
Florida, Cornell, J, Pl	1970-1972	155	3.50	Unknown
Georgia, Rufo, J, Pl	1970-1972	155	3.50	Unknown
Hawaii, Nathan, J, Pl	1970-1972	155	3.50	Unknown
Idaho, Jones, J, Pl	1970-1972	155	3.50	Unknown
Illinois, Nathan, J, Pl	1970-1972	155	3.50	Unknown

Indiana, Stanton, J, Pl	1970-1972	155	3.50	Unknown
Iowa, Rufo, J, Pl	1970-1972	155	3.50	Unknown
Kansas, Cornell, J, Pl	1970-1972	155	3.50	Unknown
Kentucky, Cornell, J, Pl	1970-1972	155	3.50	Unknown
Louisiana, Stanton, J, Pl	1970-1972	155	3.50	Unknown
Maine, Stanton, J, Pl	1970-1972	155	3.50	Unknown
Maryland, Rufo, J, Pl	1970-1972	155	3.50	Unknown
Massachusetts, Stanton, J, Pl	1970-1972	155	3.50	Unknown
Michigan, Cornell, J, Pl	1970-1972	155	3.50	Unknown
Minnesota, Rufo, J, Pl	1970-1972	155	3.50	Unknown
Mississippi, Rufo, J, Pl	1970-1972	155	3.50	Unknown
Missouri, Stanton, J, Pl	1970-1972	155	3.50	Unknown
Montana, Cornell, J, Pl	1970-1972	155	3.50	Unknown
Nebraska, Cornell, J, Pl	1970-1972	155	3.50	Unknown
Nevada, Cornell, J, Pl	1970-1972	155	3.50	Unknown
New Hampshire, Nathan, J, Pl	1970-1972	155	3.50	Unknown
New Jersey, Cornell, J, Pl	1970-1972	155	3.50	Unknown
New Mexico, Cornell, J, Pl	1970-1972	155	3.50	Unknown
New York, Stanton, J, Pl	1970-1972	155	3.50	Unknown
North Carolina, Rufo, J, Pl	1970-1972	155	3.50	Unknown
North Dakota, Stanton, J, Pl	1970-1972	155	3.50	Unknown
Ohio, Rufo, J, Pl	1970-1972	155	3.50	Unknown
Oklahoma, Rufo, J, Pl	1970-1972	155	3.50	Unknown
Oregon, Cornell, J, Pl	1970-1972	155	3.50	Unknown
Pennsylvania, Cornell, J, Pl	1970-1972	155	3.50	Unknown
Rhode Island, Cornell, J, Pl	1970-1972	155	3.50	Unknown
South Carolina, Stanton, J, Pl	1970-1972	155	3.50	Unknown
South Dakota, Stanton, J, Pl	1970-1972	155	3.50	Unknown
Tennessee, Stanton, J, Pl	1970-1972	155	3.50	Unknown
Texas, Cornell, J, Pl	1970-1972	155	3.50	Unknown
Utah, Rufo, J, Pl	1970-1972	155	3.50	Unknown
Vermont, Nathan, J, Pl	1970-1972	155	3.50	Unknown
Virginia, Stanton, J, Pl	1970-1972	155	3.50	Unknown
Washington, Rufo, J, Pl	1970-1972	155	3.50	Unknown
West Virginia, Cornell, J, Pl	1970-1972	155	3.50	Unknown
Wisconsin, Cornell, J, Pl	1970-1972	155	3.50	Unknown
Wyoming, Cornell, J, Pl	1970-1972	155	3.50	Unknown

Franklin Mint Medals, Great American Landmarks

Air Force Academy, Lauser, 39mm., D, P	1971-1972	1337	9.50	15.00
Alamo, Cornell, 39mm., D, P	1971-1972	1337	9.50	15.00
Cape Kennedy, Lauser, 39mm., D, P	1971-1972	1337	9.50	15.00
French Quarter, Nathan, 39mm., D, P	1971-1972	1337	9.50	15.00
Gateway Arch, Cornell, 39mm., D, P	1971-1972	1337	9.50	15.00
Golden Gate Bridge, Rufo, 39mm., D, P	1971-1972	1337	9.50	15.00
Grand Canyon, Miller, 39mm., D, P	1971-1972	1337	9.50	15.00
Hoover Dam, Cornell, 39mm., D, P	1971-1972	1337	9.50	15.00
Independence Hall, Stanton, 39mm., D, P	1971-1972	1337	9.50	15.00
Lincoln's Log Cabin, Nathan, 39mm., D, P	1971-1972	1337	9.50	15.00
Mackinac Island, Rufo, 39mm., D, P	1971-1972	1337	9.50	15.00
Mount Rushmore, Cornell, 39mm., D, P	1971-1972	1337	9.50	15.00
Mount Vernon, Jones, 39mm., D, P	1971-1972	1337	9.50	15.00
Niagara Falls, Stanton, 39mm., D, P	1971-1972	1337	9.50	15.00
Old Faithful, Stanton, 39mm., D, P	1971-1972	1337	9.50	15.00
Old Ironsides, Nathan, 39mm., D, P	1971-1972	1337	9.50	15.00
Space Needle, Rufo, 39mm., D, P	1971-1972	1337	9.50	15.00
Statue Of Liberty, Faulkner, 39mm., D, P	1971-1972	1337	9.50	15.00
Stone Mountain, Nathan, 39mm., D, P	1971-1972	1337	9.50	15.00
U.S.Capitol, Rufo, 39mm., D, P	1971-1972	1337	9.50	15.00

Air Force Academy, Lauser, 39mm., D, Pl	1971-1972	2482	9.50	15.00
Alamo, Cornell, 39mm., D, Pl	1971-1972	2482	9.50	15.00
Cape Kennedy, Lauser, 39mm., D, Pl	1971-1972	2482	9.50	15.00
French Quarter, Nathan, 39mm., D, Pl	1971-1972	2482	9.50	15.00
Gateway Arch, Cornell, 39mm., D, Pl	1971-1972	2482	9.50	15.00
Golden Gate Bridge, Rufo, 39mm., D, Pl	1971-1972	2482	9.50	15.00
Grand Canyon, Miller, 39mm., D, Pl	1971-1972	2482	9.50	15.00
Hoover Dam, Cornell, 39mm., D, Pl	1971-1972	2482	9.50	15.00
Independence Hall, Stanton, 39mm., D, Pl	1971-1972	2482	9.50	15.00
Lincoln's Log Cabin, Nathan, 39mm., D, Pl	1971-1972	2482	9.50	15.00

Mackinac Island, Rufo, 39mm., D, Pl	1971-1972	2482	9.50	15.00
Mount Rushmore, Cornell, 39mm., D, Pl	1971-1972	2482	9.50	15.00
Mount Vernon, Jones, 39mm., D, Pl	1971-1972	2482	9.50	15.00
Niagara Falls, Stanton, 39mm., D, Pl	1971-1972	2482	9.50	15.00
Old Faithful, Stanton, 39mm., D, Pl	1971-1972	2482	9.50	15.00
Old Ironsides, Nathan, 39mm., D, Pl	1971-1972	2482	9.50	15.00
Space Needle, Rufo, 39mm., D, Pl	1971-1972	2482	9.50	15.00
Statue Of Liberty, Faulkner, 39mm., D, Pl	1971-1972	2482	9.50	15.00
Stone Mountain, Nathan, 39mm., D, Pl	1971-1972	2482	9.50	15.00
U.S.Capitol, Rufo, 39mm., D, Pl	1971-1972	2482	9.50	15.00
Air Force Academy, Lauser, 39mm., F, P	1971-1972	347	14.50	Unknown
Alamo, Cornell, 39mm., F, P	1971-1972	347	14.50	Unknown
Cape Kennedy, Lauser, 39mm., F, P	1971-1972	347	14.50	Unknown
French Quarter, Nathan, 39mm., F, P	1971-1972	347	14.50	Unknown
Gateway Arch, Cornell, 39mm., F, P	1971-1972	347	14.50	Unknown
Golden Gate Bridge, Rufo, 39mm., F, P	1971-1972	347	14.50	Unknown
Grand Canyon, Miller, 39mm., F, P	1971-1972	347	14.50	Unknown
Hoover Dam, Cornell, 39mm., F, P	1971-1972	347	14.50	Unknown
Independence Hall, Stanton, 39mm., F, P	1971-1972	347	14.50	Unknown
Lincoln's Log Cabin, Nathan, 39mm., F, P	1971-1972	347	14.50	Unknown
Mackinac Island, Rufo, 39mm., F, P	1971-1972	347	14.50	Unknown
Mount Rushmore, Cornell, 39mm., F, P	1971-1972	347	14.50	Unknown
Mount Vernon, Jones, 39mm., F, P	1971-1972	347	14.50	Unknown
Niagara Falls, Stanton, 39mm., F, P	1971-1972	347	14.50	Unknown
Old Faithful, Stanton, 39mm., F, P	1971-1972	347	14.50	Unknown
Old Ironsides, Nathan, 39mm., F, P	1971-1972	347	14.50	Unknown
Space Needle, Rufo, 39mm., F, P	1971-1972	347	14.50	Unknown
Statue Of Liberty, Faulkner, 39mm., F, P	1971-1972	347	14.50	Unknown
Stone Mountain, Nathan, 39mm., F, P	1971-1972	347	14.50	Unknown
U.S.Capitol, Rufo, 39mm., F, P	1971-1972	347	14.50	Unknown
Air Force Academy, Lauser, 39mm., F, Pl	1971-1972	1662	14.50	Unknown
Alamo, Cornell, 39mm., F, Pl	1971-1972	1662	14.50	Unknown
Cape Kennedy, Lauser, 39mm., F, Pl	1971-1972	1662	14.50	Unknown
French Quarter, Nathan, 39mm., F, Pl	1971-1972	1662	14.50	Unknown
Gateway Arch, Cornell, 39mm., F, Pl	1971-1972	1662	14.50	Unknown
Golden Gate Bridge, Rufo, 39mm., F, Pl	1971-1972	1662	14.50	Unknown
Grand Canyon, Miller, 39mm., F, Pl	1971-1972	1662	14.50	Unknown
Hoover Dam, Cornell, 39mm., F, Pl	1971-1972	1662	14.50	Unknown
Independence Hall, Stanton, 39mm., F, Pl	1971-1972	1662	14.50	Unknown
Lincoln's Log Cabin, Nathan, 39mm., F, Pl	1971-1972	1662	14.50	Unknown
Mackinac Island, Rufo, 39mm., F, Pl	1971-1972	1662	14.50	Unknown
Mount Rushmore, Cornell, 39mm., F, Pl	1971-1972	1662	14.50	Unknown
Mount Vernon, Jones, 39mm., F, Pl	1971-1972	1662	14.50	Unknown
Niagara Falls, Stanton, 39mm., F, Pl	1971-1972	1662	14.50	Unknown
Old Faithful, Stanton, 39mm., F, Pl	1971-1972	1662	14.50	Unknown
Old Ironsides, Nathan, 39mm., F, Pl	1971-1972	1662	14.50	Unknown
Space Needle, Rufo, 39mm., F, Pl	1971-1972	1662	14.50	Unknown
Statue Of Liberty, Faulkner, 39mm., F, Pl	1971-1972	1662	14.50	Unknown
Stone Mountain, Nathan, 39mm., F, Pl	1971-1972	1662	14.50	Unknown
U.S.Capitol, Rufo, 39mm., F, Pl	1971-1972	1662	14.50	Unknown

Franklin Mint, Great American Victories Series, see Franklin Mint Medals, American Legion Treasury of Great American Victories

Franklin Mint, Great Americans Series, see Franklin Mint Medals Gallery of Great Americans

Franklin Mint, Hall of Fame Series, see Franklin Mint Medals, Patriots Hall of Fame

Franklin Mint Medals, History of Flight

History Of Flight, Set Of 100, D, P, Each	1973	Year	12.50	12.50

Franklin Mint Medals, History of Mankind

History Of Mankind, Set Of 100, F, P, Each	1974	Year	25.00	25.00

Franklin Mint Medals, History of the American Revolution

Allen's Men Capture Ticonderoga, D, P	1970-1971	6246	3.75	5.00 to 7.00
Americans Fail In Assault On Quebec, D, P	1970-1971	6246	3.75	5.00 to 7.00
Americans Learn Of Arnold's Treason, D, P	1970-1971	6246	3.75	5.00 to 7.00

Arnold's Ships At Valcour, D, P	1970-1971	6246	3.75	5.00 to 7.00
Backwoodsmen Thrash Tories In South, D, P	1970-1971	6246	3.75	5.00 to 7.00
Blockade Seals French At Newport, D, P	1970-1971	6246	3.75	5.00 to 7.00
Both Sides Sign Treaty At Paris, D, P	1970-1971	6246	3.75	5.00 to 7.00
British Crush Garrison, Charleston, D, P	1970-1971	6246	3.75	5.00 to 7.00
British Enforce Customs Laws, D, P	1970-1971	6246	3.75	5.00 to 7.00
British Move South, Savannah, D, P	1970-1971	6246	3.75	5.00 to 7.00
British Occupy New York City, D, P	1970-1971	6246	3.75	5.00 to 7.00
British Soldiers Leave New York, D, P	1970-1971	6246	3.75	5.00 to 7.00
British Troops Evacuate Boston, D, P	1970-1971	6246	3.75	5.00 to 7.00
Bunker Hill Inspires Patriots, D, P*	1970-1971	6246	3.75	5.00 to 7.00
Burgoyne's Men At Saratoga, D, P	1970-1971	6246	3.75	5.00 to 7.00
Clark Captures Vincennes, D, P	1970-1971	6246	3.75	5.00 to 7.00
Congress Adopts Confederation Plan, D, P	1970-1971	6246	3.75	5.00 to 7.00
Congress Flees Philadelphia, D, P	1970-1971	6246	3.75	5.00 to 7.00
Congress Names 5 For Peace, D, P	1970-1971	6246	3.75	5.00 to 7.00
Congress Seeks Support From Abroad, D, P	1970-1971	6246	3.75	5.00 to 7.00
Cornwallis Surrenders At Yorktown, D, P	1970-1971	6246	3.75	5.00 to 7.00
Cruel Winter At Valley Forge, D, P	1970-1971	6246	3.75	5.00 to 7.00
Declaration Of Rights, D, P	1970-1971	6246	3.75	5.00 to 7.00
Dispute Leads To Boston Tea Party, D, P	1970-1971	6246	3.75	5.00 to 7.00
Franklin Gains Support Of France, D, P	1970-1971	6246	3.75	5.00 to 7.00
George III Proclaims Rebellion, D, P	1970-1971	6246	3.75	5.00 to 7.00
Hancock, Declaration Of Independence, D, P	1970-1971	6246	3.75	5.00 to 7.00
House Of Commons Votes To End War, D, P	1970-1971	6246	3.75	5.00 to 7.00
Howe's Troops Put Down Mutiny, D, P	1970-1971	6246	3.75	5.00 to 7.00
Indians Massacre Pennsylvania, D, P	1970-1971	6246	3.75	5.00 to 7.00
John Paul Jones Defeats Serapis, D, P	1970-1971	6246	3.75	5.00 to 7.00
Lafayette Joins Fight For Freedom, D, P	1970-1971	6246	3.75	5.00 to 7.00
Lee Demands Freedom For Colonies, D, P	1970-1971	6246	3.75	5.00 to 7.00
Molly Pitcher Helps Win Key Battle, D, P	1970-1971	6246	3.75	5.00 to 7.00
Paine's Common Sense Assails King, D, P	1970-1971	6246	3.75	5.00 to 7.00
Patrick Henry Calls For Liberty, D, P	1970-1971	6246	3.75	5.00 to 7.00
Patriots At Princeton, D, P	1970-1971	6246	3.75	5.00 to 7.00
Patriots Oppose Stamp Act, D, P	1970-1971	6246	3.75	5.00 to 7.00
Paul Revere Alerts Patriots, D, P	1970-1971	6246	3.75	5.00 to 7.00
Proclamation Bars Colonists, D, P	1970-1971	6246	3.75	5.00 to 7.00
Redcoats Hang Nathan Hale As Spy, D, P	1970-1971	6246	3.75	5.00 to 7.00
Second Congress In Philadelphia, D, P	1970-1971	6246	3.75	5.00 to 7.00
Taxation Without Representation, D, P	1970-1971	6246	3.75	5.00 to 7.00
Tension Triggers Boston Massacre, D, P	1970-1971	6246	3.75	5.00 to 7.00
Townshend Acts Lead To Violence, D, P	1970-1971	6246	3.75	5.00 to 7.00
War Begins At Lexington, D, P	1970-1971	6246	3.75	5.00 to 7.00
Washington Bids Farewell To Army, D, P	1970-1971	6246	3.75	5.00 to 7.00
Washington Crosses Delaware, D, P	1970-1971	6246	3.75	5.00 to 7.00
Washington Takes Command Of Troops, D, P	1970-1971	6246	3.75	5.00 to 7.00
Washington Unfurls 1st Flag, D, P	1970-1971	6246	3.75	5.00 to 7.00
Allen's Men Capture Ticonderoga, J, P	1970-1971	2674	1.50	Unknown
Americans Fail In Assault On Quebec, J, P	1970-1971	2674	1.50	Unknown
Americans Learn Of Arnold's Treason, J, P	1970-1971	2674	1.50	Unknown
Arnold's Ships At Valcour, J, P	1970-1971	2674	1.50	Unknown
Backwoodsmen Thrash Tories In South, J, P	1970-1971	2674	1.50	Unknown
Blockade Seals French At Newport, J, P	1970-1971	2674	1.50	Unknown
Both Sides Sign Treaty At Paris, J, P	1970-1971	2674	1.50	Unknown
British Crush Garrison, Charleston, J, P	1970-1971	2674	1.50	Unknown
British Enforce Customs Laws, J, P	1970-1971	2674	1.50	Unknown
British Move South, Take Savannah, J, P	1970-1971	2674	1.50	Unknown
British Occupy New York City, J, P	1970-1971	2674	1.50	Unknown
British Soldiers Leave New York, J, P	1970-1971	2674	1.50	Unknown
British Troops Evacuate Boston, J, P	1970-1971	2674	1.50	Unknown
Bunker Hill Inspires Patriots, J, P	1970-1971	2674	1.50	Unknown
Burgoyne's Men At Saratoga, J, P	1970-1971	2674	1.50	Unknown
Clark Captures Vincennes, J, P	1970-1971	2674	1.50	Unknown
Congress Adopts Confederation Plan, J, P	1970-1971	2674	1.50	Unknown
Congress Flees Philadelphia, J, P	1970-1971	2674	1.50	Unknown
Congress Names 5 For Peace, J, P	1970-1971	2674	1.50	Unknown
Congress Seeks Support From Abroad, J, P	1970-1971	2674	1.50	Unknown
Cornwallis Surrenders At Yorktown, J, P	1970-1971	2674	1.50	Unknown
Cruel Winter At Valley Forge, J, P	1970-1971	2674	1.50	Unknown

Franklin Mint, History Of The American Revolution,
Bunker Hill Inspires Patriots

Franklin Mint, History Of The American Revolution,
Taxation Without Representation

Declaration Of Rights, J, P	1970-1971	2674	1.50	Unknown
Dispute Leads To Boston Tea Party, J, P	1970-1971	2674	1.50	Unknown
Franklin Gains Support Of France, J, P	1970-1971	2674	1.50	Unknown
George III Proclaims Rebellion, J, P	1970-1971	2674	1.50	Unknown
Hancock, Declaration Of Independence, J, P	1970-1971	2674	1.50	Unknown
House Of Commons Votes To End War, J, P	1970-1971	2674	1.50	Unknown
Howe's Troops Put Down Mutiny, J, P	1970-1971	2674	1.50	Unknown
Indians Massacre Pennsylvania, J, P	1970-1971	2674	1.50	Unknown
John Paul Jones Defeats The Serapis, J, P	1970-1971	2674	1.50	Unknown
Lafayette Joins Fight For Freedom, J, P	1970-1971	2674	1.50	Unknown
Lee Demands Freedom For Colonies, J, P	1970-1971	2674	1.50	Unknown
Molly Pitcher Helps Win Key Battle, J, P	1970-1971	2674	1.50	Unknown
Paine's Common Sense Assails King, J, P	1970-1971	2674	1.50	Unknown
Patrick Henry Calls For Liberty, J, P	1970-1971	2674	1.50	Unknown
Patriots At Princeton, J, P	1970-1971	2674	1.50	Unknown
Patriots Oppose Stamp Act, J, P	1970-1971	2674	1.50	Unknown
Paul Revere Alerts Patriots, J, P	1970-1971	2674	1.50	Unknown
Proclamation Bars Colonists, J, P	1970-1971	2674	1.50	Unknown
Redcoats Hang Nathan Hale As Spy, J, P	1970-1971	2674	1.50	Unknown
Second Congress In Philadelphia, J, P	1970-1971	2674	1.50	Unknown
Taxation Without Representation, J, P*	1970-1971	2674	1.50	Unknown
Tension Triggers Boston Massacre, J, P	1970-1971	2674	1.50	Unknown
Townshend Acts Lead To Violence, J, P	1970-1971	2674	1.50	Unknown
War Begins At Lexington, J, P	1970-1971	2674	1.50	Unknown
Washington Bids Farewell To Army, J, P*	1970-1971	2674	1.50	Unknown
Washington Crosses Delaware, J, P	1970-1971	2674	1.50	Unknown
Washington Takes Command Of Troops, J, P*	1970-1971	2674	1.50	Unknown
Washington Unfurls 1st Flag, J, P	1970-1971	2674	1.50	Unknown
Allen's Men Capture Ticonderoga, D, Pl	1971-1972	525	3.75	Unknown
Americans Fail Assault On Quebec, D, Pl	1971-1972	525	3.75	Unknown
Americans Learn Arnold's Treason, D, Pl	1971-1972	525	3.75	Unknown
Arnold's Ships At Valcour, D, Pl	1971-1972	525	3.75	Unknown
Backwoodsmen Beat Tories In South, D, Pl	1971-1972	525	3.75	Unknown
Blockade Seals French At Newport, D, Pl	1971-1972	525	3.75	Unknown
Both Sides Sign Treaty At Paris, D, Pl	1971-1972	525	3.75	Unknown
British Crush Garrison, Charleston, D, Pl	1971-1972	525	3.75	Unknown
British Enforce Customs Laws, D, Pl	1971-1972	525	3.75	Unknown
British Leave New York, D, Pl	1971-1972	525	3.75	Unknown
British Occupy New York City, D, Pl	1971-1972	525	3.75	Unknown
British Take Savannah, D, Pl	1971-1972	525	3.75	Unknown
British Troops Evacuate Boston, D, Pl	1971-1972	525	3.75	Unknown
Bunker Hill Inspires Patriots, D, Pl	1971-1972	525	3.75	Unknown
Burgoyne's Men At Saratoga, D, Pl	1971-1972	525	3.75	Unknown
Clark Captures Vincennes, D, Pl	1971-1972	525	3.75	Unknown
Congress Adopts Confederation Plan, D, Pl	1971-1972	525	3.75	Unknown
Congress Flees Philadelphia, D, Pl	1971-1972	525	3.75	Unknown
Congress Names 5 For Peace, D, Pl	1971-1972	525	3.75	Unknown
Congress Seeks Support From Abroad, D, Pl	1971-1972	525	3.75	Unknown
Cornwallis Surrenders At Yorktown, D, Pl	1971-1972	525	3.75	Unknown
Cruel Winter At Valley Forge, D, Pl	1971-1972	525	3.75	Unknown
Declaration Of Rights, D, Pl	1971-1972	525	3.75	Unknown
Dispute Leads To Boston Tea Party, D, Pl	1971-1972	525	3.75	Unknown
Franklin Gains Support Of France, D, Pl	1971-1972	525	3.75	Unknown
George III Proclaims Rebellion, D, Pl	1971-1972	525	3.75	Unknown
Hancock, Independence Declaration, D, Pl	1971-1972	525	3.75	Unknown
House Of Commons Votes To End War, D, Pl	1971-1972	525	3.75	Unknown
Howe's Troops Put Down Mutiny, D, Pl	1971-1972	525	3.75	Unknown
Indians Massacre Pennsylvania, D, Pl	1971-1972	525	3.75	Unknown
John Paul Jones Defeats Serapis, D, Pl	1971-1972	525	3.75	Unknown
Lafayette Joins Fight For Freedom, D, Pl	1971-1972	525	3.75	Unknown
Lee Demands Freedom For Colonies, D, Pl	1971-1972	525	3.75	Unknown
Molly Pitcher Helps Win Key Battle, D, Pl	1971-1972	525	3.75	Unknown
Paine's Common Sense Assails King, D, Pl	1971-1972	525	3.75	Unknown
Patrick Henry Calls For Liberty, D, Pl	1971-1972	525	3.75	Unknown
Patriots At Princeton, D, Pl	1971-1972	525	3.75	Unknown
Patriots Oppose Stamp Act, D, Pl	1971-1972	525	3.75	Unknown
Paul Revere Alerts Patriots, D, Pl	1971-1972	525	3.75	Unknown
Proclamation Bars Colonists, D, Pl	1971-1972	525	3.75	Unknown
Redcoats Hang Nathan Hale As Spy, D, Pl	1971-1972	525	3.75	Unknown

Franklin Mint, History Of The American Revolution, Washington Bids Farewell

Franklin Mint, History Of The American Revolution, Washington Takes Command

Second Congress In Philadelphia, D, Pl	1971-1972	525	3.75	Unknown
Taxation Without Representation, D, Pl	1971-1972	525	3.75	Unknown
Tension Triggers Boston Massacre, D, Pl	1971-1972	525	3.75	Unknown
Townshend Acts Lead To Violence, D, Pl	1971-1972	525	3.75	Unknown
War Begins At Lexington, D, Pl	1971-1972	525	3.75	Unknown
Washington Bids Farewell To Army, D, Pl	1971-1972	525	3.75	Unknown
Washington Crosses Delaware, D, Pl	1971-1972	525	3.75	Unknown
Washington Takes Command Of Troops, D, Pl	1971-1972	525	3.75	Unknown
Washington Unfurls 1st Flag, D, Pl	1971-1972	525	3.75	Unknown

Franklin Mint Medals, History of the United States

Signing Of The Declaration Of Independence, D	1968	10000	9.75	Unknown
The Stars & Stripes Are Born, 1777, Faulkner, D	1968	10000	9.75	Unknown
Winter At Valley Forge, 1778, Faulkner, D*	1968	10000	9.75	Unknown
John Paul Jones' Great Naval Victory, 1779, D	1968	10000	9.75	Unknown
Washington Joined By French Army, Newport, D	1968	10000	9.75	Unknown
British Capitulate At Yorktown, 1781, Nathan, D	1968	10000	9.75	Unknown
Preliminary Articles Of Peace Signed, 1782, D	1968	10000	9.75	Unknown
Washington Takes Leave Of His Officers, D	1968	10000	9.75	Unknown
Congress Ratifies Peace Treaty, 1784, Nathan, D	1968	10000	9.75	Unknown
Land Ordinance Becomes Law, 1785, Faulkner, D	1968	10000	9.75	Unknown
Shays' Rebellion, 1786, Cornell, D	1968	10000	9.75	Unknown
The Constitution Approved, 1787, Faulkner, D	1968	10000	9.75	Unknown
U.S.Constitution Ratified, 1788, Cornell, D	1968	10000	9.75	Unknown
Washington Inaugurated 1st President, 1789, D	1968	10000	9.75	Unknown
Hamilton & Jefferson Agree On Debt, 1790, D	1968	10000	9.75	Unknown
Bill Of Rights Guarantees Freedoms, 1791, D	1968	10000	9.75	Unknown
First U.S.Mint Established, 1792, Cornell, D	1968	10000	9.75	Unknown
Eli Whitney Invents The Cotton Gin, 1793, D	1968	10000	9.75	Unknown
Jay's Treaty Secures Northwest Forts, 1794, D	1969	10000	9.75	Unknown
Pinckney's Treaty, Mississippi Commerce, D	1969	10000	9.75	Unknown
Washington Writes His Farewell Address, D	1969	10000	9.75	Unknown
1st Vessel Of New Navy Launched, 1797, D	1969	10000	9.75	Unknown
Alien & Sedition Acts Curtail Liberties, D	1969	10000	9.75	Unknown
Death Of George Washington, 1799, Cornell, D	1969	10000	9.75	Unknown
Federal Government Moves To Washington, D	1969	10000	9.75	Unknown
Election Of Jefferson Decided By Congress, D	1969	10000	9.75	Unknown
U.S.Military Academy Established, 1802, D	1969	10000	9.75	Unknown
Louisiana Territory Purchased From France, D	1969	10000	9.75	Unknown
Hamilton & Burr Feud Ends In Duel, 1804, D	1969	10000	9.75	Unknown
Lewis & Clark Reach The Pacific, 1805, D	1969	10000	9.75	Unknown
Zebulon Pike Sights Pike's Peak, 1806, D	1969	10000	9.75	Unknown
Fulton's Clermont Proves Successful, 1807, D	1969	10000	9.75	Unknown
Importation Of Slaves Prohibited, 1808, D	1969	10000	9.75	Unknown
Supreme Court Defends Federal Authority, D	1969	10000	9.75	Unknown
First Country Fair Held, 1810, Lauser, D	1969	10000	9.75	Unknown
Battle Of Tippecanoe Against Indians, 1811, D	1969	10000	9.75	Unknown
Constitution Defeats Guerriere, 1812, D	1969	10000	9.75	Unknown
Battle Of Lake Erie, 1813, Nathan, D	1969	10000	9.75	Unknown
National Anthem Inspired At Fort Mchenry, D	1969	10000	9.75	Unknown
Jackson Repels British At New Orleans, 1815, D	1969	10000	9.75	Unknown
Second Bank Of U.S.Chartered, 1816, Stanton, D	1969	10000	9.75	Unknown
Construction Begins On Erie Canal, 1817, D	1969	10000	9.75	Unknown
Northern Boundary Set At 49th Parallel, D	1970	10000	9.75	Unknown
Spain Cedes Florida To U.S., 1819, Nathan, D	1970	10000	9.75	Unknown
Missouri Compromise Limits Slavery, 1820, D	1970	10000	9.75	Unknown
Santa Fe Trail Opened To Trade, 1821, Lauser, D	1970	10000	9.75	Unknown
Factory Towns Begin In U.S., 1822, Nathan, D	1970	10000	9.75	Unknown
Monroe Doctrine Sets Foreign Policy, 1823, D	1970	10000	9.75	Unknown
Lafayette Begins Hero's Tour Of U.S., 1824, D	1970	10000	9.75	Unknown
Completion Of Erie Canal Celebrated, 1825, D	1970	10000	9.75	Unknown
Nation Celebrates 50th Anniversary, 1826, D	1970	10000	9.75	Unknown
Beginning Of U.S.Labor Movement, 1827, D	1970	10000	9.75	Unknown
1st Stone On Baltimore & Ohio Railroad, D	1970	10000	9.75	Unknown
Andrew Jackson Becomes President, 1829, D	1970	10000	9.75	Unknown
1st Train Passenger Service Inaugurated, D	1970	10000	9.75	Unknown
The Liberator Published To Fight Slavery, D	1970	10000	9.75	Unknown
South Carolina Votes For Nullification, D	1970	10000	9.75	Unknown
1st National Temperance Convention, 1833, D	1970	10000	9.75	Unknown

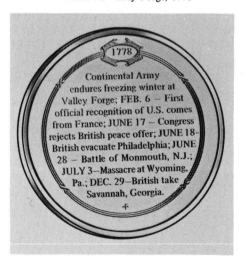

Franklin Mint, History Of The United States,
Winter At Valley Forge, 1778

Cyrus McCormick Patents His Reaper, 1834, D	1970	10000	9.75	Unknown
Liberty Bell Tolls Death Of John Marshall, D	1970	10000	9.75	Unknown
Texas Wins Its Independence, 1836, Baldwin, D	1970	10000	9.75	Unknown
Industry Paralyzed By Depression, 1837, D	1970	10000	9.75	Unknown
Forcible Removal Of Indians To West, 1838, D	1970	10000	9.75	Unknown
1st Use Of Photography In U.S., 1839, Lauser, D	1970	10000	9.75	Unknown
Wilke's Expedition Reaches Antarctic, 1840, D	1970	10000	9.75	Unknown
1st Whig President Inaugurated, 1841, D	1970	10000	9.75	Unknown
Fremont Begins Mapping West, 1842, Nathan, D	1971	10000	9.75	Unknown
Great Migration To Oregon Begins, 1843, D	1971	10000	9.75	Unknown
Morse Proves Telegraph To Congress, 1844, D	1971	10000	9.75	Unknown
Texas Annexed As State, 1845, Rufo, D	1971	10000	9.75	Unknown
War Declared Between U.S.& Mexico, 1846, D	1971	10000	9.75	Unknown
U.S.Forces Occupy Mexico City, 1847, Lauser, D	1971	10000	9.75	Unknown
Immigration Swelled By Famine & Revolution, D	1971	10000	9.75	Unknown
49ers Seek El Dorado In California, 1849, D	1971	10000	9.75	Unknown
Compromise Of 1850 Debated In Senate, 1850, D	1971	10000	9.75	Unknown
Clipper Ships Vie For Supremacy Of Seas, D	1971	10000	9.75	Unknown
Uncle Tom's Cabin Shows Slavery's Evils, D	1971	10000	9.75	Unknown
Crystal Palace Exhibition Opens, 1853, Jones, D	1971	10000	9.75	Unknown
Perry Opens Trade With Japan, 1854, Ferrell, D	1971	10000	9.75	Unknown
Year Of Engineering Feats, 1855, Lauser, D	1971	10000	9.75	Unknown
Slavery Dispute Brings Violence To Kansas, D	1971	10000	9.75	Unknown
Supreme Court Decision Favors Slavery, 1857, D	1971	10000	9.75	Unknown
Lincoln-Douglas Debates, 1858, Ferrell, D	1971	10000	9.75	Unknown
Beginning Of U.S.Oil Industry, 1859, Lauser, D	1971	10000	9.75	Unknown
News Of Lincoln's Election By Pony Express, D	1971	10000	9.75	Unknown
Civil War Opens With Attack On Fort Sumter, D	1971	10000	9.75	Unknown
1st Battle Of Ironclads, 1862, Schroeder, D	1971	10000	9.75	Unknown
Tide Turns At Gettysburg, 1863, Schroeder, D	1971	10000	9.75	Unknown
Sherman's March Brings Destruction, 1864, D	1971	10000	9.75	Unknown
General Lee Surrenders At Appomattox, 1865, D	1971	10000	9.75	Unknown
Atlantic Cable Connects U.S.& Europe, 1866, D	1972	10000	9.75	Unknown
Alaska Purchased From Russia, 1867, Faulkner, D	1972	10000	9.75	Unknown
Impeachment Of Johnson, 1868, Ferrell, D	1972	10000	9.75	Unknown
East & West Joined By Railroad, 1869, Lauser, D	1972	10000	9.75	Unknown
15th Amendment Guarantees Right To Vote, D	1972	10000	9.75	Unknown
Chicago Laid Waste By Fire, 1871, Ferrell, D	1972	10000	9.75	Unknown
Yellowstone National Park Established, 1872, D	1972	10000	9.75	Unknown
Thousands Ruined By Financial Panic, 1873, D	1972	10000	9.75	Unknown
Barbed Wire Fences The West, 1874, Lauser, D	1972	10000	9.75	Unknown
Great Religious Revivals Begin, 1875, Nemeth, D	1972	10000	9.75	Unknown
Telephone Demonstrated At Centennial, 1876, D	1972	10000	9.75	Unknown
Hayes-Tilden Election Decided, 1877, D	1972	10000	9.75	Unknown
Knights Of Labor Emerge As National Union, D	1972	10000	9.75	Unknown
Electric Light Comes Of Age, 1879, Shoyer, D	1972	10000	9.75	Unknown
Farmer's Alliance Organized, 1880, Nemeth, D	1972	10000	9.75	Unknown
American Red Cross Organized, 1881, Shoyer, D	1972	10000	9.75	Unknown
The Buffalo Nears Extinction, 1882, Baldwin, D	1972	10000	9.75	Unknown
Government Civil Service Based On Merit, D	1972	10000	9.75	Unknown
Skyscraper Forecasts Changing City, 1884, D	1972	10000	9.75	Unknown
Washington Monument Dedicated, 1885, D	1972	10000	9.75	Unknown
Liberty Welcomes The World, 1886, Faulkner, D	1972	10000	9.75	Unknown
Interstate Commerce Act Passed, 1887, Shoyer, D	1972	10000	9.75	Unknown
Great Blizzard Parlyzes East, 1888, Lauser, D	1972	10000	9.75	Unknown
Settlers Rush To Oklahoma, 1889, Schole, D	1972	10000	9.75	Unknown
Signing Of The Declaration Of Independence, J	1968	24836	3.00	Unknown
The Stars & Stripes Are Born, 1777, Faulkner, J	1968	24836	3.00	Unknown
Winter At Valley Forge, 1778, Faulkner, J*	1968	24836	3.00	Unknown
John Paul Jones' Great Naval Victory, 1779, J	1968	24836	3.00	Unknown
Washington Joined By French Army, Newport, J	1968	24836	3.00	Unknown
British Capitulate At Yorktown, 1781, Nathan, J	1968	24836	3.00	Unknown
Preliminary Articles Of Peace Signed, 1782, J	1968	24836	3.00	Unknown
Washington Takes Leave Of His Officers, J	1968	24836	3.00	Unknown
Congress Ratifies Peace Treaty, 1784, Nathan, J	1968	24836	3.00	Unknown
Land Ordinance Becomes Law, 1785, Faulkner, J	1968	24836	3.00	Unknown
Shays' Rebellion, 1786, Cornell, J	1968	24836	3.00	Unknown
The Constitution Approved, 1787, Faulkner, J	1968	24836	3.00	Unknown

U.S.Constitution Ratified, 1788, Cornell, J	1969	24836	3.00	Unknown
Washington Inaugurated 1st President, 1789, J	1969	24836	3.00	Unknown
Hamilton & Jefferson Agree On Debt, 1790, J	1969	24836	3.00	Unknown
Bill Of Rights Guarantees Freedoms, 1791, J	1969	24836	3.00	Unknown
1st U.S.Mint Established, 1792, Cornell, J	1969	24836	3.00	Unknown
Eli Whitney Invents The Cotton Gin, 1793, J	1969	24836	3.00	Unknown
Jay's Treaty Secures Northwest Forts, 1794, J	1969	24836	3.00	Unknown
Pinckney's Treaty, Mississippi Commerce, J	1969	24836	3.00	Unknown
Washington Writes His Farewell Address, J	1969	24836	3.00	Unknown
1st Vessel Of New Navy Launched, 1797, J	1969	24836	3.00	Unknown
Alien & Sedition Acts Curtail Liberties, J	1969	24836	3.00	Unknown
Death Of George Washington, 1799, Cornell, J	1969	24836	3.00	Unknown
Federal Government Moves To Washington, J	1969	24836	3.00	Unknown
Election Of Jefferson Decided By Congress, J	1969	24836	3.00	Unknown
U.S.Military Academy Established, 1802, J	1969	24836	3.00	Unknown
Louisiana Territory Purchased From France, J	1969	24836	3.00	Unknown
Hamilton & Burr Feud Ends In Duel, 1804, J	1969	24836	3.00	Unknown
Lewis & Clark Reach The Pacific, 1805, J	1969	24836	3.00	Unknown
Zebulon Pike Sights Pike's Peak, 1806, J	1969	24836	3.00	Unknown
Fulton's Clermont Proves Successful, 1807, J	1969	24836	3.00	Unknown
Importation Of Slaves Prohibited, 1808, J	1969	24836	3.00	Unknown
Supreme Court Defends Federal Authority, J	1969	24836	3.00	Unknown
1st County Fair Held, 1810, Lauser, J	1969	24836	3.00	Unknown
Battle Of Tippecanoe Against Indians, 1811, J	1969	24836	3.00	Unknown
Constitution Defeats Guerriere, 1812, J	1970	24836	3.00	Unknown
Battle Of Lake Erie, 1813, Nathan, J	1970	24836	3.00	Unknown
National Anthem Inspired At Fort Mchenry, J	1970	24836	3.00	Unknown
Jackson Repels British At New Orleans, 1815, J	1970	24836	3.00	Unknown
Second Bank Of U.S.Chartered, 1816, Stanton, J	1970	24836	3.00	Unknown
Construction Begins On Erie Canal, 1817, J	1970	24836	3.00	Unknown
Northern Boundary Set At 49th Parallel, J	1970	24836	3.00	Unknown
Spain Cedes Florida To U.S., 1819, Nathan, J	1970	24836	3.00	Unknown
Missouri Compromise Limits Slavery, 1820, J	1970	24836	3.00	Unknown
Santa Fe Trail Opened To Trade, 1821, Lauser, J	1970	24836	3.00	Unknown
Factory Towns Begin In U.S., 1822, Nathan, J	1970	24836	3.00	Unknown
Monroe Doctrine Sets Foreign Policy, 1823, J	1970	24836	3.00	Unknown
Lafayette Begins Hero's Tour Of U.S., 1824, J	1970	24836	3.00	Unknown
Completion Of Erie Canal Celebrated, 1825, J	1970	24836	3.00	Unknown
Nation Celebrates 50th Anniversary, 1826, J	1970	24836	3.00	Unknown
Beginning Of U.S.Labor Movement, 1827, J	1970	24836	3.00	Unknown
1st Stone On Baltimore & Ohio Railroad, J	1970	24836	3.00	Unknown
Andrew Jackson Becomes President, 1829, J	1970	24836	3.00	Unknown
1st Train Passenger Service Inaugurated, J	1970	24836	3.00	Unknown
The Liberator Published To Fight Slavery, J	1970	24836	3.00	Unknown
South Carolina Votes For Nullification, J	1970	24836	3.00	Unknown
1st National Temperance Convention, 1833, J	1970	24836	3.00	Unknown
Cyrus McCormick Patents His Reaper, 1834, J	1970	24836	3.00	Unknown
Liberty Bell Tolls Death Of John Marshall, J	1970	24836	3.00	Unknown
Texas Wins Its Independence, 1836, Baldwin, J	1971	24836	3.00	Unknown
Industry Paralyzed By Depression, 1837, J	1971	24836	3.00	Unknown
Forcible Removal Of Indians To West, 1838, J	1971	24836	3.00	Unknown
1st Use Of Photography In U.S., 1839, Lauser, J	1971	24836	3.00	Unknown
Wilke's Expedition Reaches Antarctic, 1840, J	1971	24836	3.00	Unknown
1st Whig President Inaugurated, 1841, J	1971	24836	3.00	Unknown
Fremont Begins Mapping West, 1842, J	1971	24836	3.00	Unknown
Great Migration To Oregon Begins, 1843, J	1971	24836	3.00	Unknown
Morse Proves Telegraph To Congress, 1844, J	1971	24836	3.00	Unknown
Texas Annexed As State, 1845, Rufo, J	1971	24836	3.00	Unknown
War Declared Between U.S.& Mexico, 1846, J	1971	24836	3.00	Unknown
U.S.Forces Occupy Mexico City, 1847, Lauser, J	1971	24836	3.00	Unknown
Immigration Swelled By Famine & Revolution, J	1971	24836	3.00	Unknown
49ers Seek El Dorado In California, 1849, J	1971	24836	3.00	Unknown
Compromise Of 1850 Debated In Senate, 1850, J	1971	24836	3.00	Unknown
Clipper Ships Vie For Supremacy Of Seas, J	1971	24836	3.00	Unknown
Uncle Tom's Cabin Shows Slavery's Evils, J	1971	24836	3.00	Unknown
Crystal Palace Exhibition Opens, 1853, Jones, J	1971	24836	3.00	Unknown
Perry Opens Trade With Japan, 1854, Ferrell, J	1971	24836	3.00	Unknown
Year Of Engineering Feats, 1855, Lauser, J	1971	24836	3.00	Unknown

Royal Copenhagen, Year Mug, 1973, Large

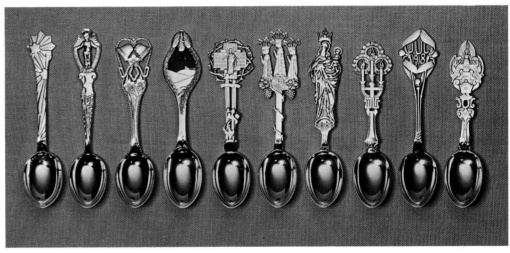

Royal Copenhagen, Year Mug, 1973, Small

Michelsen, Christmas Spoons,
1910 - 1919 Left To Right

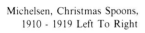

Michelsen, Christmas Spoons,
1920 -1929 Left To Right

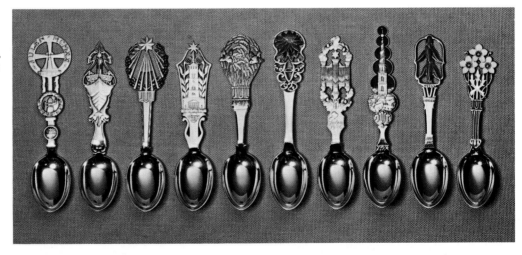

Michelsen, Christmas Spoons,
1930 -1939 Left To Right

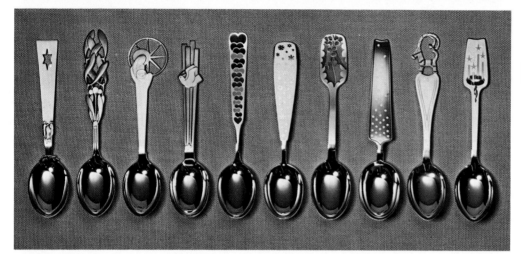

Michelsen, Christmas Spoons,
1940 - 1949 Left To Right

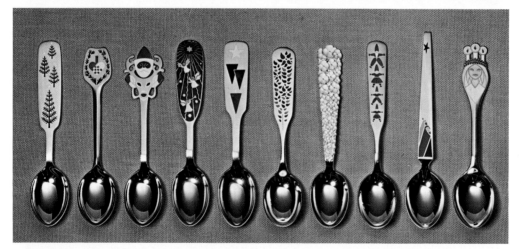

Michelsen, Christmas Spoons,
1950 - 1959 Left To Right

Michelsen, Christmas Spoons,
1960 - 1969 Left To Right

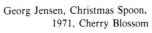
Georg Jensen, Christmas Spoon,
1971, Cherry Blossom

Michelsen, Christmas Fork And Spoon, 1972

Michelsen, Christmas Fork And Spoon,
1973

Michelsen, Christmas Spoon, 1971

Georg Jensen, Christmas Spoon,
1972, Cornflower

Michelsen, Christmas Fork And Spoon, 1974

Michelsen, Christmas Fork And Spoon,
1970

Georg Jensen, Christmas Spoon, 1973,
Corn Marigold

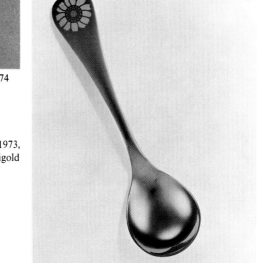

Ispanky, Abraham

Ispanky, Love Letters

Ispanky, Dragon, Emerald

Ispanky, Maid Of The Mist

Boehm, Brown Pelican

Borsato, Morsels Of Wisdom

Boehm, Mute Swans (Bird Of Peace)

Boehm, E.M.Boehm Orchid Centerpiece

Boehm, Hooded Mergansers

Boehm, Canadian Warbler, Fledgling

Boehm, Rufous Hummingbirds

Lenox, Boehm Wildlife Plate, 1973, Racoons

Lenox, Boehm Bird Plate, 1970, Wood Thrush

Lenox, Boehm Bird Plate, 1971, Goldfinch

Rosenthal, Christmas Plate,
1973

Holmegaard, Kylle Svanlund Deep Bowl, Crystal

Holmegaard,
Kylle Svanlund Glass Sculptures, Pair

Holmegaard,
Kylle Svanlund Centerpiece Bowl, Purple

Holmegaard,
Kylle Svanlund Oblong Glass Sculpture

Van Son,
Commemorative Paperweight, 1972

Pairpoint,
Red, White And Blue Crown Paperweight

Pairpoint, Faceted Red Rose Paperweight

Pairpoint, Peachblow Bell, 1973

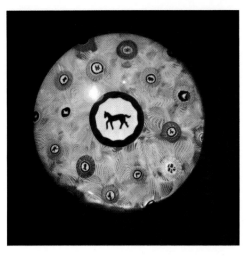

Baccarat, Gridel Horse

Baccarat, Millefiori, Regular

Baccarat, Harry S. Truman, Overlay

Baccarat, Complex Flower

Baccarat, Gridel Squirrel
Baccarat, Millefiori, Concentric

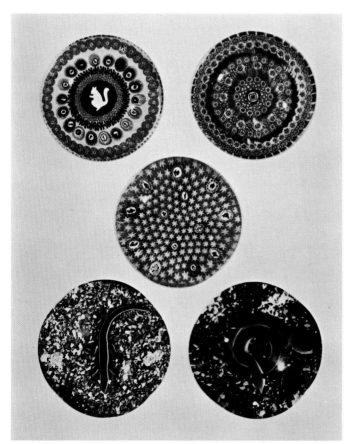

Baccarat, Carpet Ground
With Zodiac Signs

Royal Bayreuth, Christmas Plate, 1973

Baccarat, Salamander
Baccarat, Snake

Slavery Dispute Brings Violence To Kansas, J	1971	24836	3.00	Unknown
Supreme Court Decision Favors Slavery, 1857, J	1971	24836	3.00	Unknown
Lincoln-Douglas Debates, 1858, Ferrell, J	1971	24836	3.00	Unknown
Beginning Of U.S.Oil Industry, 1859, Lauser, J	1971	24836	3.00	Unknown
News Of Lincoln's Election By Pony Express, J	1972	24836	3.00	Unknown
Civil War Opens With Attack On Fort Sumter, J	1972	24836	3.00	Unknown
1st Battle Of Ironclads, 1862, Schroeder, J	1972	24836	3.00	Unknown
Tide Turns At Gettysburg, 1863, Schroeder, J	1972	24836	3.00	Unknown
Sherman's March Brings Destruction, 1864, J	1972	24836	3.00	Unknown
General Lee Surrenders At Appomattox, 1865, J	1972	24836	3.00	Unknown
Atlantic Cable Connects U.S.& Europe, 1866, J	1972	24836	3.00	Unknown
Alaska Purchased From Russia, 1867, Faulkner, J	1972	24836	3.00	Unknown
Impeachment Of Johnson, 1868, Ferrell, J	1972	24836	3.00	Unknown
East & West Joined By Railroad, 1869, Lauser, J	1972	24836	3.00	Unknown
15th Amendment Guarantees Right To Vote, J	1972	24836	3.00	Unknown
Chicago Laid Waste By Fire, 1871, Ferrell, J	1972	24836	3.00	Unknown
Yellowstone National Park Established, 1872, J	1972	24836	3.00	Unknown
Thousands Ruined By Financial Panic, 1873, J	1972	24836	3.00	Unknown
Barbed Wire Fences The West, 1874, Lauser, J	1972	24836	3.00	Unknown
Great Religious Revivals Begin, 1875, Nemeth, J	1972	24836	3.00	Unknown
Telephone Demonstrated At Centennial, 1876, J	1972	24836	3.00	Unknown
Hayes-Tilden Election Decided, 1877, J	1972	24836	3.00	Unknown
Knights Of Labor Emerge As National Union, J	1972	24836	3.00	Unknown
Electric Light Comes Of Age, 1879, Shoyer, J	1972	24836	3.00	Unknown
Farmer's Alliance Organized, 1880, Nemeth, J	1972	24836	3.00	Unknown
American Red Cross Organized, 1881, Shoyer, J	1972	24836	3.00	Unknown
The Buffalo Nears Extinction, 1882, Baldwin, J	1972	24836	3.00	Unknown
Government Civil Service Based On Merit, J	1972	24836	3.00	Unknown

Franklin Mint Medals, Holiday Season

Dove Of Peace, Gilroy Roberts, D	1965	250	5.00	Unknown
Praying Hands, Stanley Fine, D	1966	500	10.01	Unknown
Three Angels, Gilroy Roberts, D	1966	500	10.01	Unknown
Three Wise Men, Harold Faulkner, D	1966	500	10.01	Unknown
Christmas Carolers, Gilroy Roberts, D	1967	1000	5.05	Unknown
Mother & Child, Alex Hromych, D	1967	1000	7.00	Unknown
Peace On Earth, Richard Baldwin, D	1967	1000	9.74	Unknown
English Coaching Scene, Philip Nathan, D	1968	1000	18.52	Unknown
Manger Scene, Gilroy Roberts, D	1968	1000	18.52	Unknown
Peace, Harold Faulkner, D	1968	1000	18.52	Unknown
Lion & Lamb, William Cousins, D	1969	1000	31.81	Unknown
Praying Child, Richard Baldwin, D	1969	1000	31.81	Unknown
Winter Scene, Philip Nathan, D	1969	1000	31.81	Unknown
Snow Scene, Ernest Lauser, D	1970	1000	30.38	15.00
The Menorah, Daniel Stapleford, D	1970	1000	34.88	15.00
The Nativity, James Ferrell, D	1970	1000	40.62	15.00
Youth For Peace, Lumen Martin Winter, D	1970	1000	170.15	15.00
Doves Of Peace, Philip Nathan, D	1971	1000	77.61	15.00
Hanukkah Medal, Ernest Schroeder, D	1971	1000	68.96	15.00
Holiday Scene, James Ferrell, D	1971	1000	91.12	15.00
The Nativity, Ernest Schroeder, D	1971	1000	87.64	15.00
Adoration Of The Magi, Vincent Miller, D	1972	1000		11.00
Dove Of Peace, Harold Faulkner, D	1972	1000		11.00
Festival Of Lights, William Shoyer, D	1972	1000		11.00
Home For Christmas, Richard Baldwin, D	1972	1000		11.00
Country Christmas, Lunger, D, P	1973	Year	11.00	11.00
Lighting The Menorah, Lauser, D, P	1973	Year	11.00	11.00
Peace On Earth, De Roose, D, P	1973	Year	11.00	11.00
The Nativity, Schroeder, D, P	1973	Year	11.00	11.00

Franklin Mint Medals, Hollywood Hall of Fame Series

Bogart, Humphrey, Cornell, 39mm., D, P	1971	521	10.00	Unknown
Cooper, Gary, Grove, 39mm., D, P	1971	508	10.00	Unknown
Fields, W.C., Grove, 39mm., D, P	1971	567	10.00	Unknown
Flynn, Errol, Grove, 39mm., D, P	1971	477	10.00	Unknown
Gable, Clark, Cornell, 39mm., D, P	1971	579	10.00	Unknown
Garland, Judy, Baldwin, 39mm., D, P	1971	498	10.00	Unknown
Harlow, Jean, Grove, 39mm., D, P	1971	487	10.00	Unknown
Laughton, Charles, Cornell, 39mm., D, P	1971	468	10.00	Unknown
Monroe, Marilyn, Cornell, 39mm., D, P	1971	537	10.00	Unknown

Tracy, Spencer, Grove, 39mm., D, P	1971	532	10.00	Unknown

Franklin Mint Coin-Medals, Indian Tribal Nations

Apache, C, P	1973	9500	16.00	16.00
Crow, C, P	1973	9500	16.00	16.00
Havusapai, C, P	1973	9500	16.00	16.00
Hopi, C, P	1973	9500	16.00	16.00
Navajo, C, P	1973	9500	16.00	16.00
Osage, C, P	1973	9500	16.00	16.00
Paiute, C, P	1973	9500	16.00	16.00
Papago, C, P	1973	9500	16.00	16.00
Sioux, C, P	1973	9500	16.00	16.00
Yakima, C, P	1973	9500	16.00	16.00

Franklin Mint Medals, Kings & Queens of England

Edward I, 45mm., D, P	1970-1972	6713	12.00	Unknown
Edward II, 45mm., D, P	1970-1972	6713	12.00	Unknown
Edward III, 45mm., D, P	1970-1972	6713	12.00	Unknown
Edward IV, 45mm., D, P	1970-1972	6713	12.00	Unknown
Edward V, 45mm., D, P	1970-1972	6713	12.00	Unknown
Edward VI, 45mm., D, P	1970-1972	6713	12.00	Unknown
Edward The Confessor, 45mm., D, P	1970-1972	6713	12.00	Unknown
Harold, 45mm., D, P	1970-1972	6713	12.00	Unknown
Henry I, 45mm., D, P	1970-1972	6713	12.00	Unknown
Henry II, 45mm., D, P	1970-1972	6713	12.00	Unknown
Henry III, 45mm., D, P	1970-1972	6713	12.00	Unknown
Henry IV, 45mm., D, P	1970-1972	6713	12.00	Unknown
Henry V, 45mm., D, P	1970-1972	6713	12.00	Unknown
Henry VI, 45mm., D, P	1970-1972	6713	12.00	Unknown
Henry VII, 45mm., D, P	1970-1972	6713	12.00	Unknown
Henry VIII, 45mm., D, P	1970-1972	6713	12.00	Unknown
John, 45mm., D, P	1970-1972	6713	12.00	Unknown
Lady Jane Grey, 45mm., D, P	1970-1972	6713	12.00	Unknown
Mary I, 45mm., D, P	1970-1972	6713	12.00	Unknown
Richard I, 45mm., D, P	1970-1972	6713	12.00	Unknown
Richard II, 45mm., D, P	1970-1972	6713	12.00	Unknown
Richard III, 45mm., D, P	1970-1972	6713	12.00	Unknown
Stephen, 45mm., D, P	1970-1972	6713	12.00	Unknown
William I, 45mm., D, P	1970-1972	6713	12.00	Unknown
William II, 45mm., D, P	1970-1972	6713	12.00	Unknown
Anne, 45mm., D, P	1973	6713	12.00	12.00
Charles I, 45mm., D, P	1973	6713	12.00	12.00
Charles II, 45mm., D, P	1973	6713	12.00	12.00
Elizabeth I, 45mm., D, P	1973	6713	12.00	12.00
George I, 45mm., D, P	1973	6713	12.00	12.00
George II, 45mm., D, P	1973	6713	12.00	12.00
George III, 45mm., D, P	1973	6713	12.00	12.00
George IV, 45mm., D, P	1973	6713	12.00	12.00
James I, 45mm., D, P	1973	6713	12.00	12.00
James II, 45mm., D, P	1973	6713	12.00	12.00
Mary II, 45mm., D, P	1973	6713	12.00	12.00
William III, 45mm., D, P	1973	6713	12.00	12.00
Edward VII, 45mm., D, P	1974	6713	12.00	12.00
Edward VIII, 45mm., D, P	1974	6713	12.00	12.00
George V, 45mm., D, P	1974	6713	12.00	12.00
George VI, 45mm., D, P	1974	6713	12.00	12.00
Victoria, 45mm., D, P	1974	6713	12.00	12.00
William IV, 45mm., D, P	1974	6713	12.00	12.00

Franklin Mint Medals, L'Antico Testamento di Monti

Abraham Offers Isaac, 45mm., D, A	1973-1974	1269	12.50	12.50
Adam & Eve, 45mm., D, A	1973-1974	1269	12.50	12.50
Cain & Abel, 45mm., D, A	1973-1974	1269	12.50	12.50
Daniel In The Lion's Den, 45mm., D, A	1973-1974	1269	12.50	12.50
David & Goliath, 45mm., D, A	1973-1974	1269	12.50	12.50
David Plays For King Saul, 45mm., D, A	1973-1974	1269	12.50	12.50
Elijah Entering Heaven, 45mm., D, A	1973-1974	1269	12.50	12.50
Esther Pleads For Her People, 45mm., D, A	1973-1974	1269	12.50	12.50
Jacob Buys Esau's Birthright, 45mm., D, A	1973-1974	1269	12.50	12.50
Jacob Sees The Ladder, 45mm., D, A	1973-1974	1269	12.50	12.50

Jonah & The Whale, 45mm., D, A	1973-1974	1269	12.50	12.50
Joseph Sold Into Slavery, 45mm., D, A	1973-1974	1269	12.50	12.50
Joshua & The Walls Of Jericho, 45mm., D, A	1973-1974	1269	12.50	12.50
Lot's Choice, 45mm., D, A	1973-1974	1269	12.50	12.50
Moses & The Burning Bush, 45mm., D, A	1973-1974	1269	12.50	12.50
Moses Brings 10 Commandments, 45mm., D, A	1973-1974	1269	12.50	12.50
Noah's Ark, 45mm., D, A	1973-1974	1269	12.50	12.50
Samson & Delilah, 45mm., D, A	1973-1974	1269	12.50	12.50
Solomon Building The Temple, 45mm., D, A	1973-1974	1269	12.50	12.50
The Creation, 45mm., D, A	1973-1974	1269	12.50	12.50
The Golden Calf, 45mm., D, A	1973-1974	1269	12.50	12.50
The Marriage Of Ruth & Boaz, 45mm., D, A	1973-1974	1269	12.50	12.50
The Testing Of Job, 45mm., D, A	1973-1974	1269	12.50	12.50
The Tower Of Babel, 45mm., D, A	1973-1974	1269	12.50	12.50
Abraham Offers Isaac, 45mm., J, A	1973-1974	829	5.00	5.00
Adam & Eve, 45mm., J , A	1973-1974	829	5.00	5.00
Cain & Abel, 45mm., J, A	1973-1974	829	5.00	5.00
Daniel In The Lion's Den, 45mm., J, A	1973-1974	829	5.00	5.00
David & Goliath, 45mm., J, A	1973-1974	829	5.00	5.00
David Plays For King Saul, 45mm., J, A	1973-1974	829	5.00	5.00
Elijah Entering Heaven, 45mm., J, A	1973-1974	829	5.00	5.00
Esther Pleads For Her People, 45mm., J, A	1973-1974	829	5.00	5.00
Jacob Buys Esau's Birthright, 45mm., J, A	1973-1974	829	5.00	5.00
Jacob Sees The Ladder, 45mm., J, A	1973-1974	829	5.00	5.00
Jonah & The Whale, 45mm., J, A	1973-1974	829	5.00	5.00
Joseph Sold Into Slavery, 45mm., J, A	1973-1974	829	5.00	5.00
Joshua & The Walls Of Jericho, 45mm., J, A	1973-1974	829	5.00	5.00
Lot's Choice, 45mm., J, A	1973-1974	829	5.00	5.00
Moses & The 10 Commandments, 45mm., J, A	1973-1974	829	5.00	5.00
Moses & The Burning Bush, 45mm., J, A	1973-1974	829	5.00	5.00
Noah's Ark, 45mm., J, A	1973-1974	829	5.00	5.00
Samson & Delilah, 45mm., J, A	1973-1974	829	5.00	5.00
Solomon Building The Temple, 45mm., J, A	1973-1974	829	5.00	5.00
The Creation, 45mm., J, A	1973-1974	829	5.00	5.00
The Golden Calf, 45mm., J, A	1973-1974	829	5.00	5.00
The Marriage Of Ruth & Boaz, 45mm., J, A	1973-1974	829	5.00	5.00
The Testing Of Job, 45mm., J, A	1973-1974	829	5.00	5.00
The Tower Of Babel, 45mm., J, A	1973-1974	829	5.00	5.00

Franklin Mint, Louvre Series, see Franklin Mint Medals, Treasures of the Louvre

Franklin Mint, Mankind Series, see Franklin Mint Medals, History of Mankind

Franklin Mint, Mayors' Conference Series, see Franklin Mint Medals, Official Mayors of U.S. Conference of Mayors

Franklin Mint, Medallic Bible Series, see Franklin Mint Medals, Thomason Medallic Bible

Franklin Mint, Michelangelo Series, see Franklin Mint Medals, Genius of Michelangelo

Franklin Mint Medals, Mother's Day Issues

Oh The Love Of A Mother, 39mm., D, P	1971	5083	9.50	30.00 to 35.00
The Love Of A Mother, 39mm., D, P	1972	7089	9.50	25.00 to 30.00
Mother's Day, 39mm., D, P	1973	Year	16.75	20.00
Mother's Day, 39mm., D, P	1974	Year	16.75	16.75

Franklin Mint Medals, Norman Rockwell's Spirit of Scouting

A Scout Is Brave, 39mm., D, P	1972	26971	9.75	20.00
A Scout Is Cheerful, 39mm., D, P	1972	26971	9.75	20.00
A Scout Is Clean, 39mm., D, P	1972	26971		20.00
A Scout Is Courteous, 39mm., D, P	1972	26971	9.75	20.00
A Scout Is Friendly, 39mm., D, P	1972	26971	9.75	20.00
A Scout Is Helpful, 39mm., D, P	1972	26971	9.75	20.00
A Scout Is Kind, 39mm., D, P	1972	26971	9.75	20.00
A Scout Is Loyal, 39mm., D, P	1972	26971	9.75	20.00
A Scout Is Obedient, 39mm., D, P	1972	26971	9.75	20.00
A Scout Is Reverent, 39mm., D, P	1972	26971	9.75	20.00
A Scout Is Thrifty, 39mm., D, P	1972	26971	9.75	20.00
A Scout Is Trustworthy, 39mm., D, P	1972	26971	9.75	20.00

Franklin Mint Medals, Official 1972 Presidential Campaign

McGovern, George S., 39mm., D, P	1972	2629	15.00	Unknown
Nixon, Richard M., 39mm., D, P	1972	5007	15.00	Unknown
Nixon, Richard M., 39mm., J, Pl	1972	108044		Unknown

Franklin Mint Medals, Official Mayors of U.S. Conference of Mayors

Atlanta, Georgia, Mafko, 39mm., D, P	1971	2109	9.50	Unknown
Baltimore, Maryland, Lunger, 39mm., D, P	1971	2109	9.50	Unknown
Birmingham, Alabama, Nemeth, 39mm., D, P	1971	2109	9.50	Unknown
Boston, Massachusetts, Caimi, 39mm., D, P	1971	2109	9.50	Unknown
Buffalo, New York, Deroos, 39mm., D, P	1971	2109	9.50	Unknown
Chicago, Illinois, Shoyer, 39mm., D, P	1971	2109	9.50	Unknown
Cincinnati, Ohio, Schroeder, 39mm., D, P	1971	2109	9.50	Unknown
Dallas, Texas, Shoyer, 39mm., D, P	1971	2109	9.50	Unknown
Denver, Colorado, Douglas, 39mm., D, P	1971	2109	9.50	Unknown
Cleveland, Ohio, Faulkner, 39mm., D, P	1971	2109	9.50	Unknown
Columbus, Ohio, Lunger, 3.Mm., D, P	1971	2109	9.50	Unknown
Detroit, Michigan, Rufo, 39mm., D, P	1971	2109	9.50	Unknown
El Paso, Texas, Jones, 39mm., D, P	1971	2109	9.50	Unknown
Fort Worth, Texas, Miller, 39mm., D, P	1971	2109	9.50	Unknown
Honolulu, Hawaii, Caimi, 39mm., D, P	1971	2109	9.50	Unknown
Houston, Texas, Mafko, 39mm., D, P	1971	2109	9.50	Unknown
Indianapolis, Indiana, Blaker, 39mm., D, P	1971	2109	9.50	Unknown
Jacksonville, Florida, Miller, 39mm., D, P	1971	2109	9.50	Unknown
Kansas City, Missouri, Greenwood, 39mm., D, P	1971	2109	9.50	Unknown
Long Beach, California, Ferrell, 39mm., D, P	1971	2109	9.50	Unknown
Los Angeles, California, Blaker, 39mm., D, P	1971	2109	9.50	Unknown
Louisville, Kentucky, Caimi, 39mm., D, P	1971	2109	9.50	Unknown
Memphis, Tennessee, Ferrell, 39mm., D, P	1971	2109	9.50	Unknown
Miami, Florida, Caimi, 39mm., D, P	1971	2109	9.50	Unknown
Milwaukee, Wisconsin, Ferrell, 39mm., D, P	1971	2109	9.50	Unknown
Minneapolis, Minnesota, Rufo, 39mm., D, P	1971	2109	9.50	Unknown
Nashville, Tennessee, Greenwood, 39mm., D, P	1971	2109	9.50	Unknown
New Orleans, Louisiana, Rufo, 39mm., D, P	1971	2109	9.50	Unknown
New York, New York, Mafko, 39mm., D, P	1971	2109	9.50	Unknown
Newark, New Jersey, Shoyer, 39mm., D, P	1971	2109	9.50	Unknown
Norfolk, Virginia, Caimi, 39mm., D, P	1971	2109	9.50	Unknown
Oakland, California, Mafko, 39mm., D, P	1971	2109	9.50	Unknown
Oklahoma City, Oklahoma, Mafko, 39mm., D, P	1971	2109	9.50	Unknown
Omaha, Nebraska, Park, 39mm., D, P	1971	2109	9.50	Unknown
Philadelphia, Pennsylvania, Monnaies, 39mm., D,	1971	2109	9.50	Unknown
Phoenix, Arizona, Nemeth, 39mm., D, P	1971	2109	9.50	Unknown
Pittsburgh, Pennsylvania, Jones, 39mm., D, P	1971	2109	9.50	Unknown
Portland, Oregon, Rufo, 39mm., D, P	1971	2109	9.50	Unknown
Rochester, New York, Caimi, 39mm., D, P	1971	2109	9.50	Unknown
San Antonio, Texas, Lunger, 39mm., D, P	1971	2109	9.50	Unknown
San Diego, California, Nathan, 39mm., D, P	1971	2109	9.50	Unknown
San Francisco, California, Jones, 39mm., D, P	1971	2109	9.50	Unknown
San Jose, California, Miller, 39mm., D, P	1971	2109	9.50	Unknown
Seattle, Washington, Mafko, 39mm., D, P	1971	2109	9.50	Unknown
St.Louis, Missouri, Nemeth, 39mm., D, P	1971	2109	9.50	Unknown
St.Paul, Minnesota, Mafko, 39mm., D, P	1971	2109	9.50	Unknown
Tampa, Florida, Lunger, 39mm., D, P	1971	2109	9.50	Unknown
Toledo, Ohio, Weiland, 39mm., D, P	1971	2109	9.50	Unknown
Tulsa, Oklahoma, Lauser, 39mm., D, P	1971	2109	9.50	Unknown
Washington, D.C., Monnaies, 39mm., D, P	1971	2109	9.50	Unknown
Atlanta, Georgia, Mafko, 39mm., F, P	1971	1274	14.50	Unknown
Baltimore, Maryland, Lunger, 39mm., F, P	1971	1274	14.50	Unknown
Birmingham, Alabama, Nemeth, 39mm., F, P	1971	1274	14.50	Unknown
Boston, Massachusetts, Caimi, 39mm., F, P	1971	1274	14.50	Unknown
Buffalo, New York, Deroos, 39mm., F, P	1971	1274	14.50	Unknown
Chicago, Illinois, Shoyer, 39mm., F, P	1971	1274	14.50	Unknown
Cincinnati, Ohio, Schroeder, 39mm., F, P	1971	1274	14.50	Unknown
Cleveland, Ohio, Faulkner, 39mm., F, P	1971	1274	14.50	Unknown
Columbus, Ohio, Lunger, 39mm., F, P	1971	1274	14.50	Unknown
Dallas, Texas, Shoyer, 39mm., F, P	1971	1274	14.50	Unknown
Denver, Colorado, Douglas, 39mm., F, P	1971	1274	14.50	Unknown
Detroit, Michigan, Rufo, 39mm., F, P	1971	1274	14.50	Unknown

El Paso, Texas, Jones, 39mm., F, P	1971	1274	14.50	Unknown
Fort Worth, Texas, Miller, 39mm., F, P	1971	1274	14.50	Unknown
Honolulu, Hawaii, Caimi, 39mm., F, P	1971	1274	14.50	Unknown
Houston, Texas, Mafko, 39mm., F, P	1971	1274	14.50	Unknown
Indianapolis, Indiana, Blaker, 39mm., F, P	1971	1274	14.50	Unknown
Jacksonville, Florida, Miller, 39mm., F, P	1971	1274	14.50	Unknown
Kansas City, Missouri, Greenwood, 39mm., F, P	1971	1274	14.50	Unknown
Long Beach, California, Ferrell, 39mm., F, P	1971	1274	14.50	Unknown
Los Angeles, California, Blaker, 39mm., F, P	1971	1274	14.50	Unknown
Louisville, Kentucky, Caimi, 39mm., F, P	1971	1274	14.50	Unknown
Memphis, Tennessee, Ferrell, 39mm., F, P	1971	1274	14.50	Unknown
Miami, Florida, Caimi, 39mm., F, P	1971	1274	14.50	Unknown
Milwaukee, Wisconsin, Ferrell, 39mm., F, P	1971	1274	14.50	Unknown
Minneapolis, Minnesota, Rufo, 39mm., F, P	1971	1274	14.50	Unknown
Nashville, Tennessee, Greenwood, 39mm., F, P	1971	1274	14.50	Unknown
New Orleans, Louisiana, Rufo, 39mm., F, P	1971	1274	14.50	Unknown
New York, New York, Mafko, 39mm., F, P	1971	1274	14.50	Unknown
Newark, New Jersey, Shoyer, 39mm., F, P	1971	1274	14.50	Unknown
Norfolk, Virginia, Caimi, 39mm., F, P	1971	1274	14.50	Unknown
Oakland, California, Mafko, 39mm., F, P	1971	1274	14.50	Unknown
Oklahoma City, Oklahoma, Mafko, 39mm., F, P	1971	1274	14.50	Unknown
Omaha, Nebraska, Park, 39mm., F, P	1971	1274	14.50	Unknown
Philadelphia, Pennsylvania, Monnaies, 39mm., F,	1971	1274	14.50	Unknown
Phoenix, Arizona, Nemeth, 39mm., F, P	1971	1274	14.50	Unknown
Pittsburgh, Pennsylvania, Jones, 39mm., F, P	1971	1274	14.50	Unknown
Portland, Oregon, Rufo, 39mm., F, P	1971	1274	14.50	Unknown
Rochester, New York, Caimi, 39mm., F, P	1971	1274	14.50	Unknown
San Antonio, Texas, Lunger, 39mm., F, P	1971	1274	14.50	Unknown
San Diego, California, Nathan, 39mm., F, P	1971	1274	14.50	Unknown
San Francisco, California, Jones, 39mm., F, P	1971	1274	14.50	Unknown
San Jose, California, Miller, 39mm., F, P	1971	1274	14.50	Unknown
Seattle, Washington, Mafko, 39mm., F, P	1971	1274	14.50	Unknown
St.Louis, Missouri, Nemeth, 39mm., F, P	1971	1274	14.50	Unknown
St.Paul, Minnesota, Mafko, 39mm., F, P	1971	1274	14.50	Unknown
Tampa, Florida, Lunger, 39mm., F, P	1971	1274	14.50	Unknown
Toledo, Ohio, Weiland, 39mm., F, P	1971	1274	14.50	Unknown
Tulsa, Oklahoma, Lauser, 39mm., F, P	1971	1274	14.50	Unknown
Washington, D.C., Monnaies, 39mm., F, P	1971	1274	14.50	Unknown

Franklin Mint Medals, Official Signers

Bartlett, Josiah, New Hampshire, 39mm., D,	1971-1972	14038	9.50	Unknown
Chase, Samuel, Maryland, 39mm., D, P	1971-1972	14038	9.50	Unknown
Floyd, William, New York, 39mm., D, P	1971-1972	14038	9.50	Unknown
Gwinnett, Button, Georgia, 39mm., D, P	1971-1972	14038	9.50	Unknown
Hancock, John, Massachusetts, 39mm., D, P	1971-1972	14038	9.50	Unknown
Hooper, William, North Carolina, 39mm., D,	1971-1972	14038	9.50	Unknown
Hopkins, Stephen, Rhode Island, 39mm., D, P	1971-1972	14038	9.50	Unknown
Jefferson, Thomas, Virginia, 39mm., D, P	1971-1972	14038	9.50	Unknown
Morris, Robert, Pennsylvania, 39mm., D, P	1971-1972	14038	9.50	Unknown
Rodney, Caesar, Delaware, 39mm., D, P	1971-1972	14038	9.50	Unknown
Rutledge, Edward, S.Carolina, 39mm., D, P	1971-1972	14038	9.50	Unknown
Sherman, Roger, Connecticut, 39mm., D, P	1971-1972	14038	9.50	Unknown
Stockton, Richard, New Jersey, 39mm., D, P	1971-1972	14038	9.50	Unknown
Adams, Samuel, Massachusetts, 39mm., D, P	1973	14038	9.50	9.50
Ellery, William, Rhode Island, 39mm., D, P	1973	14038	9.50	9.50
Harrison, Benjamin, Virginia, 39mm., D, P	1973	14038	9.50	9.50
Hewes, Joseph, North Carolina, 39mm., D, P	1973	14038	9.50	9.50
Heyward, Thomas, Jr., South Carolina, 39mm.D, P	1973	14038	9.50	9.50
Huntington, Samuel, Connecticut, 39mm., D, P	1973	14038	9.50	9.50
Livingston, Philip, New York, 39mm., D, P	1973	14038	9.50	9.50
Paca, William, Maryland, 39mm., D, P	1973	14038	9.50	9.50
Read, George, Delaware, 39mm., D, P	1973	14038	9.50	9.50
Rush, Benjamin, Pennsylvania, 39mm., D, P	1973	14038	9.50	9.50
Whipple, William, New Hampshire, 39mm., D, P	1973	14038	9.50	9.50
Witherspoon, John, New Jersey, 39mm., D, P	1973	14038	9.50	9.50
Adams, John, Massachusetts, 39mm., D, P	1974	14038	9.50	9.50
Franklin, Benjamin, Pennsylvania, 39mm., D, P	1974	14038	9.50	9.50
Hall, Lyman, Georgia, 39mm., D, P	1974	14038	9.50	9.50
Hopkinson, Francis, New Jersey, 39mm., D, P	1974	14038	9.50	9.50

Lewis, Francis, New York, 39mm., D, P	1974	14038	9.50	9.50
Lynch, Thomas, South Carolina, 39mm., D, P	1974	14038	9.50	9.50
McKean, Thomas, Delaware, 39mm., D, P	1974	14038	9.50	9.50
Nelson, Thomas, Jr., Virginia, 39mm., D, P	1974	14038	9.50	9.50
Penn, John, North Carolina, 39mm., D, P	1974	14038	9.50	9.50
Stone, Thomas, Maryland, 39mm., D, P	1974	14038	9.50	950.
Thornton, Matthew, New Hampshire, 39mm., D, P	1974	14038	9.50	9.50
Williams, William, Connecticut, 39mm., D, P	1974	14038	9.50	9.50

Franklin Mint Medals, Official United Nations 25th Anniversary Commemorative

Chinese Version, 39mm., D, Pl	1970	237	10.00	Unknown
Chinese Version, 39mm., J, M	1970	585	2.75	Unknown
English Version, 39mm., D, P	1970	40286	10.00	Unknown
English Version, 32mm., D, Pl	1970	56730	5.00	Unknown
English Version, 39mm., D, Pl	1970	30743	10.00	Unknown
English Version, 32mm., J, M	1970	19223	1.00	Unknown
English Version, 39mm., J, M	1970	4705	2.75	Unknown
English Version, 64mm., D, Pl	1970	10778	30.00	Unknown
French Version, 39mm., D, Pl	1970	237	10.00	Unknown
French Version, 39mm., J, M	1970	585	2.75	Unknown
Russian Version, 39mm., D, Pl	1970	152	10.00	Unknown
Russian Version, 39mm., J, M	1970	263	2.75	Unknown
Set Of 5, Each Version, 39mm., D, P	1970	11362	55.00	50.00 to 60.00
Spanish Version, 39mm., D, Pl	1970	56	10.00	Unknown
Spanish Version, 39mm., J, M	1970	591	2.75	Unknown

Franklin Mint Medals, Official United Nations Commemorative

World Youth Assembly, 39mm., D, P	1970	17015	10.00	Unknown
World Youth Assembly, 39mm., J, Pl	1970	11014	5.00	Unknown
Peace, 39mm., D, P	1971	29734	12.00	Unknown
Peace, 39mm., D, Pl	1971	4001	12.00	Unknown
Peace, Easel Card, 39mm., J, Pl	1971	22400	2.00	Unknown
Peace, Holder & Necklace, 39mm., J, Pl	1971	22400	5.00	Unknown
Unicef Silver Anniversary, 39mm., D, P	1971	8498	12.00	Unknown
Unicef Silver Anniversary, 39mm., D, Pl	1971	100		Unknown
Unicef Silver Anniversary, 39mm., J, Pl	1971	8355	5.00	Unknown
Chinese Version, 39mm., D, P	1972	2261	12.00	Unknown
English Version, 39mm., D, P	1972	2261	12.00	Unknown
English Version, European Economic, 39mm., D, P	1972	20195	12.50	Unknown
English Version, Human Environment, 39mm., D, P	1972	20195	12.50	Unknown
English Version, Nuclear Weapons, 39mm., D, P	1972	20195	12.50	Unknown
English Version, Sert Mural, 39mm., D, P	1972	20195	12.50	Unknown
English Version, World Health Day, 39mm., D, P	1972	20195	12.50	Unknown
French Version, 39mm., D, P	1972	2261	12.00	Unknown
Russian Version, 39mm., D, P	1972	2261	12.00	Unknown
Spanish Version, 39mm., D, P	1972	2261	12.00	Unknown
Peace, 39mm., D, P	1972	25645	12.00	Unknown
Peace, 39mm., D, Pl	1972-1973		12.00	24.00
Chinese Version, 39mm., D, P	1973	1596	12.00	12.00
English Version, 39mm., D, P	1973	1596	12.00	12.00
English Version, Disarmament, 39mm., D, P	1973	16478	12.50	12.00
English Version, Human Rights, 39mm., D, P	1973	16478	12.50	12.00
English Version, Namibia, 39mm., D, P	1973	19478	12.50	12.00
English Version, Narcotics, 39mm., D, P	1973	16478	12.50	12.00
English Version, Volunteers, 39mm., D, P	1973	16478	12.50	12.00
French Version, 39mm., D, P	1973	1596	12.00	12.00
Russian Version, 39mm., D, P	1973	1596	12.00	12.00
Spanish Version, 39mm., D, P	1973	1596	12.00	12.00

Franklin Mint Olympic Series, see Franklin Mint Medals, United States Olympic Team XX Olympiad, XI Olympic Winter Games, XX Summer Games in Munich

Franklin Mint Medals, Opera's Most Beautiful Moments

Opera's Moments, Set Of 60, F, P, Each	1973	Year	18.50	18.50

**Franklin Mint Medals, Patriots Hall of Fame Series, Builders
of Our Nation**

Adams, John Q., Lunger, 39mm., D, P	1972-1973	1336	9.50	Unknown
Baldwin, Osceola, 39mm., D, P	1972-1973	1336	9.50	Unknown
Calhoun, John, Shoyer, 39mm., D, P	1972-1973	1336	9.50	Unknown
Clay, Henry, Park, 39mm., D, P	1972-1973	1336	9.50	Unknown
Decatur, Stephen, Park, 39mm., D, P	1972-1973	1336	9.50	Unknown
Fulton, Robert, Lunger, 39mm., D, P	1972-1973	1336	9.50	Unknown
Harrison, William Henry, Lunger, 39mm., D,	1972-1973	1336	9.50	Unknown
Houston, Sam, Jones, 39mm., D, P	1972-1973	1336	9.50	Unknown
Jackson, Andrew, Hromych, 39mm., D, P	1972-1973	1336	9.50	Unknown
Lawrence, James, Ferrell, 39mm., D, P	1972-1973	1336	9.50	Unknown
Lewis & Clark, Park, 39mm., D, P	1972-1973	1336	9.50	Unknown
Madison, James, Ponter, 39mm., D, P	1972-1973	1336	9.50	Unknown
Mann, Horace, Faulkner, 39mm., D, P	1972-1973	1336	9.50	Unknown
Marshall, John, Miller, 39mm., D, P	1972-1973	1336	9.50	Unknown
Monroe, James, Nemeth, 39mm., D, P	1972-1973	1336	9.50	Unknown
Oliver, Perry H., Hromych, 39mm., D, P	1972-1973	1336	9.50	Unknown
Scott, Winfield, Blaker, 39mm., D, P	1972-1973	1336	9.50	Unknown
Taylor, Zachary, Blaker, 39mm., D, P	1972-1973	1336	9.50	Unknown
Webster, Daniel, Park, 39mm., D, P	1972-1973	1336	9.50	Unknown
Whitney, Eli, Lunger, 39mm., D, P	1972-1973	1336	9.50	Unknown

**Franklin Mint Medals, Patriots Hall of Fame Series, Defenders
of Freedom**

Adams, John, Faulkner, 39mm., D, P	1971-1972	2648	9.50	Unknown
Adams, Samuel, Cornell, 39mm., D, P	1971-1972	2648	9.50	Unknown
Allen, Ethan, Faulkner, 39mm., D, P	1971-1972	2648	9.50	Unknown
Barry, John, Nemeth, 39mm., D, P	1971-1972	2648	9.50	Unknown
Clark, George Rogers, Lauser, 39mm., D, P	1971-1972	2648	9.50	Unknown
Franklin, Benjamin, Nathan, 39mm., D, P	1971-1972	2648	9.50	Unknown
Hale, Nathan, Nemeth, 39mm., D, P	1971-1972	2648	9.50	Unknown
Hamilton, Alexander, Faulkner, 39mm., D, P	1971-1972	2648	9.50	Unknown
Hancock, John, Monnaies, 39mm., D, P	1971-1972	2648	9.50	Unknown
Henry, Patrick, Rufo, 39mm., D, P	1971-1972	2648	9.50	Unknown
Jay, John, Faulkner, 39mm., D, P	1971-1972	2648	9.50	Unknown
Jefferson, Thomas, Park, 39mm., D, P	1971-1972	2648	9.50	Unknown
Jones, John Paul, Monnaies, 39mm., D, P	1971-1972	2648	9.50	Unknown
Marion, Francis, Stanton, 39mm., D, P	1971-1972	2648	9.50	Unknown
Paine, Thomas, Lauser, 39mm., D, P	1971-1972	2648	9.50	Unknown
Pitcher, Molly, Nathan, 39mm., D, P	1971-1972	2648	9.50	Unknown
Revere, Paul, Monnaies, 39mm., D, P	1971-1972	2648	9.50	Unknown
Salem, Peter, Cornell, 39mm., D, P	1971-1972	2648	9.50	Unknown
Washington, George, Monnaies, 39mm., D, P	1971-1972	2648	9.50	Unknown
Wayne, Anthony, Cornell, 39mm., D, P	1971-1972	2648	9.50	Unknown
Adams, John, Faulkner, 39mm., D, Pl	1971-1972	307	9.50	Unknown
Adams, Samuel, Cornell, 39mm., D, Pl	1971-1972	307	9.50	Unknown
Allen, Ethan, Faulkner, 39mm., D, Pl	1971-1972	307	9.50	Unknown
Barry, John, Nemeth, 39mm., D, Pl	1971-1972	307	9.50	Unknown
Clark, George Rogers, Lauser, 39mm., D, Pl	1971-1972	307	9.50	Unknown
Franklin, Benjamin, Nathan, 39mm., D, Pl	1971-1972	307	9.50	Unknown
Hale, Nathan, Nemeth, 39mm., D, Pl	1971-1972	307	9.50	Unknown
Hamilton, Alexander, Faulkner, 39mm., D, Pl	1971-1972	307	9.50	Unknown
Hancock, John, Monnaies, 39mm., D, Pl	1971-1972	307	9.50	Unknown
Henry, Patrick, Rufo, 39mm., D, Pl	1971-1972	307	9.50	Unknown
Jay, John, Faulkner, 39mm., D, Pl	1971-1972	307	9.50	Unknown
Jefferson, Thomas, Park, 39mm., D, Pl	1971-1972	307	9.50	Unknown
Jones, John Paul, Monnaies, 39mm., D, Pl	1971-1972	307	9.50	Unknown
Marion, Francis, Stanton, 39mm., D, Pl	1971-1972	307	9.50	Unknown
Paine, Thomas, Lauser, 39mm., D, Pl	1971-1972	307	9.50	Unknown
Pitcher, Molly, Nathan, 39mm., D, Pl	1971-1972	307	9.50	Unknown
Revere, Paul, Monnaies, 39mm., D, Pl	1971-1972	307	9.50	Unknown
Salem, Peter, Cornell, 39mm., D, Pl	1971-1972	307	9.50	Unknown
Washington, George, Monnaies, 39mm., D, Pl	1971-1972	307	9.50	Unknown
Wayne, Anthony, Cornell, 39mm., D, Pl	1971-1972	307	9.50	Unknown
Adams, John, Faulkner, 39mm., F, Pl	1971-1972	253	14.50	Unknown
Adams, Samuel, Cornell, 39mm., F, Pl	1971-1972	253	14.50	Unknown
Allen, Ethan, Faulkner, 39mm., F, Pl	1971-1972	253	14.50	Unknown

Barry, John, Nemeth, 39mm., F, Pl	1971-1972	253	14.50	Unknown
Clark, George Rogers, Lauser, 39mm., F, Pl	1971-1972	253	14.50	Unknown
Franklin, Benjamin, Nathan, 39mm., F, Pl	1971-1972	253	14.50	Unknown
Hale, Nathan, Nemeth, 39mm., F, Pl	1971-1972	253	14.50	Unknown
Hamilton, Alexander, Faulkner, 39mm., F, Pl	1971-1972	253	14.50	Unknown
Hancock, John, Monnaies, 39mm., F, Pl	1971-1972	253	14.50	Unknown
Henry, Patrick, Rufo, 39mm., F, Pl	1971-1972	253	14.50	Unknown
Jay, John, Faulkner, 39mm., F, Pl	1971-1972	253	14.50	Unknown
Jefferson, Thomas, Park, 39mm., F, Pl	1971-1972	253	14.50	Unknown
Jones, John Paul, Monnaies, 39mm., F, Pl	1971-1972	253	14.50	Unknown
Marion, Francis, Stanton, 39mm., F, Pl	1971-1972	253	14.50	Unknown
Paine, Thomas, Lauser, 39mm., F, Pl	1971-1972	253	14.50	Unknown
Pitcher, Molly, Nathan, 39mm., F, Pl	1971-1972	253	14.50	Unknown
Revere, Paul, Monnaies, 39mm., F, Pl	1971-1972	253	14.50	Unknown
Salem, Peter, Cornell, 39mm., F, Pl	1971-1972	253	14.50	Unknown
Washington, George, Monnaies, 39mm., F, Pl	1971-1972	253	14.50	Unknown
Wayne, Anthony, Cornell, 39mm., F, Pl	1971-1972	253	14.50	Unknown

Franklin Mint Medals, Patriots Hall of Fame, Division and Reunion

Anthony, Susan B., D, P	1973	Year	11.00	11.00
Barton, Clara, D, P	1973	Year	11.00	11.00
Chamberlain, Joshua, D, P	1973	Year	11.00	11.00
Dewey, George, D, P	1973	Year	11.00	11.00
Douglass, Frederick, D, P	1973	Year	11.00	11.00
Farragut, David, D, P	1973	Year	11.00	11.00
Funston, Frederick, D, P	1973	Year	11.00	11.00
Garrison, William Lloyd, D, P	1973	Year	11.00	11.00
Grant, Ulysses, S., D, P	1973	Year	11.00	11.00
Greeley, Horace, D, P	1973	Year	11.00	11.00
Lee, Robert E., D, P	1973	Year	11.00	11.00
Lincoln, Abraham, D, P	1973	Year	11.00	11.00
Reed, Walter, D, P	1973	Year	11.00	11.00
Ross, Edmund G., D, P	1973	Year	11.00	11.00
Schurz, Carl, D, P	1973	Year	11.00	11.00
Seward, William Henry, D, P	1973	Year	11.00	11.00
Sheridan, Philip H., D, P	1973	Year	11.00	11.00
Sherman, William T., D, P	1973	Year	11.00	11.00
Stowe, Harriet Beecher, D, P	1973	Year	11.00	11.00
Washington, Booker T., D, P	1973	Year	11.00	11.00

Franklin Mint, Presidential Campaign Series, see Franklin Mint
Medals, Official 1972 Presidential Campaign

Franklin Mint Medals, Presidential Series, American Express
Edition

Presidents, Set Of 36, 39mm., D	1970-1971	60709	225.00	288.00

Franklin Mint Medals, Presidential Series, Proof Edition

Presidents, Set Of 36, 32mm., D	1967	1088	126.00	Unknown
Presidents, Set Of 36, 39mm., D	1967	2525	207.00	432.00 to 468.00

Franklin Mint Medals, Presidential Series, White House
Historical Association Edition

Adams, John, 45mm., D, P	1972-1975	7764	12.50	12.50
Adams, John Quincy, 45mm., D, P	1972-1975	7764	12.50	12.50
Arthur, Chester A., 45mm., D, P	1972-1975	7764	12.50	12.50
Buchanan, James, 45mm., D, P	1972-1975	7764	12.50	12.50
Cleveland, Grover, 45mm., D, P	1972-1975	7764	12.50	12.50
Coolidge, Calvin, 45mm., D, P	1972-1975	7764	12.50	12.50
Eisenhower, Dwight D., 45mm., D, P	1972-1975	7764	12.50	12.50
Fillmore, Millard, 45mm., D, P	1972-1975	7764	12.50	12.50
Garfield, James A., 45mm., D, P	1972-1975	7764	12.50	12.50
Grant, Ulysses S., 45mm., D, P	1972-1975	7764	12.50	12.50
Harding, Warren G., 45mm., D, P	1972-1975	7764	12.50	12.50
Harrison, Benjamin, 45mm., D, P	1972-1975	7764	12.50	12.50
Harrison, William H., 45mm., D, P	1972-1975	7764	12.50	12.50
Hayes, Rutherford B., 45mm., D, P	1972-1975	7764	12.50	12.50
Hoover, Herbert, 45mm., D, P	1972-1975	7764	12.50	12.50
Jackson, Andrew, 45mm., D, P	1972-1975	7764	12.50	12.50
Jefferson, Thomas, 45mm., D, P	1972-1975	7764	12.50	12.50
Johnson, Andrew, 45mm., D, P	1972-1975	7764	12.50	12.50
Johnson, Lyndon B., 45mm., D, P	1972-1975	7764	12.50	12.50

Kennedy, John F., 45mm., D, P	1972-1975	7764	12.50	12.50
Lincoln, Abraham, 45mm., D, P	1972-1975	7764	12.50	12.50
Madison, James, 45mm., D, P	1972-1975	7764	12.50	12.50
McKinley, William, 45mm., D, P	1972-1975	7764	12.50	12.50
Monroe, James, 45mm., D, P	1972-1975	7764	12.50	12.50
Nixon, Richard, 45mm., D, P	1972-1975	7764	12.50	12.50
Pierce, Franklin, 45mm., D, P	1972-1975	7764	12.50	12.50
Polk, James K., 45mm., D, P	1972-1975	7764	12.50	12.50
Roosevelt, Franklin D., 45mm., D, P	1972-1975	7764	12.50	12.50
Roosevelt, Theodore, 45mm., D, P	1972-1975	7764	12.50	12.50
Taft, William H., 45mm., D, P	1972-1975	7764	12.50	12.50
Taylor, Zachary, 45mm., D, P	1972-1975	7764	12.50	12.50
Truman, Harry S., 45mm., D, P	1972-1975	7764	12.50	12.50
Tyler, John, 45mm., D, P	1972-1975	7764	12.50	12.50
Van Buren, Martin, 45mm., D, P	1972-1975	7764	12.50	12.50
Washington, George, 45mm., D, P	1972-1975	7764	12.50	12.50
Wilson, Woodrow, 45mm., D, P	1972-1975	7764	12.50	12.50
Adams, John, 45mm., F, P	1972-1975	5999	17.50	17.50
Adams, John Quincy, 45mm., F, P	1972-1975	5999	17.50	17.50
Arthur, Chester A., 45mm., F, P	1972-1975	5999	17.50	17.50
Buchanan, James, 45mm., F, P	1972-1975	5999	17.50	17.50
Cleveland, Grover, 45mm., F, P	1972-1975	5999	17.50	17.50
Coolidge, Calvin, 45mm., F, P	1972-1975	5999	17.50	17.50
Eisenhower, Dwight D., 45mm., F, P	1972-1975	5999	17.50	17.50
Fillmore, Millard, 45mm., F, P	1972-1975	5999	17.50	17.50
Garfield, James A., 45mm., F, P	1972-1975	5999	17.50	17.50
Grant, Ulysses S., 45mm., F, P	1972-1975	5999	17.50	17.50
Harding, Warren G., 45mm., F, P	1972-1975	5999	17.50	17.50
Harrison, Benjamin, 45mm., F, P	1972-1975	5999	17.50	17.50
Harrison, William H., 45mm., F, P	1972-1975	5999	17.50	17.50
Hayes, Rutherford B., 45mm., F, P	1972-1975	5999	17.50	17.50
Hoover, Herbert, 45mm., F, P	1972-1975	5999	17.50	17.50
Jackson, Andrew, 45mm., F, P	1972-1975	5999	17.50	17.50
Jefferson, Thomas, 45mm., F, P	1972-1975	5999	17.50	17.50
Johnson, Andrew, 45mm., F, P	1972-1975	5999	17.50	17.50
Johnson, Lyndon B., 45mm., F, P	1972-1975	5999	17.50	17.50
Kennedy, John F., 45mm., F, P	1972-1975	5999	17.50	17.50
Lincoln, Abraham, 45mm., F, P	1972-1975	5999	17.50	17.50
Madison, James, 45mm., F, P	1972-1975	5999	17.50	17.50
McKinley, William, 45mm., F, P	1972-1975	5999	17.50	17.50
Monroe, James, 45mm., F, P	1972-1975	5999	17.50	17.50
Nixon, Richard, 45mm., F, P	1972-1975	5999	17.50	17.50
Pierce, Franklin, 45mm., F, P	1972-1975	5999	17.50	17.50
Polk, James, K., 45mm., F, P	1972-1975	5999	17.50	17.50
Roosevelt, Franklin D., 45mm., F, P	1972-1975	5999	17.50	17.50
Roosevelt, Theodore, 45mm., F, P	1972-1975	5999	17.50	17.50
Taft, William H., 45mm., F, P	1972-1975	5999	17.50	17.50
Taylor, Zachary, 45mm., F, P	1972-1975	5999	17.50	17.50
Truman, Harry S., 45mm., F, P	1972-1975	5999	17.50	17.50
Tyler, John, 45mm., F, P	1972-1975	5999	17.50	17.50
Van Buren, Martin, 45mm., F, P	1972-1975	5999	17.50	17.50
Washington, George, 45mm., F, P	1972-1975	5999	17.50	17.50
Wilson, Woodrow, 45mm., F, P	1972-1975	5999	17.50	17.50

Franklin Mint Medals, Presidential Series, 26mm. Edition

Presidents, Set Of 36, 26mm., D	1968	20193	61.25	Unknown

Franklin Mint Medals, Pro Football's Immortals

1920-Jim Thorpe, 39mm., D, P	1972	1946	9.50	Unknown
1921-Joe Carr, NFL President, 39mm., D, P	1972	1946	9.50	Unknown
1922-Wilbur (Pete) Henry, 39mm., D, P	1972	1946	9.50	Unknown
1923-John (Paddy) Driscoll, 39mm., D, P	1972	1946	9.50	Unknown
1924-Guy Chamberlin, 39mm., D, P	1972	1946	9.50	Unknown
1925-Harold (Red) Grange, 39mm., D, P	1972	1946	9.50	Unknown
1926-Ernie Nevers, 39mm., D, P	1972	1946	9.50	Unknown
1920-Jim Thorpe, 39mm., J, P	1972	1802	3.50	Unknown
1921-Joe Carr, NFL President, 39mm., J, P	1972	1802	3.50	Unknown
1922-Wilbur (Pete) Henry, 39mm., J, P	1972	1802	3.50	Unknown
1923-John (Paddy) Driscoll, 39mm., J, P	1972	1802	3.50	Unknown

1924-Guy Chamberlin, 39mm., J, P	1972	1802	3.50	Unknown
1925-Harold (Red) Grange, 39mm., J, P	1972	1802	3.50	Unknown
1926-Ernie Nevers, 39mm., J, P	1972	1802	3.50	Unknown
1927-Steve Owens, 39mm., J, P	1972	1802	3.50	Unknown
1928-Jimmy Conzelman, 39mm., D, P	1973	1946	9.50	9.50
1929-Earl (Curly) Lambeau, 39mm., D, P	1973	1946	9.50	9.50
1930-Johnny (Blood) McNally, 39mm., D, P	1973	1946	9.50	9.50
1931-Robert (Cal) Hubbard, 39mm., D, P	1973	1946	9.50	9.50
1932-Bronco Nagurski, 39mm., D, P	1973	1946	9.50	9.50
1933-Bill Hewitt, 39mm., D, P	1973	1946	9.50	9.50
1934-Ken Strong, 39mm., D, P	1973	1946	9.50	9.50
1935-Earl (Dutch) Clark, 39mm., D, P	1973	1946	9.50	9.50
1936-Clarke Hinkle, 39mm., D, P	1973	1946	9.50	9.50
1937-Cliff Battles, 39mm., D, P	1973	1946	9.50	9.50
1938-Mel Hein, 39mm., D, P	1973	1946	9.50	9.50
1939-Dan Fortmann, 39mm., D, P	1973	1946	9.50	9.50
1940-Sid Luckman, 39mm., D, P	1973	1946	9.50	9.50
1941-George McAfee, 39mm., D, P	1973	1946	9.50	9.50
1942-Clyde (Bulldog) Turner, 39mm., D, P	1973	1946	9.50	9.50
1943-Sammy Baugh, 39mm., D, P	1973	1946	9.50	9.50
1944-Don Hutson, 39mm.D, P	1973	1946	9.50	9.50
1945-Bob Waterfield, 39mm., D, P	1973	1946	9.50	9.50
1946-Bill Dudley, 39mm., D, P	1973	1946	9.50	9.50
1947-Charley Trippi, 39mm., D, P	1973	1946	9.50	9.50
1948-Steve Van Buren, 39mm., D, P	1973	1946	9.50	9.50
1949-Pete Pihos, 39mm., D, P	1973	1946	9.50	9.50
1950-Marion Motley, 39mm., D, P	1973	1946	9.50	9.50
1951-Elroy (Crazylegs) Hirsch, 39mm., D, P	1973	1946	9.50	9.50
1928-Jimmy Conzelman, 39mm., J, P	1973	1802	3.50	3.50
1929-Earl (Curly) Lambeau, 39mm., J, P	1973	1802	3.50	3.50
1930-Johnny (Blood) McNally, 39mm., J, P	1973	1802	3.50	3.50
1931-Robert (Cal) Hubbard, 39mm., J, P	1973	1802	3.50	3.50
1932-Bronco Nagurski, 39mm., J, P	1973	1802	3.50	3.50
1933-Bill Hewitt, 39mm., J, P	1973	1802	3.50	3.50
1934-Ken Strong, 39mm., J, P	1973	1802	3.50	3.50
1935-Earl (Dutch) Clark, 39mm., J, P	1973	1802	3.50	3.50
1936-Clarke Hinkle, 39mm., J, P	1973	1802	3.50	3.50
1937-Cliff Battles, 39mm., J, P	1973	1802	3.50	3.50
1938-Mel Hein, 39mm., J, P	1973	1802	3.50	3.50
1939-Dan Fortmann, 39mm., J, P	1973	1802	3.50	3.50
1940-Sid Luckman, 39mm., J, P	1973	1802	3.50	3.50
1941-George McAfee, 39mm., J, P	1973	1802	3.50	3.50
1942-Clyde (Bulldog) Turner, 39mm., J, P	1973	1802	3.50	3.50
1943-Sammy Baugh, 39mm., J, P	1973	1802	3.50	3.50
1944-Don Hutson, 39mm., J, P	1973	1802	3.50	3.50
1945-Bob Waterfield, 39mm.J, P	1973	1802	3.50	3.50
1946-Bill Dudley, 39mm., J, P	1973	1802	3.50	3.50
1947-Charley Trippi, 39mm., J, P	1973	1802	3.50	3.50
1948-Steve Van Buren, 39mm., J, P	1973	1802	3.50	3.50
1949-Pete Pihos, 39mm., J, P	1973	1802	3.50	3.50
1950-Marion Motley, 39mm., J, P	1973	1802	3.50	3.50
1951-Elroy (Crazylegs) Hirsch, 39mm., J, P	1973	1802	3.50	3.50
1952-Hugh McElhenny, 39mm., D, P	1974	1946	9.50	9.50
1953-Bobby Layne, 39mm., D, P	1974	1946	9.50	9.50
1954-Joe Perry, 39mm., D, P	1974	1946	9.50	9.50
1955-Otto Graham, 39mm., D, P	1974	1946	9.50	9.50
1956-Chuck Bednarik, 39mm., D, P	1974	1946	9.50	9.50
1957-Leo Nomellini, 39mm.D, P	1974	1946	9.50	9.50
1958-Art Donovan, 39mm., D, P	1974	1946	9.50	9.50
1959-Bert Bell, NFL Commissioner, 39mm., D, P	1974	1946	9.50	9.50
1960-Norm Van Brocklin, 39mm., D, P	1974	1946	9.50	9.50
1961-Emlen Tunnell, 39mm., D, P	1974	1946	9.50	9.50
1962-Andy Robustelli, 39mm., D, P	1974	1946	9.50	9.50
1963-Y.A.Tittle, 39mm., D, P	1974	1946	9.50	9.50
1964-Gino Marchetti, 39mm., D, P	1974	1946	9.50	9.50
1965-Ollie Matson, 39mm., D, P	1974	1946	9.50	9.50
1966-Lamar Hunt, AFL Founder, 39mm., D, P	1974	1946	9.50	9.50

1967-Vince Lombardi, Coach, 39mm., D, P	1974	1946	9.50	9.50
1968-Paul Brown, Coach, 39mm., D, P	1974	1946	9.50	9.50
1969-George Halas, NFL Coorganizer, 3977.D, P	1974	1946	9.50	9.50
1952-Hugh McElhenny, 39mm., J, P	1974	1802	3.50	3.50
1953-Bobby Layne, 39mm., J, P	1974	1802	3.50	3.50
1954-Joe Perry, 39mm., J, P	1974	1802	3.50	3.50
1955-Otto Graham, 39mm., J, P	1974	1802	3.50	3.50
1956-Chuck Bednarik, 39mm., J, P	1974	1802	3.50	3.50
1957-Leo Nomellini, 39mm., J, P	1974	1802	3.50	3.50
1958-Art Donovan, 39mm., J, P	1974	1802	3.50	3.50
1959-Bert Bell, NFL Commissioner, 39mm., J, P	1974	1802	3.50	3.50
1960-Norm Van Brocklin, 39mm., J, P	1974	1802	3.50	3.50
1961-Emlen Tunnell, 39mm., J, P	1974	1802	3.50	3.50
1962-Andy Robustelli, 39mm., J, P	1974	1802	3.50	3.50
1963-Y.A.Tittle, 39mm., J, P	1974	1802	3.50	3.50
1964-Gino Marchetti, 39mm., J, P	1974	1802	3.50	3.50
1965-Ollie Matson, 39mm., J, P	1974	1802	3.50	3.50
1966-Lamar Hunt, AFL Founder, 39mm., J, P	1974	1802	3.50	3.50
1967-Vince Lombardi, Coach, 39mm., J, P	1974	1802	3.50	3.50
1968-Paul Brown, Coach, 39mm., J, P	1974	1802	3.50	3.50
1969-George Halas, NFL Coorganizer, 39mm.J, P	1974	1802	3.50	3.50

Franklin Mint Medals, Project Apollo Series

Command Ship Separation, Nemeth, D, Pl	1970	4967	4.25	13.50 to 15.00
Descent To The Moon, Lauser, D, Pl	1970	4967	4.25	13.50 to 15.00
Docking Maneuver, Stanton, D, Pl	1970	4967	4.25	13.50 to 15.00
Earth Orbit, Lauser, D, Pl	1970	4967	4.25	13.50 to 15.00
Fiery Reentry, Baldwin, D, Pl	1970	4967	4.25	13.50 to 15.00
Final Module Separation, Nathan, D, Pl	1970	4967	4.25	13.50 to 15.00
Lift-Off To The Moon, Nemeth, D, Pl	1970	4967	4.25	13.50 to 15.00
LM Extraction, Stanton, D, Pl	1970	4967	4.25	13.50 to 15.00
LM Jettisoned, Pere, D, Pl	1970	4967	4.25	13.50 to 15.00
LM Launched To The Moon, Rufo, D, Pl	1970	4967	4.25	13.50 to 15.00
Lunar Exploration, Jones, D, Pl	1970	4967	4.25	13.50 to 15.00
Lunar Landing, Lauser, D, Pl	1970	4967	4.25	13.50 to 15.00
Lunar Lift-Off, Jones, D, Pl	1970	4967	4.25	13.50 to 15.00
Lunar Orbit, Rufo, D, Pl	1970	4967	4.25	13.50 to 15.00
Lunar Trajectory, Nemeth, D, Pl	1970	4967	4.25	13.50 to 15.00
Recovery, Stapleford, D, Pl	1970	4967	4.25	13.50 to 15.00
Rendezvous In Space, Pere, D, Pl	1970	4967	4.25	13.50 to 15.00
Return To Earth, Nathan, D, Pl	1970	4967	4.25	13.50 to 15.00
Second Stage Ignition, Nemeth, D, Pl	1970	4967	4.25	13.50 to 15.00
Splash-Down, Jones, D, Pl	1970	4967	4.25	13.50 to 15.00

Franklin Mint, Rembrandt Series, see Franklin Mint Medals, Genius of Rembrandt

Franklin Mint Medals, Roberts' Bird Series

Chickadees, 51mm., D, P	1970	13448	20.00	50.00
Great Horned Owls, 51mm., D, P	1970	14995	20.00	50.00
Ospreys, 51mm., D, P	1970	12435	20.00	50.00
Ring-Necked Pheasants, 51mm., D, P	1970	12227	20.00	50.00
Swallows, 51mm., D, P	1970	11577	20.00	50.00
Albatross, 51mm., D, P	1971	7474	20.00	40.00 to 45.00
Avocets, 51mm., D, P	1971	7580	20.00	40.00 to 45.00
Bald Eagles, 51mm., D, P	1971	11164	20.00	40.00 to 45.00
Barn Owls, 51mm., D, P	1971	8954	20.00	40.00 to 45.00
Black Skimmers, 51mm., D, P	1971	7671	20.00	40.00 to 45.00
Blue Jays, 51mm., D, P	1971	8618	20.00	40.00 to 45.00
Brown Thrashers, 51mm., D, P	1971	8550	20.00	40.00 to 45.00
European Robin, 51mm., D, P	1971	7955	20.00	40.00 to 45.00
Goshawk, 51mm., D, P	1971	8259	20.00	40.00 to 45.00
Greater Flamingo, 51mm., D, P	1971	11015	20.00	40.00 to 45.00
Nightingales, 51mm., D, P	1971	7704	20.00	40.00 to 45.00
Pelicans, 51mm., D, P	1971	8515	20.00	40.00 to 45.00
Peregrine Falcon, 51mm., D, P	1971	12113	20.00	40.00 to 45.00
Pileated Woodpeckers, 51mm., D, P	1971	8000	20.00	40.00 to 45.00
Quail, 51mm., D, P	1971	9055	20.00	40.00 to 45.00
Roadrunner, 51mm., D, P	1971	13124	20.00	40.00 to 45.00
Ruby-Throated Hummingbird, 51mm., D, P	1971	12540	20.00	40.00 to 45.00

Ruffed Grouse, 51mm., D, P	1971	11441	20.00	40.00 to 45.00
Skylark, 51mm., D, P	1971	7437	20.00	40.00 to 45.00
Woodcock, 51mm., D, P	1971	7544	20.00	40.00 to 45.00
American Egret, 51mm., D, P	1972	Year	20.00	35.00 to 40.00
Cardinal, 51mm., D, P	1972	Year	20.00	35.00 to 40.00
Mourning Dove, 51mm., D, P	1972	Year	20.00	35.00 to 40.00
Scissor-Tailed Fly Catcher, 51mm., D, P	1972	Year	20.00	35.00 to 40.00
Swallow-Tailed Kite, 51mm., D, P	1972	Year	20.00	35.00 to 40.00
Belted Kingfisher, D, P	1973	Year	25.00	25.00 to 30.00
California Quail, D, P	1973	Year	25.00	25.00 to 30.00
House Wren, D, P	1973	Year	25.00	25.00 to 30.00
Marsh Hawk, D, P	1973	Year	25.00	25.00 to 30.00
Mockingbird, D, P	1973	Year	25.00	25.00 to 30.00

Franklin Mint Medals, Roberts' Zodiac Series

Aquarius, 32mm., D, P	1968	1221	6.50	Unknown
Aries, 32mm., D, P	1968	1221	6.50	Unknown
Cancer, 32mm., D, P	1968	1469	6.50	Unknown
Capricorn, 32mm., D, P	1968	1211	6.50	Unknown
Gemini, 32mm., D, P	1968	1211	6.50	Unknown
Leo, 32mm., D, P	1968	1215	6.50	Unknown
Libra, 32mm., D, P	1968	1214	6.50	Unknown
Pisces, 32mm., D, P	1968	1283	6.50	Unknown
Sagittarius, 32mm., D, P	1968	1221	6.50	Unknown
Scorpio, 32mm., D, P	1968	1217	6.50	Unknown
Taurus, 32mm, D, P	1968	1233	6.50	Unknown
Virgo, 32mm., D, P	1968	1221	6.50	Unknown
Aquarius, 39mm., D, P	1968	1221	10.00	Unknown
Aries, 39mm., D, P	1968	1221	10.00	Unknown
Cancer, 39mm., D, P	1968	1469	10.00	Unknown
Capricorn, 39mm., D, P	1968	1211	10.00	Unknown
Gemini, 39mm., D, P	1968	1211	10.00	Unknown
Leo, 39mm., D, P	1968	1215	10.00	Unknown
Libra, 39mm., D, P	1968	1214	10.00	Unknown
Pisces, 39mm., D, P	1968	1283	10.00	Unknown
Sagittarius, 39mm., D, P	1968	1221	10.00	Unknown
Scorpio, 39mm., D, P	1968	1217	10.00	Unknown
Taurus, 39mm., D, P	1968	1233	10.00	Unknown
Virgo, 39mm., D, P	1968	1221	10.00	Unknown
Aquarius, 39mm., D, P	1970	4185	8.00	Unknown
Aries, 39mm., D, P	1970	4185	8.00	Unknown
Cancer, 39mm., D, P	1970	4185	8.00	Unknown
Capricorn, 39mm., D, P	1970	4185	8.00	Unknown
Gemini, 39mm., D, P	1970	4185	8.00	Unknown
Leo, 39mm., D, P	1970	4185	8.00	Unknown
Libra, 39mm., D, P	1970	4185	8.00	Unknown
Pisces, 39mm., D, P	1970	4185	8.00	Unknown
Sagittarius, 39mm., D, P	1970	4185	8.00	Unknown
Scorpio, 39mm., D, P	1970	4185	8.00	Unknown
Taurus, 39mm., D, P	1970	4185	8.00	Unknown
Virgo, 39mm., D, P	1970	4185	8.00	Unknown
Aquarius, J, P	1970	1760	3.00	Unknown
Aries, J, P	1970	1760	3.00	Unknown
Cancer, J, P	1970	1760	3.00	Unknown
Capricorn, J, P	1970	1760	3.00	Unknown
Gemini, J, P	1970	1760	3.00	Unknown
Leo, J, P	1970	1760	3.00	Unknown
Libra, J, P	1970	1760	3.00	Unknown
Pisces, J, P	1970	1760	3.00	Unknown
Sagittarius, J, P	1970	1760	3.00	Unknown
Scorpio, J, P	1970	1760	3.00	Unknown
Taurus, J, P	1970	1760	3.00	Unknown
Virgo, J, P	1970	1760	3.00	Unknown

Franklin Mint Medals, Shakespeare

A Midsummer Night's Dream, 45mm., D, P	1971-1972	3287	12.00	Unknown
As You Like It, 45mm., D, P	1971-1972	3287	12.00	Unknown

Coriolanus, 45mm., D, P	1971-1972	3287	12.00	Unknown
Hamlet, 45mm., D, P	1971-1972	3287	12.00	Unknown
King Henry IV, Part 1, 45mm., D, P	1971-1972	3287	12.00	Unknown
King Henry IV, Part 2, 45mm., D, P	1971-1972	3287	12.00	Unknown
King Henry VI, Part 1, 45mm., D, P	1971-1972	3287	12.00	Unknown
King John, 45mm., D, P	1971-1972	3287	12.00	Unknown
King Lear, 45mm., D, P	1971-1972	3287	12.00	Unknown
King Richard II, 45mm., D, P	1971-1972	3287	12.00	Unknown
Life Of Henry V, 45mm., D, P	1971-1972	3287	12.00	Unknown
Macbeth, 45mm., D, P	1971-1972	3287	12.00	Unknown
Merry Wives Of Windsor, 45mm., D, P	1971-1972	3287	12.00	Unknown
Romeo & Juliet, 45mm., D, P	1971-1972	3287	12.00	Unknown
The Taming Of The Shrew, 45mm., D, P	1971-1972	3287	12.00	Unknown
The Tempest, 45mm., D, P	1971-1972	3287	12.00	Unknown
Timon Of Athens, 45mm., D, P	1971-1972	3287	12.00	Unknown
Titus Andronicus, 45mm., D, P	1971-1972	3287	12.00	Unknown
Twelfth Night, 45mm., D, P	1971-1972	3287	12.00	Unknown
Winter's Tale, 45mm., D, P	1971-1972	3287	12.00	Unknown
A Midsummer Night's Dream, 45mm., F, P	1971-1972	2173	18.00	Unknown
As You Like It, 45mm., F, P	1971-1972	2173	18.00	Unknown
Coriolanus, 45mm., F, P	1971-1972	2173	18.00	Unknown
Hamlet, 45mm., F, P	1971-1972	2173	18.00	Unknown
King Henry IV, Part 1, 45mm.F, P	1971-1972	2173	18.00	Unknown
King Henry IV, Part 2, 45mm., F, P	1971-1972	2173	18.00	Unknown
King Henry VI, Part 1, 45mm., F, P	1971-1972	2173	18.00	Unknown
King John, 45mm., F, P	1971-1972	2173	18.00	Unknown
King Lear, 45mm., F, P	1971-1972	2173	18.00	Unknown
King Richard II, 45mm., F, P	1971-1972	2173	18.00	Unknown
Life Of Henry V, 45mm., F, P	1971-1972	2173	18.00	Unknown
Macbeth, 45mm., F, P	1971-1972	2173	18.00	Unknown
Merry Wives Of Windsor, 45mm., F, P	1971-1972	2173	18.00	Unknown
Romeo & Juliet, 45mm., F, P	1971-1972	2173	18.00	Unknown
The Taming Of The Shrew, 45mm., F, P	1971-1972	2173	18.00	Unknown
The Tempest, 45mm., F, P	1971-1972	2173	18.00	Unknown
Timon Of Athens, 45mm., F, P	1971-1972	2173	18.00	Unknown
Titus Andronicus, 45mm., F, P	1971-1972	2173	18.00	Unknown
Twelfth Night, 45mm., F, P	1971-1972	2173	18.00	Unknown
Winter's Tale, 45mm., F, P	1971-1972	2173	18.00	Unknown
Comedy Of Errors, 45mm., D, P	1973	3287	12.00	12.00
Cymbeline, 45mm., D, P	1973	3287	12.00	12.00
Julius Caesar, 45mm., D, P	1973	3287	12.00	12.00
King Henry VI, Part 2, 45mm., D, P	1973	3287	12.00	12.00
King Henry VI, Part 3, 45mm., D, P	1973	3287	12.00	12.00
King Henry VIII, 45mm., D, P	1973	3287	12.00	12.00
King Richard III, 45mm., D, P	1973	3287	12.00	12.00
Love's Labours Lost, 45mm., D, P	1973	3287	12.00	12.00
Measure For Measure, 45mm., D, P	1973	3287	12.00	12.00
Merchant Of Venice, 45mm., D, P	1973	3287	12.00	12.00
Othello, 45mm., D, P	1973	3287	12.00	12.00
Pericles, 45mm., D, P	1973	3287	12.00	12.00
Comedy Of Errors, 45mm., F, P	1973	2173	18.00	18.00
Cymbeline, 45mm., F, P	1973	2173	18.00	18.00
Julius Caesar, 45mm., F, P	1973	2173	18.00	18.00
King Henry VI-Part 2, 45mm., F, P	1973	2173	18.00	18.00
King Henry VI-Part 3, 45mm., F, P	1973	2173	18.00	18.00
King Henry VIII, 45mm., F, P	1973	2173	18.00	18.00
King Richard III, 45mm., F, P	1973	2173	18.00	18.00
Love's Labours Lost, 45mm., F, P	1973	2173	18.00	18.00
Measure For Measure, 45mm., F, P	1973	2173	18.00	18.00
Merchant Of Venice, 45mm., F, P	1973	2173	18.00	18.00
Othello, 45mm., F, P	1973	2173	18.00	18.00
Pericles, 45mm., F, P	1973	2173	18.00	18.00
All's Well That Ends Well, 45mm., D, P	1974	3287	12.00	12.00
Antony & Cleopatra, 45mm., D, P	1974	3287	12.00	12.00
Much Ado About Nothing, 45mm., D, P	1974	3287	12.00	12.00
Troilus & Cressida, 45mm., D, P	1974	3287	12.00	12.00

Two Gentlemen Of Verona, 45mm., D, P	1974	3287	12.00	12.00
Two Noble Kinsmen, 45mm., D, P	1974	3287	12.00	12.00
				12.00
All's Well That Ends Well, 45mm., F, P	1974	2173	18.00	18.00
Antony & Cleopatra, 45mm., F, P	1974	2173	18.00	18.00
Much Ado About Nothing, 45mm., F, P	1974	2173	18.00	18.00
Troilus & Cressida, 45mm., F, P	1974	2173	18.00	18.00
Two Gentlemen Of Verona, 45mm., F, P	1974	2173	18.00	18.00
Two Noble Kinsmen, 45mm., F, P	1974	2173	18.00	18.00

Franklin Mint, Signers of the Declaration of Independence Series,

See Franklin Mint Medals, Official Signers

Franklin Mint Medals, Societe de la Sculpture de Medailles

Sports In Sweden, 64mm., D, A	1971	1002	50.00	75.00
Boat Against The Waves, 64mm., D, A	1972	557	50.00	75.00
Bunraku, 64mm., D, A	1972	387	50.00	75.00
Copenhagen Castle, 64mm., D, A	1972	Year	50.00	75.00
Creation Of The World, 64mm., D, A	1971	1060	50.00	75.00
Crest Of The Wave, 64mm., D, A	1972	318	50.00	75.00
Escolas De Samba, 64mm., D, A	1972	361	50.00	75.00
Lapland In Summer, 64mm., D, A	1972	914	50.00	75.00
Man In The Field, 64mm., D, A	1972	Year	50.00	75.00
Modern Design, 64mm., D, A	1972	742	50.00	75.00
New Zealand, 64mm., D, A	1971	1561	50.00	75.00
Noh Player, 64mm., D, A	1972	872	50.00	75.00
Peace & Tranquility, 64mm., D, A	1972	Year	50.00	75.00
Progression, 64mm., D, A	1972	354	50.00	75.00
Spirit Of Portugal, 64mm., D, A	1972	287	50.00	75.00

Franklin Mint Medals, Special Commemorative Issues

American Airlines 747 Astroliner, Lauser, D	1970	7507	6.25	Unknown
American British Numismatic Society, D	1970	7507	6.25	Unknown
American Prestige Arts, Norman Nemeth, D	1970	7507	6.25	Unknown
Apollo 13, Lumen Martin Winter, D	1970	7507	6.25	Unknown
Army & Air Force Employees' Assoc., D	1970	7507	6.25	Unknown
English-Speaking Union Of The U.S., Newell, D	1970	7507	6.25	Unknown
Fulton County Historical Society, Faulkner, D	1970	7507	6.25	Unknown
German-American National Congress, D	1970	7507	6.25	Unknown
Governor William T.Cahill, Inaugural, D	1970	7507	6.25	Unknown
Group W, Westinghouse Broadcasting Company, D	1970	7507	6.25	Unknown
League Of Women Voters Of The U.S., D	1970	7507	6.25	Unknown
Lincoln Center For The Performing Arts, D	1970	7507	6.25	Unknown
Los Alamos Kiwanis Club, Stapleford, D	1970	7507	6.25	Unknown
MacArthur Memorial Foundation, D	1970	7507	6.25	Unknown
Mayor John V.Lindsay, Faulkner, D	1970	7507	6.25	Unknown
Milwaukee World Festival, Salute To Mexico, D	1970	7507	6.25	Unknown
Miss America Pageant, Lauser, D	1970	7507	6.25	Unknown
Museum Of The Confederacy, D	1970	7507	6.25	Unknown
Ohio State University, Anthony Jones, D	1970	7507	6.25	Unknown
Organization Of International Numismatists, D	1970	7507	6.25	Unknown
Philadelphia Convention & Tourist Bureau, D	1970	7507	6.25	Unknown
RCA, Defense Electronic Products, Caimi, D	1970	7507	6.25	Unknown
Ringling Bros. & Barnum & Bailey, Faulkner, D	1970	7507	6.25	Unknown
Society Of Sons & Daughters Of Pilgrims, D	1970	7507	6.25	Unknown
Steamship Historical Society Of America, D	1970	7507	6.25	Unknown
The Bostonian Society, Richard Baldwin, D	1970	7507	6.25	Unknown
The Cavalry, General George S.Patton, D	1970	7507	6.25	Unknown
Token & Medal Society, James Ferrell, D	1970	7507	6.25	Unknown
Untronic Systems Corporation, Anthony Jones, D	1970	7507	6.25	Unknown
Wilberforce University, Philip Nathan, D	1970	7507	6.25	Unknown
American Airlines 747 Astroliner, Lauser, J	1970	2490	2.75	Unknown
American-British Numismatic Society, J	1970	2490	2.75	Unknown
American Prestige Arts, Nemeth, J	1970	2490	2.75	Unknown
Apollo 13, Lumen Martin Winter, J	1970	2490	2.75	Unknown
Army & Air Force Employees' Assoc., J	1970	2490	2.75	Unknown
Bostonian Society, J	1970	2490	2.75	Unknown
Cavalry, General George S.Patton, J	1970	2490	2.75	Unknown
English-Speaking Union Of The U.S., Newell, J	1970	2490	2.75	Unknown
Fulton County Historical Society, Faulkner, J	1970	2490	2.75	Unknown
German-American National Congress, J	1970	2490	2.75	Unknown

Governor William T.Cahill, Inaugural, J	1970	2490	2.75	Unknown
Group W, Westinghouse Broadcasting Company, J	1970	2490	2.75	Unknown
League Of Women Voters Of The U.S., J	1970	2490	2.75	Unknown
Lincoln Center For The Performing Arts, J	1970	2490	2.75	Unknown
Los Alamos Kiwanis Club, Stapleford, J	1970	2490	2.75	Unknown
MacArthur Memorial Foundation, J	1970	2490	2.75	Unknown
Mayor John V.Lindsay, Faulkner, J	1970	2490	2.75	Unknown
Milwaukee World Festival, Salute To Mexico, J	1970	2490	2.75	Unknown
Miss America Pageant, Lauser, J	1970	2490	2.75	Unknown
Museum Of The Confederacy, J	1970	2490	2.75	Unknown
Ohio State University, Jones, J	1970	2490	2.75	Unknown
Organization Of International Numismatists, J	1970	2490	2.75	Unknown
Philadelphia Convention & Tourist Bureau, J	1970	2490	2.75	Unknown
Rca, Defense Electronic Products, Caimi, J	1970	2490	2.75	Unknown
Ringling Bros. & Barnum & Bailey, Faulkner, J	1970	2490	2.75	Unknown
Society Of Sons & Daughters Of Pilgrims, J	1970	2490	2.75	Unknown
Steamship Historical Society Of America, J	1970	2490	2.75	Unknown
Token & Medal Society, Ferrell, J	1970	2490	2.75	Unknown
Untronic Systems Corporation, Jones, J	1970	2490	2.75	Unknown
Wilberforce University, Philip Nathan, J	1970	2490	2.75	Unknown
American Medical Women's Association, D	1971	6281	6.60	Unknown
American Red Cross, Clara Barton, Shoyer, D	1971	6281	6.60	Unknown
American Stock Exchange, Baldwin, D	1971	6281	6.60	Unknown
Apollo 14, Lauser, D	1971	6281	6.60	Unknown
Apollo, 15, Nemeth, D	1971	6281	6.60	Unknown
Arkansas River Waterway, Nemeth, D	1971	6281	6.60	Unknown
Arlington National Cemetery, Shoyer, D	1971	6281	6.60	Unknown
Azteca Numismatica, Rufo, D	1971	6281	6.60	Unknown
Big Brothers Of America, Miller & Baldwin, D	1971	6281	6.60	Unknown
British Columbia Centennial Commission, D	1971	6281	6.60	Unknown
Canterbury Museum, Berry, D	1971	6281	6.60	Unknown
CARE, 25th Anniversary, Miller, D	1971	6281	6.60	Unknown
Disabled American Veterans, Rufo & Caimi, D	1971	6281	6.60	Unknown
Friendly Sons Of St.Patrick, Park, D	1971	6281	6.60	Unknown
Hagley Museum, Miller & Lunger, D	1971	6281	6.60	Unknown
Hayden Planetarium, Faulkner, D	1971	6281	6.60	Unknown
Inter-Tribal Indian Ceremonial, Rufo, D	1971	6281	6.60	Unknown
Italian Culture Council, Dante, 650th, D	1971	6281	6.60	Unknown
Lincoln Center For The Performing Arts, D	1971	6281	6.60	Unknown
Lowell Art Association, Lauser, D	1971	6281	6.60	Unknown
Multiple Sclerosis Society, Lauser, D	1971	6281	6.60	Unknown
New Mexico Historical Society, Nemeth, D	1971	6281	6.60	Unknown
New Orleans Jazz Museum, Louis Armstrong, D	1971	6281	6.60	Unknown
Oklahoma Inaugural Committee, David Hall, D	1971	6281	6.60	Unknown
Order Of Ahepa, Greek Independence, D	1971	6281	6.60	Unknown
Peace Corps, 10th Anniversary, Dehoff, D	1971	6281	6.60	Unknown
Pensacola Historical Society, Caimi & Jones, D	1971	6281	6.60	Unknown
Philadelphia Convention & Tourist Bureau, D	1971	6281	6.60	Unknown
Royal Society Of New Zealand, Berry, D	1971	6281	6.60	Unknown
Scott Memorial Foundation, Pinches, D	1971	6281	6.60	Unknown
Sons & Daughters Of The Pilgrims, Miller, D	1971	6281	6.60	Unknown
Token & Medal Society Convention, Faulkner, D	1971	6281	6.60	Unknown
United Automobile Workers, Lauser & Jones, D	1971	6281	6.60	Unknown
United States Figure Skating Association, D	1971	6281	6.60	Unknown
Virgin Islands, Governor Evans, Baldwin, D	1971	6281	6.60	Unknown
Voste National Committee, Lauser, D	1971	6281	6.60	Unknown
American Medical Women's Association, J	1971	1726	3.00	Unknown
American Red Cross, Clara Barton, Shoyer, J	1971	1726	3.00	Unknown
American Stock Exchange, Baldwin, J	1971	1726	3.00	Unknown
Apollo 14, Lauser, J	1971	1726	3.00	Unknown
Apollo 15, Nemeth, J	1971	1726	3.00	Unknown
Arkansas River Waterway, Nemeth, J	1971	1726	3.00	Unknown
Arlington National Cemetery, Shoyer, J	1971	1726	3.00	Unknown
Azteca Numismatica, Rufo, J	1971	1726	3.00	Unknown
Big Brothers Of America, Miller & Baldwin, J	1971	1726	3.00	Unknown
British Columbia Centennial Commission, J	1971	1726	3.00	Unknown
Canterbury Museum, Berry, J	1971	1726	3.00	Unknown
CARE, 25th Anniversary, Miller, J	1971	1726	3.00	Unknown
Disabled American Veterans, Rufo & Caimi, J	1971	1726	3.00	Unknown

Friendly Sons Of St.Patrick, Park, J	1971	1726	3.00	Unknown
Hagley Museum, Miller & Lunger, J	1971	1726	3.00	Unknown
Hayden Planetarium, Faulkner, J	1971	1726	3.00	Unknown
Inter-Tribal Indian Ceremonial, Rufo, J	1971	1726	3.00	Unknown
Italian Culture Council, Lauser & Ferrell, J	1971	1726	3.00	Unknown
Lincoln Center For The Performing Arts, J	1971	1726	3.00	Unknown
Lowell Art Association, Lauser, J	1971	1726	3.00	Unknown
Multiple Sclerosis Society, Lauser, J	1971	1726	3.00	Unknown
New Mexico Historical Society, Nemeth, J	1971	1726	3.00	Unknown
New Orleans Jazz Museum, Louis Armstrong, J	1971	1726	3.00	Unknown
Oklahoma Inaugural Committee, Lauser, J	1971	1726	3.00	Unknown
Order Of Ahepa, Greek Independence, J	1971	1726	3.00	Unknown
Peace Corps, 10th Anniversary, Dehoff, J	1971	1726	3.00	Unknown
Pensacola Historical Society, Caimi & Jones, J	1971	1726	3.00	Unknown
Philadelphia Convention & Tourist Bureau, J	1971	1726	3.00	Unknown
Royal Society Of New Zealand, Berry, J	1971	1726	3.00	Unknown
Scott Memorial Foundation, Pinches, J	1971	1726	3.00	Unknown
Sons & Daughters Of Pilgrims, Miller, J	1971	1726	3.00	Unknown
Token & Medal Society Convention, Faulkner, J	1971	1726	3.00	Unknown
United Automobile Workers, Lauser & Jones, J	1971	1726	3.00	Unknown
United States Figure Skating Association, J	1971	1726	3.00	Unknown
Virgin Islands, Governor Evans, Baldwin, J	1971	1726	3.00	Unknown
Votes National Committee, Lauser, J	1971	1726	3.00	Unknown
Air Force Sergeants Association, Miller, D	1972	3861	6.60	Unknown
American Aviation Historical Society, D	1972	3861	6.60	Unknown
American Public Health Association, Aron, D	1972	3861	6.60	Unknown
Apollo 16, De Roos, D	1972	3861	6.60	Unknown
Bostonian Society, Hromych, D	1972	3861	6.60	Unknown
Brazil-American Society, Lunger, D	1972	3861	6.60	Unknown
Calvin Coolidge Memorial Foundation, D	1972	3861	6.60	Unknown
Castillo De San Marcos, Shoyer, D	1972	3861	6.60	Unknown
Committee On Employment Of Handicapped, D	1972	3861	6.60	Unknown
Comsat, Blaker, D	1972	3861	6.60	Unknown
Eleanor Roosevelt Memorial Foundation, D	1972	3861	6.60	Unknown
Friendly Sons Of St.Patrick, Faulkner, D	1972	3861	6.60	Unknown
Galena, Illinois, Chamber Of Commerce, Lauser, D	1972	3861	6.60	Unknown
George C.Marshall Research Foundation, Rufo, D	1972	3861	6.60	Unknown
Harold Prince Productions, Lauser, D	1972	3861	6.60	Unknown
Historic Annapolis, Inc., Blaker, D	1972	3861	6.60	Unknown
International Bible Collectors Soc., Rufo, D	1972	3861	6.60	Unknown
Lincoln Memorial University, Miller, D	1972	3861	6.60	Unknown
National Railroad Historical Association, D	1972	3861	6.60	Unknown
North Dakota Historical Society, Miller, D	1972	3861	6.60	Unknown
Northbrook, Illinois, Skater, Hromych, D	1972	3861	6.60	Unknown
Office Of The Mayor Of New Orleans, Shoyer, D	1972	3861	6.60	Unknown
Philadelphia College Of Physicians, Schule, D	1972	3861	6.60	Unknown
Red Cloud School & Sioux Indian Museum, D	1972	3861	6.60	Unknown
Rhode Island Historical Society, Schroeder, D	1972	3861	6.60	Unknown
San Juan Island Historical Park, Ponter, D	1972	3861	6.60	Unknown
U.S.Lawn Tennis Association, Ponter, D	1972	3861	6.60	Unknown
Watauga Historical Association, Lauser, D	1972	3861	6.60	Unknown
Wyoming State Archives, Shoyer, D	1972	3861	6.60	Unknown
Air Force Sergeants Association, Miller, J	1972	1104	3.00	Unknown
American Aviation Historical Society, J	1972	1104	3.00	Unknown
American Public Health Association, Aron, J	1972	1104	3.00	Unknown
Apollo 16, De Roos, J	1972	1104	3.00	Unknown
Bostonian Society, Hromych, J	1972	1104	3.00	Unknown
Brazil-American Society, Lunger, J	1972	1104	3.00	Unknown
Calvin Coolidge Memorial Foundation, J	1972	1104	3.00	Unknown
Castillo De San Marcos, Shoyer, J	1972	1104	3.00	Unknown
Committee On Employment Of Handicapped, J	1972	1104	3.00	Unknown
Comsat, Blaker, J	1972	1104	3.00	Unknown
Eleanor Roosevelt Memorial Foundation, J	1972	1104	3.00	Unknown
Friendly Sons Of St.Patrick, Faulkner, J	1972	1104	3.00	Unknown
Galena, Illinois, Chamber Of Commerce, Lauser, J	1972	1104	3.00	Unknown
George C.Marshall Research Foundation, Rufo, J	1972	1104	3.00	Unknown
Harold Prince Productions, Lauser, J	1972	1104	3.00	Unknown
Historic Annapolis, Inc., Blaker, J	1972	1104	3.00	Unknown

International Bible Collectors Society, J	1972	1104	3.00	Unknown
Lincoln Memorial University, Ponter, J	1972	1104	3.00	Unknown
National Railroad Historical Association, J	1972	1104	3.00	Unknown
North Dakota Historical Society, Miller, J	1972	1104	3.00	Unknown
Northbrook, Illinois, Skater, Hromych, J	1972	1104	3.00	Unknown
Office Of The Mayor Of New Orleans, Shoyer, J	1972	1104	3.00	Unknown
Philadelphia College Of Physicians, Schule, J	1972	1104	3.00	Unknown
Red Cloud School & Sioux Indian Museum, J	1972	1104	3.00	Unknown
Rhode Island Historical Society, Schroeder, J	1972	1104	3.00	Unknown
San Juan Island Historical Park, Ponter, J	1972	1104	3.00	Unknown
U.S.Lawn Tennis Association, Ponter, J	1972	1104	3.00	Unknown
Watauga Historical Association, Lauser, J	1972	1104	3.00	Unknown
Wyoming State Archives, Shoyer, J	1972	1104	3.00	Unknown

Franklin Mint Medals, States of the Union

Alabama, Rufo, D, P	1969	30422	3.75	5.00
Alaska, Cornell, D, P	1969	30422	3.75	5.00
Arizona, Cornell, D, P	1969	30422	3.75	5.00
Arkansas, Stanton, D, P	1969	30422	3.75	5.00
California, Rufo, D, P	1969	30422	3.75	5.00
Colorado, Rufo, D, P	1969	30422	3.75	5.00
Connecticut, Cornell, D, P	1969	30422	3.75	5.00
Delaware, Jones, D, P	1969	30422	3.75	5.00
Florida, Cornell, D, P	1969	30422	3.75	5.00
Georgia, Rufo, D, P	1969	30422	3.75	5.00
Hawaii, Nathan, D, P	1969	30422	3.75	5.00
Idaho, Jones, D, P	1969	30422	3.75	5.00
Illinois, Nathan, D, P	1969	30422	3.75	5.00
Indiana, Stanton, D, P	1969	30422	3.75	5.00
Iowa, Rufo, D, P	1969	30422	3.75	5.00
Kansas, Cornell, D, P	1969	30422	3.75	5.00
Kentucky, Cornell, D, P	1969	30422	3.75	5.00
Louisiana, Stanton, D, P	1969	30422	3.75	5.00
Maine, Stanton, D, P	1969	30422	3.75	5.00
Maryland, Rufo, D, P	1969	30422	3.75	5.00
Massachusetts, Stanton, D, P	1969	30422	3.75	5.00
Michigan, Cornell, D, P	1969	30422	3.75	5.00
Minnesota, Rufo, D, P	1969	30422	3.75	5.00
Mississippi, Rufo, D, P	1969	30422	3.75	5.00
Missouri, Stanton, D, P	1969	30422	3.75	5.00
Montana, Cornell, D, P	1969	30422	3.75	5.00
Nebraska, Cronell, D, P	1969	30422	3.75	5.00
Nevada, Cornell, D, P	1969	30422	3.75	5.00
New Hampshire, Nathan, D, P	1969	30422	3.75	5.00
New Jersey, Cornell, D, P	1969	30422	3.75	5.00
New Mexico, Rufo, D, P	1969	30422	3.75	5.00
New York, Stanton, D, P	1969	30422	3.75	5.00
North Carolina, Rufo, D, P	1969	30422	3.75	5.00
North Dakota, Stanton, D, P	1969	30422	3.75	5.00
Ohio, Rufo, D, P	1969	30422	3.75	5.00
Oklahoma, Rufo, D, P	1969	30422	3.75	5.00
Oregon, Cornell, D, P	1969	30422	3.75	5.00
Pennsylvania, Cornell, D, P	1969	30422	3.75	5.00
Rhode Island, Cornell, D, P	1969	30422	3.75	5.00
South Carolina, Stanton, D, P	1969	30422	3.75	5.00
South Dakota, Stanton, D, P	1969	30422	3.75	5.00
Tennessee, Stanton, D, P	1969	30422	3.75	5.00
Texas, Cornell, D, P	1969	30422	3.75	5.00
Utah, Rufo, D, P	1969	30422	3.75	5.00
Vermont, Nathan, D, P	1969	30422	3.75	5.00
Virginia, Stanton, D, P	1969	30422	3.75	5.00
Washington, Rufo, D, P	1969	30422	3.75	5.00
West Virginia, Cornell, D, P	1969	30422	3.75	5.00
Wisconsin, Cornell, D, P	1969	30422	3.75	5.00
Wyoming, Cornell, D, P	1969	30422	3.75	5.00
Alabama, Rufo, J, P	1969	14118	1.50	Unknown
Alaska, Cornell, J, P	1969	14118	1.50	Unknown
Arizona, Cornell, J, P	1969	14118	1.50	Unknown
Arkansas, Stanton, J, P	1969	14118	1.50	Unknown
California, Rufo, J, P	1969	14118	1.50	Unknown

Colorado, Rufo, J, P	1969	14118	1.50	Unknown
Connecticut, Cornell, J, P	1969	14118	1.50	Unknown
Delaware, Jones, J, P	1969	14118	1.50	Unknown
Florida, Cornell, J, P	1969	14118	1.50	Unknown
Georgia, Rufo, J, P	1969	14118	1.50	Unknown
Hawaii, Nathan, J, P	1969	14118	1.50	Unknown
Idaho, Jones, J, P	1969	14118	1.50	Unknown
Illinois, Nathan, J, P	1969	14118	1.50	Unknown
Indiana, Stanton, J, P	1969	14118	1.50	Unknown
Iowa, Rufo, J, P	1969	14118	1.50	Unknown
Kansas, Cornell, J, P	1969	14118	1.50	Unknown
Kentucky, Cornell, J, P	1969	14118	1.50	Unknown
Louisiana, Stanton, J, P	1969	14118	1.50	Unknown
Maine, Stanton, J, P	1969	14118	1.50	Unknown
Maryland, Rufo, J, P	1969	14118	1.50	Unknown
Massachusetts, Stanton, J, P	1969	14118	1.50	Unknown
Michigan, Cornell, J, P	1969	14118	1.50	Unknown
Minnesota, Rufo, J, P	1969	14118	1.50	Unknown
Mississippi, Rufo, J, P	1969	14118	1.50	Unknown
Missouri, Stanton, J, P	1969	14118	1.50	Unknown
Montana, Cornell, J, P	1969	14118	1.50	Unknown
Nebraska, Cornell, J, P	1969	14118	1.50	Unknown
Nevada, Cornell, J, P	1969	14118	1.50	Unknown
New Hampshire, Nathan, J, P	1969	14118	1.50	Unknown
New Jersey, Cornell, J, P	1969	14118	1.50	Unknown
New Mexico, Rufo, J, P	1969	14118	1.50	Unknown
New York, Stanton, J, P	1969	14118	1.50	Unknown
North Carolina, Rufo, J, P	1969	14118	1.50	Unknown
North Dakota, Stanton, J, P	1969	14118	1.50	Unknown
Ohio, Rufo, J, P	1969	14118	1.50	Unknown
Oklahoma, Rufo, J, P	1969	14118	1.50	Unknown
Oregon, Cornell, J, P	1969	14118	1.50	Unknown
Pennsylvania, Cornell, J, P	1969	14118	1.50	Unknown
Rhode Island, Cornell, J, P	1969	14118	1.50	Unknown
South Carolina, Stanton, J, P	1969	14118	1.50	Unknown
South Dakota, Stanton, J, P	1969	14118	1.50	Unknown
Tennessee, Stanton, J, P	1969	14118	1.50	Unknown
Texas, Cornell, J, P	1969	14118	1.50	Unknown
Utah, Rufo, J, P	1969	14118	1.50	Unknown
Vermont, Nathan, J, P	1969	14118	1.50	Unknown
Virginia, Stanton, J, P	1969	14118	1.50	Unknown
Washington, Rufo, J, P	1969	14118	1.50	Unknown
West Virginia, Cornell, J, P	1969	14118	1.50	Unknown
Wisconsin, Cornell, J, P	1969	14118	1.50	Unknown
Wyoming, Cornell, J, P	1969	14118	1.50	Unknown
Alabama, Rufo, D, Pl	1970	1853	4.25	5.25
Alaska, Cornell, D, Pl	1970	1853	4.25	5.25
Arizona, Cornell, D, Pl	1970	1853	4.25	5.25
Arkansas, Stanton, D, Pl	1970	1853	4.25	5.25
California, Rufo, D, Pl	1970	1853	4.25	5.25
Colorado, Rufo, D, Pl	1970	1853	4.25	5.25
Connecticut, Cornell, D, Pl	1970	1853	4.25	5.25
Delaware, Jones, D, Pl	1970	1853	4.25	5.25
Florida, Cornell, D, Pl	1970	1853	4.25	5.25
Georgia, Rufo, D, Pl	1970	1853	4.25	5.25
Hawaii, Nathan, D, Pl	1970	1853	4.25	5.25
Idaho, Jones, D, Pl	1970	1853	4.25	5.25
Illinois, Nathan, D, Pl	1970	1853	4.25	5.25
Indiana, Stanton, D, Pl	1970	1853	4.25	5.25
Iowa, Rufo, D, Pl	1970	1853	4.25	5.25
Kansas, Cornell, D, Pl	1970	1853	4.25	5.25
Kentucky, Cornell, D, Pl	1970	1853	4.25	5.25
Louisiana, Stanton, D, Pl	1970	1853	4.25	5.25
Maine, Stanton, D, Pl	1970	1853	4.25	5.25
Maryland, Rufo, D, Pl	1970	1853	4.25	5.25
Massachusetts, Stanton, D, Pl	1970	1853	4.25	5.25
Michigan, Cornell, D, Pl	1970	1853	4.25	5.25
Minnesota, Rufo, D, Pl	1970	1853	4.25	5.25
Mississippi, Rufo, D, Pl	1970	1853	4.25	5.25

Missouri, Stanton, D, Pl	1970	1853	4.25	5.25
Montana, Cornell, D, Pl	1970	1853	4.25	5.25
Nebraska, Cornell, D, Pl	1970	1853	4.25	5.25
Nevada, Cornell, D, Pl	1970	1853	4.25	5.25
New Hampshire, Nathan, D, Pl	1970	1853	4.25	5.25
New Jersey, Cornell, D, Pl	1970	1853	4.25	5.25
New Mexico, Rufo, D, Pl	1970	1853	4.25	5.25
New York, Stanton, D, Pl	1970	1853	4.25	5.25
North Carolina, Rufo, D, Pl	1970	1853	4.25	5.25
North Dakota, Stanton, D, Pl	1970	1853	4.25	5.25
Ohio, Rufo, D, Pl	1970	1853	4.25	5.25
Oklahoma, Rufo, D, Pl	1970	1853	4.25	5.25
Oregon, Cornell, D, Pl	1970	1853	4.25	5.25
Pennsylvania, Cornell, D, Pl	1970	1853	4.25	5.25
Rhode Island, Cornell, D, Pl	1970	1853	4.25	5.25
South Carolina, Stanton, D, Pl	1970	1853	4.25	5.25
South Dakota, Stanton, D, Pl	1970	1853	4.25	5.25
Tennessee, Stanton, D, Pl	1970	1853	4.25	5.25
Texas, Cornell, D, Pl	1970	1853	4.25	5.25
Utah, Rufo, D, Pl	1970	1853	4.25	5.25
Vermont, Nathan, D, Pl	1970	1853	4.25	5.25
Virginia, Stanton, D, Pl	1970	1853	4.25	5.25
Washington, Rufo, D, Pl	1970	1853	4.25	5.25
West Virginia, Cornell, D, Pl	1970	1853	4.25	5.25
Wisconsin, Cornell, D, Pl	1970	1853	4.25	5.25
Wyoming, Cornell, D, Pl	1970	1853	4.25	5.25
Alabama, Rufo, J, Pl	1970	290	1.75	Unknown
Alaska, Cornell, J, Pl	1970	290	1.75	Unknown
Arizona, Cornell, J, Pl	1970	290	1.75	Unknown
Arkansas, Stanton, J, Pl	1970	290	1.75	Unknown
California, Rufo, J, Pl	1970	290	1.75	Unknown
Colorado, Rufo, J, Pl	1970	290	1.75	Unknown
Connecticut, Cornell, J, Pl	1970	290	1.75	Unknown
Delaware, Jones, J, Pl	1970	290	1.75	Unknown
Florida, Cornell, J, Pl	1970	290	1.75	Unknown
Georgia, Rufo, J, Pl	1970	290	1.75	Unknown
Hawaii, Nathan, J, Pl	1970	290	1.75	Unknown
Idaho, Jones, J, Pl	1970	290	1.75	Unknown
Illinois, Nathan, J, Pl	1970	290	1.75	Unknown
Indiana, Stanton, J, Pl	1970	290	1.75	Unknown
Iowa, Rufo, J, Pl	1970	290	1.75	Unknown
Kansas, Cornell, J, Pl	1970	290	1.75	Unknown
Kentucky, Cornell, J, Pl	1970	290	1.75	Unknown
Louisiana, Stanton, J, Pl	1970	290	1.75	Unknown
Maine, Stanton, J, Pl	1970	290	1.75	Unknown
Maryland, Rufo, J, Pl	1970	290	1.75	Unknown
Massachusetts, Stanton, J, Pl	1970	290	1.75	Unknown
Michigan, Cornell, J, Pl	1970	290	1.75	Unknown
Minnesota, Rufo, J, Pl	1970	290	1.75	Unknown
Mississippi, Rufo, J, Pl	1970	290	1.75	Unknown
Missouri, Stanton, J, Pl	1970	290	1.75	Unknown
Montana, Cornell, J, Pl	1970	290	1.75	Unknown
Nebraska, Cornell, J, Pl	1970	290	1.75	Unknown
Nevada, Cornell, J, Pl	1970	290	1.75	Unknown
New Hampshire, Nathan, J, Pl	1970	290	1.75	Unknown
New Jersey, Cornell, J, Pl	1970	290	1.75	Unknown
New Mexico, Rufo, J, Pl	1970	290	1.75	Unknown
New York, Stanton, J, Pl	1970	290	1.75	Unknown
North Carolina, Rufo, J, Pl	1970	290	1.75	Unknown
North Dakota, Stanton, J, Pl	1970	290	1.75	Unknown
Ohio, Rufo, J, Pl	1970	290	1.75	Unknown
Oklahoma, Rufo, J, Pl	1970	290	1.75	Unknown
Oregon, Cornell, J, Pl	1970	290	1.75	Unknown
Pennsylvania, Cornell, J, Pl	1970	290	1.75	Unknown
Rhode Island, Cornell, J, Pl	1970	290	1.75	Unknown
South Carolina, Stanton, J, Pl	1970	290	1.75	Unknown
South Dakota, Stanton, J, Pl	1970	290	1.75	Unknown
Tennessee, Stanton, J, Pl	1970	290	1.75	Unknown
Texas, Cornell, J, Pl	1970	290	1.75	Unknown
Utah, Rufo, J, Pl	1970	290	1.75	Unknown

Vermont, Nathan, J, Pl	1970	290	1.75	Unknown
Virginia, Stanton, J, Pl	1970	290	1.75	Unknown
Washington, Rufo, J, Pl	1970	290	1.75	Unknown
West Virginia, Cornell, J, Pl	1970	290	1.75	Unknown
Wisconsin, Cornell, J, Pl	1970	290	1.75	Unknown
Wyoming, Cornell, J, Pl	1970	290	1.75	Unknown

Franklin Mint Medals, Ten Greatest Men of American Business

Baruch, Bernard, Ferrell, 39mm., D, P	1971	266	9.50	Unknown
Bell, Alexander Graham, Lauser, 39mm., D, P	1971	266	9.50	Unknown
Carnegie, Andrew, Ferrell, 39mm., D, P	1971	266	9.50	Unknown
Disney, Walt, Miller, 39mm., D, P	1971	266	9.50	Unknown
Eastman, George, Baldwin, 39mm., D, P	1971	266	9.50	Unknown
Edison, Thomas, Park, 39mm., D, P	1971	266	9.50	Unknown
Ford, Henry, Man, Baldwin, 39mm., D, P	1971	266	9.50	Unknown
Franklin, Benjamin, Faulkner, 39mm., D, P	1971	266	9.50	Unknown
Rockefeller, John D., Sr., Caimi, 39mm., D, P	1971	266	9.50	Unknown
Watson, Thomas J., Sr., Nemeth, 39mm., D, P	1971	266	9.50	Unknown
Baruch, Bernard, Ferrell, 39mm., F, P	1971	1722	14.50	Unknown
Bell, Alexander Graham, Lauser, 39mm., F, P	1971	1722	14.50	Unknown
Carnegie, Andrew, Ferrell, 39mm., F, P	1971	1722	14.50	Unknown
Disney, Walt, Miller, 39mm., F, P	1971	1722	14.50	Unknown
Eastman, George, Baldwin, 39mm., F, P	1971	1722	14.50	Unknown
Edison, Thomas, Park, 39mm., F, P	1971	1722	14.50	Unknown
Ford, Henry, Nemeth, 39mm., F, P	1971	1722	14.50	Unknown
Franklin, Benjamin, Faulkner, 39mm., F, P	1971	1722	14.50	Unknown
Rockefeller, John D., Sr., Caimi, 39mm., F, P	1971	1722	14.50	Unknown
Watson, Thomas J., Sr., Nemeth, 39mm., D, P	1971	1722	14.50	Unknown
Baruch, Bernard, Ferrell, 39mm., J, Pl	1971	203	4.00	Unknown
Bell, Alexander Graham, Lauser, 39mm., J, Pl	1971	203	4.00	Unknown
Carnegie, Andrew, Ferrell, 39mm., J, Pl	1971	203	4.00	Unknown
Disney, Walt, Miller, 39mm., J, Pl	1971	203	4.00	Unknown
Eastman, George, Baldwin, 39mm., J, Pl	1971	203	4.00	Unknown
Edison, Thomas, Park, 39mm., J, Pl	1971	203	4.00	Unknown
Ford, Henry, Nemeth, 39mm., J, Pl	1971	203	4.00	Unknown
Franklin, Benjamin, Faulkner, 39mm., J, Pl	1971	203	4.00	Unknown
Rockefeller, John D., Sr., Caimi, 39mm., J, Pl	1971	203	4.00	Unknown
Watson, Thomas J., Sr., Nemeth, 39mm., J, Pl	1971	203	4.00	Unknown

Franklin Mint Medals, Thomason Medallic Bible

Abraham Buried In The Cave, D	1967-1970	2090	9.50	10.00 to 13.00
Abraham Offering His Son Isaac, D	1967-1970	2090	9.50	10.00 to 13.00
Absalom Slain, D	1967-1970	2090	9.50	10.00 to 13.00
Adam Gave Names To The Animals, D	1967-1970	2090	9.50	10.00 to 13.00
Balaam Smiting The Ass, D	1967-1970	2090	9.50	10.00 to 13.00
Cain Slaying His Brother Abel, D	1967-1970	2090	9.50	10.00 to 13.00
Daniel In The Lion's Den, D	1967-1970	2090	9.50	10.00 to 13.00
David Defeats Goliath, D	1967-1970	2090	9.50	10.00 to 13.00
Elijah Carried Into Heaven, D	1967-1970	2090	9.50	10.00 to 13.00
Elijah Fed By Ravens, D	1967-1970	2090	9.50	10.00 to 13.00
Enoch Carried Up Into Heaven, D	1967-1970	2090	9.50	10.00 to 13.00
Eve Presenting The Forbidden Fruit, D	1967-1970	2090	9.50	10.00 to 13.00
Isaac Blessing Jacob, D	1967-1970	2090	9.50	10.00 to 13.00
Jacob & Esau, D	1967-1970	2090	9.50	10.00 to 13.00
Jacob On His Deathbed, D	1967-1970	2090	9.50	10.00 to 13.00
Jael Driving The Nail, D	1967-1970	2090	9.50	10.00 to 13.00
Jephthah's Rash Vow, D	1967-1970	2090	9.50	10.00 to 13.00
Jeroboam Ordering Man Of God Seized, D	1967-1970	2090	9.50	10.00 to 13.00
Job In Distress, D	1967-1970	2090	9.50	10.00 to 13.00
Jonah And The Whale, D	1967-1970	2090	9.50	10.00 to 13.00
Joseph Maketh Himself Known, D	1967-1970	2090	9.50	10.00 to 13.00
Joseph Sold By His Brethren, D	1967-1970	2090	9.50	10.00 to 13.00
Joseph's Interpretation, D	1967-1970	2090	9.50	10.00 to 13.00
Joshua Commanding The Sun, D	1967-1970	2090	9.50	10.00 to 13.00
Joshua Dividing The Waters, D	1967-1970	2090	9.50	10.00 to 13.00
Judgment Of Solomon, D	1967-1970	2090	9.50	10.00 to 13.00
Lot & His Two Daughters, D	1967-1970	2090	9.50	10.00 to 13.00
Lot Parting From Abraham, D	1967-1970	2090	9.50	10.00 to 13.00
Moses Discovered, D	1967-1970	2090	9.50	10.00 to 13.00

Moses Smote The Rock, D	1967-1970	2090	9.50	10.00 to 13.00
Moses' Brazen Serpent, D	1967-1970	2090	9.50	10.00 to 13.00
Noah Buildeth An Altar, D	1967-1970	2090	9.50	10.00 to 13.00
Noah's Ark, D	1967-1970	2090	9.50	10.00 to 13.00
Pharaoh Drowned, D	1967-1970	2090	9.50	10.00 to 13.00
Rebecca Drawing Water, D	1967-1970	2090	9.50	10.00 to 13.00
Samson & The Gates Of Gaza, D	1967-1970	2090	9.50	10.00 to 13.00
Samson Killing The Lion, D	1967-1970	2090	9.50	10.00 to 13.00
Saul Visits The Witch, D	1967-1970	2090	9.50	10.00 to 13.00
Shadrach, Meshach, & Abednego In Fire, D	1967-1970	2090	9.50	10.00 to 13.00
Solomon's Temple, D	1967-1970	2090	9.50	10.00 to 13.00
The Adoration Of The Wise Men, D	1967-1970	2090	9.50	10.00 to 13.00
The Agony Of Christ, D	1967-1970	2090	9.50	10.00 to 13.00
The Ark Of The Covenant, D	1967-1970	2090	9.50	10.00 to 13.00
The Army Of Sennacherib, D	1967-1970	2090	9.50	10.00 to 13.00
The Ascension, D	1967-1970	2090	9.50	10.00 to 13.00
The Baptism Of Christ, D	1967-1970	2090	9.50	10.00 to 13.00
The Crucifixion, D	1967-1970	2090	9.50	10.00 to 13.00
The Divine Psalmist, D	1967-1970	2090	9.50	10.00 to 13.00
The Expulsion Of Adam & Eve, D	1967-1970	2090	9.50	10.00 to 13.00
The First-Born Slain, D	1967-1970	2090	9.50	10.00 to 13.00
The Flight Into Egypt, D	1967-1970	2090	9.50	10.00 to 13.00
The Last Supper, D	1967-1970	2090	9.50	10.00 to 13.00
The Murder Of Julius Caesar, D	1967-1970	2090	9.50	10.00 to 13.00
The Raising Of Lazarus, D	1967-1970	2090	9.50	10.00 to 13.00
The Rod Of Moses, D	1967-1970	2090	9.50	10.00 to 13.00
The Sacrifice Of The Red Heifer, D	1967-1970	2090	9.50	10.00 to 13.00
The Son Restored To Life, D	1967-1970	2090	9.50	10.00 to 13.00
The Tower Of Babel, D	1967-1970	2090	9.50	10.00 to 13.00
Travels Of The Children Of Israel, D	1967-1970	2090	9.50	10.00 to 13.00
Worshipping The Molten Calf, D	1967-1970	2090	9.50	10.00 to 13.00
Abraham Buried In The Cave, J	1967-1970	2023	2.75	Unknown
Abraham Offering His Son Isaac, J	1967-1970	2023	2.75	Unknown
Absalom Slain, J	1967-1970	2023	2.75	Unknown
Adam Gave Names To The Animals, J	1967-1970	2023	2.75	Unknown
Balaam Smiting The Ass, J	1967-1970	2023	2.75	Unknown
Cain Slaying His Brother Abel, J	1967-1970	2023	2.75	Unknown
Daniel In The Lion's Den, J	1967-1970	2023	2.75	Unknown
David Defeats Goliath, J	1967-1970	2023	2.75	Unknown
Elijah Carried Into Heaven, J	1967-1970	2023	2.75	Unknown
Elijah Fed By Ravens, J	1967-1970	2023	2.75	Unknown
Enoch Carried Up Into Heaven, J	1967-1970	2023	2.75	Unknown
Eve Presenting The Forbidden Fruit, J	1967-1970	2023	2.75	Unknown
Isaac Blessing Jacob, J	1967-1970	2023	2.75	Unknown
Jacob & Esau, J	1967-1970	2023	2.75	Unknown
Jacob On His Deathbed, J	1967-1970	2023	2.75	Unknown
Jael Driving The Nail, J	1967-1970	2023	2.75	Unknown
Jephthah's Rash Vow, J	1967-1970	2023	2.75	Unknown
Jeroboam Ordering Man Of God Seized, J	1967-1970	2023	2.75	Unknown
Job In Distress, J	1967-1970	2023	2.75	Unknown
Jonah & The Whale, J	1967-1970	2023	2.75	Unknown
Joseph Maketh Himself Known, J	1967-1970	2023	2.75	Unknown
Joseph Sold By His Brethren, J	1967-1970	2023	2.75	Unknown
Joseph's Interpretation, J	1967-1970	2023	2.75	Unknown
Joshua Commanding The Sun, J	1967-1970	2023	2.75	Unknown
Joshua Dividing The Waters, J	1967-1970	2023	2.75	Unknown
Judgment Of Solomon, J	1967-1970	2023	2.75	Unknown
Lot & His Two Daughters, J	1967-1970	2023	2.75	Unknown
Lot Parting From Abraham, J	1967-1970	2023	2.75	Unknown
Moses Discovered, J	1967-1970	2023	2.75	Unknown
Moses Smote The Rock, J	1967-1970	2023	2.75	Unknown
Moses' Brazen Serpent, J	1967-1970	2023	2.75	Unknown
Noah Buildeth An Altar, J	1967-1970	2023	2.75	Unknown
Noah's Ark, J	1967-1970	2023	2.75	Unknown
Pharaoh Drowned, J	1967-1970	2023	2.75	Unknown
Rebecca Drawing Water, J	1967-1970	2023	2.75	Unknown
Samson & The Gates Of Gaza, J	1967-1970	2023	2.75	Unknown
Samson Killing The Lion, J	1967-1970	2023	2.75	Unknown
Saul Visits The Witch, J	1967-1970	2023	2.75	Unknown
Shadrach, Meshach, & Abednego In Fire, J	1967-1970	2023	2.75	Unknown

Solomon's Temple, J	1967-1970	2023	2.75	Unknown
The Adoration Of The Wise Men, J	1967-1970	2023	2.75	Unknown
The Agony Of Christ, J	1967-1970	2023	2.75	Unknown
The Ark Of The Covenant, J	1967-1970	2023	2.75	Unknown
The Army Of Sennacherib, J	1967-1970	2023	2.75	Unknown
The Ascension, J	1967-1970	2023	2.75	Unknown
The Baptism Of Christ, J	1967-1970	2023	2.75	Unknown
The Crucifixion, J	1967-1970	2023	2.75	Unknown
The Divine Psalmist, J	1967-1970	2023	2.75	Unknown
The Expulsion Of Adam & Eve, J	1967-1970	2023	2.75	Unknown
The First-Born Slain, J	1967-1970	2023	2.75	Unknown
The Flight Into Egypt, J	1967-1970	2023	2.75	Unknown
The Last Supper, J	1967-1970	2023	2.75	Unknown
The Murder Of Julius Caesar, J	1967-1970	2023	2.75	Unknown
The Raising Of Lazarus, J	1967-1970	2023	2.75	Unknown
The Rod Of Moses, J	1967-1970	2023	2.75	Unknown
The Sacrifice Of The Red Heifer, J	1967-1970	2023	2.75	Unknown
The Son Restored To Life, J	1967-1970	2023	2.75	Unknown
The Tower Of Babel, J	1967-1970	2023	2.75	Unknown
Travels Of The Children Of Israel, J	1967-1970	2023	2.75	Unknown
Worshipping The Molten Calf, J	1967-1970	2023	2.75	Unknown
Abraham Buried In The Cave, J, M	1970	7008	3.25	Unknown
Abraham Offering His Son Isaac, J, M	1970	7008	3.25	Unknown
Absalom Slain, J, M	1970	7008	3.25	Unknown
Adam Gave Names To The Animals, J, M	1970	7008	3.25	Unknown
Balaam Smiting The Ass, J, M	1970	7008	3.25	Unknown
Cain Slaying His Brother Abel, J, M	1970	7008	3.25	Unknown
Daniel In The Lion's Den, J, M	1970	7008	3.25	Unknown
David Defeats Goliath, J, M	1970	7008	3.25	Unknown
Elijah Carried Into Heaven, J, M	1970	7008	3.25	Unknown
Elijah Fed By Ravens, J, M	1970	7008	3.25	Unknown
Enoch Carried Up Into Heaven, J, M	1970	7008	3.25	Unknown
Eve Presenting The Forbidden Fruit, J, M	1970	7008	3.25	Unknown
Isaac Blessing Jacob, J, M	1970	7008	3.25	Unknown
Jacob & Esau, J, M	1970	7008	3.25	Unknown
Jacob On His Deathbed, J, M	1970	7008	3.25	Unknown
Jael Driving The Nail, J, M	1970	7008	3.25	Unknown
Jephthah's Rash Vow, J, M	1970	7008	3.25	Unknown
Jeroboam Ordering Man Of God Seized, J, M	1970	7008	3.25	Unknown
Job In Distress, J, M	1970	7008	3.25	Unknown
Jonah & The Whale, J, M	1970	7008	3.25	Unknown
Joseph Maketh Himself Known, J, M	1970	7008	3.25	Unknown
Joseph Sold By His Brethren, J, M	1970	7008	3.25	Unknown
Joseph's Interpretation, J, M	1970	7008	3.25	Unknown
Joshua Commanding The Sun, J, M	1970	7008	3.25	Unknown
Joshua Dividing The Waters, J, M	1970	7008	3.25	Unknown
Judgment Of Solomon, J, M	1970	7008	3.25	Unknown
Lot & His Two Daughters, J, M	1970	7008	3.25	Unknown
Lot Parting From Abraham, J, M	1970	7008	3.25	Unknown
Moses Discovered, J, M	1970	7008	3.25	Unknown
Moses Smote The Rock, J, M	1970	7008	3.25	Unknown
Moses' Brazen Serpent, J, M	1970	7008	3.25	Unknown
Noah Buildeth An Altar, J, M	1970	7008	3.25	Unknown
Noah's Ark, J, M	1970	7008	3.25	Unknown
Pharaoh Drowned, J, M	1970	7008	3.25	Unknown
Rebecca Drawing Water, J, M	1970	7008	3.25	Unknown
Samson & The Gates Of Gaza, J, M	1970	7008	3.25	Unknown
Samson Killing The Lion, J, M	1970	7008	3.25	Unknown
Saul Visits The Witch, J, M	1970	7008	3.25	Unknown
Shadrach, Meshach, & Abednego In Furnace, J, M	1970	7008	3.25	Unknown
Solomon's Temple, J, M	1970	7008	3.25	Unknown
The Adoration Of The Wise Men, J, M	1970	7008	3.25	Unknown
The Agony Of Christ, J, M	1970	7008	3.25	Unknown
The Ark Of The Covenant, J, M	1970	7008	3.25	Unknown
The Army Of Sennacherib, J, M	1970	7008	3.25	Unknown
The Ascension, J, M	1970	7008	3.25	Unknown
The Baptism Of Christ, J, M	1970	7008	3.25	Unknown
The Crucifixion, J, M	1970	7008	3.25	Unknown
The Divine Psalmist, J, M	1970	7008	3.25	Unknown
The Expulsion Of Adam & Eve, J, M	1970	7008	3.25	Unknown

The First-Born Slain, J, M	1970	7008	3.25	Unknown
The Flight Into Egypt, J, M	1970	7008	3.25	Unknown
The Last Supper, J, M	1970	7008	3.25	Unknown
The Murder Of Julius Caesar, J, M	1970	7008	3.25	Unknown
The Raising Of Lazarus, J, M	1970	7008	3.25	Unknown
The Rod Of Moses, J, M	1970	7008	3.25	Unknown
The Sacrifice Of The Red Heifer, J, M	1970	7008	3.25	Unknown
The Son Restored To Life, J, M	1970	7008	3.25	Unknown
The Tower Of Babel, J, M	1970	7008	3.25	Unknown
Travels Of The Children Of Israel, J, M	1970	7008	3.25	Unknown
Worshipping The Molten Calf, J, M	1970	7008	3.25	Unknown

Franklin Mint Medals, Treasures of the Louvre

Bouquetin Aile, 45mm., D, P	1971-1972	7792	12.00	Unknown
Charles V, 45mm., D, P	1971-1972	7792	12.00	Unknown
Esclave Rebelle, 45mm., D, P	1971-1972	7792	12.00	Unknown
La Code De Hammourabi, 45mm., D, P	1971-1972	7792	12.00	Unknown
La Grande Porteuse D'auge, 45mm., D, P	1971-1972	7792	12.00	Unknown
La Joconde, 45mm., D, P	1971-1972	7792	12.00	Unknown
La Victoire De Samothrace, 45mm., D, P	1971-1972	7792	12.00	Unknown
Le Scribe Accroupi, 45mm., D, P	1971-1972	7792	12.00	Unknown
L'homme Dit Le Condottiere, 45mm., D, P	1971-1972	7792	12.00	Unknown
Portrait D'Anne De Cleves, 45mm., D, P	1971-1972	7792	12.00	Unknown
Portrait D'Erasme, 45mm., D, P	1971-1972	7792	12.00	Unknown
Portrait De Francois I, 45mm., D, P	1971-1972	7792	12.00	Unknown
Portrait De L'artiste, 45mm., D, P	1971-1972	7792	12.00	Unknown
Projet De Medaille, 45mm., D, P	1971-1972	7792	12.00	Unknown
St.Michel Et Le Dragon, 45mm., D, P	1971-1972	7792	12.00	Unknown
Tete De Saint, 45mm., D, P	1971-1972	7792	12.00	Unknown
Un Vieillard Et Son Petit-Fils, 45mm.D, P	1971-1972	7792	12.00	Unknown

Alexandre Brongniart Enfant, 45mm., D, P	1973	7792	12.00	12.00
Buste De La Comtesse Du Barry, 45mm., D, P 1974	1973	7792	12.00	12.00
Charles Premier D'Angleterre, 45mm., D, P	1973	7792	12.00	12.00
Diane D'Anet, 45mm., D, P	1973	7792	12.00	12.00
Diane Sortant Du Bain, 45mm., D, P	1973	7792	12.00	12.00
Eve Tendant La Pomme, 45mm., D, P	1973	7792	12.00	12.00
Femme A Demi-Nue, 45mm., D, P	1973	7792	12.00	12.00
Helena Fourment Et Ses Enfants, 45mm., D, P	1973	7792	12.00	12.00
L'aigle De Suger, 45mm., D, P	1973	7792	12.00	12.00
L'amour Et Psyche, 45mm., D, P	1973	7792	12.00	12.00
L'inspiration Du Poete, 45mm., D, P	1973	7792	12.00	12.00
La Bohemienne, 45mm., D, P	1973	7792	12.00	12.00
La Dentelliere, 45mm., D, P	1973	7792	12.00	12.00
La Venus De Milo, 45mm., D, P	1973	7792	12.00	12.00
Le Benedicite, 45mm., D, P	1973	7792	12.00	12.00
Le Jeune Mediant, 45mm., D, P	1973	7792	12.00	12.00
Le Repas Des Paysans, 45mm., D, P	1973	7792	12.00	12.00
Leda Et Le Cygne, 45mm., D, P	1973	7792	12.00	12.00
Les Pelerins D'Emmaus, 45mm., D, P	1973	7792	12.00	12.00
Milon De Crotone, 45mm., D, P	1973	7792	12.00	12.00
Portrait De Claude Deruet, 45mm., D, P	1973	7792	12.00	12.00
Saint Joseph Charpentier, 45mm., D, P	1973	7792	12.00	12.00
Tete D'une Princesse Amarnienne, 45mm., D, P	1973	7792	12.00	12.00
Tete De Michel-Ange, 45mm., D, P	1973	7792	12.00	12.00

Franklin Mint, United Nations Commemorative Series, see Franklin Mint Medals, Official United Nations Commemorative

Franklin Mint, United Nations 25th Anniversary Commemorative, see Franklin Mint Medals, Official United Nations 25th Anniversary Commemorative

Franklin Mint Medals, United States Olympic Team, XX Olympiad

VI Pan-American Games, Colombia, 39mm., D, Pl	1971	9377	8.33	Unknown
XI Winter Games, Sapporo, Japan, 39mm., D, Pl	1971	9377	8.33	Unknown
XX Olympiad, Munich, Germany, 39mm., D, Pl	1971	9377	8.33	Unknown
VI Pan-American Games, Colombia, 39mm., D, Pl	1972	Year	8.33	Unknown
XI Winter Games, Sapporo, Japan, 39mm., D, Pl	1972	Year	8.33	Unknown
XX Olympiad, Munich, Germany, 39mm., D, Pl	1972	Year	8.33	Unknown

Franklin Mint Medals, Vita Christi

Jesus Before Pilate, 57mm., D, A	1971-1972	2588	24.00	35.00 to 58.00

The Annunciation, 57mm., D, A	1971-1972	2588	24.00	35.00 to 58.00
The Ascension, 57mm., D, A	1971-1972	2588	24.00	35.00 to 58.00
The Baptism Of Jesus, 57mm., D, A	1971-1972	2588	24.00	35.00 to 58.00
The Crucifixion, 57mm., D, A	1971-1972	2588	24.00	35.00 to 58.00
The Descent From The Cross, 57mm., D, A	1971-1972	2588	24.00	35.00 to 58.00
The Entry Into Jerusalem, 57mm., D, A	1971-1972	2588	24.00	35.00 to 58.00
The Flight Into Egypt, 57mm., D, A	1971-1972	2588	24.00	35.00 to 58.00
The Last Supper, 57mm., D, A	1971-1972	2588	24.00	35.00 to 58.00
The Nativity, 57mm., D, A	1971-1972	2588	24.00	35.00 to 58.00
The Resurrection, 57mm., D, A	1971-1972	2588	24.00	35.00 to 58.00
The Sermon On The Mount, 57mm., D, A	1971-1972	2588	24.00	35.00 to 58.00
Jesus Before Pilate, 57mm., J, A	1971-1972	912	9.00	Unknown
The Annunciation, 57mm., J, A	1971-1972	912	9.00	Unknown
The Ascension, 5mmm., J, A	1971-1972	912	9.00	Unknown
The Baptism Of Jesus, 57mm., J, A	1971-1972	912	9.00	Unknown
The Crucifixion, 57mm., J, A	1971-1972	912	9.00	Unknown
The Descent From The Cross, 57mm., J, A	1971-1972	912	9.00	Unknown
The Entry Into Jerusalem, 57mm., J, A	1971-1972	912	9.00	Unknown
The Flight Into Egypt, 57mm., J, A	1971-1972	912	9.00	Unknown
The Last Supper, 57mm., J, A	1971-1972	912	9.00	Unknown
The Nativity, 57mm., J, A	1971-1972	912	9.00	Unknown
The Resurrection, 57mm., J, A	1971-1972	912	9.00	Unknown
The Sermon On The Mount, 57mm., J, A	1971-1972	912	9.00	Unknown

Franklin Mint, Wild Life Series, see Franklin Mint Medals, East African Wild Life Society

Franklin Mint Medals, Wonders of Mankind, Encyclopaedia Britannica

Austria, The Uhrturm, Lunger, 39mm., D, P	1971-1972	3563	9.50	9.50 to 12.50
Brazil, Christ The Redeemer, 39mm., D, P	1971-1972	3563	9.50	9.50 to 12.50
Burma, Shwe Dagon Pagoda, 39mm., D, P	1971-1972	3563	9.50	9.50 to 12.50
Canada, Old Quebec City, Park, 39mm., D, P	1971-1972	3563	9.50	9.50 to 12.50
Chile, Easter Island Monoliths, 39mm., D, P	1971-1972	3563	9.50	9.50 to 12.50
China, The Great Wall, Lauser, 39mm., D, P	1971-1972	3563	9.50	9.50 to 12.50
Czechoslovakia, Karlstein, 39mm., D, P	1971-1972	3563	9.50	9.50 to 12.50
Egypt, The Pyramids, Stanton, 39mm., D, P	1971-1972	3563	9.50	9.50 to 12.50
England, Houses Of Parliament, 39mm., D, P	1971-1972	3563	9.50	9.50 to 12.50
France, The Eiffel Tower, Jones, 39mm., D,	1971-1972	3563	9.50	9.50 to 12.50
Germany, Cologne Cathedral, 39mm., D, P	1971-1972	3563	9.50	9.50 to 12.50
Greece, The Parthenon, Park, 39mm., D, P	1971-1972	3563	9.50	9.50 to 12.50
India, The Taj Mahal, Stanton, 39mm., D, P	1971-1972	3563	9.50	9.50 to 12.50
Ireland, Rock Of Cashel, Rufo, 39mm., D, P	1971-1972	3563	9.50	9.50 to 12.50
Italy, The Colosseum, Nemeth, 39mm., D, P	1971-1972	3563	9.50	9.50 to 12.50
Japan, Itsuku Island Torii, 39mm., D, P	1971-1972	3563	9.50	9.50 to 12.50
Mexico, Aztec Ruins, Bergier, 39mm., D, P	1971-1972	3563	9.50	9.50 to 12.50
Panama, Panama Canal, Rufo, 39mm., D, P	1971-1972	3563	9.50	9.50 to 12.50
Russia, The Kremlin, Rufo, 39mm., D, P	1971-1972	3563	9.50	9.50 to 12.50
Spain, The Alcazar In Segovia, 39mm., D, P	1971-1972	3563	9.50	9.50 to 12.50
Switzerland, Lion Monument, 39mm., D, P	1971-1972	3563	9.50	9.50 to 12.50
Thailand, Temple Of The Dawn, 39mm., D, P	1971-1972	3563	9.50	9.50 to 12.50
Tibet, Potala Palace, Mafko, 39mm., D, P	1971-1972	3563	9.50	9.50 to 12.50
U.S., Mount Rushmore, Lauser, 39mm., D, P	1971-1972	3563	9.50	9.50 to 12.50
Austria, The Uhrturm, Lunger, 39mm., D, Pl	1971-1972	186	9.50	Unknown
Brazil, Christ The Redeemer, 39mm., D, Pl	1971-1972	186	9.50	Unknown
Burma, Shwe Dagon Pagoda, 39mm., D, Pl	1971-1972	186	9.50	Unknown
Canada, Old Quebec City, Park, 39mm., D, Pl	1971-1972	186	9.50	Unknown
Chile, Easter Island Monolith, 39mm., D, Pl	1971-1972	186	9.50	Unknown
China, The Great Wall, Lauser, 39mm., D, Pl	1971-1972	186	9.50	Unknown
Czechoslovakia, Karlstein, 39mm., D, Pl	1971-1972	186	9.50	Unknown
Egypt, The Pyramids, Stanton, 39mm., D, Pl	1971-1972	186	9.50	Unknown
England, Houses Of Parliament, 39mm., D, Pl	1971-1972	186	9.50	Unknown
France, The Eiffel Tower, 39mm., D, Pl	1971-1972	186	9.50	Unknown
Germany, Cologne Cathedral, 39mm., D, Pl	1971-1972	186	9.50	Unknown
Greece, The Parthenon, Park, 39mm., D, Pl	1971-1972	186	9.50	Unknown
India, The Taj Mahal, Stanton, 39mm., D, Pl	1971-1972	186	9.50	Unknown
Ireland, Rock Of Cashel, Rufo, 39mm., D, Pl	1971-1972	186	9.50	Unknown
Italy, The Colosseum, Nemeth, 39mm., D, Pl	1971-1972	186	9.50	Unknown
Japan, Itsuku Island Torii, 39mm., D, Pl	1971-1972	186	9.50	Unknown
Mexico, Aztec Ruins, Bergier, 39mm., D, Pl	1971-1972	186	9.50	Unknown

Panama, Panama Canal, Rufo, 39mm., D, Pl	1971-1972	186	9.50	Unknown
Russia, The Kremlin, Rufo, 39mm., D, Pl	1971-1972	186	9.50	Unknown
Spain, The Alcazar In Segovia, 39mm., D, Pl	1971-1972	186	9.50	Unknown
Switzerland, Lion Monument, 39mm., D, Pl	1971-1972	186	9.50	Unknown
Thailand, Temple Of The Dawn, 39mm., D, Pl	1971-1972	186	9.50	Unknown
Tibet, Potala Palace, Mafko, 39mm., D, Pl	1971-1972	186	9.50	Unknown
U.S., Mount Rushmore, Lauser, 39mm., D, Pl	1971-1972	186	9.50	Unknown
Austria, The Uhrturm, Lunger, 39mm., F, P	1971-1972	2436	14.50	Unknown
Brazil, Christ The Redeemer, 39mm., F, P	1971-1972	2436	14.50	Unknown
Burma, Shwe Dagon Pagoda, 39mm., F, P	1971-1972	2436	14.50	Unknown
Canada, Old Quebec City, Park, 39mm., F, P	1971-1972	2436	14.50	Unknown
Chile, Easter Island Monoliths, 39mm., F, P	1971-1972	2436	14.50	Unknown
China, The Great Wall, Lauser, 39mm., F, P	1971-1972	2436	14.50	Unknown
Czechoslovakia, Karlstein, 39mm., F, P	1971-1972	2436	14.50	Unknown
Egypt, The Pyramids, Stanton, 39mm., F, P	1971-1972	2436	14.50	Unknown
England, Houses Of Parliament, 39mm., F, P	1971-1972	2436	14.50	Unknown
France, The Eiffel Tower, Jones, 39mm., F,	1971-1972	2436	14.50	Unknown
Germany, Cologne Cathedral, 39mm., F, P	1971-1972	2436	14.50	Unknown
Greece, The Parthenon, Park, 39mm., F, P	1971-1972	2436	14.50	Unknown
India, The Taj Mahal, Stanton, 39mm., F, P	1971-1972	2436	14.50	Unknown
Ireland, Rock Of Cashel, Rufo, 39mm., F, P	1971-1972	2436	14.50	Unknown
Italy, The Colosseum, Nemeth, 39mm., F, P	1971-1972	2436	14.50	Unknown
Japan, Itsuku Island Torii, 39mm., F, P	1971-1972	2436	14.50	Unknown
Mexico, Aztec Ruins, Bergier, 39mm., F, P	1971-1972	2436	14.50	Unknown
Panama, Panama Canal, Rufo, 39mm., F, P	1971-1972	2436	14.50	Unknown
Spain, The Alcazar In Segovia, 39mm., F, P	1971-1972	2436	14.50	Unknown
Switzerland, Lion Monument, 39mm., F, P	1971-1972	2436	14.50	Unknown
Thailand, Temple Of The Dawn, 39mm., F, P	1971-1972	2436	14.50	Unknown
Tibet, Potala Palace, Mafko, 39mm., F, P	1971-1972	2436	14.50	Unknown
Russia, The Kremlin, Rufo, 39mm., F, P	1971-1972	2436	14.50	Unknown
U.S., Mount Rushmore, Lauser, 39mm., F, P	1971-1972	2436	14.50	Unknown
Austria, The Uhrturm, Lunger, 39mm., F, Pl	1971-1972	186	14.50	Unknown
Brazil, Christ The Redeemer, 39mm., F, Pl	1971-1972	186	14.50	Unknown
Burma, Shwe Dagon Pagoda, 39mm., F, Pl	1971-1972	186	14.50	Unknown
Canada, Old Quebec City, Park, 39mm., F, Pl	1971-1972	186	14.50	Unknown
Chile, Easter Island Monolith, 39mm., F, Pl	1971-1972	186	14.50	Unknown
China, The Great Wall, Lauser, 39mm., F, Pl	1971-1972	186	14.50	Unknown
Czechoslovakia, Karlstein, 39mm., F, Pl	1971-1972	186	14.50	Unknown
Egypt, The Pyramids, Stanton, 39mm., F, Pl	1971-1972	186	14.50	Unknown
England, Houses Of Parliament, 39mm., F, Pl	1971-1972	186	14.50	Unknown
France, The Eiffel Tower, 39mm., F, Pl	1971-1972	186	14.50	Unknown
Germany, Cologne Cathedral, 39mm., F, Pl	1971-1972	186	14.50	Unknown
Greece, The Parthenon, Park, 39mm., F, Pl	1971-1972	186	14.50	Unknown
India, The Taj Mahal, Stanton, 39mm., F, Pl	1971-1972	186	14.50	Unknown
Ireland, Rock Of Cashel, Rufo, 39mm., F, Pl	1971-1972	186	14.50	Unknown
Italy, The Colosseum, Nemeth, 39mm., F, Pl	1971-1972	186	14.50	Unknown
Japan, Itsuku Island Torii, 39mm., F, Pl	1971-1972	186	14.50	Unknown
Mexico, Aztec Ruins, Bergier, 39mm., F, Pl	1971-1972	186	14.50	Unknown
Panama, Panama Canal, Rufo, 39mm., F, Pl	1971-1972	186	14.50	Unknown
Spain, The Alcazar In Segovia, 39mm., F, Pl	1971-1972	186	14.50	Unknown
Switzerland, Lion Monument, 39mm., F, Pl	1971-1972	186	14.50	Unknown
Thailand, Temple Of The Dawn, 39mm., F, Pl	1971-1972	186	14.50	Unknown
Tibet, Potala Palace, Mafko, 39mm., F, Pl	1971-1972	186	14.50	Unknown
Russia, The Kremlin, Rufo, 39mm., F, Pl	1971-1972	186	14.50	Unknown
U.S., Mount Rushmore, Lauser, 39mm., F, Pl	1971-1972	186	14.50	Unknown

Franklin Mint, Zodiac Series, see Franklin Mint, Roberts' Zodiac

Franklin Mint Medals, XI Olympic Winter Games

Biathlon, 32mm., D, P	1972	1537	7.00	Unknown
Bobsled Racing, 32mm., D, P	1972	1537	7.00	Unknown
Cross-Country, 32mm., D, P	1972	1537	7.00	Unknown
Downhill, 32mm., D, P	1972	1537	7.00	Unknown
Figure Skating, 32mm., D, P	1972	1537	7.00	Unknown
Ice Hockey, 32mm., D, P	1972	1537	7.00	Unknown
Ski Jumping, 32mm., D, P	1972	1537	7.00	Unknown
Slalom, 32mm., D, P	1972	1537	7.00	Unknown
Speed Skating, 32mm., D, P	1972	1537	7.00	Unknown
Toboggan Racing, 32mm., D, P	1972	1537	7.00	Unknown

Franklin Mint Medals, XX Summer Olympic Games in Munich

Basketball, 32mm., C, P	1972	Year	7.00	Unknown
Boxing, 32mm., C, P	1972	Year	7.00	Unknown
Broad Jump, 32mm., C, P	1972	Year	7.00	Unknown
Canoeing, 32mm., C, P	1972	Year	7.00	Unknown
Cycling, 32mm., C, P	1972	Year	7.00	Unknown
Equestrian, 32mm., C, P	1972	Year	7.00	Unknown
Fencing, 32mm., C, P	1972	Year	7.00	Unknown
Gymnastics, 32mm., C, P	1972	Year	7.00	Unknown
Hurdles, 32mm., C, P	1972	Year	7.00	Unknown
Pole Vault, 32mm., C, P	1972	Year	7.00	Unknown
Rowing, 32mm., C, P	1972	Year	7.00	Unknown
Running, 32mm., C, P	1972	Year	7.00	Unknown
Shot Put, 32mm., C, P	1972	Year	7.00	Unknown
Soccer, 32mm., C, P	1972	Year	7.00	Unknown
Swimming, 32mm., C, P	1972	Year	7.00	Unknown
Yachting, 2, 32mm., C, P	1972	Year	7.00	Unknown
Yachting, 4, 32mm., C, P	1972	Year	7.00	Unknown

Freedom Founders Series, see WNW Mint Medals

Official Inaugural Medal, Gerald R. Ford

Gorham Silver Co., of Providence, Rhode Island, was founded in 1831. Crystal and China were added in 1970. The first limited edition item, a silver Christmas ornament, was introduced in 1970. Limited edition porcelain plates were issued in 1971. Ingots and medals were first made by the Gorham Mint division in 1973.

See listing for Gorham in Figurine, Plate, and Bar & Ingot sections

Gorham Mint Medals

Bicentennial, Signers, Silver, Set Of 13	1974	5000	150.00	150.00

Great Men of Medicine Series, see Presidential Art Medals, Inc. Medals, Men of Medicine

Great Religions of the World Series, see Presidential Art Medals, Inc. Medals, Great Religions

Hall of Fame Medals, see Medallic Art Company Medals

Hamilton Mint of Arlington Heights, Illinois, is a private mint. Limited edition gold and silver plates, medals, and ingots were introduced in 1972. Editions are serially numbered on the back. When an edition is completed, the die is destroyed.

See listing for Hamilton Mint in Plate and Bar & Ingot sections

Hamilton Mint Medals

Christmas Pendant, Gold	1973		35.00	35.00
Christmas Pendant, Sterling	1973		25.00	25.00
District Of Columbia, Bronze	1973		2.75	2.75
District Of Columbia, Gold	1973	1000	20.00	20.00
District Of Columbia, Silver	1973	10000	10.00	10.00
Mother's Day, Silver	1973		15.00	15.00
St.Patrick's Day	1973		25.00	25.00

History of Money and Banking Series, see Schulman Coin & Mint Company Medals

Indian Chief Series, see WNW Mint Medals

Inaugural Medals, Official

Coolidge, Bronze	1925			1500.00 to 2000.00
Eisenhower, Bronze, 70mm.	1953	25685		85.00 to 100.00
Eisenhower, Bronze, 70mm.	1957	21705		85.00 to 100.00
Eisenhower, Gold, 21mm.	1953	18		Unknown
Eisenhower, Gold, 31mm.	1953	1		Unknown
Eisenhower, Gold, 70mm.	1953	2		Unknown
Eisenhower, Gold, 21mm.	1957	4		Unknown
Eisenhower, Gold, 27mm.	1957	6		Unknown
Eisenhower, Gold, 30mm.	1957	2		Unknown
Eisenhower, Gold, 70mm.	1957	3		Unknown
Eisenhower, Silver, 70mm.	1953	782		Unknown
Eisenhower, Silver, 70mm.	1957	1031		Unknown
Ford, Gerald R., Gold On Silver	1974	1000	75.00	75.00
Ford, Gerald R., Silver, A*	1974	2500	55.00	55.00
Ford, Gerald R.Silver, P	1974	2500	60.00	60.00

Harding, Bronze	1921		1500.00 to 2000.00
Hoover, Bronze	1929	1000	750.00 to 900.00
Hoover, Gold	1929	2	Unknown
Johnson, Bronze, 27mm.	1965	1000	U to KNOWN.
Johnson, Bronze, 70mm.	1965	26275	Unknown
Johnson, Gold, 27mm.	1965	9	Unknown
Johnson, Gold, 70mm.	1965	1	Unknown
Johnson, Silver, 64mm.	1965	7695	Unknown
Kennedy, Bronze, 70mm	1961	53331	Unknown
Kennedy, Gold, 21mm.	1961	1	Unknown
Kennedy, Gold, 24mm.	1961	1	Unknown
Kennedy, Gold, 27mm.	1961	5	Unknown
Kennedy, Gold, 70mm.	1961	1	Unknown
Kennedy, Silver, 70mm.	1961	7500	70.00 to 80.00
McKinley, Bronze	1901	3500	150.00 to 175.00
McKinley, Gold	1901	2	Unknown
McKinley, Silver	1901		Unknown
Nixon, Bronze, 14mm., Jewelry Item	1969	500	Unknown
Nixon, Bronze, 38mm.	1969	1000	Unknown
Nixon, Bronze, 70mm.	1969	78529	Unknown
Nixon, Gold, 14mm.Jewelry Item	1969	650	Unknown
Nixon, Gold, 29mm.	1969	5	Unknown
Nixon, Gold, 70mm.	1969	1	Unknown
Nixon, Silver, 14mm., Jewelry Item	1969	2000	Unknown
Nixon, Silver, 64mm.	1969	15000	Unknown
Nixon, Silver, 70mm.	1969	1	Unknown
Nixon, Silver	1972	45.00	70.00 to 80.00
Roosevelt, Franklin D., Bronze	1933	1550	475.00 to 525.00
Roosevelt, Franklin D., Bronze	1937	1025	475.00 to 525.00
Roosevelt, Franklin D., Bronze, Type 1	1941	1000	250.00 to 300.00
Roosevelt, Franklin D., Bronze, Type 2	1941	2000	250.00 to 300.00
Roosevelt, Franklin D., Bronze	1945	3500	250.00 to 300.00
Roosevelt, Franklin D., Gold	1933	2	Unknown
Roosevelt, Franklin D., Gold	1937	2	Unknown
Roosevelt, Franklin D., Gold	1941	1	Unknown
Roosevelt, Franklin D., Gold	1945	2	Unknown
Roosevelt, Franklin D., Silver	1933	2	Unknown
Roosevelt, Franklin D., Silver	1937	2	Unknown
Roosevelt, Franklin D., Silver	1941	2	Unknown
Roosevelt, Franklin D., Silver	1945	2	Unknown
Roosevelt, Theodore, Davison Medal, Bronze	1905	3000	200.00 to 250.00
Roosevelt, Theodore, Tiffany Medal, Bronze	1905	120	3000.00 to 4000.00
Roosevelt, Theodore, Tiffany Medal, Gold	1905	2	Unknown
Taft, Bronze	1909	3000	275.00 to 325.00
Taft, Gold	1909	3	Unknown
Truman, Bronze	1949	7500	275.00 to 325.00
Truman, Gold	1949	2	Unknown
Truman, Silver	1949	9	Unknown
Wilson, Bronze	1913	3000	250.00 to 300.00
Wilson, Bronze	1917		900.00 to 1100.00
Wilson, Gold	1913	3	Unknown
Wilson, Gold	1917	3	Unknown
Wilson, Silver	1913	30	Unknown
Wilson, Silver	1917		Unknown

International Mint Medals

Living Free, Silver, Set Of 3, Each	1972	9.75	9.75
Nation Of Riflemen, Silver, Set Of 30, Each	1970	3200	12.00	12.00
Pilgrim Heritage, Silver, Set Of 12, Each	1970	400	12.00	12.00

*The International Numismatic Agency of New York City has designed
and marketed limited edition art medals since 1962. Many of the medals are
produced by Medallic Art Company of Danbury, Connecticut. Silver
bars were introduced in 1973.*

See listing for International Numismatic in Bar & Ingot section

International Numismatic Agency Medals

Apollo 12 Lunar Exploration, Silver	1969	1000	35.00	Unknown
Christ In The Holy Land, Set Of 4, Bronze	1962	25000	34.95	Unknown
Christ In The Holy Land, 4, Nickel Silver	1962	1500	39.95	Unknown
Christ In The Holy Land, Set Of 4, Silver	1962	1500	150.00	Unknown

International Numismatic Agency,
John F. Kennedy Memorial, Set Of 4

International Numismatic Agency,
Douglas MacArthur

International Numismatic Agency,
NASA Space Series, Set Of 13

International Numismatic Agency,
Peace In Vietnam

Churchill, Sir Winston, Silver	1969	2500	50.00	Unknown
Da Vinci, Silver		500	50.00	Unknown
Democracy At Work, Gold Vermeil, Set Of 3	1972	500	60.00	Unknown
Democracy At Work, Silver, Set Of 3	1972	10000	45.00	45.00
Documents Of Freedom, Silver, Pair		2000	39.95	39.95
Ford, Gerald R., Inaugural, Gold Vermeil	1974	1000	75.00	75.00
Heroes Of Israel, Silver, Pair	1973	2500	40.00	40.00
Journey For Peace, Silver	1972	15000	50.00	50.00
Kennedy, John F., Memorial, Set Of 4, Bronze	1973	2500	12.95	12.95
Kennedy, John F., Memorial, Set Of 4, Silver*	1973	2000	40.00	40.00
King, Martin Luther, Silver	1968		60.00	Unknown
Kissinger, Henry, Gold Vermeil	1973	1000	85.00	85.00
Kissinger, Henry, Silver	1973	5000	65.00	65.00
Lion Of Israel, Silver	1969	1000	30.00	Unknown
MacArthur, Douglas, Silver*	1972	5000	50.00	50.00
Man's Conquest Of Space, Silver		10000	50.00	50.00
Masterpieces In Medals, Silver, Set Of 3		500	150.00	Unknown
Moon Landing, Silver	1972	10000	50.00	50.00
Mt. Rushmore, Silver	1972	1000	30.00	Unknown
NASA Space Series, Set Of 13, Pewter	1973		45.00	45.00
NASA Space Series, Set Of 13, Silver*	1973		150.00	150.00
Peace In Vietnam, Gold Vermeil	1973	2500	55.00	55.00 to 60.00
Peace In Vietnam, Silver*	1973	15000	45.00	45.00 to 50.00
Rembrandt, Silver		500	50.00	Unknown
Return Of Our POWS, Gold Vermeil	1973	2500	60.00	60.00
Return Of Our POWS, Silver	1973	15000	50.00	50.00
Return Of The A.E.F., Doughboy, Silver		1500	25.00	Unknown
Salute To Harry Truman, Gold Vermeil, Pair		2500	50.00	50.00
Salute To Harry Truman, Silver, Pair		10000	40.00	40.00
Salute To Ike, Gold Vermeil, Pair		2500	50.00	50.00
Salute To Ike, Silver, Pair		10000	40.00	40.00
Salute To Israel, Silver*	1973	3000	50.00	50.00
Salute To Israel, Silver & Bronze Set	1973	300	125.00	12.50
Salute To Joe Louis, Silver*		5000	53.00	53.00
Salute To L.B.J., Gold Vermeil, Pair	1972	2500	50.00	50.00
Salute To L.B.J., Silver, Pair*	1972	10000	40.00	40.00
Tribute To Apollo 17, Silver*	1973	10000	50.00	50.00
White House, Silver		1000	30.00	Unknown

Israeli Commemorative Society Medals

12 Tribes Of Israel, Bronze, Set Of 12, Each	1973	5733	25.00	25.00
12 Tribes Of Israel, Silver, Set Of 12, Each	1973	5733	50.00	50.00

Jefferson Mint of Amador City, California, introduced limited edition silver plates and bars in 1972. Medals in bronze and silver were added in 1973.

Jefferson Mint Medals

Bicentennial, Bronze, Set Of 6, Each	1973	6000	4.50	4.50
Bicentennial, Silver, Set Of 6, Each	1973	600	13.50	13.50
S.H. Sesquicentennial, Bronze	1973	2000	5.00	5.00
S.H. Sesquicentennial, Silver	1972	200	15.00	15.00

John F. Kennedy Center for the Performing Arts Medals

J.F.K. Gold-Filled & Silver Set, 63mm.	1971	1000	200.00	Unknown
J.F.K., Gold-Filled & Silver Set, 44mm.	1971	1000	100.00	Unknown
J.F.K., Gold-Filled, 44mm.	1971	5000	50.00	Unknown
J.F.K., Gold-Filled, 63mm.	1971	2000	100.00	Unknown
J.F.K., Silver, 44mm.	1971	10000	25.00	Unknown
J.F.K., Silver, 63mm.*	1971	5000	50.00	Unknown

Judah L. Magnes Memorial Museum Medals

Brandeis, Louis, Bronze		1000	6.50	9.50
Brandeis, Louis, Silver		500	25.00	37.50
Einstein, Albert, Bronze		1000	6.50	9.50
Einstein, Albert, Silver		500	25.00	37.50
Gershwin, George, Bronze		1000	6.50	9.50
Gershwin, George, Silver		500	25.00	37.50
Lehman, Herbert, Bronze		1000	9.50	9.50
Lehman, Herbert, Silver		500	37.50	37.50
Magnes, Judah L., Commemorative, Bronze	1971	1000	6.50	9.50
Magnes, Judah L., Commemorative, Silver	1971	500	25.00	37.50
Salomon, Haym, Bronze		1000	12.50	12.50

Salomon, Haym, Silver		500	32.50	38.50

The Judaic Heritage Society first made medals commemorating Jewish traditions in 1969. Limited edition plates were introduced in 1972.

See listing for Judaic Heritage in Plate section

Judaic Heritage Society Medals

History Of Jewish People, Silver, Set Of 120	1969	1858	9.50	9.50 to 15.00

International Numismatic Agency,
Salute To Israel

Kennedy Center for the Performing Arts, see John F. Kennedy Center for the Performing Arts Medals

Letcher Mint of Lancaster, California, started to make bas relief gold on silver medals in 1974.

Letcher Mint Medals, 12 Great Americans, Silver

Edison, Thomas A.	1974	9800	25.00	30.00
Eisenhower, Dwight D.	1974	9800	25.00	30.00
Franklin, Benjamin	1974	9800	25.00	30.00
Hamilton, Alexander	1974	9800	25.00	30.00
Jones, John Paul	1974	9800	25.00	30.00
Kennedy, John F.	1974	9800	25.00	30.00
Lee, Robert E.	1974	9800	25.00	30.00
Lincoln, Abraham	1974	9800	25.00	30.00
Lindbergh, Charles A.	1974	9800	25.00	30.00
Roosevelt, Theodore	1974	9800	25.00	30.00
Twain, Mark	1974	9800	25.00	30.00
Washington, George	1974	9800	25.00	30.00

International Numismatic Agency,
Salute To Joe Louis

Life of Christ Series, see Danbury Mint Medals

Lincoln Center for the Performing Arts Medals

10th Anniversary, Silver, 70mm.	1973	500	60.00	60.00

Lincoln Heritage Medal, see Richard Newman Associates Medals

Lincoln Memorial University Medals

Lincoln Memorial University, Bronze, Small	1972	5000	3.50	Unknown
Lincoln Memorial University, Silver, Large	1972	250	75.00	Unknown

The Lincoln Mint of Chicago, Illinois, entered the limited edition field in 1971. Gold, silver, and vermeil plates, medals, and ingots are made. Lincoln Mint has produced official state bicentennial and governors medals for a number of states.

See listing for Lincoln Mint in Plate and Bar & Ingot sections

International Numismatic Agency,
Salute To L.B.J., Pair

Lincoln Mint Medals, A Prophecy Fulfilled

Balfour Declaration Of 1917, Gold Plate	1973	5000	17.50	17.50
Founder Of Zionism, Gold Plate	1973	5000	17.50	17.50
Hashomer, The Watchman, Gold Plate	1973	5000	17.50	17.50
Six Days War, Gold Plate	1973	5000	17.50	17.50
State Of Israel Proclaimed, Gold	1973	5000	17.50	17.50
Balfour Declaration Of 1917, Sterling	1973	5000	12.50	12.50
Founder Of Zionism, Sterling	1973	5000	12.50	12.50
Hashomer, The Watchman, Sterling	1973	5000	12.50	12.50
Six Days War, Sterling	1973	5000	12.50	12.50
State Of Israel Proclaimed, Sterling	1973	5000	12.50	7 12.50

Lincoln Mint Medals, Great Events of 1972

Great Events Of 1972, Bronze, Set Of 12, Each	1972	5000	6.25	6.25
Great Events Of 1972, Silver, Set Of 12, Each	1972	5000	12.50	13.50

Lincoln Mint Medals, Great Events of 1973

Great Events Of 1973, Bronze, Set Of 12, Each	1973	5000	6.25	6.25
Great Events Of 1973, Gold Plate, 12, Each	1973	5000	19.50	19.50
Great Events Of 1973, Silver, Set Of 12, Each	1973	5000	12.50	13.50

International Numismatic Agency,
Tribute To Apollo 17

John F. Kennedy Center
For The Performing Arts Medal, J.F.K

Lincoln Mint Medals, History of the Civil War

History Of The Civil War, Silver, Set Of 40	1971	5000	8.50	8.50 to 9.50

Lincoln Mint Medals, Legacy of JFK

Legacy Of JFK, Silver, Set Of 36, Each	1973	5000	12.50	12.50

Lincoln Mint Medals, President Lincoln Series

Black Hawk War, Gold On Silver	1974	5000	14.50	14.50
Commander-In-Chief, Gold On Silver	1974	5000	14.50	14.50
Debates With Douglas, Gold On Silver	1974	5000	14.50	14.50
Emancipation Proclamation, Gold On Silver	1974	5000	14.50	14.50

Medallic Art Company,
Apollo 11, John F. Kennedy, Silver

Medallic Art Company,
College Football Centennial

Medallic Art Company,
Civil War Centennial, Silver

Medallic Art Company, Pablo Casals

Farewell To Springfield, Gold On Silver	1974	5000	14.50	14.50
First Inaugural, Gold On Silver	1974	5000	14.50	14.50
Ford's Theatre, Gold On Silver	1974	5000	14.50	14.50
Gettysburg Address, Gold On Silver	1974	5000	14.50	14.50
Illinois Legislator, Gold On Silver	1974	5000	14.50	14.50
Indiana Years, Gold On Silver	1974	5000	14.50	14.50
Kentucky Birth, Gold On Silver	1974	5000	14.50	14.50
Marriage To Mary Todd, Gold On Silver	1974	5000	14.50	14.50
Move To Illinois, Gold On Silver	1974	5000	14.50	14.50
Nomination For President, Gold On Silver	1974	5000	14.50	14.50
Postmaster & Surveyor, Gold On Silver	1974	5000	14.50	14.50
Presidential Election, Gold On Silver	1974	5000	14.50	14.50
Second Inaugural, Gold On Silver	1974	5000	14.50	14.50
Sister Sara, Gold On Silver	1974	5000	14.50	14.50
Springfield Lawyer, Gold On Silver	1974	5000	14.50	14.50
The House Divided, Gold On Silver	1974	5000	14.50	14.50
The Lincoln Family, Gold On Silver	1974	5000	14.50	14.50
The Memorial, Gold On Silver	1974	5000	14.50	14.50
Trip To New Orleans, Gold On Silver	1974	5000	14.50	14.50
United States Congressman, Silver	1974	5000	11.50	11.50
Black Hawk War, Silver	1974	5000	11.50	11.50
Commander-In-Chief, Silver	1974	5000	11.50	11.50
Debates With Douglas, Silver	1974	5000	11.50	11.50
Emancipation Proclamation, Silver	1974	5000	11.50	11.50
Farewell To Springfield, Silver	1974	5000	11.50	11.50
First Inaugural, Silver	1974	5000	11.50	11.50
Ford's Theatre, Silver	1974	5000	11.50	11.50
Gettysburg Address, Silver	1974	5000	11.50	11.50
Illinois Legislator, Silver	1974	5000	11.50	11.50
Indiana Years, Silver	1974	5000	11.50	11.50
Kentucky Birth, Silver	1974	5000	11.50	11.50
Marriage To Mary Todd, Silver	1974	5000	11.50	11.50
Move To Illinois, Silver	1974	5000	11.50	11.50
Nomination For President, Silver	1974	5000	11.50	11.50
Postmaster & Surveyor, Silver	1974	5000	11.50	11.50
Presidential Election, Silver	1974	5000	11.50	11.50
Second Inaugural, Silver	1974	5000	11.50	11.50
Sister Sara, Silver	1974	5000	11.50	11.50
Springfield Lawyer, Silver	1974	5000	11.50	11.5
The House Divided, Silver	1974	5000	11.50	11.50
The Lincoln Family, Silver	1974	5000	11.50	11.50
The Memorial, Silver	1974	5000	11.50	11.50
Trip To New Orleans, Silver	1974	5000	11.50	11.50
United States Congressman, Gold On Silver	1974	5000	14.50	14.50

Lincoln Mint Medals, Top Sports Figures

Top Sports Figures, Bronze, Set Of 16, Each	1971	5000	6.00	6.00 to 6.25
Top Sports Figures, Silver, Set Of 16, Each	1971	5000	8.50	13.50

The Lombardo Mint of Quebec, Canada, is a private mint. Limited and non-limited medals, bars, and posta ingettes are produced. Posta ingettes are silver or bronze replicas of presidential stamps.

See listing for Lombardo Mint in Bar & Ingot section

Lombardo Mint Medals

Peace, Set Of Bronze & Silver, Pair	1970	500	14.00	14.00

The Medallic Art Company of Danbury, Connecticut, was established by Henri and Felix Weil around the turn of the century. The name Medallic Art Company was first used in 1909. Prominent medals produced by Medallic Art include Pulitzer Prize medals, official presidential inaugural medals, city and state bicentennial medals and many others. Medallic Art also produces medals for Presidential Art Medals, Society of Medalists, International Numismatic Agency, Medical Heritage Society and many other organizations.

Medallic Art Company, City and State Medals, see City and State Medals, Official

Medallic Art Company, Inaugural Medals, see Inaugural Medals, Official

Medallic Art Company, Dodgers Baseball, Silver

Medallic Art Company Medals

American Legion, 50th Anniversary, Silver	1968	20000	10.00	Unknown
Apollo 11, John F.Kennedy, Silver*	1969	10000	39.95	39.95
Casals, Pablo, Gold On Silver	1973	500	45.00	45.00
Casals, Pablo, Silver*	1973	1000	30.00	30.00
Cattlemens' Centennial, Bronze	1967	10750		Unknown
Cattlemens' Centennial, Silver, Not Numbered	1967	500		Unknown
Cattlemens' Centennial, Silver, Numbered	1967	1000		Unknown
Cheyenne Centennial, Silver	1967	1500	15.00	Unknown
Chicago Coin Club, 50th Anniversary, Silver	1968	100	20.00	Unknown
Civil War Centennial, Bronze	1961	31150	4.00	4.00
Civil War Centennial, Silver*	1961	12500	30.00	35.00
College Football Centennial, Bronze, Large	1969	3925	6.00	Unknown
College Football Centennial, Bronze, Small	1969	10000	2.00	Unknown
College Football Centennial, Silver*	1969	500	9.00	Unknown
Consecration Armenian Church, American, Silver	1968	100	16.00	Unknown
Consecration Armenian Church, English, Silver	1968	100	16.00	Unknown
Dodgers Baseball, Bronze	1962	1000	5.00	Unknown
Dodgers Baseball, Silver*	1962	1000	30.00	35.00
Eisenhower, Dwight D., Silver Dollar, Silver*	1969	10000	39.95	Unknown
Gloucester Fishing Schooner, Set Of 5, Silver*	1973		50.00	50.00
Golden Gate Bridge, Bronze	1962	2000	4.00	Unknown
Golden Gate Bridge, Silver*	1962	1000	30.00	40.00
Indianapolis Speedway, 50th Anniv., Bronze	1966	10000		Unknown
Ives, Charles, Danbury Coin Club, Bronze	1968	500	3.50	7.50
Ives, Charles, Danbury Coin Club, Silver	1968	100		Unknown
King, Martin Luther, Jr., Bronze & Silver Set	1968	500	39.95	Unknown
Naval Aviation, 50th Anniversary, Bronze	1961	5000	4.00	4.00
Naval Aviation, 50th Anniversary, Silver*	1961	2016	30.00	Unknown
Niagara Falls, 75th Anniversary, Bronze	1967	10000	1.50	Unknown
Niagara Falls, 75th Anniversary, Silver	1967	50	10.00	Unknown
Spirit Of St.Louis, 40th Anniversary, Silver	1967	2000	10.00	Unknown
Stone Mountain, Silver, 39mm.	1970	25000	12.35	Unknown
Stone Mountain, Silver, 70mm.*	1970	5000	36.60	Unknown
U.S.S.Enterprise, Bronze	1960	10200	4.00	4.00
U.S.S.Enterprise, Silver*	1960	3998	30.00	35.00
101st Airborne Division, 25th Anniv., Set	1969	2500	15.00	Unknown
101st Airborne Division, 25th Anniv., Silver*	1969	10000	10.00	Unknown

Medallic Art Company,
Dwight D.Eisenhower Silver Dollar

Medallic Art Company Medals, Hall of Fame

Adams, John	1963-1974	7500	17.50	17.50
Adams, John Quincy	1963-1974	7500	17.50	17.50
Addams, Jane	1963-1974	7500	17.50	17.50
Agassiz, Louis	1963-1974	7500	17.50	17.50
Anthony, Susan B.	1963-1974	7500	17.50	17.50
Audubon, John James	1963-1974	7500	17.50	17.50
Bancroft, George	1963-1974	7500	17.50	17.50
Beecher, Henry Ward	1963-1974	7500	17.50	17.50
Bell, Alexander Graham	1963-1974	7500	17.50	17.50
Boone, Daniel	1963-1974	7500	17.50	17.50
Booth, Edwin	1963-1974	7500	17.50	17.50
Brooks, Phillips	1963-1974	7500	17.50	17.50
Bryant, William Cullen	1963-1974	7500	17.50	17.50
Channing, William Ellery	1963-1974	7500	17.50	17.50
Choate, Rufus	1963-1974	7500	17.50	17.50
Clay, Henry	1963-1974	7500	17.50	17.50
Clemens, Samuel	1963-1974	7500	17.50	17.50
Cleveland, Grover	1963-1974	7500	17.50	17.50
Cooper, James Fenimore	1963-1974	7500	17.50	17.50
Cooper, Peter	1963-1974	7500	17.50	17.50
Cushman, Charlotte	1963-1974	7500	17.50	17.50
Eads, James Buchanan	1963-1974	7500	17.50	17.50
Edison, Thomas Alva	1963-1974	7500	17.50	17.50
Edwards, Jonathan	1963-1974	7500	17.50	17.50
Emerson, Ralph Waldo*	1963-1974	7500	17.50	17.50
Farragut, David Glasgow*	1963-1974	7500	17.50	17.50
Foster, Stephen	1963-1974	7500	17.50	17.50
Franklin, Benjamin	1963-1974	7500	17.50	17.50
Fulton, Robert	1963-1974	7500	17.50	17.50
Gibbs, Josiah Willard	1963-1974	7500	17.50	17.50

Medallic Art Company,
Gloucester Fishing Schooner Set

Medallic Art Company,
Golden Gate Bridge, Silver

Medallic Art Company,
Naval Aviation, 50th Anniversary

Medallic Art Company, Stone Mountain

Medallic Art Company, 101st Airborne Division

Medallic Art Company, U.S.S.Enterprise

Medallic Art Company, Hall Of Fame,
David Glasgow Farragut

Medallic Art Company, Hall Of Fame,
Ralph Waldo Emerson

Gorgas, William	1963-1974	7500	17.50	17.50
Grant, Ulysses S.	1963-1974	7500	17.50	17.50
Gray, Asa	1963-1974	7500	17.50	17.50
Hamilton, Alexander	1963-1974	7500	17.50	17.50
Hawthorne, Nathaniel	1963-1974	7500	17.50	17.50
Henry, Joseph	1963-1974	7500	17.50	17.50
Henry, Patrick	1963-1974	7500	17.50	17.50
Holmes, Oliver Wendell, Jr.	1963-1974	7500	17.50	17.50
Holmes, Oliver Wendell, Sr.	1963-1974	7500	17.50	17.50
Hopkins, Mark	1963-1974	7500	17.50	17.50
Howe, Elias	1963-1974	7500	17.50	17.50
Irving, Washington	1963-1974	7500	17.50	17.50
Jackson, Andrew*	1963-1974	7500	17.50	17.50
Jackson, Stonewall	1963-1974	7500	17.50	17.50
Jefferson, Thomas	1963-1974	7500	17.50	17.50
Jones, John Paul	1963-1974	7500	17.50	17.50
Kent, James	1963-1974	7500	17.50	17.50
Lanier, Sidney	1963-1974	7500	17.50	17.50
Lee, Robert E.	1963-1974	7500	17.50	17.50
Lincoln, Abraham	1963-1974	7500	17.50	17.50
Longfellow, Henry Wadsworth	1963-1974	7500	17.50	17.50
Lowell, James Russell	1963-1974	7500	17.50	17.50
Lyon, Mary	1963-1974	7500	17.50	17.50
MacDowell, Edward	1963-1974	7500	17.50	17.50
Madison, James	1963-1974	7500	17.50	17.50
Mann, Horace	1963-1974	7500	17.50	17.50
Marshall, John	1963-1974	7500	17.50	17.50
Matley, John Lothrop	1963-1974	7500	17.50	17.50
Maury, Matthew	1963-1974	7500	17.50	17.50
Michelson, Albert A.	1963-1974	7500	17.50	17.50
Mitchell, Maria	1963-1974	7500	17.50	17.50
Monroe, James	1963-1974	7500	17.50	17.50
Morse, Samuel	1963-1974	7500	17.50	17.50
Morton, William T.G.	1963-1974	7500	17.50	17.50
Newcomb, Simon	1963-1974	7500	17.50	17.50
Paine, Thomas	1963-1974	7500	17.50	17.50
Palmer, Alice Freeman	1963-1974	7500	17.50	17.50
Parkman, Francis	1963-1974	7500	17.50	17.50
Peabody, George	1963-1974	7500	17.50	17.50
Penn, William	1963-1974	7500	17.50	17.50
Poe, Edgar Allan	1963-1974	7500	17.50	17.50
Reed, Walter	1963-1974	7500	17.50	17.50
Roosevelt, Theodore	1963-1974	7500	17.50	17.50
Saint-Gaudens, Augustus	1963-1974	7500	17.50	17.50
Sherman, William Tecumseh	1963-1974	7500	17.50	17.50
Story, Joseph	1963-1974	7500	17.50	17.50
Stowe, Harriet Beecher	1963-1974	7500	17.50	17.50
Stuart, Gilbert Charles	1963-1974	7500	17.50	17.50
Thayer, Sylvanus	1963-1974	7500	17.50	17.50
Thoreau, Henry David	1963-1974	7500	17.50	17.50
Wald, Lillian*	1963-1974	7500	17.50	17.50
Washington, Booker T.*	1963-1974	7500	17.50	17.50
Washington, George	1963-1974	7500	17.50	17.50
Webster, Daniel	1963-1974	7500	17.50	17.50
Westinghouse, George	1963-1974	7500	17.50	17.50
Whistler, James McN.*	1963-1974	7500	17.50	17.50
Whitman, Walt*	1963-1974	7500	17.50	17.50
Whitney, Eli	1963-1974	7500	17.50	17.50
Whittier, John Greenleaf	1963-1974	7500	17.50	17.50
Willard, Emma	1963-1974	7500	17.50	17.50
Willard, Frances	1963-1974	7500	17.50	17.50
Williams, Roger	1963-1974	7500	17.50	17.50
Wilson, Woodrow	1963-1974	7500	17.50	17.50
Wright, Orville & Wilbur	1963-1974	7500	17.50	17.50

Medical Heritage Society Medals

Dentistry Series, Set Of 50, Gold Plate, Each	1971	25.00	Unknown
Dentistry Series, Set Of 50, Silver	1971	12.50	Unknown
Medical Series, Set Of 60, Bronze, Each	1969	4.50	Unknown
Medical Series, Set Of 60, Silver, Each	1969	12.50	Unknown
Pharmacy Series, Set Of 36, Bronze, Each	1970	4.50	4.50

Medals

Pharmacy Series, Set Of 36, Gold Plate, Each	1970	361	25.00	40.00
Pharmacy Series, Set Of 36, Silver, Each	1970		12.50	Unknown
Physicians Series, Set Of 4, Bronze	1971	1200	165.00	Unknown
Physicians Series, Set Of 4, Gold Over Gold	1971	180	580.00	Unknown
Physicians Series, Set Of 4, Silver	1971	480	380.00	Unknown
Science History, Set Of 75, Bronze, Each	1972	3000	5.00	Unknown
Science History, Set Of 75, Gold Filled, Each	1972	100	38.00	Unknown
Science History, Set Of 75, Gold Plate, Each	1972	750	23.50	Unknown
Science History, Set Of 75, Silver, Each	1972	1500	14.00	Unknown
Surgery Series, Set Of 36, Bronze, Each	1971		6.50	Unknown
Surgery Series, Set Of 36, Gold Plate, Each	1971		28.50	Unknown
Surgery Series, Set Of 36, Silver, Each	1971		18.50	18.50

Medical Series, see Medical Heritage Society Medals

Museum of the City of New York Medals

50th Anniv.Musuem Of New York, Bronze	1972	350	15.00	Unknown
50th Anniv.Museum Of New York, Silver	1972	15	100.00	Unknown

National Parks Centennial Medals

National Parks, Silver, Set Of 36, Each	1972	15000	14.75	Unknown

New York Democrat Club Medals

Humphrey-Muskie, Silver	1968	12.00	Unknown

New York Republican Club Medals

Nixon-Agnew, Silver	1968	12.00	Unknown

Oakland County, Michigan Sesquicentennial Medals

Chief Pontiac, Bronze & Silver Set	1970	1000	12.50	Unknown
Chief Pontiac, Silver*	1970	5000	10.00	Unknown

Pharmacy Series, see Medical Heritage Society Medals
President Lincoln Series, see Lincoln Mint

Presidential Art Medals, Inc., of Vandalia, Ohio, has produced limited edition high-relief art medals since the 1960s. All medals are struck by the Medallic Art Company.

Presidential Art Medals Inc. Medals, Apollo, .999 Silver

Apollo 11*	1969-1973	10000	35.00	175.00
Apollo 12	1969-1973	10000	35.00	45.00
Apollo 13	1969-1973	10000	35.00	45.00
Apollo 14	1969-1973	10000	35.00	45.00
Apollo 15	1969-1973	10000	35.00	45.00
Apollo 16	1969-1973	10000	35.00	45.00
Apollo 17	1969-1973	10000	35.00	45.00

Presidential Art Medals Inc. Medals, Aviation

Allen, Gold-Filled	1971-	250	50.00	Unknown
Allen, Silver	1971-	2500	25.00	25.00
Cochran, Gold-Filled	1971-	250	50.00	Unknown
Cochran, Silver	1971-	2500	25.00	25.00
Doolittle, Gold-Filled	1971-	250	50.00	Unknown
Doolittle, Silver	1971-	2500	25.00	25.00
Earhart, Gold-Filled	1971-	250	50.00	Unknown
Earhart, Silver	1971-	2500	25.00	25.00
Kenney, Gold-Filled	1971-	250	50.00	Unknown
Kenney, Silver	1971-	2500	25.00	25.00
Lindbergh, Gold-Filled	1971-	250	50.00	Unknown
Lindbergh, Silver	1971-	2500	25.00	25.00
Loening, Gold-Filled	1971-	250	50.00	Unknown
Loening, Silver	1971-	2500	25.00	25.00
Rickenbacker, Gold-Filled	1971-	250	50.00	Unknown
Rickenbacker, Silver*	1971-	2500	25.00	25.00

Presidential Art Medals Inc. Medals, Great Religions

Bahai Faith, Gold-Filled	1971-	500	40.00	Unknown
Bahai Faith, Silver	1971-	5000	20.00	20.00
Baptist, Gold-Filled	1971-	500	40.00	Unknown
Baptist, Silver	1971-	5000	20.00	20.00
Buddhism, Gold-Filled	1971-	500	40.00	Unknown
Buddhism, Silver	1971-	5000	20.00	20.00
Catholic, Gold-Filled	1971-	500	40.00	Unknown

Medallic Art Company, Hall Of Fame,
Andrew Jackson

Medallic Art Company, Hall Of Fame, Lillian Wald

Medallic Art Company, Hall Of Fame,
Booker T.Washington

Medallic Art Company, Hall Of Fame,
James McN.Whistler

Medallic Art Company, Hall Of Fame, Walt Whitman

Oakland County, Michigan Sesquicentennial Medal,
Chief Pontiac

Presidential Art Medals, Apollo 11

Presidential Art Medals, Aviation, Rickenbacker

Presidential Art Medals, Great Religions, Lutheran

Presidential Art Medals, Men Of Medicine, Galen

Catholic, Silver	1971-	5000	20.00	20.00
Christian Church, Gold-Filled	1971-	500	40.00	Unknown
Christian Church, Silver	1971-	5000	20.00	20.00
Christian Science, Gold-Filled	1971-	500	40.00	Unknown
Christian Science, Silver	1971-	5000	20.00	20.00
Episcopal, Gold-Filled	1971-	500	40.00	Unknown
Episcopal, Silver	1971-	5000	20.00	20.00
Greek Orthodox, Gold-Filled	1971-	500	40.00	Unknown
Greek Orthodox, Silver	1971-	5000	20.00	20.00
Islam, Gold-Filled	1971-	500	40.00	Unknown
Islam, Silver	1971-	5000	20.00	20.00
Judaism, Gold-Filled	1971-	500	40.00	Unknown
Judaism, Silver	1971-	5000	20.00	20.00
Lutheran, Gold-Filled	1971-	500	40.00	Unknown
Lutheran, Silver*	1971-	5000	20.00	20.00
Mormons, Gold-Filled	1971-	500	40.00	Unknown
Mormons, Silver	1971-	5000	20.00	20.00
Presbyterian, Gold-Filled	1971-	500	40.00	Unknown
Presbyterian, Silver	1971-	5000	20.00	20.00
Quakers, Gold-Filled	1971-	500	40.00	Unknown
Quakers, Silver	1971-	5000	20.00	20.00
Seventh-Day Adventists, Gold-Filled	1971-	500	40.00	Unknown
Seventh-Day Adventists, Silver	1971-	5000	20.00	20.00
United Methodist, Gold-Filled	1971-	500	40.00	Unknown
United Methodist, Silver	1971-	5000	20.00	20.00

Presidential Art Medals Inc. Medals, Men of Medicine, .999 Silver

Addison	1969-1974	5000	17.50	20.00
Bernard	1969-1974	5000	17.50	20.00
Boerhaave	1969-1974	5000	17.50	20.00
Bright	1969-1974	5000	17.50	20.00
Cajal	1969-1974	5000	17.50	20.00
Charcot	1969-1974	5000	17.50	20.00
Dioscorides	1969-1974	5000	17.50	20.00
Ehrlich	1969-1974	5000	17.50	20.00
Freud	1969-1974	5000	17.50	20.00
Galen*	1969-1974	5000	17.50	20.00
Graves	1969-1974	5000	17.50	20.00
Harvey	1969-1974	5000	17.50	20.00
Hippocrates	1969-1974	5000	17.50	20.00
Hodgkin	1969-1974	5000	17.50	20.00
Hunter	1969-1974	5000	17.50	20.00
Jenner	1969-1974	5000	17.50	20.00
Koch	1969-1974	5000	17.50	20.00
Larrey	1969-1974	5000	17.50	20.00
Lavoisier	1969-1974	5000	17.50	20.00
Lister	1969-1974	5000	17.50	20.00
Louis	1969-1974	5000	17.50	20.00
Maimonides	1969-1974	5000	17.50	20.00
Mitchell	1969-1974	5000	17.50	20.00
Morgagni	1969-1974	5000	17.50	20.00
Morton	1969-1974	5000	17.50	20.00
Osler	1969-1974	5000	17.50	20.00
Paracelsus	1969-1974	5000	17.50	20.00
Pare	1969-1974	5000	17.50	20.00
Pasteur	1969-1974	5000	17.50	20.00
Pavlov	1969-1974	5000	17.50	20.00
Pinel	1969-1974	5000	17.50	20.00
Reed	1969-1974	5000	17.50	20.00
Rush	1969-1974	5000	17.50	20.00
Scarpa	1969-1974	5000	17.50	20.00
Scheele	1969-1974	5000	17.50	20.00
Semmelweis	1969-1974	5000	17.50	20.00
Sims	1969-1974	5000	17.50	20.00
Snow	1969-1974	5000	17.50	20.00
Sydenham	1969-1974	5000	17.50	20.00
Van Leeuwenhoek	1969-1974	5000	17.50	20.00
Vesalius	1969-1974	5000	17.50	20.00
Virchow	1969-1974	5000	17.50	20.00
Von Roentgen	1969-1974	5000	17.50	20.00
Welch	1969-1974	5000	17.50	20.00

Withering	1969-1974	5000	17.50	20.00

Presidential Art Medals Inc. Medals, Miscellaneous

Assassinated Presidents, Silver		1000		50.00
Churchill, Sir Winston, Memorial, Silver	1972	5000		45.00
Hoover, J.Edgar, Gold-Filled	1972	500	75.00	Unknown
Hoover, J.Edgar, Silver*	1972	5000	35.00	40.00
Kennedy, John F., Memorial, Silver		1500		17.50
Kennedy, Robert F., Memorial, Silver		1500		17.50
Menconi, Ralph J., Gold-Filled	1972	250		125.00
Menconi, Ralph J., Silver	1972	2500	45.00	45.00
Official Nixon Inaugural Medal, Silver	1969	15000		100.00
Pope Paul VI, Silver		5000		Unknown
Skylab I, Silver	1974	10000	45.00	45.00
Spellman, Cardinal, Silver	1974	10000	45.00	45.00

Presidential Art Medals, J.Edgar Hoover

Presidential Art Medals, Inc. Medals, Presidential, .999 Silver

Adams	1961-1970	6500	10.00	13.50
Adams, J.Q.	1961-1970	6500	10.00	13.50
Arthur	1961-1970	6500	10.00	13.50
Buchanan	1961-1970	6500	10.00	13.50
Cleveland	1961-1970	6500	10.00	13.50
Coolidge	1961-1970	6500	10.00	13.50
Eisenhower	1961-1970	6500	10.00	13.50
Fillmore	1961-1970	6500	10.00	13.50
Garfield	1961-1970	6500	10.00	13.50
Grant	1961-1970	6500	10.00	13.50
Harding	1961-1970	6500	10.00	13.50
B.Harrison	1961-1970	6500	10.00	13.50
Harrison, W.	1961-1970	6500	10.00	13.50
Hayes	1961-1970	6500	10.00	13.50
Hoover	1961-1970	6500	10.00	13.50
Jackson	1961-1970	6500	10.00	13.50
Jefferson	1961-1970	6500	10.00	13.50
Johnson, A.	1961-1970	6500	10.00	13.50
Johnson, L.B.*	1961-1970	6500	10.00	13.50
Kennedy	1961-1970	6500	10.00	25.00
Lincoln	1961-1970	6500	10.00	25.00
Madison	1961-1970	6500	10.00	13.50
McKinley	1961-1970	6500	10.00	13.50
Monroe	1961-1970	6500	10.00	13.50
Nixon*	1961-1970	6500	10.00	13.50
Pierce	1961-1970	6500	10.00	13.50
Polk	1961-1970	6500	10.00	13.50
Roosevelt, F.	1961-1970	6500	10.00	25.00
Roosevelt, T.	1961-1970	6500	10.00	13.50
Taft	1961-1970	6500	10.00	13.50
Taylor	1961-1970	6500	10.00	13.50
Truman	1961-1970	6500	10.00	13.50
Tyler	1961-1970	6500	10.00	13.50
Van Buren	1961-1970	6500	10.00	13.50
Washington	1961-1970	6500	10.00	25.00
Wilson	1961-1970	6500	10.00	13.50

Presidential Art Medals, Presidential, L. B. Johnson

Presidential Art Medals, Presidential, Nixon

Presidential Art Medals Inc. Medals, Signers, .999 Silver

Adams, J.	1962-1974	7500	10.00	13.50
Adams, S.	1962-1974	7500	10.00	13.50
Bartlett	1962-1974	7500	10.00	13.50
Braxton	1962-1974	7500	10.00	13.50
Carroll	1962-1974	7500	10.00	13.50
Chase	1962-1974	7500	10.00	13.50
Clark	1962-1974	7500	10.00	13.50
Clymer	1962-1974	7500	10.00	13.50
Ellery	1962-1974	7500	10.00	13.50
Floyd	1962-1974	7500	10.00	13.50
Franklin	1962-1974	7500	10.00	13.50
Gerry	1962-1974	7500	10.00	13.50
Hancock	1962-1974	7500	10.00	13.50
Harrison	1962-1974	7500	10.00	13.50
Hart	1962-1974	7500	10.00	13.50
Hewes	1962-1974	7500	10.00	13.50
Heyward, Jr.	1962-1974	7500	10.00	13.50

Hooper	1962-1974	7500	10.00	13.50
Hopkins	1962-1974	7500	10.00	13.50
Hopkinson	1962-1974	7500	10.00	13.50
Huntington	1962-1974	7500	10.00	13.50
Jefferson*	1962-1974	7500	10.00	13.50
Lee, F.	1962-1974	7500	10.00	13.50
Lee, R.H.	1962-1974	7500	10.00	13.50
Lewis	1962-1974	7500	10.00	13.50
Livingston	1962-1974	7500	10.00	13.50
Lynch, Jr.	1962-1974	7500	10.00	13.50
McKean	1962-1974	7500	10.00	13.50
Middleton	1962-1974	7500	10.00	13.50
Morris, L.	1962-1974	7500	10.00	13.50
Morris, R.	1962-1974	7500	10.00	13.50
Morton	1962-1974	7500	10.00	13.50
Nelson, Jr.	1962-1974	7500	10.00	13.50
Paca	1962-1974	7500	10.00	13.50
Paine	1962-1974	7500	10.00	13.50
Penn	1962-1974	7500	10.00	13.50
Read	1962-1974	7500	10.00	13.50
Rodney	1962-1974	7500	10.00	13.50
Ross	1962-1974	7500	10.00	13.50
Rush	1962-1974	7500	10.00	13.50
Rutledge	1962-1974	7500	10.00	13.50
Sherman	1962-1974	7500	10.00	13.50
Smith	1962-1974	7500	10.00	13.50
Stockton	1962-1974	7500	10.00	13.50
Stone	1962-1974	7500	10.00	13.50
Taylor	1962-1974	7500	10.00	13.50
Thornton	1962-1974	7500	10.00	13.50
Whipple	1962-1974	7500	10.00	13.50
Williams	1962-1974	7500	10.00	13.50
Wilson	1962-1974	7500	10.00	13.50
Witherspoon	1962-1974	7500	10.00	13.50
Wolcott	1962-1974	7500	10.00	13.50
Wythe	1962-1974	7500	10.00	13.50

Presidential Art Medals, Signers, Jefferson

Presidential Art Medals Inc. Medals, Statehood, .999 Silver

Alabama	1962-1973	7500	10.00	13.50
Alaska	1962-1973	7500	10.00	13.50
Arizona	1962-1973	7500	10.00	13.50
Arkansas	1962-1973	7500	10.00	13.50
California	1962-1973	7500	10.00	13.50
Colorado	1962-1973	7500	10.00	13.50
Connecticut	1962-1973	7500	10.00	13.50
Delaware	1962-1973	7500	10.00	13.50
Florida	1962-1973	7500	10.00	13.50
Georgia	1962-1973	7500	10.00	13.50
Hawaii	1962-1973	7500	10.00	13.50
Idaho	1962-1973	7500	10.00	13.50
Illinois	1962-1973	7500	10.00	13.50
Indiana	1962-1973	7500	10.00	13.50
Iowa	1962-1973	7500	10.00	13.50
Kansas	1962-1973	7500	10.00	13.50
Kentucky	1962-1973	7500	10.00	13.50
Louisiana	1962-1973	7500	10.00	13.50
Maine	1962-1973	7500	10.00	13.50
Maryland	1962-1973	7500	10.00	13.50
Massachusetts	1962-1973	7500	10.00	13.50
Michigan	1962-1973	7500	10.00	13.50
Minnesota	1962-1973	7500	10.00	13.50
Mississippi	1962-1973	7500	10.00	13.50
Missouri	1962-1973	7500	10.00	13.50
Montana	1962-1973	7500	10.00	13.50
Nebraska	1962-1973	7500	10.00	13.50
Nevada	1962-1973	7500	10.00	13.50
New Hampshire	1962-1973	7500	10.00	13.50
New Jersey	1962-1973	7500	10.00	13.50
New Mexico	1962-1973	7500	10.00	13.50
New York	1962-1973	7500	10.00	13.50
North Carolina	1962-1973	7500	10.00	13.50

North Dakota	1962-1973	7500	10.00	13.50
Ohio	1962-1973	7500	10.00	13.50
Oklahoma*	1962-1973	7500	10.00	13.50
Oregon	1962-1973	7500	10.00	13.50
Pennsylvania	1962-1973	7500	10.00	13.50
Rhode Island	1962-1973	7500	10.00	13.50
South Carolina	1962-1973	7500	10.00	13.50
South Dakota	1962-1973	7500	10.00	13.50
Tennessee	1962-1973	7500	10.00	13.50
Texas	1962-1973	7500	10.00	13.50
Utah	1962-1973	7500	10.00	13.50
Vermont	1962-1973	7500	10.00	13.50
Virginia	1962-1973	7500	10.00	13.50
Washington	1962-1973	7500	10.00	13.50
West Virginia	1962-1973	7500	10.00	13.50
Wisconsin	1962-1973	7500	10.00	13.50
Wyoming	1962-1973	7500	10.00	13.50

Presidential Art Medals, Statehood, Oklahoma

Presidential Art Medals Inc. Medals, World War II, .999 Silver

Air Battle Of Britain	1966-1970	2500		20.00
Air War In China Burma	1966-1970	2500		20.00
Air War Over Europe	1966-1970	2500		20.00
Bastogne	1966-1970	2500		20.00
Battle Of Leyte	1966-1970	2500		20.00
Battle Of Midway	1966-1970	2500		20.00
China-Burma Campaign	1966-1970	2500		20.00
Commemorating Civilians	1966-1970	2500		20.00
Commemorating Military	1966-1970	2500		20.00
Doolittle Raid	1966-1970	2500		20.00
Dunkirk	1966-1970	2500		20.00
El-Alemein	1966-1970	2500		20.00
End Of African Campaign	1966-1970	2500		20.00
Guadalcanal	1966-1970	2500		20.00
Hiroshima	1966-1970	2500		20.00
Invasion Of Italy	1966-1970	2500		20.00
Invasion Of Sicily	1966-1970	2500		20.00
Iwo Jima	1966-1970	2500		20.00
Landing On Luzon*	1966-1970	2500		20.00
Liberation Of Paris	1966-1970	2500		20.00
Normandy Invasion	1966-1970	2500		20.00
Okinawa	1966-1970	2500		20.00
Pearl Harbor	1966-1970	2500		20.00
Philippines	1966-1970	2500		20.00
Remagen Bridgehead	1966-1970	2500		20.00
St.Lo Breakout	1966-1970	2500		20.00
Stalingrad	1966-1970	2500		20.00
Tarawa	1966-1970	2500		20.00
VE Day	1966-1970	2500		20.00
VJ Day	1966-1970	2500		20.00

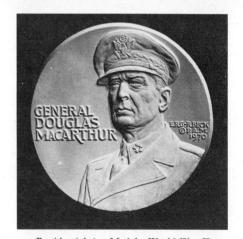

Presidential Art Medals, World War II,
Landing On Luzon

Presidential Inaugural Medals, see Inaugural Medals, Official

Prophecy Fulfilled Series, see Lincoln Mint Medals

Richard Newman Associates Medals

Lincoln Heritage Trail, Silver, 1 1/2 In.	1969	10000	10.00	Unknown
Lincoln Heritage Trail, Bronze, 1 1/2 In.	1970	105000	2.00	Unknown
Lincoln Heritage Trail, Bronze, 2 1/2 In.	1970		7.50	Unknown
Lincoln Heritage Trail, Silver, 1 1/2 In.	1970	7500	12.50	Unknown
Lincoln Heritage Trail, Silver, 2 1/2 In.	1970		35.00	Unknown
Mississippi River Parkway, Silver, 1 1/2 In	1970	15000	10.00	Unknown

Schulman Coin & Mint Company Medals

Money & Banking, Silver, Set Of 12, Each	1972	1025		25.00

Signers Series, see Franklin Mint Medals, Official Signers,

Presidential Art Medals, Inc. Medals, Signers

The Society of Medalists of Weston, Connecticut, is a non-profit organization founded in 1930 to promote the art of medallic sculpture. Each year the society commissions artists to design the Society's two annual medals. Bronze medals are not limited. Silver replicas of the 1930-1940 bronze medals were issued in 1973. The remainder of the bronze medals will be issued in silver in a limited edition of 700.

U.S.Capitol Historical Society Medal,
U.S.Capitol Building

Philadelphia Mint,
American Museum Of Immigration

Philadelphia Mint, Castle Clinton

Philadelphia Mint, Ellis Island

Philadelphia Mint, Federal Hall

Society of Medalists Medals

America, Turkey, Silver	1973	700	47.50	47.50
Aphrodite, Silver	1973	700	47.50	47.50
Dionysus, Silver	1973	700	47.50	47.50
Gloria, Silver	1973	700	47.50	47.50
Hunter & Dog, Silver	1973	700	47.50	47.50
Indian Prayer For Rain, Silver	1973	700	47.50	47.50
Lindbergh, Charles A., Silver	1973	700	47.50	47.50
No Easy Way To Stars, Silver	1973	700	47.50	47.50
Whatsoever Man Soweth, Silver	1973	700	47.50	47.50
Youth Fishing, Silver	1973	700	47.50	47.50

State Centennial Medals, see City and State Medals, Official

Statehood Series, see Franklin Mint Medals, States of the Union,
Presidential Art Medals, Inc. Medals, Statehood

Surgery Series, see Medical Heritage Society Medals

Texas Ranger Sesquicentennial Series, see WNW Mint Medals

Token & Medal Society Medals, Past Presidents Series

Culver, Virginia, Bronze	1968	150	Unknown
Culver, Virginia, Silver	1968	25	Unknown
Curtis, Jane S., Bronze	1968	150	Unknown
Curtis, Jane S., Silver	1968	25	Unknown
Fuld, Dr.George, Bronze	1968	100	Unknown
Fuld, Dr.George, Silver	1968	25	Unknown
Hamm, Paul, Bronze	1968	150	Unknown
Hamm, Paul, Silver	1968	25	Unknown

Trova Medallions

Mickey Mouse, Empire Builder*		50	350.00	500.00 to 600.00

United Nations Medals

20th Anniversary United Nations, Silver	1965	7500	14.00	Unknown

United States Capitol Historical Society Medals

U.S.Capitol Building, Gold On Silver	1973	1976	180.00	180.00
U.S.Capitol Building, Silver*	1973		45.00	45.00

*Commemorative medals struck by the official United States Government
Mint require approval through special legislative bills passed by Congress
and signed by the president. Most U. S. Mint medals commemorate
various city, state, and national celebrations. Official presidential
inaugural and city and state medals struck by the U.S. Mint are listed
separately under Inaugural Medals, Official, and City and State
Medals, Official. The medals are struck at the Philadelphia branch of
the mint.*

United States Mint Special Commemorative Medals

American Museum Of Immigration, Silver*	1965	5000	10.00	Unknown
Castle Clinton, Silver*	1965	5000	10.00	Unknown
Dartmouth College Bicentennial, Bronze	1969	5000	10.00	10.00
Ellis Island, Silver*	1967	5000	10.00	Unknown
Federal Hall, Silver*	1965	5000	10.00	Unknown
Golden Spike Centennial, Bronze, 1 15/16 In.	1968	118700		Unknown
Golden Spike Centennial, Bronze, 2 1/2 In.	1968	4750		Unknown
Golden Spike Centennial, Silver, 2 1/2 In.	1968	3000		Unknown
International Exposition Hemisfair, Bronze	1966	15500		Unknown
International Exposition Hemisfair, Silver	1966	13320		Unknown
International Ladies' Garment Workers, Bronze	1962	2000		Unknown
MacArthur Memorial, Bronze, 1 15/16 In.	1962	10000		Unknown
MacArthur Memorial, Bronze, 3 In.	1962	1000		Unknown
Nevada Silver Centennial, Silver	1959	1000		Unknown
New York City Shrines, Silver	1964	18000		Unknown
Ohio Northern University Centennial, Bronze	1971	1000		Unknown
Ohio Northern University Centennial, Silver	1971	2000		Unknown
Pony Express Centennial, Bronze, 1 15/16 In.	1960	50000		Unknown
Pony Express Centennial, Bronze, 2 1/4 In.	1960	1000		Unknown
Pony Express Centennial, Silver, 1 15/16 In.	1960	5000		Unknown
Pony Express Centennial, Silver, 2 1/4 In.	1960	3000		Unknown
Stone Mountain Memorial, Matched Set Of 4	1970	500	67.00	110.00
Stone Mountain Memorial, Silver, 1 9/16 In.	1970	1000	13.50	21.50
Stone Mountain Memorial, Silver, 3 In.	1970	1000	38.00	80.00

Transpo '72, Bronze	1972	90000	.50	.50
Winston Churchill Memorial, Bronze	1969	8000		Unknown
Winston Churchill Memorial, Silver	1969	5000		Unknown
250th Anniversary, Padre Serra, Bronze	1963	82000		Unknown
250th Anniversary, Padre Serra, Silver	1963	10000		Unknown

*The Van Brook Mint of Lexington, Kentucky, designs and produces
a variety of privately commissioned medals for many organizations.*

Van Brook Mint Medals

Churchill, Gold Plate On Sterling, Set Of 2	1973	500		50.00
Churchill, Nickel Silver	1973			5.00
Clay County, 1873-1973, Bronze	1973			2.00 to 5.00
Clay County, 1873-1973, Sterling	1973	300		25.00
Confederate Half Dollar, Gold On Bronze	1973			4.95
Confederate Half Dollar, Sterling	1973			14.50
Drum & Bugle Corps, Bronze	1973			3.00
Drum & Bugle Corps, Sterling	1973	2500		13.00
FAA Administration, Bronze	1972			3.00
FAA Administration, Nickel Silver	1972			5.00
FAA Administration, Sterling	1972	5000		12.00
Godfrey, Arthur, Bronze	1973			5.00
Godfrey, Arthur, Nickel Silver	1973			10.00
Godfrey, Arthur, Sterling	1973	25000		25.00
Holland Land Co., Bronze	1973			2.00
Holland Land Co., Sterling	1973			10.00
Johnson, L.B., Gold Plate On Silver	1973			10.00
Johnson, L.B., Nickel Silver	1973			5.00 to 10.00
Johnson, L.B., Sterling & 24K Gold, Pair	1973	1000		50.00
Keystone Of The North, Nickel Silver	1972			4.00 to 5.00
Keystone Of The North, Sterling	1972	10000		12.00
Little Caesar's Casino, Sterling	1973	100		60.00
Miami Dolphins, Gold Plate On Silver	1973	10000		25.00
Miami Dolphins, Sterling	1973	10000		20.00
N.W.Public Service Company, Bronze	1973			5.00
N.W.Public Service Company, Sterling	1973	200		20.00
Pan Am, 747, Sterling	1973	100		1200.00
Sanctus Eligius, Bronze	1973	2000	4.00	4.00
Sanctus Eligius, Gold On Silver	1973	500	25.00	25.00
Sanctus Eligius, Sterling	1973	1000	20.00	20.00
Sesquicentennial Festival, Bronze	1973			2.00
Sesquicentennial Festival, Sterling	1973			10.00
Sisters Of Mercy Hospital, Bronze	1973			2.00
Sisters Of Mercy Hospital, Sterling	1973			25.00
United States Seal, Gold On Bronze	1973		5.20	5.20
United States Seal, Gold On Bronze, Proof Set	1973		22.50	22.50
United States Seal, Gold On Silver, Proof Set	1973		39.50	39.50
United States Seal, Sterling	1973		7.50	7.50
United States Seal, Sterling, Proof Set Of 3	1973		29.50	29.50
Wildcat Club, Sterling	1973			10.25
Y-Indian Guides, Sterling, Set Of 2	1972	1500	25.00	25.00

Veraflex Medals

Carver, George Washington, Silver*	1970	7500	12.00	Unknown
Evers, Medgar, Silver*	1970	7500	12.00	Unknown
King, Dr.Martin Luther, Silver*	1970	7500	12.00	Unknown
Malcolm X, Silver*	1970	7500	12.00	Unknown
Washington, Booker, T., Silver*	1970	7500	12.00	Unknown

Wittnauer Mint Medals, American National Legacy

American Legacy Series, Gold On Silver, 36	1973		850.00	850.00

Wittnauer Mint Medals, Presidential Signature Series

Presidential Series, Silver, Set Of 36	1973		475.00	475.00

Wittnauer Mint Medals, The Scout Oath

The Scout Oath, Gold On Silver	1974	Year	23.50	23.50
The Scout Oath, Silver	1974	Year	18.50	18.50
On My Honor, Gold On Silver	1974	Year	23.50	23.50
On My Honor, Silver	1974	Year	18.50	18.50
I Will Do My Best, Gold On Silver	1974	Year	23.50	23.50
I Will Do My Best, Silver	1974	Year	18.50	18.50
To Do My Duty To God, Gold On Silver	1974	Year	23.50	23.50

Veraflex,
George Washington Carver

Veraflex,
Booker T.Washington

Veraflex,
Medgar Evers

Veraflex,
Martin Luther King, Jr.

Veraflex,
Malcolm X

To Do My Duty To God, Silver	1974	Year	18.50	18.50
And My Country, Gold On Silver	1974	Year	23.50	23.50
And My Country, Silver	1974	Year	18.50	18.50
Be Prepared, Gold On Silver	1974	Year	23.50	23.50
Be Prepared, Silver	1974	Year	18.50	18.50
To Obey The Scout Law, Gold On Silver	1974	Year	23.50	23.50
To Obey The Scout Law, Silver	1974	Year	18.50	18.50
Do A Good Turn Daily, Gold On Silver	1974	Year	23.50	23.50
Do A Good Turn Daily, Silver	1974	Year	18.50	18.50
To Help Others At All Times, Gold On Silver	1974	Year	23.50	23.50
To Help Others At All Times, Silver	1974	Year	18.50	18.50
To Keep Physically Strong, Gold On Silver	1974	Year	23.50	23.50
To Keep Physically Strong, Silver	1974	Year	18.50	18.50
Mentally Awake, Gold On Silver	1974	Year	23.50	23.50
Mentally Awake, Silver	1974	Year	18.50	18.50
And Morally Straight, Gold On Silver	1974	Year	23.50	23.50
And Morally Straight, Silver	1974	Year	18.50	18.50

WNW Mint Industries of Amarillo, Texas, introduced limited edition silver plates in 1972. Limited edition medals in bronze and silver were first issued in 1971.

See listing for WNW Mint in Plate section

WNW Mint Medals

Freedom Founders, Bronze, Set Of 56, Each	1973	Year	4.00	4.00
Freedom Founders, Silver, Set Of 56, Each	1973	Year	15.00	15.00
Indian Chief, Bronze, Set Of 51, Each	1973	350	3.00	3.00
Indian Chief, Silver, Set Of 51, Each	1973	150	15.00	15.00
Texas Ranger Hall Of Fame, Bronze	1974	5000	3.00	3.00
Texas Ranger Hall Of Fame, Gold On Silver	1974	250	25.00	25.00
Texas Ranger Hall Of Fame, Silver	1974	2500	15.00	15.00
Texas Ranger Sesquicentennial, Bronze	1973	100000	1.50	1.50
Texas Ranger Sesquicentennial, Silver*	1973	13000	11.00	11.00

World War II Series, see Presidential Art Medals, World War II

5

Bars and Ingots

Title	Date of Issue	Issue Limi- tation	Issue Price	Current Price
Adams Company Bars				
Elongated Kennedy Half-Dollar, Bronze	1973	800		3.50 to 4.50
Elongated Kennedy Half-Dollar, Silver	1973	200		15.00
America the Beautiful ingots, see Hamilton Mint				
America's Greatest Events ingots, see Hamilton Mint				
American Numismatic Association bars, see Coin Gallery of San Francisco				
American Silver Editions, Ltd. Silver Bars, 1 oz.				
Pope John XXIII	1973	4000		20.00
Pope John XXIII, Gold Over Silver	1973	1000		30.00
Roosevelt, Eleanor	1973	4000		15.00 to 20.00
Roosevelt, Eleanor, Gold Over Silver	1973	1000		25.00 to 30.00
Anniversary bars, see Washington Mint				
Barry Hepsley, see Hepsley				
Belford Silver Bars				
Peacemaker	1973	15000		5.00 to 6.00
Winchester	1973	15000		5.00 to 6.00
Bradford Silver Bars				
Quarter Horse, Silver, 1 Oz.	1973	1000		12.50 to 15.00
Buffalo Silver Ingot, Ltd. Silver Bars				
Israel, 25th Anniversary, Enameled	1973			15.00
Carson City Mint Spikes				
Virginia & Truckee Railroad Silver Spike*	1969	1000	150.00	150.00
Ceeco Mint Silver Bars				
Birthday	1973-1974		9.95	9.95
Go Go Bar	1973	15000		8.00 to 9.50
I Love You, Enamel Decoration	1974		9.95	9.95
Labor Day, Pregnant Woman	1973	4500		17.50
Laurel & Hardy			5.95	5.95
Women's Lib	1973	9500		10.00
Clover Coin Company Silver Bars				
Israel, 25th Anniversary, Shalom	1973	2000	25.00	25.00
Coin-A-Rama Silver Bars, 1 oz.				
Coin-A-Rama City	1973	15000		8.50 to 9.50
Four Seasons, Autumn	1973			12.50
Four Seasons, Spring	1973			12.50
Four Seasons, Summer	1973			12.50

Continental Mint, Last Supper

Continental Mint, David, Michelangelo

Continental Mint, La Pieta

Continental Mint, Mona Lisa

Four Seasons, Winter	1973			12.50

Coin Gallery Silver Bars, Winners of the Triple Crown

Assault, 1946	1973	2500	20.00	20.00
Citation, 1948	1973	2500	20.00	20.00
Count Fleet, 1943	1973	2500	20.00	20.00
Gallant Fox, 1930	1973	2500	20.00	20.00
Omaha, 1935	1973	2500	20.00	20.00
Secretariat, 1973	1973	2500	20.00	20.00
Sir Barton, 1919	1973	2500	20.00	20.00
Trophy Bar, 1973	1973	2500	20.00	20.00
War Admiral, 1937	1973	2500	20.00	20.00
Whirlaway, 1941	1973	2500	20.00	20.00

Coin Gallery of San Francisco Silver Bars

American Numismatic Association, Pine Tree	1973	500		10.75
82nd Anniversary Of ANA Convention	1973	7500		6.50 to 8.00

Coin Gallery of San Francisco Silver Bars, San Francisco Historical

Barbary Coast	1973	2500		6.50 to 8.00
Barbary Coast, Error	1973			30.00 to 35.00
Emperor Norton	1973	2500		6.50 to 7.50
Mammy Pleasant's House Of Pleasure	1973			6.50 to 8.00
Vigilantes	1973	1500		6.50 to 8.00

Colonial Mint Ingots

Brooklyn Bridge, Silver				
Mitchell, John, Silver	1973	15000		7.00 to 10.00
Mitchell, Martha, Queen Of Watergate, Bronze	1973			3.00
Mitchell, Martha, Queen Of Watergate, Silver	1973			5.50 to 12.50
Nixon-Brezhnev	1973			450. to 9.50
Nixon-Mao	1973	10000		9.50
Secretariat, Silver	1973	2500		45.00
Watergate Gang, Bronze	1973			3.00
Watergate Gang, Silver	1973			3.00

Colony Coin Shop Silver Bars

J.F.K., 10th Anniversary, Gold Plate	1973	200	30.00	30.00
J.F.K., 10th Anniversary, Silver	1973	2300	12.50	12.50

The Columbus Mint of Pataskala, Ohio, issued its first silver bar in 1973. The bars are produced for Columbus Mint by Wendall's Manufacturing Company.

Columbus Mint Bars

Christmas, Bronze	1973	1000	1.95	1.95
Christmas, Gold On Nickel Silver	1973	250	4.25	4.25
Christmas, Nickel Silver	1973	1000	2.95	2.95
Christmas, Silver	1973	300	15.00	5.50 to 15.00
Columbus Day, Bronze	1973	1500	1.95	1.95
Columbus Day, Gold On Nickel Silver	1973	1000	4.25	4.25
Columbus Day, Nickel Silver, Proof	1973	5000	2.95	2.95
Columbus Day, Silver, Proof	1973	500	15.00	15.00
Thanksgiving, Bronze	1973	1000	1.95	1.95
Thanksgiving, Gold On Nickel Silver	1973	1500	4.25	4.25
Thanksgiving, Nickel Silver	1973	5000	2.95	2.95
Thanksgiving, Silver	1973	500	15.00	15.00

The Continental Mint of Panorama City, California, has made limited edition medals since the 1960s. Silver bars were first made in 1972.

See listing for Continental Mint in Medal section

Continental Mint Silver Bars, 2 1/2 oz.

Adoration Of Mary	1973	2000	25.00	25.00
Apollo & Daphne	1973	2000	25.00	25.00
Baptism Of Christ	1973	2000	25.00	25.00
David, Michelangelo*	1973	2000	25.00	25.00
La Pieta*	1973	2000	25.00	25.00
Last Supper*	1973	2000	25.00	25.00
Madonna Del Parto	1973	2000	25.00	25.00
Mona Lisa*	1973	2000	25.00	25.00
Perseus, Cellini	1973	2000	25.00	25.00

Continental Mint, Skylab

Pioneer F	1973	2000	25.00	25.00
Skylab*	1973	2000	25.00	25.00
Tahitian Women	1973	2000	25.00	25.00
The Kiss, Rodin*	1973	2000	25.00	25.00
Three Graces	1973	2000	25.00	25.00
Venus De Milo*	1973	2000	25.00	25.00
1898 Renault*	1973	2000	25.00	25.00
1908 Model T Ford*	1973	2000	25.00	25.00
1913 Rolls-Royce*	1973	2000	25.00	25.00
1922 Lancia-Lambda	1973	2000	25.00	25.00
1930 Alfa Romeo	1973	2000	25.00	25.00
1934 Citroen	1973	2000	25.00	25.00
1939 Volkswagen	1973	2000	25.00	25.00
1946 Chrysler*	1973	2000	25.00	25.00
1957 Fiat Nuova 500	1973	2000	25.00	25.00
1960 Mini Minor*	1973	2000	25.00	25.00
1971 Lunar Rover*	1973	2000	25.00	25.00

Corinthian Mint Bars

Secretariat, Bronze, Set Of 3	1973		90.00
Secretariat, Gold Over Silver, Set Of 3	1973	2000	283.50
Secretariat, Silver, Set Of 3	1973	10000	202.50

Crabtree Mint Silver Bars

Crabtree Mint	1973		6.00
Happy Anniversary	1973	4.95	5.25 to 6.75
Happy Anniversary	1974	4.95	4.95
I Love You	1973		4.95

Continental Mint, The Kiss,
Rodin

Danbury Mint, a division of Glendinning Companies, Inc., creates and markets art medals and limited edition plates. All limited editions are struck for the Danbury Mint by other organizations. Limited edition plates were first introduced in 1972. Danbury Mint State ingots were introduced in 1972 at 22 dollars for the 2,500 grain ingot and 40 dollars for the 5,000 grain ingot. Because of the increase in the price of silver, issue prices were raised in 1973 to 29 dollars and 50 cents and fifty-five dollars. The combined 1972 and 1973 production of the State ingot series was 6,800.

See listing for Danbury Mint in Plate and Medal sections

Danbury Mint Silver Ingots, State

State, 2, 500 Grains, Set Of 50	1972-1976	6800	22.00	Unknown
State, 2, 500 Grains, Set Of 50	1973	6800	29.50	Unknown
State, 5, 000 Grains, Set Of 50	1972-1976	6800	40.00	Unknown
State, 5, 000 Grains, Set Of 50	1973	6800	55.00	Unknown

Don Adams, see Adams Company

Englehard Silver Bars

Canada	1972		6.50 to 10.00
United States			6.50 to 7.00

First National Bank of Chicago Silver Bars

Drover's Bank	1973	15000	10.00 to 18.00
First National Bank Of Chicago	1973	13000	16.00
First Wisconsin Center	1973	10000	16.00 to 18.00
Middlesex Mint	1973		17.50

Continental Mint,
Venus De Milo

Foster & Co. Silver Bars

Buffalo	1970		65.00 to 75.00
Donkey Pulling Ore Car	1969		10.00
Flag, 1/2 Oz.	1973		35.00
Mining Companies, 1968 Series, Set Of 5, 3 Oz.	1968	2650	200.00
Mining Companies, 1969 Series, Set Of 5, 3 Oz.	1969	2650	200.00
Mining Companies, 1970 Series, Set Of 5, 3 Oz.	1970		200.00
Silver Eagle Series, Set Of 10, 10 Oz.	1969		250.00

Continental Mint, 1898 Renault

Franklin Mint was organized in the early 1960s by Joseph Segel and Gilroy Roberts, chief sculptor engraver for the U.S. Mint. It is located in Franklin Center, Pennsylvania. Franklin Mint introduced the first sterling silver collector's plate on the market in 1970. Medals have been made since the 1960s. The official Franklin Mint code is used to describe the composition of the medals. The code is translated as follows A-Platinum, B-Gold, C-Fine Silver .999, D-Sterling

Continental Mint, 1908 Model T Ford

Continental Mint, 1913 Rolls-Royce

Continental Mint, 1946 Chrysler

Continental Mint, 1960 Mini Minor

Continental Mint, 1971 Lunar Roving Vehicle

Silver .925, F-Gold on Sterling, J-Franklin Bronze,
N-commercial bronze. Letters A, M, P, or Pl following the first
code letter refer to Antique, Mint, Proof, or Proof-Like finish.
There are 25.4 mm. to an inch.

See listing for Franklin Mint in Plate and Medal sections

Franklin Mint Ingots, Bank, 1,000 Grains Silver

Alaska National, Fairbanks, Alaska, P	1970	8014	10.00	10.00 to 16.00
Amalgamated Trust & Savings, Chicago, P	1970	8014	10.00	10.00 to 16.00
Bank Of Nevada, Las Vegas, Nevada, P	1970	8014	10.00	10.00 to 16.00
Bank Of Yakima, Washington, P	1970	8014	10.00	10.00 to 16.00
Bankers Trust Company, Des Moines, Iowa, P	1970	8014	10.00	10.00 to 16.00
Boatmen's National, St.Louis, Missouri, P	1970	8014	10.00	10.00 to 16.00
Box Elder County, Brigham City, Utah, P	1970	8014	10.00	10.00 to 16.00
Central Bank & Trust Co., Lexington, Ky., P	1970	8014	10.00	10.00 to 16.00
Central National, Cleveland, Ohio, P	1970	8014	10.00	10.00 to 16.00
Charleston National, Charleston, W.V., P	1970	8014	10.00	10.00 to 16.00
Cheshire National, Keene, New Hampshire, P	1970	8014	10.00	10.00 to 16.00
Citizens & Southern National, Savannah, Ga., P	1970	8014	10.00	10.00 to 16.00
City Bank Of Honolulu, Hawaii, P	1970	8014	10.00	10.00 to 16.00
Clovis National, Clovis, New Mexico, P	1970	8014	10.00	10.00 to 16.00
Colorado Springs National, Colorado, P	1970	8014	10.00	10.00 to 16.00
Exchange National, Atchison, Kansas, P	1970	8014	10.00	10.00 to 16.00
Farmers & Mechanics National, Frederick, Md., P	1970	8014	10.00	10.00 to 16.00
Federal Trust Company, Waterville, Maine, P	1970	8014	10.00	10.00 to 16.00
Fidelity Bank & Trust Co., Minneapolis, P	1970	8014	10.00	10.00 to 16.00
Fidelity National, Baton Rouge, Louisiana, P	1970	8014	10.00	10.00 to 16.00
First Citizens Bank & Trust Co., S.C., P	1970	8014	10.00	10.00 to 16.00
First National Bank & Trust Co., Tulsa, P	1970	8014	10.00	10.00 to 16.00
First National Bank & Trust Co. Of Wyoming, P	1970	8014	10.00	10.00 to 16.00
First National, Birmingham, Alabama, P	1970	8014	10.00	10.00 to 16.00
First National, Grand Forks, N.D., P	1970	8014	10.00	10.00 to 16.00
First National, Jackson, Mississippi, P	1970	8014	10.00	10.00 to 16.00
First National, Little Rock, Arkansas, P	1970	8014	10.00	10.00 to 16.00
First National, Omaha, Nebraska, P	1970	8014	10.00	10.00 to 16.00
First National, Orlando, Florida, P	1970	8014	10.00	10.00 to 16.00
Franklin National, New York, N.Y., P	1970	8014	10.00	10.00 to 16.00
Hartford National & Trust Company, Conn., P	1970	8014	10.00	10.00 to 16.00
Harvard Trust Co., Cambridge, Mass., P	1970	8014	10.00	10.00 to 16.00
Imperial, Los Angeles, California, P	1970	8014	10.00	10.00 to 16.00
Marine, Milwaukee, Wisconsin, P	1970	8014	10.00	10.00 to 16.00
Mechanics & Farmers, Durham, N.C., P	1970	8014	10.00	10.00 to 16.00
Midland National, Billings, Montana, P	1970	8014	10.00	10.00 to 16.00
National Of Memphis, Tennessee, P	1970	8014	10.00	10.00 to 16.00
National State, Elizabeth, N.J., P	1970	8014	10.00	10.00 to 16.00
Pierre National, South Dakota, P	1970	8014	10.00	10.00 to 16.00
Pontiac State, Pontiac, Michigan, P	1970	8014	10.00	10.00 to 16.00
Proctor Trust Co., Proctor/Poultney, Vt., P	1970	8014	10.00	10.00 to 16.00
Provident National, Philadelphia, Penn., P	1970	8014	10.00	10.00 to 16.00
Rhode Island Hospital Trust National, P	1970	8014	10.00	10.00 to 16.00
St.Joseph Valley, Elkhart, Indiana, P	1970	8014	10.00	10.00 to 16.00
Texas Commerce, Houston, Texas, P	1970	8014	10.00	10.00 to 16.00
Thunderbird, Glendale, Arizona, P	1970	8014	10.00	10.00 to 16.00
Twin Falls Bank & Trust Company, Idaho, P	1970	8014	10.00	10.00 to 16.00
U.S.National, Portland, Oregon, P	1970	8014	10.00	10.00 to 16.00
United Virginia, Richmond, Va., P	1970	8014	10.00	10.00 to 16.00
Wilmington Trust Company, Delaware, P	1970	8014	10.00	10.00 to 16.00
Aberdeen National, South Dakota, P	1971	8014	11.00	12.00 to 16.00
Albuquerque National, New Mexico, P	1971	8014	11.00	12.00 to 16.00
American Bank & Trust Co., Racine, Wisconsin, P	1971	8014	11.00	12.00 to 16.00
American National Bank & Trust, Michigan, P	1971	8014	11.00	12.00 to 16.00
Amoskeag Banks, Manchester, N.H., P	1971	8014	11.00	12.00 to 16.00
B.M.Behrends, Juneau, Alaska, P	1971	8014	11.00	12.00 to 16.00
Bank Of America, San Francisco, California, P	1971	8014	11.00	12.00 to 16.00
Bank Of Clarksdale, Mississippi, P	1971	8014	11.00	12.00 to 16.00
Bank Of North Dakota, Bismarck, P	1971	8014	11.00	12.00 to 16.00
Burke & Herbert Bank & Trust Co., Virginia, P	1971	8014	11.00	12.00 to 16.00
Central National, Des Moines, Iowa, P	1971	8014	11.00	12.00 to 16.00
Central Pacific, Honolulu, Hawaii, P	1971	8014	11.00	12.00 to 16.00
Chittenden Trust Co., Burlington, Vt., P	1971	8014	11.00	12.00 to 16.00

Commercial Bank, Salem, Oregon, P	1971	8014	11.00	12.00 to 16.00
Equimark, Pittsburgh, Pennsylvania, P	1971	8014	11.00	12.00 to 16.00
Eutaw Savings, Baltimore, Maryland, P	1971	8014	11.00	12.00 to 16.00
Farmers Bank, Wilmington, Delaware, P	1971	8014	11.00	12.00 to 16.00
First Bank, Minneapolis, Minnesota, P	1971	8014	11.00	12.00 to 16.00
First Bank, Springfield, Mass., P	1971	8014	11.00	12.00 to 16.00
First Metals Bank & Trust, Butte, Montana, P	1971	8014	11.00	12.00 to 16.00
First National, Abilene, Texas, P	1971	8014	11.00	12.00 to 16.00
First National, Boulder, Colorado, P	1971	8014	11.00	12.00 to 16.00
First National, Kansas City, Missouri, P	1971	8014	11.00	12.00 to 16.00
First National, Laramie, Wyoming, P	1971	8014	11.00	12.00 to 16.00
First National, Reno, Nevada, P	1971	8014	11.00	12.00 to 16.00
First National, Toledo, Ohio, P	1971	8014	11.00	12.00 to 16.00
First Peoples' Bank, Johnson City, Tennessee, P	1971	8014	11.00	12.00 to 16.00
Fort Wayne National, Indiana, P	1971	8014	11.00	12.00 to 16.00
Fourth National, Wichita, Kansas, P	1971	8014	11.00	12.00 to 16.00
Georgia Railroad Bank &&trust, Augusta, Ga., P	1971	8014	11.00	12.00 to 16.00
Great Western Bank & Trust, Phoenix, Arizona, P	1971	8014	11.00	12.00 to 16.00
Greater Providence Trust, Rhode Island, P	1971	8014	11.00	12.00 to 16.00
Harris Trust, Chicago, Illinois, P	1971	8014	11.00	12.00 to 16.00
Hibernia National, New Orleans, Louisiana, P	1971	8014	11.00	12.00 to 16.00
Idaho Bank Of Commerce, Rexburg, Idaho, P	1971	8014	11.00	12.00 to 16.00
Kanawha Valley, Charleston, W.V., P	1971	8014	11.00	12.00 to 16.00
Liberty Bank, Oklahoma City, Oklahoma, P	1971	8014	11.00	12.00 to 16.00
McIlroy, Fayetteville, Arkansas, P	1971	8014	11.00	12.00 to 16.00
Merchants National, Mobile, Ala., P	1971	8014	11.00	12.00 to 16.00
New Jersey National, Trenton, P	1971	8014	11.00	12.00 to 16.00
Northeast Bankshare Association, Me., P	1971	8014	11.00	12.00 to 16.00
Omaha National, Nebraska, P	1971	8014	11.00	12.00 to 16.00
Peoples National, Greenville, S.C., P	1971	8014	11.00	12.00 to 16.00
Planters National, Rocky Mount, N.C., P	1971	8014	11.00	12.00 to 16.00
Rochester Savings, N.Y., P	1971	8014	11.00	12.00 to 16.00
Seattle First National, Washington, P	1971	8014	11.00	12.00 to 16.00
Second National, Ashland, Kentucky, P	1971	8014	11.00	12.00 to 16.00
Tallahassee Bank, Florida, P	1971	8014	11.00	12.00 to 16.00
Tracy Collins Bank & Trust, Salt Lake City, P	1971	8014	11.00	12.00 to 16.00
Union Trust, Stamford, Connecticut, P	1971	8014	11.00	12.00 to 16.00
Aberdeen National, South Dakota, Pl	1971	5061	11.00	12.00 to 16.00
Albuquerque National, New Mexico, Pl	1971	5061	11.00	12.00 to 16.00
American Bank & Trust Co., Wisconsin, Pl	1971	5061	11.00	12.00 to 16.00
American National & Trust Co. Of Michigan, Pl	1971	5061	11.00	12.00 to 16.00
Amoskeag Banks, Manchester, N.H., Pl	1971	5061	11.00	12.00 to 16.00
B.M.Behrends Bank, Juneau, Alaska, Pl	1971	5061	11.00	12.00 to 16.00
Bank Of America, San Francisco, California, Pl	1971	5061	11.00	12.00 to 16.00
Bank Of Clarksdale, Mississippi, Pl	1971	5061	11.00	12.00 to 16.00
Bank Of North Dakota, Bismarck, Pl	1971	5061	11.00	12.00 to 16.00
Burke & Herbert Bank & Trust Co., Virginia, Pl	1971	5061	11.00	12.00 to 16.00
Central National, Des Moines, Iowa, Pl	1971	5061	11.00	12.00 to 16.00
Central Pacific Bank, Honolulu, Hawaii, Pl	1971	5061	11.00	12.00 to 16.00
Chittenden Trust Co., Burlington, Vt., Pl	1971	5061	11.00	12.00 to 16.00
Commercial Bank, Salem, Oregon, Pl	1971	5061	11.00	12.00 to 16.00
Equimark, Pittsburgh, Pennsylvania, Pl	1971	5061	11.00	12.00 to 16.00
Eutaw Savings, Baltimore, Maryland, Pl	1971	5061	11.00	12.00 to 16.00
Farmers Bank, Wilmington, Delaware, Pl	1971	5061	11.00	12.00 to 16.00
First Bank, Minneapolis, Minnesota, Pl	1971	5061	11.00	12.00 to 16.00
First Bank, Springfield, Mass., Pl	1971	5061	11.00	12.00 to 16.00
First Metals Bank & Trust, Butte, Montana, Pl	1971	5061	11.00	12.00 to 16.00
First National, Abilene, Texas, Pl	1971	5061	11.00	12.00 to 16.00
First National, Boulder, Colorado, Pl	1971	5061	11.00	12.00 to 16.00
First National, Kansas City, Missouri, Pl	1971	5061	11.00	12.00 to 16.00
First National, Laramie, Wyoming, Pl	1971	5061	11.00	12.00 to 16.00
First National, Reno, Nevada, Pl	1971	5061	11.00	12.00 to 16.00
First National, Toledo, Ohio, Pl	1971	5061	11.00	12.00 to 16.00
First Peoples, Johnson City, Tennessee, Pl	1971	5061	11.00	12.00 to 16.00
Fort Wayne National, Indiana, Pl	1971	5061	11.00	12.00 to 16.00
Fourth National, Wichita, Kansas, Pl	1971	5061	11.00	12.00 to 16.00
Georgia Railroad Bank & Trust, Augusta, Pl	1971	5061	11.00	12.00 to 16.00
Great Western Bank & Trust, Phoenix, Ariz., Pl	1971	5061	11.00	12.00 to 16.00
Greater Providence Trust, Rhode Island, Pl	1971	5061	11.00	12.00 to 16.00
Harris Trust, Chicago, Illinois, Pl	1971	5061	11.00	12.00 to 16.00

Franklin Mint, Christmas, 1970,
The Skaters

Franklin Mint, Christmas, 1971, Sleighing Scene

Franklin Mint, Christmas, 1972,
Hauling In The Yule Log

Franklin Mint, Christmas, 1973, The Carolers

Hibernia National, New Orleans, Louisiana, Pl	1971	5061	11.00	12.00 to 16.00
Idaho Bank Of Commerce, Rexburg, Idaho, Pl	1971	5061	11.00	12.00 to 16.00
Kanawha Valley, Charleston, W.V., Pl	1971	5061	11.00	12.00 to 16.00
Liberty Bank, Oklahoma City, Oklahoma, Pl	1971	5061	11.00	12.00 to 16.00
McIlroy, Fayetteville, Arkansas, Pl	1971	5061	11.00	12.00 to 16.00
Merchants National, Mobile, Alabama, Pl	1971	5061	11.00	12.00 to 16.00
New Jersey National, Trenton, N.J., Pl	1971	5061	11.00	12.00 to 16.00
Northeast Bankshare Association, Me., Pl	1971	5061	11.00	12.00 to 16.00
Omaha National, Nebraska, Pl	1971	5061	11.00	12.00 to 16.00
Peoples National, Greenville, S.C., Pl	1971	5061	11.00	12.00 to 16.00
Planters National, Rocky Mount, N.C., Pl	1971	5061	11.00	12.00 to 16.00
Rochester Savings, Rochester, N.Y., Pl	1971	5061	11.00	12.00 to 16.00
Seattle 1st National, Seattle, Washington, Pl	1971	5061	11.00	12.00 to 16.00
Second National, Ashland, Kentucky, Pl	1971	5061	11.00	12.00 to 16.00
Tallahassee Bank, Florida, Pl	1971	5061	11.00	12.00 to 16.00
Tracy Collins Bank & Trust, Salt Lake City, Pl	1971	5061	11.00	12.00 to 16.00
Union Trust, Stamford, Connecticut, Pl	1971	5061	1.00	12.00 to 16.00
				12.00 to 16.00
Alexandria National, Virginia, P	1972	8014	11.00	13.00 to 15.00
American National, Gadsden, Alabama, P	1972	8014	11.00	13.00 to 15.00
Bancohio Corporation, Columbus, Ohio, P	1972	8014	11.00	13.00 to 15.00
Bank Of Idaho, Boise, P	1972	8014	11.00	13.00 to 15.00
Central, Monroe, Louisiana, P	1972	8014	11.00	13.00 to 15.00
Citizens & Southern National, N.C., P	1972	8014	11.00	13.00 to 15.00
Citizens Fidelity Bank & Trust, Ky., P	1972	8014	11.00	13.00 to 15.00
Citizens National, Englewood, New Jersey, P	1972	8014	11.00	13.00 to 15.00
Commerce, Kansas City, Missouri, P	1972	8014	11.00	13.00 to 15.00
Commercial Security, Ogden, Utah, P	1972	8014	11.00	13.00 to 15.00
Concord National, New Hampshire, P	1972	8014	11.00	13.00 to 15.00
Connecticut Bank & Trust Co., Hartford, P	1972	8014	11.00	13.00 to 15.00
Continental, Philadelphia, Pa., P	1972	8014	11.00	13.00 to 15.00
Continental Illinois National, Chicago, P	1972	8014	11.00	13.00 to 15.00
Detroit Bank & Trust, Michigan, P	1972	8014	11.00	13.00 to 15.00
Farmers & Merchants, Huron, South Dakota, P	1972	8014	11.00	13.00 to 15.00
First Hawaiian, Honolulu, P	1972	8014	11.00	13.00 to 15.00
First National Bank & Trust, Fargo, N.D., P	1972	8014	11.00	13.00 to 15.00
First National, Amarillo, Texas, P	1972	8014	11.00	13.00 to 15.00
First National, Oregon, Portland, P	1972	8014	11.00	13.00 to 15.00
First National, Santa Fe, New Mexico, P	1972	8014	11.00	13.00 to 15.00
First National, Topeka, Kansas, P	1972	8014	11.00	13.00 to 15.00
First Wisconsin National, Milwaukee, P	1972	8014	11.00	13.00 to 15.00
Great Falls National, Montana, P	1972	8014	11.00	13.00 to 15.00
Greeley National, Greeley, Colorado, P	1972	8014	11.00	13.00 to 15.00
Hancock, Gulfport, Mississippi, P	1972	8014	11.00	13.00 to 15.00
Maine National, Portland, P	1972	8014	11.00	13.00 to 15.00
Manufacturers-Hanover Trust, New York, N.Y., P	1972	8014	11.00	13.00 to 15.00
Marquette National, Minneapolis, Minn., P	1972	8014	11.00	13.00 to 15.00
Maryland National, Baltimore, P	1972	8014	11.00	13.00 to 15.00
Milford Trust Co., Delaware, P	1972	8014	11.00	13.00 to 15.00
National Bank Of Alaska, Anchorage, P	1972	8014	11.00	13.00 to 15.00
National Bank Of Commerce, Seattle, Wash., P	1972	8014	11.00	13.00 to 15.00
National Of Tulsa, Oklahoma, P	1972	8014	11.00	13.00 to 15.00
North Carolina National, Charlotte, P	1972	8014	11.00	13.00 to 15.00
Northern Bank & Trust Co., Little Rock, Ark., P	1972	8014	11.00	13.00 to 15.00
Old Stone, Providence, Rhode Island, P	1972	8014	11.00	13.00 to 15.00
Peoples Bank & Trust, Cedar Rapids, Iowa, P	1972	8014	11.00	13.00 to 15.00
Security Bank & Trust, Vincennes, Indiana, P	1972	8014	11.00	13.00 to 15.00
Southern Arizona, Tucson, P	1972	8014	11.00	13.00 to 15.00
State Street Bank & Trust, Boston, Mass., P	1972	8014	11.00	13.00 to 15.00
Trust Co., Atlanta, Georgia, P	1972	8014	11.00	13.00 to 15.00
U.S.National Of Omaha, Nebraska, P	1972	8014	11.00	13.00 to 15.00
Union Planters National, Memphis, Tenn., P	1972	8014	11.00	13.00 to 15.00
United Banking Group, Miami Beach, Florida, P	1972	8014	11.00	13.00 to 15.00
Valley Of Nevada, Las Vegas, P	1972	8014	11.00	13.00 to 15.00
Vermont National, Brattleboro, Vt., P	1972	8014	11.00	13.00 to 15.00
Wells Fargo, San Francisco, California, P	1972	8014	11.00	13.00 to 15.00
Wheeling Dollar, West Virginia, P	1972	8014	11.00	13.00 to 15.00
Wyoming National, Casper, P	1972	8014	11.00	13.00 to 15.00

Alexandria National, Virginia, Pl	1972	Year	11.00	13.00 to 15.00
American National, Gadsden, Alabama, Pl	1972	Year	11.00	13.00 to 15.00
Bancohio Corporation, Columbus, Ohio, Pl	1972	Year	11.00	13.00 to 15.00
Bank Of Idaho, Boise, Pl	1972	Year	11.00	13.00 to 15.00
Central, Monroe, Louisiana, Pl	1972	Year	11.00	13.00 to 15.00
Citizens & Southern National, S.C., Pl	1972	Year	11.00	13.00 to 15.00
Citizens Fidelity Bank & Trust, Kentucky, Pl	1972	Year	11.00	13.00 to 15.00
Citizens National, Englewood, N.J., Pl	1972	Year	11.00	13.00 to 15.00
Commerce, Kansas City, Missouri, Pl	1972	Year	11.00	13.00 to 15.00
Commercial Security, Ogden, Utah, Pl	1972	Year	11.00	13.00 to 15.00
Concord National, New Hampshire, Pl	1972	Year	11.00	13.00 to 15.00
Connecticut Bank & Trust, Hartford, Pl	1972	Year	11.00	13.00 to 15.00
Continental, Philadelphia, Pa., Pl	1972	Year	11.00	13.00 to 15.00
Continental Illinois National, Chicago, Pl	1972	Year	11.00	13.00 to 15.00
Detroit Bank & Trust, Michigan, Pl	1972	Year	11.00	13.00 to 15.00
Farmers & Merchants, Huron, South Dakota, Pl	1972	Year	11.00	13.00 to 15.00
First Hawaiian, Honolulu, Pl	1972	Year	11.00	13.00 to 15.00
First National Bank & Trust, Fargo, N.D., Pl	1972	Year	11.00	13.00 to 15.00
First National Of Amarillo, Texas, Pl	1972	Year	11.00	13.00 to 15.00
First National Of Oregon, Portland, Pl	1972	Year	11.00	13.00 to 15.00
First National, Santa Fe, New Mexico, Pl	1972	Year	11.00	13.00 to 15.00
First National, Topeka, Kansas, Pl	1972	Year	11.00	13.00 to 15.00
First Wisconsin National, Milwaukee, Pl	1972	Year	11.00	13.00 to 15.00
Great Falls National, Montana, Pl	1972	Year	11.00	13.00 to 15.00
Greeley National, Colorado, Pl	1972	Year	11.00	13.00 to 15.00
Hancock, Gulfport, Mississippi, Pl	1972	Year	11.00	13.00 to 15.00
Maine National, Portland, Pl	1972	Year	11.00	13.00 to 15.00
Manufacturers-Hanover Trust, New York, N.Y., Pl	1972	Year	11.00	13.00 to 15.00
Marquette National, Minneapolis, Minn., Pl	1972	Year	11.00	13.00 to 15.00
Maryland National, Baltimore, Pl	1972	Year	11.00	13.00 to 15.00
Milford Trust, Delaware, Pl	1972	Year	11.00	13.00 to 15.00
National Of Alaska, Anchorage, Pl	1972	Year	11.00	13.00 to 15.00
National Of Commerce, Seattle, Wash., Pl	1972	Year	11.00	13.00 to 15.00
National Of Tulsa, Oklahoma, Pl	1972	Year	11.00	13.00 to 15.00
North Carolina National, Charlotte, Pl	1972	Year	11.00	13.00 to 15.00
Northern Bank & Trust, Little Rock, Ark., Pl	1972	Year	11.00	13.00 to 15.00
Old Stone, Providence, Rhode Island, Pl	1972	Year	11.00	13.00 to 15.00
Peoples Bank & Trust, Cedar Rapids, Iowa, Pl	1972	Year	11.00	13.00 to 15.00
Security Bank & Trust, Vincennes, Indiana, Pl	1972	Year	11.00	13.00 to 15.00
Southern Arizona, Tucson, Pl	1972	Year	11.00	13.00 to 15.00
State Street Bank & Trust, Boston, Mass., Pl	1972	Year	11.00	13.00 to 15.00
Trust Company, Atlanta, Georgia, Pl	1972	Year	11.00	13.00 to 15.00
U.S.National Of Omaha, Nebraska, Pl	1972	Year	11.00	13.00 to 15.00
Union Planters National Of Memphis, Tenn., Pl	1972	Year	11.00	13.00 to 15.00
United Banking Group, Miami Beach, Florida, Pl	1972	Year	11.00	13.00 to 15.00
Valley Of Nevada, Las Vegas, Pl	1972	Year	11.00	13.00 to 15.00
Vermont National, Brattleboro, Vt., Pl	1972	Year	11.00	13.00 to 15.00
Wells Fargo, San Francisco, California, Pl	1972	Year	11.00	13.00 to 15.00
Wheeling Dollar, West Virginia, Pl	1972	Year	11.00	13.00 to 15.00
Wyoming National, Casper, Pl	1972	Year	11.00	13.00 to 15.00
Bank Ingot Series, Set Of 50, Each	973	8014	11.00	11.00

Franklin Mint,
Father's Day, 1971,
Father & Child Walking

Franklin Mint Ingots, Centennial Cars, 1,000 Grains Silver

Centennial Cars, Set Of 100, Each	1974	YEA	3.50	5.00

Franklin Mint Ingots, Christmas, 1,000 Grains Silver

The Skaters, Lauser, P*	1970	28897	12.00	160.00 to 220.00
Sleighing Scene, Schroeder, P*	1971	47912	12.00	50.00 to 75.00
Hauling In The Yule Log, Ferrell, P*	1972	Year	12.00	26.50 to 40.00
The Carolers, Schule, P*	1973	Year	13.50	13.50 to 16.00
Christmas	1974	YEA	17.50	17.50 to 19.00

Franklin Mint Ingots, Dow-Jones Commemorative, 1,000 Grains Silver

New York Stock Exchange, D, Pl	1973	1092	100.00	100.00

Franklin Mint, Father's Day,
1972, Carrying Child

Franklin Mint Ingots, Father's day, 1,000 Grains Silver

Father & Child Walking, Lauser, P*	1971	10259	12.50	100.00 to 175.00
Carrying Child, Ponter, Lucite Block, P*	1972	5375	18.00	50.00 to 125.00
Carrying Child, Ponter, Presentation Case, P	1972	10510	12.50	50.00 to 125.00
Father's Day	1973	YEA		25.00

Father's Day	1974	YEA		22.50

Franklin Mint Ingots, Great Flags of America, 1,000 Grains Silver

California Republic, D, P	1972-1974	4892	13.50	16.00 to 20.00
Continental Colors, D, P	1972-1974	4892	13.50	16.00 to 20.00
France, D, P	1972-1974	4892	13.50	16.00 to 20.00
Great Britain, D, P	1972-1974	4892	13.50	16.00 to 20.00
Hawaii, D, P	1972-1974	4892	13.50	16.00 to 20.00
Mexico, D, P	1972-1974	4892	13.50	16.00 to 20.00
Netherlands, D, P	1972-1974	4892	13.50	16.00 to 20.00
Republic Of West Florida, D, P	1972-1974	4892	13.50	16.00 to 20.00
Russian Empire, D, P	1972-1974	4892	13.50	16.00 to 20.00
Spain, D, P	1972-1974	4892	13.50	16.00 to 20.00
Sweden, D, P	1972-1974	4892	13.50	16.00 to 20.00
Texas Republic, D, P	1972-1974	4892	13.50	16.00 to 20.00
1st Confederate, D, P	1972-1974	4892	13.50	16.00 to 20.00
1st Official Confederate, D, P	1972-1974	4892	13.50	16.00 to 20.00
2nd Official Confederate, D, P	1972-1974	4892	13.50	16.00 to 20.00
1st U.S., D, P	1972-1974	4892	13.50	16.00 to 20.00
2nd U.S., D, P	1972-1974	4892	13.50	16.00 to 20.00
3rd U.S., D, P	1972-1974	4892	13.50	16.00 to 20.00
4th U.S., D, P	1972-1974	4892	13.50	16.00 to 20.00
5th U.S., D, P	1972-1974	4892	13.50	16.00 to 20.00
6th U.S., D, P	1972-1974	4892	13.50	16.00 to 20.00
7th U.S., D, P	1972-1974	4892	13.50	16.00 to 20.00
8th U.S., D, P	1972-1974	4892	13.50	16.00 to 20.00
9th U.S., D, P	1972-1974	4892	13.50	16.00 to 20.00
10th U.S., D, P	1972-1974	4892	13.50	16.00 to 20.00
11th U.S., D, P	1972-1974	4892	13.50	16.00 to 20.00
12th U.S., D, P	1972-1974	4892	13.50	16.00 to 20.00
13th U.S., D, P	1972-1974	4892	13.50	16.00 to 20.00
14th U.S., D, P	1972-1974	4892	13.50	16.00 to 20.00
15th U.S., D, P	1972-1974	4892	13.50	16.00 to 20.00
16th U.S., D, P	1972-1974	4892	13.50	16.00 to 20.00
17th U.S., D, P	1972-1974	4892	13.50	16.00 to 20.00
18th U.S., D, P	1972-1974	4892	13.50	16.00 to 20.00
19th U.S., D, P	1972-1974	4892	13.50	16.00 to 20.00
20th U.S., D, P	1972-1974	4892	13.50	16.00 to 20.00
21th U.S., D, P	1972-1974	4892	13.50	16.00 to 20.00
22nd U.S., D, P	1972-1974	4892	13.50	16.00 to 20.00
23rd U.S., D, P	1972-1974	4892	13.50	16.00 to 20.00
24th U.S., D, P	1972-1974	4892	13.50	16.00 to 20.00
25th U.S., D, P	1972-1974	4892	13.50	16.00 to 20.00
26th U.S., D, P	1972-1974	4892	13.50	16.00 to 20.00
27th U.S., D, P	1972-1974	4892	13.50	16.00 to 20.00
California Republic, D, Pl	1972-1974	Year	13.50	13.50
Continental Colors, D, Pl	1972-1974	Year	13.50	13.50
France, D, Pl	1972-1974	Year	13.50	13.50
Great Britain, D, Pl	1972-1974	Year	13.50	13.50
Hawaii, D, Pl	1972-1974	Year	13.50	13.50
Mexico, D, Pl	1972-1974	Year	13.50	13.50
Netherlands, D, Pl	1972-1974	Year	13.50	13.50
Republic Of West Florida, D, Pl	1972-1974	Year	13.50	13.50
Russian Empire, D, Pl	1972-1974	Year	13.50	13.50
Spain, D, Pl	1972-1974	Year	13.50	13.50
Sweden, D, Pl	1972-1974	Year	13.50	13.50
Texas Republic, D, Pl	1972-1974	Year	13.50	13.50
1st Confederate, D, Pl	1972-1974	Year	13.50	13.50
1st Official Confederate, D, Pl	1972-1974	Year	13.50	13.50
2nd Official Confederate, D, Pl	1972-1974	Year	13.50	13.50
1st U.S., D, Pl	1972-1974	Year	13.50	13.50
2nd U.S., D, Pl	1972-1974	Year	13.50	13.50
3rd U.S., D, Pl	1972-1974	Year	13.50	13.50
4th U.S., D, Pl	1972-1974	Year	13.50	13.50
5th U.S., D, Pl	1972-1974	Year	13.50	13.50
6th U.S., D, Pl	1972-1974	Year	13.50	13.50
7th U.S., D, Pl	1972-1974	Year	13.50	13.50
8th U.S., D, Pl	1972-1974	Year	13.50	13.50
9th U.S., D, Pl	1972-1974	Year	13.50	13.50
10th U.S., D, Pl	1972-1974	Year	13.50	13.50

11th U.S., D, Pl	1972-1974	Year	13.50	13.50
12th U.S., D, Pl	1972-1974	Year	13.50	13.50
13th U.S., D, Pl	1972-1974	Year	13.50	13.50
14th U.S., D, Pl	1972-1974	Year	13.50	13.50
15th U.S., D, Pl	1972-1974	Year	13.50	13.50
16th U.S., D, Pl	1972-1974	Year	13.50	13.50
17th U.S., D, Pl	1972-1974	Year	13.50	13.50
18th U.S., D, Pl	1972-1974	Year	13.50	13.50
19th U.S., D, Pl	1972-1974	Year	13.50	13.50
20th U.S., D, Pl	1972-1974	Year	13.50	13.50
21th U.S., D, Pl	1972-1974	Year	13.50	13.50
22nd U.S., D, Pl	1972-1974	Year	13.50	13.50
23rd U.S., D, Pl	1972-1974	Year	13.50	13.50
24th U.S., D, Pl	1972-1974	Year	13.50	13.50
25th U.S., D, Pl	1972-1974	Year	13.50	13.50
26th U.S., D, Pl	1972-1974	Year	13.50	13.50
27th U.S., D, Pl	1972-1974	Year	13.50	13.50

Franklin Mint Ingots, Great Sailing Ships of History, 1,500 Grains Silver

Great Sailing Ships, Set Of 50, Each	1973	Year	25.00	25.00

Franklin Mint Ingots, Historic, 10, 000 Grains Silver

Benjamin Franklin, Roberts, M	1970	7452	105.00	300.00

Franklin Mint Ingots, Norman Rockwell's Fondest Memories, 1, 500 Grains Silver

Boy Scouts Of America, P	1973	Year	25.00	35.00 to 45.00
Carving The Turkey, P	1973	Year	25.00	35.00 to 45.00
Checkers At The General Store, P	1973	Year	25.00	35.00 to 45.00
Doctor Visiting Lady, Examining Doll, P	1973	Year	25.00	35.00 to 45.00
Fishing, P	1973	Year	25.00	35.00 to 45.00
Grandma Knitting, Talking To Child, P	1973	Year	25.00	35.00 to 45.00
Sled Riding, P	1973	Year	25.00	35.00 to 45.00
The Hair Cut, P	1973	Year	25.00	35.00 to 45.00
The Swimming Hole, P	1973	Year	25.00	35.00 to 45.00
Valentine's Day, P	1973	Year	25.00	35.00 to 45.00

Franklin Mint Ingots, Presidential, 1,000 Grains Silver

Adams, John, Faulkner, P	1972-1973	2360	11.35	11.35
Adams, John Quincy, Faulkner, P	1972-1973	2360	11.35	11.35
Arthur, Chester, Faulkner, P	1972-1973	2360	11.35	11.35
Buchanan, James, Faulkner, P	1972-1973	2360	11.35	11.35
Cleveland, Grover, Faulkner, P	1972-1973	2360	11.35	11.35
Coolidge, Calvin, Faulkner, P	1972-1973	2360	11.35	11.35
Eisenhower, Dwight D., Faulkner, P	1972-1973	2360	11.35	11.35
Fillmore, Millard, Faulkner, P	1972-1973	2360	11.35	11.35
Garfield, James, Faulkner, P	1972-1973	2360	11.35	11.35
Grant, Ulysses S., Faulkner, P	1972-1973	2360	11.35	11.35
Harding, Warren, Faulkner, P	1972-1973	2360	11.35	11.35
Harrison, Benjamin, Faulkner, P	1972-1973	2360	11.35	11.35
Harrison, William Henry, Faulkner, P	1972-1973	2360	11.35	11.35
Hayes, Rutherford, Faulkner, P	1972-1973	2360	11.35	11.35
Hoover, Herbert, Faulkner, P	1972-1973	2360	11.35	11.35
Jackson, Andrew, Faulkner, P	1972-1973	2360	11.35	11.35
Jefferson, Thomas, Faulkner, P	1972-1973	2360	11.35	11.35
Johnson, Andrew, Faulkner, P	1972-1973	2360	11.35	11.35
Johnson, Lyndon B., Faulkner, P	1972-1973	2360	11.35	11.35
Kennedy, John F., Faulkner, P	1972-1973	2360	11.35	11.35
Lincoln, Abraham, Faulkner, P	1972-1973	2360	11.35	11.35
Madison, James, Faulkner, P	1972-1973	2360	11.35	11.35
McKinley, William, Faulkner, P	1972-1973	2360	11.35	11.35
Monroe, James, Faulkner, P	1972-1973	2360	11.35	11.35
Nixon, Richard M., Faulkner, P	1972-1973	2360	11.35	11.35
Pierce, Franklin, Faulkner, P	1972-1973	2360	11.35	11.35
Polk, James Knox, Faulkner, P	1972-1973	2360	11.35	11.35
Roosevelt, Franklin D., Faulkner, P	1972-1973	2360	11.35	11.35
Roosevelt, Theodore, Faulkner, P	1972-1973	2360	11.35	11.35
Taft, William H., Faulkner, P	1972-1973	2360	11.35	11.35
Taylor, Zachary, Faulkner, P	1972-1973	2360	11.35	11.35
Truman, Harry S., Faulkner, P	1972-1973	2360	11.35	11.35
Tyler, John, Faulkner, P	1972-1973	2360	11.35	11.35
Van Buren, Martin, Faulkner, P	1972-1973	2360	11.35	11.35

Washington, George, Faulkner, P	1972-1973	2360	11.35	11.35
Wilson, Woodrow, Faulkner, P	1972-1973	2360	11.35	11.35
Adams, John, Faulkner, Pl	1972-1974	Year	11.35	11.35
Adams, John Quincy, Faulkner, Pl	1972-1974	Year	11.35	11.35
Arthur, Chester, Faulkner, Pl	1972-1974	Year	11.35	11.35
Buchanan, James, Faulkner, Pl	1972-1974	Year	11.35	11.35
Cleveland, Grover, Faulkner, Pl	1972-1974	Year	11.35	11.35
Coolidge, Calvin, Faulkner, Pl	1972-1974	Year	11.35	11.35
Eisenhower, Dwight D., Faulkner, Pl	1972-1974	Year	11.35	11.35
Fillmore, Millard, Faulkner, Pl	1972-1974	Year	11.35	11.35
Garfield, James, Faulkner, Pl	1972-1974	Year	11.35	11.35
Grant, Ulysses S., Faulkner, Pl	1972-1974	Year	11.35	11.35
Harding, Warren, Faulkner, Pl	1972-1974	Year	11.35	11.35
Harrison, Benjamin, Faulkner, Pl	1972-1974	Year	11.35	11.35
Harrison, William Henry, Faulkner, Pl	1972-1974	Year	11.35	11.35
Hayes, Rutherford, Faulkner, Pl	1972-1974	Year	11.35	11.35
Hoover, Herbert, Faulkner, Pl	1972-1974	Year	11.35	11.35
Jackson, Andrew, Faulkner, Pl	1972-1974	Year	11.35	11.35
Jefferson, Thomas, Faulkner, Pl	1972-1974	Year	11.35	11.35
Johnson, Andrew, Faulkner, Pl	1972-1974	Year	11.35	11.35
Johnson, Lyndon B., Faulkner, Pl	1972-1974	Year	11.35	11.35
Kennedy, John F., Faulkner, Pl	1972-1974	Year	11.35	11.35
Lincoln, Abraham, Faulkner, Pl	1972-1974	Year	11.35	11.35
Madison, James, Faulkner, Pl	1972-1974	Year	11.35	11.35
McKinley, William, Faulkner, Pl	1972-1974	Year	11.35	11.35
Monroe, James, Faulkner, Pl	1972-1974	Year	11.35	11.35
Nixon, Richard M., Faulkner, P	1972-1974	Year	11.35	11.35
Pierce, Franklin, Faulkner, Pl	1972-1974	Year	11.35	11.35
Polk, James Knox, Faulkner, Pl	1972-1974	Year	11.35	11.35
Roosevelt, Franklin D., Faulkner, Pl	1972-1974	Year	11.35	11.35
Roosevelt, Theodore, Faulkner, Pl	1972-1974	Year	11.35	11.35
Taft, William H., Faulkner, Pl	1972-1974	Year	11.35	11.35
Taylor, Zachary, Faulkner, Pl 1972	1974	Year	11.35	11.35
Truman, Harry S., Faulkner, Pl	1972-1974	Year	11.35	11.35
Tyler, John, Faulkner, Pl	1972-1974	Year	11.35	11.35
Van Buren, Martin, Faulkner, Pl	1972-1974	Year	11.35	11.35
Washington, George, Faulkner, Pl	1972-1974	Year	11.35	11.35
Wilson, Woodrow, Faulkner, Pl	1972-1974	Year	11.35	11.35

Franklin Mint Ingots, Presidential, 5,000 Grains Silver

Adams, John, Faulkner, P	1972-1974	906	44.50	44.50
Adams, John Quincy, Faulkner, P	1972-1974	906	44.50	44.50
Arthur, Chester, Faulkner, P	1972-1974	906	44.50	44.50
Buchanan, James, Faulkner, P	1972-1974	906	44.50	44.50
Cleveland, Grover, Faulkner, P	1972-1974	906	44.50	44.50
Coolidge, Calvin, Faulkner, P	1972-1974	906	44.50	44.50
Eisenhower, Dwight D., Faulkner, P	1972-1974	906	44.50	44.50
Fillmore, Millard, Faulkner, P	1972-1974	906	44.50	44.50
Garfield, James, Faulkner, P	1972-1974	906	44.50	44.50
Grant, Ulysses S., Faulkner, P	1972-1974	906	44.50	44.50
Harding, Warren, Faulkner, P	1972-1974	906	44.50	44.50
Harrison, Benjamin, Faulkner, P	1972-1974	906	44.50	44.50
Harrison, William Henry, Faulkner, P	1972-1974	906	44.50	44.50
Hayes, Rutherford, Faulkner, P	1972-1974	906	44.50	44.50
Hoover, Herbert, Faulkner, P	1972-1974	906	44.50	44.50
Jackson, Andrew, Faulkner, P	1972-1974	906	44.50	44.50
Jefferson, Thomas, Faulkner, P	1972-1974	906	44.50	44.50
Johnson, Andrew, Faulkner, P	1972-1974	906	44.50	44.50
Johnson, Lyndon B., Faulkner, P	1972-1974	906	44.50	44.50
Kennedy, John F., Faulkner, P	1972-1974	906	44.50	44.50
Lincoln, Abraham, Faulkner, P	1972-1974	906	44.50	44.50
Madison, James, Faulkner, P	1972-1974	906	44.50	44.50
McKinley, William, Faulkner, P	1972-1974	906	44.50	44.50
Monroe, James, Faulkner, P	1972-1974	906	44.50	44.50
Nixon, Richard M., Faulkner, P	1972-1974	906	44.50	44.50
Pierce, Franklin, Faulkner, P	1972-1974	906	44.50	44.50
Polk, James Knox, Faulkner, P	1972-1974	906	44.50	44.50
Roosevelt, Franklin D., Faulkner, P	1972-1974	906	44.50	44.50
Roosevelt, Theodore, Faulkner, P	1972-1974	906	44.50	44.50
Taft, William H., Faulkner, P	1972-1974	906	44.50	44.50
Taylor, Zachary, Faulkner, P	1972-1974	906	44.50	44.50

Truman, Harry S., Faulkner, P	1972-1974	906	44.50	44.50
Tyler, John, Faulkner, P	1972-1974	906	44.50	44.50
Van Buren, Martin, Faulkner, P	1972-1974	906	44.50	44.50
Washington, George, Faulkner, P	1972-1974	906	44.50	44.50
Wilson, Woodrow, Faulkner, P	1972-1974	906	44.50	44.50
Adams, John, Faulkner, Pl	1972-1975	Year	44.50	44.50
Adams, John Quincy, Faulkner, Pl	1972-1975	Year	44.50	44.50
Arthur, Chester, Faulkner, Pl	1972-1975	Year	44.50	44.50
Buchanan, James, Faulkner, Pl	1972-1975	Year	44.50	44.50
Cleveland, Grover, Faulkner, Pl	1972-1975	Year	44.50	44.50
Coolidge, Calvin, Faulkner, Pl	1972-1975	Year	44.50	44.50
Eisenhower, Dwight D., Faulkner, Pl	1972-1975	Year	44.50	44.50
Fillmore, Millard, Faulkner, Pl	1972-1975	Year	44.50	44.50
Garfield, James, Faulkner, Pl	1972-1975	Year	44.50	44.50
Grant, Ulysses S., Faulkner, Pl	1972-1975	Year	44.50	44.50
Harding, Warren, Faulkner, Pl	1972-1975	Year	44.50	44.50
Harrison, Benjamin, Faulkner, Pl	1972-1975	Year	44.50	44.50
Harrison, William Henry, Faulkner, Pl	1972-1975	Year	44.50	44.50
Hayes, Rutherford, Faulkner, Pl	1972-1975	Year	44.50	44.50
Hoover, Herbert, Faulkner, Pl	1972-1975	Year	44.50	44.50
Jackson, Andrew, Faulkner, Pl	1972-1975	Year	44.50	44.50
Jefferson, Thomas, Faulkner, Pl	1972-1975	Year	44.50	44.50
Johnson, Andrew, Faulkner, Pl	1972-1975	Year	44.50	44.50
Johnson, Lyndon B., Faulkner, Pl	1972-1975	Year	44.50	44.50
Kennedy, John F., Faulkner, Pl	1972-1975	Year	44.50	44.50
Lincoln, Abraham, Faulkner, Pl	1972-1975	Year	44.50	44.50
Madison, James, Faulkner, Pl	1972-1975	Year	44.50	44.50
McKinley, William, Faulkner, Pl	1972-1975	Year	44.50	44.50
Monroe, James, Faulkner, Pl	1972-1975	Year	44.50	44.50
Nixon, Richard M., Faulkner, Pl	1972-1975	Year	44.50	44.50
Pierce, Franklin, Faulkner, Pl	1972-1975	Year	44.50	44.50
Polk, James Knox, Faulkner, Pl	1972-1975	Year	44.50	44.50
Roosevelt, Franklin D., Faulkner, Pl	1972-1975	Year	44.50	44.50
Roosevelt, Theodore, Faulkner, Pl	1972-1975	Year	44.50	44.50
Taft, William H., Faulkner, Pl	1972-1975	Year	44.50	44.50
Taylor, Zachary, Faulkner, Pl	1972-1975	Year	44.50	44.50
Truman, Harry S., Faulkner, Pl	1972-1975	Year	44.50	44.50
Tyler, John, Faulkner, Pl	1972-1975	Year	44.50	44.50
Van Buren, Martin, Faulkner, Pl	1972-1975	Year	44.50	44.50
Washington, George, Faulkner, Pl	1972-1975	Year	44.50	44.50
Wilson, Woodrow, Faulkner, Pl	1972-1975	Year	44.50	44.50

Franklin Mint Ingots, Ship, 1,000 Grains Silver

M.S.Boheme, P	1971	4277	11.00	14.00 to 15.00
M.S.Europa, P	1971	4277	11.00	14.00 to 15.00
M.S.Gripsholm, P	1971	4277	11.00	14.00 to 15.00
M.S.Kungsholm, P	1971	4277	11.00	14.00 to 15.00
M.S.Mermoz, P	1971	4277	11.00	14.00 to 15.00
M.S.Renaissance, P	1971	4277	11.00	14.00 to 15.00
M.S.Sagafjord, P	1971	4277	11.00	14.00 to 15.00
M.S.Sea Venture, P	1971	4277	11.00	14.00 to 15.00
M.S.Skyward, P	1971	4277	11.00	14.00 to 15.00
M.S.Song Of Norway, P	1971	4277	11.00	14.00 to 15.00
M.S.Southward, P	1971	4277	11.00	14.00 to 15.00
M.S.Starward, P	1971	4277	11.00	14.00 to 15.00
M.S.Sunward, P	1971	4277	11.00	14.00 to 15.00
M.S.Victoria, P	1971	4277	11.00	14.00 to 15.00
M.V.Cunard Adventurer, P	1971	4277	11.00	14.00 to 15.00
M.V.Freeport, P	1971	4277	11.00	14.00 to 15.00
R.H.M.S.Amerikanis, P	1971	4277	11.00	14.00 to 15.00
R.H.M.S.Atlantis, P	1971	4277	11.00	14.00 to 15.00
R.M.S.Queen Elizabeth 2, P	1971	4277	11.00	14.00 to 15.00
S.S.Arcadia, P	1971	4277	11.00	14.00 to 15.00
S.S.Ariadna, P	1971	4277	11.00	14.00 to 15.00
S.S.Canberra, P	1971	4277	11.00	14.00 to 15.00
S.S.Cristoforo Colombo, P	1971	4277	11.00	14.00 to 15.00
S.S.Empress Of Canada, P	1971	4277	11.00	14.00 to 15.00
S.S.France, P	1971	4277	11.00	14.00 to 15.00
S.S.Homeric, P	1971	4277	11.00	14.00 to 15.00
S.S.Iberia, P	1971	4277	11.00	14.00 to 15.00
S.S.Leonardo Da Vinci, P	1971	4277	11.00	14.00 to 15.00

S.S.Mariposa, P	1971	4277	11.00	14.00 to 15.00
S.S.Michelangelo, P	1971	4277	11.00	14.00 to 15.00
S.S.Montery, P	1971	4277	11.00	14.00 to 15.00
S.S.New Bahama Star, P	1971	4277	11.00	14.00 to 15.00
S.S.Nieuw Amsterdam, P	1971	4277	11.00	14.00 to 15.00
S.S.Oceanic, P	1971	4277	11.00	14.00 to 15.00
S.S.Oriana, P	1971	4277	11.00	14.00 to 15.00
S.S.Oronsay, P	1971	4277	11.00	14.00 to 15.00
S.S.Orsova, P	1971	4277	11.00	14.00 to 15.00
S.S.President Cleveland, P	1971	4277	11.00	14.00 to 15.00
S.S.President Wilson, P	1971	4277	11.00	14.00 to 15.00
S.S.Raffaello, P	1971	4277	11.00	14.00 to 15.00
S.S.Rotterdam, P	1971	4277	11.00	14.00 to 15.00
S.S.Statendam, P	1971	4277	11.00	14.00 to 15.00
T.S.Bremen, P	1971	4277	11.00	14.00 to 15.00
T.S.Carls C., P	1971	4277	11.00	14.00 to 15.00
T.S.Federico C., P	1971	4277	11.00	14.00 to 15.00
T.S.Flavia, P	1971	4277	11.00	14.00 to 15.00
T.S.Hamburg, P	1971	4277	11.00	14.00 to 15.00
T.S.Hanseatic, P	1971	4277	11.00	14.00 to 15.00
T.S.S.Olympia, P	1971	4277	11.00	14.00 to 15.00
T.S.S.Queen Anna Maria, P	1971	4277	11.00	14.00 to 15.00
M.S.Boheme, Pl	1971	Year	11.00	Unknown
M.S.Europa, Pl	1971	Year	11.00	Unknown
M.S.Gripsholm, Pl	1971	Year	11.00	Unknown
M.S.Kungsholm, Pl	1971	Year	11.00	Unknown
M.S.Mermoz, Pl	1971	Year	11.00	Unknown
M.S.Renaissance, Pl	1971	Year	11.00	Unknown
M.S.Sagafijord, Pl	1971	Year	11.00	Unknown
M.S.Sea Venture, Pl	1971	Year	11.00	Unknown
M.S.Skyward, Pl	1971	Year	11.00	Unknown
M.S.Song Of Norway, Pl	1971	Year	11.00	Unknown
M.S.Southward, Pl	1971	Year	11.00	Unknown
M.S.Starward, Pl	1971	Year	11.00	Unknown
M.S.Sunward, Pl	1971	Year	11.00	Unknown
M.S.Victoria, Pl	1971	Year	11.00	Unknown
M.V.Cunard Adventurer, Pl	1971	Year	11.00	Unknown
M.V.Freeport, Pl	1971	Year	11.00	Unknown
R.H.M.S.Amerikanis, Pl	1971	Year	11.00	Unknown
R.H.M.S.Atlantis, Pl	1971	Year	11.00	Unknown
R.M.S.Queen Elizabeth 2, Pl	1971	Year	11.00	Unknown
S.S.Arcadia, Pl	1971	Year	11.00	Unknown
S.S.Ariadne, Pl	1971	Year	11.00	Unknown
S.S.Canberra, Pl	1971	Year	11.00	Unknown
S.S.Cristoforo Colombo, Pl	1971	Year	11.00	Unknown
S.S.Empress Of Canada, Pl	1971	Year	11.00	Unknown
S.S.France, Pl	1971	Year	11.00	Unknown
S.S.Homeric, Pl	1971	Year	11.00	Unknown
S.S.Iberia, Pl	1971	Year	11.00	Unknown
S.S.Leonardo Da Vinci, Pl	1971	Year	11.00	Unknown
S.S.Mariposa, Pl	1971	Year	11.00	Unknown
S.S.Michelangelo, Pl	1971	Year	11.00	Unknown
S.S.Monterey, Pl	1971	Year	11.00	Unknown
S.S.New Bahama Star, Pl	1971	Year	11.00	Unknown
S.S.Nieuw Amsterdam, Pl	1971	Year	11.00	Unknown
S.S.Oceanic, Pl	1971	Year	11.00	Unknown
S.S.Oriana, Pl	1971	Year	11.00	Unknown
S.S.Oronsay, Pl	1971	Year	11.00	Unknown
S.S.Orsova, Pl	1971	Year	11.00	Unknown
S.S.President Cleveland, Pl	1971	Year	11.00	Unknown
S.S.President Wilson, Pl	1971	Year	11.00	Unknown
S.S.Raffaello, Pl	1971	Year	11.00	Unknown
S.S.Rotterdam, Pl	1971	Year	11.00	Unknown
S.S.Statendam, Pl	1971	Year	11.00	Unknown
T.S.Bremen, Pl	1971	Year	11.00	Unknown
T.S.Carla C., Pl	1971	Year	11.00	Unknown
T.S.Flavia, Pl	1971	Year	11.00	Unknown
T.S.Federico C., Pl	1971	Year	11.00	Unknown
T.S.Hamburg, Pl	1971	Year	11.00	Unknown
T.S.Hanseatic, Pl	1971	Year	11.00	Unknown
T.S.S.Olympia, Pl	1971	Year	11.00	Unknown

T.S.S.Queen Anna Maria, Pl	1971	Year	11.00	Unknown

Franklin Mint Ingots, Tenth Anniv. of America in Space, 1,000

Grains Silver

Eagle Soaring Through Space, Lauser, Pl	1971	37528	12.50	54.50 to 110.00

Garden State Mint Silver Bars

Energy Crisis	1974	600	19.95	19.95
Gershwin, George	1974	1000	18.95	18.95
Shrinking Dollar	1973	3000	17.50	17.50

Geneva Coinage Silver Ingots, Picasso

Dove Of Peace	1974	5000	26.95	26.95
Face Of Peace	1974	5000	26.95	26.95
Peace I	1974	5000	26.95	26.95
Peace II	1974	5000	26.95	26.95
Picasso Series, Gold On Silver, Set Of 4	1974	500	149.95	149.95

George's Coins Silver Bars

Labor Day, Lunch Box	1973	5000		12.50 to 15.00

Gerlach's Coin Shop Silver Bars

Baseball World Series	1973		25.00 to 30.00
Halloween, Witch	1973		25.00 to 30.00

Gorham Silver Co., of Providence, Rhode Island, was founded in 1831. Crystal and china were added in 1970. The first limited edition item, a silver Christmas ornament, was introduced in 1970. Limited edition porcelain plates were issued in 1971. Ingots and medals were first made by the Gorham Mint division in 1973.

See listing for Gorham in Figurine, Plate, and Medal sections

Gorham Mint Silver Ingots

Bicentennial, Betsy Ross	1973	1000	65.00 to 100.00
Bicentennial, Minute Man	1973	10000	12.50 to 16.50
Natchez Paddle Wheeler	1973	10000	12.50 to 16.50

Great Lakes Mint Silver Bars

Cent	1973	10000	4.75	4.75 to 5.00
Christmas	1973		4.75	4.75 to 5.00
Good Luck	1973	13000	4.75	4.75 to 6.50
Great Lakes Mint	1973			4.75 to 5.25
Halloween	1973		4.75	4.75 to 5.25
Happy Birthday	1973		4.75	4.75 to 5.25
High Wheeler, 1873-1973	1973	10000	4.75	4.75 to 5.00
Israel, Map & Flag	1973		4.75	5.00
Labor Day	1973	21635	4.75	4.75 to 5.25
New Years	1974		4.75	4.75 to 5.00
Ten Commandments	1973		4.75	4.75 to 5.00
Texas Rangers, 1823-1973	1973	10000	4.75	4.75 to 5.00
Valentine's Day	1974		4.95	4.95

Great Lakes Mint Silver Bars, Greek God

Apollo & Artemus	1973	10000	4.75	4.75 to 5.00
Athena	1973	10000	4.75	4.75 to 5.00
Janus	1973	10000	4.75	4.75 to 5.00
Mars	1973	10000	4.75	4.75 to 5.00
Zeus	1973	10000	4.75	4.75 to 5.00

Greatest Leaders of World War II Ingots, see Lincoln Mint

Greek God bars, see Great Lakes Mint

Green Star Mint Silver Bars

Freedom For All	1974	10000	6.95	6.95

Hamilton Mint of Arlington Heights, Illinois, is a private mint. Limited edition gold and silver plates and medallions were introduced in 1972. A serial number is inscribed on the back of each plate. When an edition is completed, the die is destroyed. Limited edition ingots were first made in 1972.

See listing for Hamilton Mint in Plate and Medal sections

Hamilton Mint Silver Ingots

Christmas	1970			175.00 to 195.00
Christmas	1973	10000	12.50	12.50
Christmas, Gold Over Silver	1973	5000	17.50	17.50

International Numismatic
Agency, Babe Ruth

International Numismatic
Agency, Charles Lindbergh

International Numismatic Agency,
Marilyn Monroe

Pilgrims' Landing	1973	15000	5.50	5.50
Prospector	1973	10000		10.00
Prospector, Gold Over Silver	1973	5000	17.50	17.50
San Francisco Cable Car	1973	5000		5.50
Thanksgiving	1972			60.00 to 65.00

Hamilton Mint Silver Ingots, America the Beautiful

American Eagle	1974	10000	7.95	7.95
American Eagle, Gold Over Silver	1974	5000	12.50	12.50
American Farm	1974	10000	7.95	7.95
American Farm, Gold Over Silver	1974	5000	12.50	12.50
Everglades	1974	10000	7.95	7.95
Everglades, Gold Over Silver	1974	5000	12.50	12.50
Grand Canyon	1974	10000	7.95	7.95
Grand Canyon, Gold Over Silver	1974	5000	12.50	12.50
Maine Seaport	1974	10000	7.95	7.95
Maine Seaport, Gold Over Silver	1974	5000	12.50	12.50

Hamilton Mint Silver Ingots, America's Greatest Events

Declaration Of Independence	1974	10000	7.95	7.95
Declaration Of Independence, Gold Over Silver	1974	10000	12.50	12.50
Gettysburg Address	1974	10000	7.95	7.95
Gettysburg Address, Gold Over Silver	1974	5000	12.50	12.50
Star-Spangled Banner	1974	10000	7.95	7.95
Star-Spangled Banner, Gold Over Silver	1974	5000	12.50	12.50
Step On The Moon	1974	10000	7.95	7.95
Step On The Moon, Gold Over Silver	1974	5000	12.50	12.50
Transcontinental Railroad	1974	10000	7.95	7.95
Transcontinental Railroad, Gold Over Silver	1974	5000	12.50	12.50

Hamilton Mint Silver Ingots, Our Greatest Americans

Edison, Thomas	1973	10000	7.95	7.95
Eisenhower, Dwight D.	1973	10000	7.95	7.95
Kennedy, John F.	1973	10000	7.95	7.95
Lincoln, Abraham	1973	10000	7.95	7.95
MacArthur, Douglas	1973	10000	7.95	7.95

Hamilton Mint Silver Ingots, Wonders of America

Delta Queen	1972	15000	5.50	5.50
Golden Gate Bridge	1973	15000	5.50	5.50
Mt. Rushmore	1973	15000	5.50	5.50
Old Faithful	1973	15000	5.50	5.50
Pikes Peak	1973	15000	5.50	5.50
Statue Of Liberty	1973	15000	5.50	5.50
Stone Mountain	1973	15000	5.50	5.50

Hartford Mint Silver Bars

Kohoutek	1974		15.00	15.00

Hepsley Silver Bars

Imperial Russian Seal	1973	10000	12.50	12.50
Texas Ranger	1973	10000	15.00	12.50 to 15.00

Heritage House Silver Bars

Bicentennial, 200 Years Of Independence	1973			5.00 to 7.00

Hollywood Years Silver Bars

Horror Classics, Set Of 12	1974	1500	200.00	200.00

*The International Numismatic Agency of New York City has designed
and marketed limited edition art medals since 1962. Many of the medals are
produced by Medallic Art Company of Danbury, Connecticut. Silver
bars were introduced in 1973.*

See listing for International Numismatic in Medal section

International Numismatic Agency Silver Bars, Folk Heroes

Babe Ruth	1973	10000	12.50	12.50
Charles Lindbergh	1973	10000	12.50	12.50
Marilyn Monroe	1973	10000	12.50	12.50

International Numismatic Agency Silver Bars, Super Heroes

Batman	1974	7500	15.00	15.00
Flash Gordon	1974	7500	15.00	15.00
Mandrake The Magician	1974	7500	15.00	15.00
Superman	1974	7500	15.00	15.00
The Phantom	1974	7500	15.00	15.00

Wonder Woman	1974	7500	15.00	15.00

International Silver Company of Meriden, Connecticut, was incorporated by a group of New England silversmiths in 1898. The company makes a large variety of silver and silver plated wares. Limited edition pewter and silver plates were first made in 1972.

See listing for International Silver Company in Plate section

International Silver Company Bank Ingots

Liberty Bank Note, 1854, Sterling*	1973	7500	150.00	150.00

International Silver Ingot Company Silver Bars

Lovable Pandas	1974		6.95	6.95
Poodle & Pussycat	1974	2500	15.00	15.00
Raggedy Ann & Andy	1974		6.95	6.95

J. S. Love Silver Bars

Grandpa	1974	10000	5.25	5.25
Tennis Centennial	1973	2500		12.00 to 13.00

J. S. Love Silver Bars, Zodiac

Aquarius	1973	10000	12.50	12.50
Aries	1973	10000	12.50	12.50
Cancer	1973	10000	12.50	12.50
Capricorn	1973	10000	12.50	12.50
Gemini	1973	10000	12.50	12.50
Leo	1973	10000	12.50	12.50
Libra	1973	10000	12.50	12.50
Pisces	1973	10000	12.50	12.50
Sagittarius	1973	10000	12.50	12.50
Scorpio	1973	10000	12.50	12.50
Taurus	1973	10000	12.50	12.50
Virgo	1973	10000	12.50	12.50

James Belford, see Belford

International Silver, Liberty Bank Note

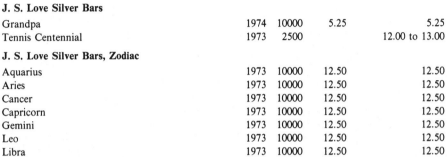

Lincoln Mint, Christmas, 1972

Jefferson Mint of Amador City, California, introduced limited edition silver plates and bars in 1972. Medals in bronze and silver were added in 1973.

Jefferson Mint Ingots

Thank You	1972	20000	4.95	4.95 to 5.25
Thank You	1973	25000	4.95	4.95

Jersey Coin Exchange Silver Bars, Seven Wonders of the World

Colossus Of Rhodes	1973	4000	10.00 to 14.00
Lighthouse	1973	2000	10.00 to 14.00
Mausoleum	1973	2000	10.00 to 14.00
Pharaohs Of Alexandria	1973	4000	10.00 to 14.00
Pyramids Of Egypt	1973	4000	10.00 to 14.00

Justice Mint Silver Bars

Bird, Bobwhite	1973		7.00 to 8.00
Bird, Mountain Quail	1973		7.00 to 8.00
Bird, Ruffed Grouse	1973		7.00 to 8.00
Churchill, Bronze	1973		22.00
Dog, Collie	1973	5000	7.00 to 80.00
Dog, Beagle	1973	5000	7.00 to 8.00
Dog, Doberman	1973	5000	7.00 to 8.00
Dog, German Shepherd	1973	5000	7.00 to 8.00
Dog, Great Dane	1973	5000	7.00 to 8.00
Easter	1973		5.25 to 6.50
Four Seasons, Set Of 4	1973		35.00 to 40.00
Go-Go Dancer	1973		5.00 to 7.00
Huck Finn	1973		5.00 to 6.50
Thanksgiving	1972		30.00 to 40.00
Unite For Peace	1973		5.00 to 7.00
Women's Lib	1973		5.00 to 6.50

Kennedy Mint Silver Bars

Bicentennial, Set Of 12	1971	2500	195.00	195.00
Eisenhower, 25 Grams	1970			17.50 to 22.50
Eisenhower, 20 Grams	1971			9.00 to 12.50
Smoky Mountains, 20 Grams	1971	1000		70.00 to 120.00
Smoky Mountains, 20 Grams	1973			26.00

Lincoln Mint, Mother's Day, 1972

Madison Mint, Balloon,
The Nassau

Madison Mint, Bar Mitzvah

Madison Mint, Cleveland Cable Car

Madison Mint, Ford Tin Lizzie

Madison Mint, Halloween, 1973

Madison Mint, Hanukkah

Kennedy Mint, Six Flights of Man Series, 300 Grains

Armstrong, Aldrin, Collins	1971		20.00 to 25.00
Byrd, Richard E.	1971		20.00 to 25.00
Da Vinci, Leonardo	1971		20.00 to 25.00
Gagarin, Yuri	1971		20.00 to 25.00
Lindbergh, Charles	1971		20.00 to 25.00
Wright Brothers	1971		20.00 to 25.00

Liberty Mint Silver Bars

Graf Zeppelin	1973	2500		6.50 to 7.50
Graf Zeppelin, Error	1973			12.00 to 13.00
Halloween	1973	1500		5.00 to 6.00
Labor Day	1973			10.00 to 12.50
Landing Of Columbus	1973			9.00 to 11.00
Valentine's Day	1974		4.95	4.95

The Lincoln Mint of Chicago, Illinois, entered the limited edition field in 1971. Gold, silver, and vermeil plates, medals, and ingots are made. Lincoln Mint has produced official state bicentennial and governors medals for a number of states.

See listing for Lincoln Mint in Plate and Medal sections

Lincoln Mint Silver Ingots

Christmas, Holy Family, Silver*	1972	5000	35.00	35.00
Mother's Day, Madonna & Child, Gold Plated	1972	5000	40.00	25.00 to 40.00
Mother's Day, Madonna & Child, Silver*	1972	5000	35.00	20.00 to 35.00
World War II, Churchill	1973	5000	13.50	13.50

Lincoln Mint Silver Ingots, Greatest Leaders of World War II

Clark	1973	5000	13.50	13.50
Doolittle	1973	5000	13.50	13.50
Eisenhower	1973	5000	13.50	13.50
Hewlett	1973	5000	13.50	13.50
Kennedy	1973	5000	13.50	13.50
MacArthur	1973	5000	13.50	13.50
Morgenthau	1973	5000	13.50	13.50
Nimitz	1973	5000	13.50	13.50
Patton	1973	5000	13.50	13.50
Roosevelt	1973	5000	13.50	13.50
Stilwell	1973	5000	13.50	13.50
Truman	1973	5000	13.50	13.50

Limited Issue Bars, Inc. Bars

Skylab, Metal	1973	2445	3.50	3.50
Watergate, Metal	1973	2445	3.50	3.50

The Lombardo Mint of Quebec, Canada, is a private mint. Limited and non-limited medals, bars, and posta ingettes are produced. Posta ingettes are silver or bronze replicas of presidential stamps.

See listing for Lombardo Mint in Medal section

Lombardo Mint Silver Bars

Christmas	1973		14.50	14.50
Posta Ingettes, Silver, Set Of 6, Each	1972-1973	5000	6.00	6.00
Posta Ingettes, Silver, Set Of 32, Each	1973-1974	5000	6.00	6.00

Long Island Coin Exchange Bars

Halloween, Bronze	1973	1000	25.00	25.00
Halloween, Gold Over Silver	1973	1000	30.00	30.00
Halloween, Silver	1973	4000	25.00	25.00

Love, see J. S. Love

Madison Mint Silver Bars

Balloon, The Nassau*	1973	17500	4.95	4.95 to 5.25
Bar Mitzvah*	1973	25000	4.95	5.00 to 5.50
Bicentennial, Buffalo	1972		4.75	4.95 to 5.25
Bicentennial, Crossed Flags, Philadelphia	1974		4.95	4.95
Bicentennial, Indian	1973		4.95	4.95 to 5.25
Bicentennial, Majestic Eagle	1973	45001	4.95	4.95 to 5.25
Chess	1974		6.25	6.25
Christmas	1972			15.00
Christmas, Joy To The World	1973	50000		5.25
Cleveland Cable Car*	1973		4.95	4.95 to 5.25

Easter	1973	53505		8.50 to 9.00
Easter	1974		8.50	8.50
Father's Day	1973	69871	4.95	4.95 to 6.50
Fire Engine	1973			4.95 to 5.25
Flags	1973	45890	1.95	4.95 to 5.25
Ford Tin Lizzie*	1973		4.95	4.95 to 5.25
Fourth Of July, Independence Day	1973	60643	4.95	4.95 to 5.50
General	1973		4.95	4.95 to 5.25
General, Error	1973	10000		70.00 to 95.00
Graduation	1973	57100	4.95	4.95 to 5.25
Halloween*	1973	45000	4.75	4.75 to 5.25
Hanukkah*	1973	15000	4.75	4.75 to 5.25
Happy Birthday	1974		8.25	8.25
Happy New Year	1974		4.95	4.95
High Wheeler	1973	17500	4.95	4.95 to 5.25
Hope, Bob	1973	5000		7.95
Liberty Bell	1973	27651	4.95	4.95 to 5.25
Liberty Bell, Large, Gold Over Silver	1973			75.00
Monroe, Marilyn	1973			9.00 to 11.00
Mother's Day	1973	78131		6.50 to 8.50
Old Ironsides*	1973		4.95	4.95 to 5.25
Spirit Of St. Louis	1973		4.95	4.95 to 5.25
St. Patrick's Day	1974		6.25	6.25
Stagecoach	1973		4.95	4.95 to 5.25
Stanley Roadster*	1973		4.95	4.95 to 5.25
Stutz Bearcat*	1973		4.95	4.95 to 5.25
Thanksgiving	1972	13505		25.00 to 50.00
Thanksgiving*	1973	23750	4.95	4.95 to 5.25
Valentine's Day	1973	40520		10.00 to 14.00
Veterans Day*	1973	25506	4.95	4.95 to 5.25
1903 Cadillac*	1973		4.95	4.95 to 5.25

Madison Mint Silver Bars, Presidential Cameo

Cleveland	1973		6.25 to 7.00
Coolidge	1973		6.25 to 7.00
Eisenhower	1973		6.25 to 7.00
Grant	1973		6.25 to 7.00
Jackson	1973		6.25 to 7.00
Jefferson	1973		6.25 to 7.00
Kennedy	1973		6.25 to 7.00
Lincoln	1973		6.25 to 7.00
Madison	1973		6.25 to 7.00
Roosevelt, Franklin D.	1973		6.25 to 7.00
Roosevelt, Theodore	1973		6.25 to 7.00
Truman	1973		6.25 to 7.00
Washington	1973		6.25 to 7.00

Mark IV Mint Silver Bars

Chevrolet	1974	6.50	6.50
Commerce On Rails	1974	6.50	6.50
De Haviland	1974	6.50	6.50
Liberty And Justice For All	1974	6.50	6.50
Marmon	1974	6.50	6.50
Model T Ford	1974	6.50	6.50
New Frontiers	1974	6.50	6.50
Readiness At Sea	1974	6.50	6.50
Star Of India	1974	6.50	6.50
14th Century English Castle	1974	6.50	6.50

Medallic Art Company, see Premium Issues

Minimint Silver Bars, 1/3 oz.

Bicentennial, Kennedy	1973	5.00	5.00
Bicentennial, Liberty Bell	1973	5.00	5.00
Carson City	1973	5.00	5.00
Fisherman	1973	5.00	5.00
Indian Head Penny, 1877	1973	5.00	5.00
Kennedy Half-Dollar	1973	5.00	5.00
Marksman	1973	5.00	5.00
Quail In Flight	1973	5.00	5.00
Sport Of Kings	1973	5.00	5.00

Mother Lode Mint Silver Bars

America's Heroes, Fire Department	1973		4.95 to 5.25

Madison Mint, Old Ironsides

Madison Mint, Stanley Roadster

Madison Mint, Stutz Bearcat

Madison Mint, Thanksgiving, 1973

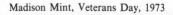

Madison Mint, Veterans Day, 1973

Madison Mint, 1903 Cadillac

San Francisco Private Mint,
Cable Car Centennial

San Francisco Private Mint,
Cable Car Centennial, Round

San Francisco Private Mint, Peace On Earth

Silver Coalition, Out-Of-Print Currency,
$1,000

Alamo	1973			4.95 to 5.25
Capitol Building	1974	4000	10.00	10.00
Christmas	1973			4.95 to 5.25
Concord Stage	1973			4.75 to 5.25
End Of Trail	1973			4.75 to 5.25
Father's Day	1973			4.75 to 5.25
First Love	1973			4.75 to 5.25
Keep Me And Never Go Broke	1973			4.75 to 5.25
Keep On Trucking	1973			4.75 to 5.25
Labor Day	1973			4.75 to 5.25
Las Vegas	1973			4.75 to 5.25
Masonic	1973			4.75 to 5.25
Mother Lode Mint	1973			4.75 to 5.25
New Orleans	1973			4.75 to 5.25
Pony Express	1973		4.75	4.75 to 5.25
Prospector	1973		4.75	4.75 to 5.25
Reno, Big 6-8	1973			4.75 to 5.25
Reno, Field 93	1973			75.00 to 100.00
Salute To History's Coinage	1973	2500		12.50 to 16.50
Thanksgiving	1973			4.75 to 5.25
Twelve Days Of Christmas, Set Of 12	1973	10000		85.00 to 90.00

Mount Everest Mint of Willow Grove, Pennsylvania, is a subsidiary of Mount Everest Corporation. Limited edition silver bars were first made in 1972.

Mt. Everest Mint Silver Bars

Boston Tea Party	1973	11500	6.00	6.00
Christmas, Building Together	1973	6(85	9.50	9.50
Christmas, Nativity	1973	12517	9.50	9.50
Christmas, One World, One Wish	1973	12671	9.50	9.50
Christmas, Star Of Wonder	1973	8875	9.50	9.50
Christmas, Taking Turns	1973	11866	9.50	9.50
Festival Of Lights	1973	5734	15.00	15.00
Kohoutek Comet	1974	Year	9.95	9.95
Mt. Everest	1973	27000	4.85	4.85
Old-Fashioned Trains, Set Of 10	1974	5000	120.00	120.00
Stonewall Jackson	1974	9999	9.95	9.95
Thanksgiving, Abundance	1973	15000	9.50	9.50
Thanksgiving, Family	1973	15000	9.50	9.50
Thanksgiving, Freedom	1973	15000	9.50	9.50
The Dreidelers	1973	5734	15.00	15.00
Valentine's Day, Barefoot In The Clouds	1974	Year	9.95	9.95
Valentine's Day, Cameo Couple	1974	Year	9.95	9.95
Valentine's Day, Chaucer	1974	Year	9.95	9.95
Wildlife, Bear Cub	1974	10000	8.25	8.25
Wildlife, Lovebirds	1974	10000	8.25	8.25
Wildlife, Owl	1974	10000	8.25	8.25
Wildlife, Raccoon	1974	10000	8.25	8.25
Wildlife, Squirrel	1974	10000	8.25	8.25
Yom Kippur War Memorial	1974		7.95	7.95

National Astronomical Archives Silver Bars

Kohoutek	1973	3500	15.00	15.00

Numismatic Exchange Silver Bars

Boone, Daniel	1973	10000	12.00	12.00

Numismatic Metals Trading Ingots, World Hockey Association, 1 oz.

Aeros, Gold	1973	100	200.00	200.00
Aeros, Silver	1973	5000	10.00	10.00
Blazers, Gold	1973	100	200.00	200.00
Blazers, Silver	1973	5000	10.00	10.00
Cougars, Gold	1973	100	200.00	200.00
Cougars, Silver	1973	5000	10.00	10.00
Fighting Saints, Gold	1973	100	200.00	200.00
Fighting Saints, Silver	1973	5000	10.00	10.00
Golden Blades, Gold	1973	100	200.00	200.00
Golden Blades, Silver	1973	5000	10.00	10.00
Jets, Gold	1973	100	200.00	200.00
Jets, Silver	1973	5000	10.00	10.00
Nordiques, Gold	1973	100	200.00	200.00
Nordiques, Silver	1973	5000	10.00	10.00

Oilers, Gold	1973	100	200.00	200.00
Oilers, Silver	1973	5000	10.00	10.00
Sharks, Gold	1973	100	200.00	200.00
Sharks, Silver	1974	5000	10.00	10.00
Toros, Gold	1973	100	200.00	200.00
Toros, Silver	1973	5000	10.00	10.00
Whalers, Gold	1973	100	200.00	200.00
Whalers, Silver	1973	5000	10.00	10.00

Ohio Mint Silver Bars

Christmas Panorama, Set Of 3	1973	44.95	44.95

United States Silver
Corporation, Agnew Who

Our Greatest Americans Ingots, see Hamilton Mint

Out-Of-Print Currency Ingots, see Silver Coalition

Patrick Mint Silver Bars

Cable Car, Centennial	1973	4.75 to 5.25
Christmas	1972	30.00 to 35.00
Christmas	1973	4.75 to 5.25
Covered Wagon	1973	4.75 to 5.25
Curtiss Biplane, Jenny	1973	4.75 to 5.25
Israel, Star	1973	6.50 to 7.50
Mercer	1973	4.75 to 5.25
Model T Ford	1973	4.75 to 5.25
Pony Express	1973	4.75 to 5.25
Prairie Schooner	1973	4.75 to 5.25
Spirit Of '76	1973	10.00
Statue Of Liberty	1973	5.25 to 6.50

United States Silver Corporation,
Belle Of Louisville

Picasso Bars, see Geneva Coin Co.

Pioneer Mint Silver Bars

Man O' War	1973	5.00 to 6.00

Premium Issue Silver Bars

Inflation, I Have No Beef With Nixon	1973	1000	25.00	25.00
Lincoln Memorial	1973	1000	20.00	20.00

Presidential Cameo Bars, see Madison Mint

Prestige Creations, see Madison Mint

Sam Sloat Silver Bars

Wartime Nickel	1973	10.00

United States Silver
Corporation, Big Ben

San Francisco Historical bars, see Coin Gallery of San Francisco

*San Francisco Private Mint of San Francisco, California, produces
silver and platinum bars and numismatic rounds. The limited edition bars
were first made in 1973.*

San Francisco Private Mint Silver Bars

San Francisco Cable Car Centennial, Bar*	1973	10000	10.00	10.00
San Francisco Cable Car Centennial, Round*	1973	800	25.00	25.00
Peace On Earth, Silver*	1973	10000	9.50	9.50
Peace On Earth, Platinum	1973	250.00	250.00

Seven Wonders of the World Bars, see Jersey Coin Exchange

Sharps-Pixley Silver Bars

Sharps-Pixley	1971	7.50 to 12.50
Sharps Pixley, Monogram	1971	15.00 to 17.50

Silver Coalition Ingots, out-of-print currency

$500 Note, Silver	1972	10000	200.00	250.00 to 300.00
$1,000 Note, Silver*	1972	10000	200.00	250.00 to 300.00
$5,000 Note, Silver	1972	10000	200.00	250.00 to 300.00
$10,000 Note, Silver	1972	10000	200.00	250.00 to 300.00

United States Silver Corporation, California Gold

United States Silver Corporation, Captain Kidd

See listing for Silver Creations in Figurine and Plate sections

Silver Creations Ingots

Churchill, Bronze	1972	340		30.00 to 60.00
Churchill, Gold Over Silver	1972	2000		20.00 to 55.00
Churchill, Silver	1972	1000		130.00 to 175.00
Happy New Year, Silver	1973	2000		12.50
Holy Bible, Gold Over Silver	1973			22.50
Holy Bible, Silver	1973	5000		17.50
Hong Kong-Shanghai, Silver, 5 Oz.	1973			28.95
Kelly, Emmett, Gold Over Silver	1973	1000	40.00	40.00

United States Silver Corporation,
Cheetah

United States Silver Corporation,
Christmas, 1973

United States Silver Corporation,
Daniel Boone

United States Silver Corporation,
Dove Of Peace

United States Silver Corporation,
Easter, 1974

Name	Year	Qty	Price	Value
Kelly, Emmett, Silver	1973	4000	35.00	35.00
Kennedy, John F., Bronze	1973	1000		12.00
Kennedy, John F., Gold Over Silver	1973	1000		23.50
Kennedy, John F., Silver	1973	2000		12.50
Picasso, Gold Over Silver	1973	1000	50.00	50.00
Picasso, Silver	1973	4000	35.00	35.00
Secretariat, Bronze, Set Of 3	1973			24.00
Secretariat, Gold Over Silver, Set Of 3	1973			60.00
Secretariat, Silver, Set Of 3				45.00
Skylab, Bronze, Set Of 3	1973			30.00
Skylab, Gold Over Silver, Set Of 3	1973			60.00
Skylab, Silver, Set Of 3	1973			45.00
Truman, Harry S., Silver	1973	4000	35.00	35.00
Watergate, Bronze, Set Of 3	1973			19.50
Watergate, Silver, Set Of 3	1973			45.00
Yalta, Bronze	1973	5000		10.00
Yalta, Gold Over Silver	1973	1000		20.00
Yalta, Silver	1973	4000		15.00

Silver Mint Silver Bars, Silver Nations, 20 grams

Name	Year	Qty	Price	Value
Australia	1973		12.50	12.50
Australia, Serially Numbered	1973	5000	15.00	15.00
Canada	1973		12.50	12.50
Canada, Serially Numbered	1973	5000	15.00	15.00
Mexico	1973		12.50	12.50
Mexico, Serially Numbered	1973	5000	15.00	15.00
Peru	1973		12.50	12.50
Peru, Serially Numbered	1973	5000	15.00	15.00
Russia	1973		12.50	12.50
Russia, Serially Numbered	1973		12.50	12.50
United States	1973		12.50	12.50
United States, Serially Numbered	1973	5000	15.00	15.00

Sloat, Sam, see Sam Sloat

Switzerland Silver Bars

Name	Year	Qty	Price	Value
California 500	1973	5000	4.95	4.95
Ecology	1973	5000	4.95	4.95
L.A. Open	1973	5000	4.95	4.95
Motorcycles	1973	5000	4.95	4.95
U.S. Golf Open	1973	5000	4.95	4.95

Symbolic American Numismatics, see Washington Mint

United States Coinage Corporation Silver Bars

Name	Year	Value
Bicentennial, Declaration Of Independence	1973	5.00 to 6.00
Bicentennial, Paul Revere's Ride	1973	5.00 to 6.00
Bicentennial, Washington At Valley Forge	1973	5.00 to 6.00
Bicentennial, Washington Crossing Delaware	1973	5.00 to 6.00
Bicentennial, Yankee Doodle	1973	5.00 to 6.00

United States Silver Corporation of Van Nuys, California, first issued limited edition silver bars in 1973.

United States Silver Corporation Silver Bars

Name	Year	Qty	Price	Value
Agnew Who*	1973	2500		14.00 to 16.00
Alaskan Pipeline	1974	2000	13.95	13.95
Belle Of Louisville*	1973	10000		6.50 to 7.50
Big Ben*	1973	5000		6.00 to 7.00
Blue Whale	1974	1750		12.50 to 14.00
Boston Tea Party	1973	20000		5.50 to 7.00
Buccanneer	1973	2500		6.00 to 7.00
Burbank, Luther	1974	5000	6.95	6.95
California Gold*	1973	12500		6.00 to 7.00
Captain Kidd*	1973	5100		5.50 to 6.50
Cheetah*	1973	1500		15.00 to 17.00
Christmas*	1973	10000		5.50 to 6.50
Cougar	1974	2800	8.95	8.95
Daniel Boone*	1973	10000		7.00 to 8.00
Dolphin	1974	2000	11.95	11.95
Dove Of Peace*	1973	2000	16.95	15.00 to 17.00
Easter*	1974	6000	5.95	5.95
Eiffel Tower*	1973	10000		6.50 to 7.50
Freemasonry	1973	10000		6.50 to 7.50
Grizzly Bear*	1972	999		42.00 to 55.00

Hallidies Cable Car	1973	7500		7.50 to 8.50
Halloween*	1973	5439		7.00 to 8.00
Happy Hanukkah*	1973	1700		8.00 to 10.00
Israel*	1973	30000		4.75 to 5.50
It's A Boy*	1973		9.95	9.95
It's A Girl*	1973		9.95	9.95
Jackalope	1974	2500	9.95	9.95
Kangaroo	1974	2000	11.95	11.95
Kitty Hawk*	1973	7500		7.00 to 8.00
Landing Of Columbus*	1973	6868		6.50 to 7.50
Last Supper*	1973	10000		15.00
Leaning Tower Of Pisa*	1973	5000		6.50 to 7.50
Leonardo Da Vinci*	1973	4500		7.50 to 8.50
Mexican Independence*	1973	13000		6.50 to 7.50
Mother's Day	1974	Year	6.50	6.50
New Year's*	1974	1312	5.95	5.95
Phoenix	1973	5000		6.50 to 7.50
Prairie Chicken	1974	2000	13.95	13.95
Reclining Nude	1973	26000		5.75 to 6.50
Rights & Liberty*	1973	15000		6.50 to 7.50
San Diego Zoo	1973	20000		5.50 to 6.50
Secretariat	1973	20000		7.00 to 8.00
Shriners	1973	5000		6.50 to 7.50
Thankfulness*	1973	7000		5.50 to 6.50
U.S.S. Constitution*	1973	2500		12.00 to 14.00
Uncle Sam*	1973	5000		9.00 to 11.00
Union & Constitution*	1973	15000		6.50 to 7.50
United Nations*	1973	4700		10.00 to 12.00
Valentine's Day	1974	6000	5.95	5.95
Wisconsin Anniversary*	1973	10000		6.50 to 7.50
World Trade & Commerce*	1973	15000		4.50 to 5.50

United States Silver Corporation Silver Bars, Zodiac

Aquarius	1973	1600	5.95
Aries	1973	1600	5.95
Cancer	1973	1600	5.95
Capricorn	1973	1600	5.95
Gemini	1973	1600	5.95
Leo	1973	1600	5.95
Libra	1973	1600	5.95
Pisces	1973	1600	5.95
Sagittarius	1973	1600	5.95
Scorpio	1973	1600	5.95
Taurus	1973	1600	5.95
Virgo	1973	1600	5.95

Valley Forge Mint of King of Prussia, Pennsylvania, issued its first limited edition silver eagle bar in 1973.

Valley Forge Mint Silver Bars

Canadian Heritage, The Beaver	1974		10.50	10.50
First Silver Eagle	1973	4000	6.00	6.00 to 7.00
Second Silver Eagle	1974		9.50	9.50

Washington D. C. Bicentennial Commission Bars, 1 oz.

Florida	1974	15000	8.95	8.95
New York	1974	15000	8.95	8.95
Pennsylvania	1974	15000	8.95	8.95
Texas	1974	15000	8.95	8.95

The Washington Mint of Beachwood, Ohio, was organized in 1970. Limited edition silver bars were first issued in 1971 and silver plates followed in 1972.

See listing for Washington Mint in Plate section

Washington Mint Silver Bars, Anniversary, 20 grams

1946-1971	1971	7000		14.00 to 15.00
1947-1972	1972	12000		12.00 to 13.00
1948-1973	1973		5.25	5.25

Washington Mint Silver Bars, Bicentennial

Columbus Discovers America	1973	10000		13.00
Paul Revere's Ride	1973	10000		13.00
Shot Heard Around The World	1973	10000		13.00

United States Silver Corporation,
Eiffel Tower

United States Silver Corporation,
Grizzly Bear

United States Silver Corporation,
Halloween, 1973

United States Silver Corporation,
Happy Hanukkah, 1973

United States Silver Corporation,
Israel

United States Silver Corporation,
It's A Girl

United States Silver Corporation,
Leaning Tower Of Pisa

United States Silver Corporation,
New Year's, 1974

United States Silver Corporation,
It's A Boy

United States Silver Corporation,
Rights & Liberty

United States Silver Corporation,
Kitty Hawk

United States Silver Corporation,
Leonardo da Vinci

United States Silver Corporation,
Thankfulness

United States Silver Corporation,
Landing Of Columbus

United States Silver Corporation,
Last Supper

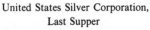

United States Silver Corporation,
Mexican Independence

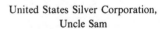

United States Silver Corporation,
Uncle Sam

United States Silver Corporation,
Union & Constitution

United States Silver Corporation,
Wisconsin Anniversary

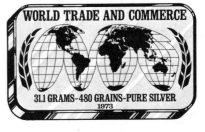

United States Silver Corporation,
U.S.S.Constitution

United States Silver Corporation,
World Trade & Commerce

United States Silver Corporation,
United Nations

Washington Mint, Great Americans

Benjamin Franklin

Abraham Lincoln

Patrick Henry

George Washington

Thomas Jefferson

James Monroe

Francis Scott Key

Washington Mint,
Symbolic American Numismatics,
Buffalo

Washington Mint,
Symbolic American Numismatics,
Draped Bust

Washington Mint,
Symbolic American Numismatics,
Indian

Washington Mint,
Symbolic American Numismatics,
Mercury Dime

Washington Mint,
Symbolic American Numismatics, Peace

Washington Mint,
Symbolic American Numismatics,
Seated Liberty

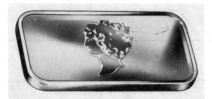

Washington Mint,
Symbolic American Numismatics,
Standing Liberty

Washington Mint,
Symbolic American Numismatics,
Walking Liberty

Washington Mint Silver Bars, Flags

Bennington	1973	5.25	5.25
Betsy Ross	1973	5.25	5.25
Bunker Hill	1973	5.25	5.25
Confederate	1973	5.25	5.25
Fifty Star Flag	1973	5.25	5.25
Fort McHenry	1973	5.25	5.25
John Paul Jones	1973	5.25	5.25
Lone Star	1973	5.25	5.25

Washington Mint Silver Bars, Great Americans, 25 grams

Abraham Lincoln*	1973	5.25
Benjamin Franklin*	1973	5.25
Francis Scott Key*	1973	5.25
George Washington*	1973	5.25
James Monroe*	1973	5.25
Patrick Henry*	1973	5.25
Thomas Jefferson*	1973	5.25

Washington Mint Silver Bars, Symbolic American Numismatics, 1 oz.

Barber	1973	5.25
Battle Of Gettysburg	1973	5.25
Buffalo*	1973	5.25
Daniel Boone	1973	5.25
Draped Bust*	1973	5.25
Draped Bust Dollar	1973	5.25
Eisenhower	1973	5.25
Flowing Hair Dollar	1973	5.25
Franklin Half	1973	5.25
Indian*	1973	5.25
Indian Eagle	1973	5.25
Indian Half Eagle	1973	5.25
Indian Princess	1973	5.25
Isabella	1973	5.25
Kennedy	1973	5.25
Lafayette	1973	5.25
Large Cent	1973	5.25
Liberty Cap Large Cent	1973	5.25
Liberty Nickel	1973	5.25
Mercury Dime*	1973	5.25
Morgan	1973	5.25
Peace*	1973	5.25
Roosevelt Dime	1973	5.25
Seated Dollar	1973	5.25
Seated Liberty*	1973	5.25
Shield Nickel	1973	5.25
St. Gaudens Double Eagle	1973	5.25
Standing Liberty*	1973	5.25
Three Cent Silver	1973	5.25
Trade Dollar	1973	5.25
Two Cent	1973	5.25
Walking Liberty*	1973	5.25
Washington Quarter	1973	5.25

Wittnauer Mint Silver Bars

Father's Day, Silver	1974	10000	23.50	23.50

Wonders of America Ingots, see Hamilton Mint

World Hockey Association Bars, see Numismatic Metals Trading

World Mint Silver Bars

Armed Forces	1974	4.95	4.95
Eagle On Globe	1974	4.95	4.95
White House	1974	7500	4.95	4.95

Worldwide Mint Silver Bars

Cantor, Eddie	1974	2500	12.50	12.50
Johnson, Lyndon	1972	5000		20.00 to 25.00
Patton, George S.	1973			17.50
Rogers, Will	1974	2500	12.50	12.50
V-Nickel	1973	10000		8.50

Yonkers Coin Exchange Silver Bars

Peace	1970		8.00 to 10.00

Zodiac bars, see J. S. Love